Paul Bowles, the romantic savage

PAUL BOWLES

Romantic Savage

Gena Dagel Caponi

Southern Illinois University Press

Carbondale and Edwardsville

Frontispiece: Paul Bowles, the romantic savage, in North
Africa, late 1940s. Courtesy Photography Collection,
Harry Ransom Humanities Research Center,
The University of Texas at Austin.

Library of Congress Cataloging-in-Publication Data

Caponi, Gena Dagel.
Paul Bowles : romantic savage / Gena Dagel Caponi.
p.   cm.
Includes bibliographical references and index.
1. Bowles, Paul, 1910–.   2. Authors, American—20th
century—Biography.   3. Composers—United States—
Biography.   I. Title.
PS3552.O874Z62   1994
813'.54—dc20
93-35581
[B]   CIP
ISBN   0-8093-1923-3

To my parents
and in memory of
Josephine Keeler Tomlinson
(1910–1988)

CONTENTS

Notes

Works by Paul Bowles

Selected Bibliography

Index

ILLUSTRATIONS

PREFACE

AS AN INTERPRETIVE BIOGRAPHY, this book offers a reading of the relations between the literary, musical, and autobiographical constructions Paul Bowles created. My aim is to penetrate to the underlying imaginative structures common to all and then to link them to a larger cultural context.

Readers will notice that I have relied on Bowles's autobiography, *Without Stopping*, to a great extent. I have done so for two reasons: first, through family letters, newspaper clippings, and his friends, I have been able to confirm many of the events he relates, enough to lead me to believe that the autobiography is largely trustworthy. In various interviews and conversations, Bowles repeated most of the same details the autobiography contains, yet *Without Stopping* remains the clearest and most elegant expression of these memories, and I felt it sensible to honor the written source. Second, *Without Stopping* is a deliberately constructed autobiography, firmly intended to present a particular persona, and no other, to the reader. I read the autobiography as another of Bowles's finely crafted fictions, and I analyze it alongside the fiction to understand the imagination that created both.

There has been little critical treatment of Bowles's work and only four book-length studies: Lawrence D. Stewart's *Paul Bowles: The Illumination of North Africa* (1974); Johannes Bertens's *Fiction of Paul Bowles: The Soul Is the Weariest Part of the Body* (1979); Wayne Pounds's *Paul Bowles: The Inner Geography* (1985); and Richard F. Patteson's *World Outside: The Fiction of Paul Bowles* (1987). Stewart's discussion of Bowles's novels and stories set in North Africa focuses on the intersection of Bowles's travels and his fiction. Bertens and Pounds both concentrate on Bowles's critique of Western civilization, with Pounds relying on R. D. Laing's *Divided Self: A Study of Sanity and Madness* for a psychological formulation of the disintegrating modern psyche. Patteson offers a method of reading Bowles through formal and thematic architectural concepts.

The definitive biography of Paul Bowles remains to be written. Christopher Sawyer-Lauçanno's *Invisible Spectator: A Biography of Paul Bowles* (1989) establishes the outline of Bowles's life and contains especially good discussions of some of Bowles's early compositions; Michelle Green's *Dream at the End of the World: Paul Bowles and the Literary Renegades in Tangier* (1991) places Bowles in the social context of Tangier in the 1950s. In this work, I avoid unnecessary duplication of their work; instead, I stress the relationships in Bowles's life that provide insight into his work—his relationships with his mentors, Aaron Copland, Gertrude Stein, and Virgil Thomson; with his editor at Random House, David McDowell; with his London editors, John Lehmann and Peter Owen; with his friend Charles Henri Ford; with his Moroccan friends Ahmed Yacoubi and Mohammed Mrabet; and with his wife, Jane Bowles—and I concentrate on defining Bowles's place in twentieth-century American culture.

Paul Bowles himself contributed to the research of this book by answering my letters, by reading one chapter and making corrections, and by spending every evening for a week answering my questions in his Tangier apartment. He showed me a hooded, camel's-hair robe and lent my husband and me a map for our trip to Fez. He could not have been kinder to someone about to write a book that would include certain issues he prefers not to discuss.

Many friends and colleagues of Paul Bowles graciously corresponded with me or allowed me to question them in person, and I am grateful to Don Bachardy, Rudy Burckhardt, Ira Cohen, David Diamond, Buffie Johnson, Bennett Lerner, Ned Rorem, Gordon Sager, Oliver Smith, Gore Vidal, and Christopher Wanklyn for their recollections and their time. I regret that others who helped me are no longer here: Aaron Copland, Maurice Grosser, Christopher Isherwood, Edouard Roditi, and Virgil Thomson. I am indebted to them all.

I would not have begun this work without encouragement and inspiration from the late Gilbert Chase, American music historian, in whose footsteps a considerable number are humbly traveling.

I am grateful to my advisers: Jeffrey Meikle, Elizabeth Fernea, William Stott, Suzanne Shelton Buckley, and Robert Abzug, who read various versions—Jeffrey and Robert, in particular, doing so out of friendship rather than duty; my colleagues: Jay Rozen and Michele Zwierski, who located scores and recordings; John Scaramelli, who uncovered leads for local history; Jennie Skerl, who provided valuable contextual suggestions and helped work through several puzzles; and Linda Schott, who gave me a job.

I also want to thank Ken Craven, Patricia Fox, Cathy Henderson, Dell Hollingsworth, and John Kirkpatrick, librarians at the Harry Ransom Humanities Research Center, who expertly assisted me; Kendall Crilly, Deborah Miller, and Harold E. Samuel at Yale University Music Library;

Bernard R. Crystal at the Rare Book and Manuscript Library at Columbia University; Timothy D. Murray in Special Collections of the University Library at the University of Delaware; Mildred K. Abraham of the Alderman Library at the University of Virginia; Flora Ito of the Department of Special Collections at the University of California, Los Angeles, who gave considerable attention to my requests; and Karl Miller at the University of Texas Fine Arts Library, who helped me find and hear Bowles's music; Curtis Clark, at Southern Illinois University Press, who answered every phone call and seemed always to believe in the manuscript; Teresa White, also at Southern Illinois University Press, who guided the manuscript and me through copyediting with estimable patience and understanding; and Catherine E. Hutchins, who transformed the writing and clarified the meaning of it.

Much appreciation also goes to John Berryhill, who kept me laughing for a year in Barcelona; Carmen Muñoz and Fransesc Beltri, who made me feel at home there; Cynthia Brandimarte, Melissa Hield, and Margaret Caffrey, who shared nearly a decade of Saturday mornings full of encouragement, practical advice, and companionship; Tina Marsh and Phyllis Liedeker, who inspired me by their example; Lisa Jones, who continued to alert me to items of interest, as she has for years; Paul and Lynn Ziese, who provided spiritual support; Mary Bell, Brenda Smith, John McLeod, and Jackie Dudley, who listened faithfully and kept in touch; and Darcy Tworek, Debbie Sanchez, Becky Fife, and Leigh Wise, who loved my children and gave me time to work.

Finally, I thank my family: Lou and Gene Dagel and Val and Marion Capone, for their constant support; Maff and Pete Caponi, for growing alongside this other baby and for making me laugh; Ingunn Larsen, our exchange student from Norway, who will always be family; and Tom Caponi, for encouraging, listening, reading, discussing, for raising the children, and for believing I would finish.

The Winnewisser family, as identified by Paul Bowles. *Left to right* starting with the
top row: Guy Ross, Emma Ross, Frederick Winnewisser; *middle row*: Claude Bowles,
Henrietta Winnewisser with child on her lap (probably Frederick Shepard, son of
Frederick Winnewisser), August Winnewisser, Ulla Danser; *bottom row*: Paul
Winnewisser, Ruth Shepard (Mrs. Frederick Winnewisser), Rena Bowles, Harold
Danser. Courtesy Photography Collection, Harry Ransom Humanities Research
Center, The University of Texas at Austin.

Paul Bowles as a child. Courtesy
Photography Collection, Harry
Ransom Humanities Research
Center, The University of Texas
at Austin.

Paul Bowles, the naïf, in St. Moritz, 14 July 1929, with an additional twenty pounds gained after escaping from his father's table. Author's Collection.

Snapshot of Paul Bowles taken in a photo booth in New York, 1929. Author's Collection.

Paul Bowles, the dandy, in New York, 1936. Courtesy Photography Collection, Harry Ransom Humanities Research Center, The University of Texas at Austin.

Paul Bowles with Mohammed Ouild Oajdi (photograph taken by
Temsamany) outside an abandoned house of pleasure in North Africa,
probably early 1950s. Courtesy Photography Collection, Harry Ransom
Humanities Research Center, The University of Texas at Austin.

Paul Bowles, the romantic savage, in North Africa, late 1940s.
Courtesy Photography Collection, Harry Ransom Humanities
Research Center, The University of Texas at Austin.

Paul Bowles and Tennessee Williams in Morocco, probably January 1949.
Courtesy Photography Collection, Harry Ransom Humanities Research
Center, The University of Texas at Austin.

Paul Bowles in Fez, 1951. Photograph by Brion Gysin.
Courtesy William Burroughs Communications.

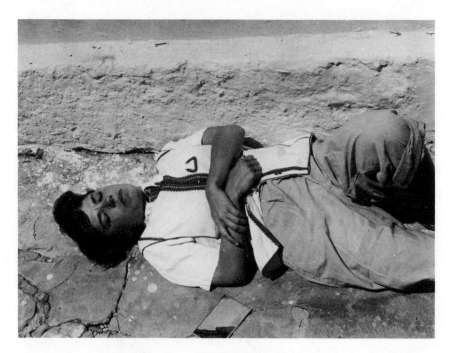

Jane Bowles on Merkala beach near Tangier, early 1950s.
Courtesy Photography Collection, Harry Ransom Humanities
Research Center, The University of Texas at Austin.

Cherifa, probably mid-1950s, in Morocco. Courtesy Photography
Collection, Harry Ransom Humanities Research Center, The
University of Texas at Austin.

Rena and Claude Bowles with chauffeur, Temsamany, in Morocco, 1957.
Courtesy Photography Collection, Harry Ransom Humanities Research
Center, The University of Texas at Austin.

The island of Taprobane. Courtesy Photography Collection, Harry Ransom
Humanities Research Center, The University of Texas at Austin.

Gore Vidal on a visit to Morocco, 1958. Courtesy Photography
Collection, Harry Ransom Humanities Research Center, The
University of Texas at Austin.

Paul Bowles, 1965. Drawing by Don Bachardy.
Courtesy of Don Bachardy.

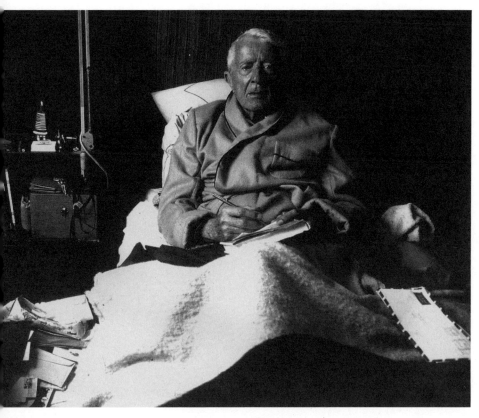

Paul Bowles in bed, Tangier, 1990. Photograph by Bernardo Perez.
Courtesy El País Internacional.

INTRODUCTION

IN **1988,** two years after I had visited Paul Bowles in Tangier, I received a letter from him in which he gently prodded, "Someone wrote me (I can't remember who) that you were planning to write my biography. I don't place any credence in the report since there's no conceivable reason why you should. I mention it only as gossip."[1]

I knew that Bowles had little respect for biography and that he certainly did not want anyone writing one about him. "I have already done that myself," he told me in Tangier, referring to his autobiography, *Without Stopping* (which William Burroughs retitled "Without Telling"). I wrote to him and explained that my book was different: "Parts of it are about your life, but mostly it is about your work and the culture it came from." I also apologized for having made him a subject for historical inquiry.

I had begun to think of him not as a biographical subject but as an artist whose life and work captured the emotional and intellectual sensibility of a group of Americans living during the middle years of the twentieth century. Though it would be impossible to name a "representative" figure for an entire era, we can find articulate people who put into expression or action preoccupations that reveal their time and society. Sometimes such mediators of culture—artists, philosophers, physicists—are able to explain more about their times because they are unlike their peers. Sigmund Freud, for example, was one of the few intellectuals during a sexually repressive era who spoke out about libido, even going so far as to develop an overarching psychological theory for which repression became the cornerstone. Freud explained the conflicts between instinct and civilization and gave scientific justification for an increasing sense of alienation and aloneness. As Freud shows us, one need not be typical in order to be significant.

I had always found Paul Bowles's writing beautiful and compelling and had wondered what kind of person could write with such clarity about confused human relations and with such detachment about wholly violent and gruesome behavior. Even more, I questioned what kind of culture could produce such an artist—one who was content only in exile, writing about the impossibility of human communication, communion, and love.

Paul Bowles would certainly be considered singular. He was born in 1910, grew up in the suburb of Jamaica, Long Island, attended the University of Virginia for less than a year, and completed his education through travel in Europe and North Africa and apprenticeships with various celebrated artists. In 1931, he showed his poetry to Gertrude Stein, who told him he was not a poet but encouraged him to go on writing his stories and to work harder at his music. He took daily composition lessons with Aaron Copland, and in 1936, after securing a job writing music for a play Orson Welles was directing, he persuaded Virgil Thomson to help him orchestrate a score. Throughout the late 1930s and early 1940s, Bowles created a brilliant career for himself, both as a composer of chamber works and theater music and as a music reviewer for the *New York Herald Tribune*. He and his wife, writer Jane Auer Bowles, circulated through the brightest New York teas, dinners, and cocktail parties. Their friends included the most gifted of American and expatriate European artists: W. H. Auden, Eugene Berman, Leonard Bernstein, John and Xenia Cage, Truman Capote, E. E. and Marion Cummings, John Latouche, John Lehmann, Oliver Smith, Kristians Tonny, Tennessee Williams, and many others less well known today.

Throughout these years Bowles traveled and occasionally settled for months at a time in various spots in Mexico: Taxco, Acapulco, Tehuantepec, Mexico City. He could not seem to adjust to life in New York City, nor was he especially happy writing music. By 1937, he had returned to the short stories Stein had preferred to his poetry.

Finally in 1947, he conceived a plan for a novel set in North Africa and sailed for Morocco. Although he returned to New York many times, usually to furnish music for a play, he spent more and more of his time abroad, eventually writing four novels and many short stories in Morocco, southern India, and Ceylon, where he bought an island to which he returned every winter for a few years. In 1958, he moved into an apartment in Tangier, where he has lived ever since.

Many aspects of Bowles's early life distinguish his childhood from a more conventional upbringing. He hated his strict father and spent much of his time with an assortment of quirky relatives. Among these were a homosexual uncle, a morphine-addicted aunt, and a great-aunt who ran a rest home for neurasthenics and held séances at which she regularly conjured up the spirit of Governor De Witt Clinton of New York.

More important than these anomalies in Bowles's childhood was his ordinary suburban upbringing. He belonged to one of the first American generations to grow up in a planned suburban development, and his unmitigated hatred of all that this life entailed provided the emotional content and the philosophical underpinning to much of his work. From his bedroom window he watched trees and marshes disappear at what he called "an alarming rate," and he grew to despise the cookie-cutter civilization that replaced the natural landscape with miles of identical houses. He relished visits to his grandparents' Massachusetts farm, where he was able to explore such woods and fields now missing from his suburban neighborhood.

Emotionally Bowles is a romantic, with the nineteenth-century artist's love of nature at its purest—untamed and unrevised. He has always been fascinated by primitive landscapes and cultures, overgrown forests and jungles, stark and hostile deserts. Like other romantics, Bowles felt the imagination was perfect without intervention and despised the corrupting influences of civilization and its institutions. Thus, Bowles's romanticism became negative and essentially antisocial: a human is at heart a savage, at best in solitary relation to nature.

Like the surrealists he admired as an adolescent, Bowles extended the romantic reverence for the imagination of the artist to a belief in the sanctity of the unconscious. He came to feel that "art is born from the unconscious; it's usually worked over subsequently to make it seem like a conscious invention, and this is often regrettable."[2] Like romantic poet William Coleridge, surrealist writer Jean Cocteau, and the North Africans he met on his travels, Bowles believed in the power of drugs to enhance the intuitive process; he came to write about a variety of states of consciousness and unconsciousness—from dreams to fever-induced hallucinations to music— and drug-induced trances. He was also interested in the imaginative powers of the unlettered mind, and he collaborated on several projects with illiterate Moroccan storytellers, bringing new voices into the global counterpoint in which his own work was a voice of dissent. The unconscious mind Bowles brought into consciousness is both Western and Oriental.

Although he holds a romantic's view of the importance of nature, Bowles does not romanticize nature in his writing. He found his truth in the solitude and barrenness of the North African desert with its unforgiving emptiness and beyond that—nothing. Nature can be indifferent and indigenous peoples often savage, yet neither tries to disguise cruelty. Having grown up in a New England family that protected children from the truth about sex and death, his discontent was with the veneer of civilization, which masked the honest cruelty of the instinctual person. Bowles believes that the barbaric savage is fully alive, while the civilized person can only question the meaning of existence. As a romantic, Bowles lives in exile from civilization; as an existentialist, he remains detached from life.

Scholar Walter Kaufmann has called existentialism more a sensibility than a philosophy, since fundamentally it has been a revolt against traditional philosophy.[3] Individualism is the soul of this sensibility, the individual a cluster of "possibilities, dread, and decisions."[4] The essence of existentialism has differed with each of its delineators; however, two characteristics remain true of all forms of existential beliefs: (1) existentialism is a philosophy that must be lived; and (2) the existentialist is entirely self-reliant and avoids self-deception. The existentialist thus abides in a heightened state of awareness, preoccupied with despair, death, and extreme situations and states of mind.

Bowles's work articulates various states of being along the continuum of existential insecurity. His reliance on the surrealist method of "unconscious writing" allows him to gain access to all regions of his mind and, like his travels across the world, is both romantic and existential in the refusal to submit to an itinerary. His interest in the splitting of personality (as in schizophrenia), in spirit possession, and in transformation owes as much to the split nature of modern reality as to his own peculiar psychological makeup, itself a reflection of his times.

Philosopher and writer Jean-Paul Sartre, explaining the doctrine of existentialism, states that a human being is "nothing else than the ensemble of his acts, nothing else than his life."[5] If one is interested in an existentialist, it makes sense to study the whole of his life, the entire ensemble of his acts. Always Bowles has been a traveler, never a tourist. For such an adventurer, there is no home to which he will return, no time frame within which to complete his journey. Free in space and time, the adventurer floats in the relativity of reality. No place has more meaning than any other, and there is all the time in the world. One cannot give meaning to existence, because existence is not about meaning. Existence is about remaining true to what one is — to one's instincts, to one's unconscious.

Bowles's existential position has its roots in a romantic quest — the search for something he has called the "lost childhood." The most fascinating memories in his autobiography are from his childhood. Adults ripped Bowles from his childhood before he had a chance to experience its essence, and he has searched for it in his art ever since. The problems of his childhood were those of many in his generation, the "post–Lost Generation," and his search is as much cultural as personal.

When I told Bowles that my book would be a form of cultural history, he replied, "You make the book you're writing sound very intriguing. I know what biographies are like, and they leave a lot to be desired, but to be 'a subject for history' is much more mysterious, and consequently more interesting."[6] Always a fan of the mysterious, Bowles once insisted that his stories and novels were nothing more than good mysteries, the mystery being the motivation for his characters' behavior.[7]

In this book I discuss what I see as the motivations behind the mystery of Bowles's life and his life's work to understand his times and ours. Sartre said,

"All that we are is the result of what we have thought."[8] The work of Paul Bowles is crucial to twentieth-century thought about who we are as individuals and as members of Western or American culture; all of his work, whether music, prose, poetry, or translations, questions cultural assumptions. Bowles denies the authority of Western culture and insists on other voices being heard. In the case of his music, he insists on other rhythms, other instruments, other harmonies, and other approaches to musical structure, as well. He has lived a life of alterity, of difference, and he has created a body of work that unceasingly ponders the question of otherness. Inescapably a product of the American suburbs, building on the nineteenth-century western European romantic tradition, he nevertheless made of himself a savage: a man with-*out* civilization.

BOOK I

THE LANDSCAPE OF THE CHILD, 1910–1929

For me, a blank wall at the end of a blind alley suggests mystery, just as being in the tiny closetlike rooms of a Moslem house in the Medina evokes the magic of early childhood games, or as the sudden call to prayer of the muezzin from his minaret is a song whose music completely transforms the moment. Such reactions, I have been told, are those of a person who refuses to grow up. If that is so, it is all right with me, to whom being childlike implies having retained the full use of the imagination.[1]

Product of the Suburbs

IN THE SPRING of 1931, twenty-year-old Paul Frederic Bowles knocked on the large double door at 27 rue de Fleurus in Paris's sixth *arrondissement* and introduced himself to the famous American expatriate poet Gertrude Stein. The monumental Stein presided over one of the world's greatest salons for painters, writers, and eccentrics, whom she collected as passionately as she did modern art. Stein and her constant companion, Alice Toklas, took to Paul immediately, although they were "sure from [his] letters that [he was] an elderly gentleman, at least seventy-five. . . . 'A highly eccentric elderly gentleman,' added Alice Toklas. 'We were certain of it.'" They insisted on calling their visitor by his younger-sounding middle name, deciding he was "really a Freddy and not a Paul."[2]

"Freddy" was pleased to elicit such a personal response from so famous a source. When his composer friend Aaron Copland arrived in Paris, Freddy proudly introduced him to Stein, who received them while seated in a high-backed, ornate chair, her legs tucked Buddha-like under her flowing gown, surrounded by paintings of Cézanne, Matisse, Picasso, Renoir, and Bonnard.[3]

Bowles spent several months traveling in Germany, and upon returning to France he joined Stein and Toklas at their country home at Bilignin, which reminded him, he said, of his grandparents' Happy Hollow Farm. He stayed there for some weeks, during which he took daily baths in icy water and ran around the courtyard dressed in lederhosen, while being pursued by Stein's giant white poodle, Basket.

Although "she was like a grandmother" in her devotion to him,[4] Bowles realized that in Stein's mind he existed primarily "as a sociological exhibit." "I provided her initial encounter with a species then rare, now the commonest of contemporary phenomena, the American suburban child with its unrelenting spleen" (*WS*:119). Within a week or so, Stein had finished her study of him and reached her verdict: Bowles was a "spoiled, insensitive, and self-indulgent young man," whose "colossal complacency in rejecting all values appalled her." And she railed at him, "If you were typical, it would be the end of our civilization. . . . You're a manufactured savage" (*WS*:119).

Stein was not the only one to attribute Bowles's behavior to a youth spent in suburbia. A few years later, he and a childhood neighbor, Max Eastman, a celebrated advocate of the Russian Revolution, debated Stalinist and Trotskyist points of view. "Listen to that, will you?" said Paul's father. "'You'd think [Paul had] been brought up in the slums of a factory town.' [Eastman] laughed. 'No, I wouldn't, Claude. I'd think he was the son of a Long Island dentist'" (*WS*:21).

Bowles had spent most of his childhood in the suburbs—one of the first American generations to do so—which was something he regretted deeply. If he was too young to know or remember the nineteenth century, his grandparents were not. He worked at being antimodern by rebelling against the emphasis on science and efficiency, and he felt he understood his Winnewisser grandparents better than their own children did. He also developed a fantasy about his grandparents' country life for his autobiography: "Gramma was not sorry for herself. It was not torture for her to live on the farm; it was merely hard work, and she was used to that. Like most New Englanders of her generation, she was very much aware of 'nature' and was happy in proximity to it. When she died, much later, her children all whispered to one another that it was the fact of having been forced to live on the farm that had killed her" (*WS*:13). This hard-working New England farm woman died while vacationing in Florida with her husband, three of their children, Emma, Frederick, and Paul, and their wives, and Paul's daughter Pauline. What her children actually whispered was that she ought never to have been allowed to go camping at her age in the dead of winter.[5] (Son-in-law, Guy Ross, who had not accompanied his wife, Emma, on the trip, wrote to Paul's mother, Rena: "Oh dear it don't seem possible. And all so unnecessary. If only they had stayed home."[6]) In an early draft of "The Frozen Fields," Bowles states that his grandparents "were not really country people and had bought the farm as an experiment." But in the same story, he writes, "For some reason [Donald] had always thought of the old house and his grandmother as two parts of the same person; it was impossible to think of one without the other."[7] Bowles treasured his summers at the Happy Hollow Farm or at his paternal grandparents' lake house in Glenora, New York.

The landscape of Bowles's childhood remained that against which he measured all others for the rest of his life. Experiences he found magical and mysterious formed an imaginary ideal that contrasted with the standardized suburban world. Jamaica, Long Island, had manicured lawns, treeless vistas, neatly marked paths, and above all, orderly, manufactured, modern middle-classness, which was a far cry from the unkempt country.

By adolescence Bowles had nothing but contempt for suburbia. It was neither country nor city; it symbolized conspicuous consumption, mass production, uniformity, ethnic dilution, and unoriginality. At the age of seventeen he left his suburban home for Paris, North Africa, Central America, Mexico, and India. Yet Paul could not so easily shed the imprint the suburbs had left on his soul. They had given him a privileged youth but had taken away from him the spirit of childhood. During the rest of his life he strove to recapture that spirit, to recover that indefinable something, which he called simply the "lost childhood."

Winnewissers and Bowleses

The child of nature, so popular an image for Rousseau romantics, had by the late nineteenth century been supplanted by a Darwinian belief in the child as a developmentally primitive being, the domestic equivalent of a savage in need of the late nineteenth-century colonizers' civilizing influence. The child, as one period expert wrote, is "destitute of any sort of conscience, its pleasures are those of the appetite, it has a short sharp temper, and will bite and 'butt' when its angry passions are aroused. . . . Ages of civilization have not succeeded in eradicating some of the most characteristic and unpleasant impulses of the brute."[8]

As an adult, Paul felt he had been pushed out of childhood far too early. Viewing him "as a captured animal of uncertain reactions" (*WS*:26), his parents adopted the commonly accepted belief that one could break the wild spirit of the untamed child through scientifically approved methods.[9] His later fascination with indigenous cultures hearkens back to his youth when a small boy was seen as a savage in need of a civilizing influence. He shared with those cultures a sense of arrested development, a destiny interrupted by an external power, and his lifelong identification with the colonized began with the premature contact with the forces of civilization.

Complementing Darwinian beliefs were the tenets of the great Age of Optimism, an era in which social reformers had faith in the ability of science and scientific methods to change society for the better. Progressive educators and social reformers urged parents to raise their children above the levels of their inherited tendencies for the good of civilization, the race, and the nation. Childhood was a laboratory, a testing ground for theories about the modern care of tomorrow's citizens. Adults came armed with myriad techniques to try out on a child. As an only child of parents from close-knit families, Paul spent time with grandparents, aunts, and uncles on both sides of his family and was subjected to a bewildering range of opinions, each of which culminated in its own particular child-rearing approach. On his father's side of the family was a long line of New England spiritualists, who encouraged proper breathing techniques and meditation; on his mother's side was a terrifying first-generation German American, who gave his grandchildren catechisms in atheism.

Paul's maternal grandmother, Henrietta Frances Barker Winnewisser, or "Etta," was from a family that had lived in New England since 1643. She was an island of secular calm in the emotional sea churned by her husband, Connecticut-born August Winnewisser, the son of German immigrant parents who had come to the United States in 1849, only seven years before his birth. Family legend had it that Great-grandfather Winnewisser had smashed the bridges of his sons' noses with a hammer when they were babies to transform or deform a distinguishing Jewish feature. Daughter Rena Winnewisser escaped the cruel ritual but not the knowledge of it or the effect; she later spent hours massaging her son's nose to reshape the delicate cartilage.

Paul seems to have rejected his cousin Marjorie's claim that his father's family was Jewish, though the possibility fascinated him, because it would have placed him farther outside the mainstream of American culture.[10] "I always want to know what people are, but it's getting harder and harder to tell," he said, with regard to ethnicity.[11] In his suburban neighborhood, there was no tradition, no sense of belonging to the past or to history; only family origins provided a sense of continuity.

The fact that August Winnewisser was a Freemason (his obituary listed him as a member of the Odd Fellows Lodge and the Amity Rebekah Lodge), an organization to which few Jews belonged, refutes the suspicion of Jewishness. Further, in his seventies, Paul Bowles wrote a friend that he had met a man from Switzerland named Winnewisser (probably the artist Rolf Winnewisser), who said that he knew of no Jewish Winnewissers (pronounced "Veenevitza") and that in the Schwartzwald, where the name was common, it meant, "he who works a plot of land."[12] Paul himself was entirely comfortable in New York Jewish culture, used Yiddish phrases naturally in conversation, and took his wife's Jewish heritage seriously. Some of Paul's friends asserted that his mother must be Jewish. John Latouche, whose own mother was Jewish and who, according to Paul, "pretended to believe that mine was too," called Paul "Friedrich von Winewitz" (*WS*:244). When Leonard Bernstein met Rena, he remarked, "She's a nice Jewish lady," and when Paul protested, he said, "Get off it. Are you pretending, don't you know she is or what?"[13]

To Paul, August Winnewisser was a "frightening man," and Paul secretly feared he might be the victim of the hammer. Winnewisser was a "moody and violent man, subject to sudden surges of temper, when his voice shook the house with bellowed imprecations in German and English." On one occasion, he called the children in from play to ask them whether they believed in God and then exploded, "Pah! There's no god. It's a lot of nonsense. Don't you believe in it" (*WS*:11).

For thirty-two years, August Winnewisser was a successful merchant in Bellows Falls, Vermont, until in 1912 an injury forced him to retire, and after moving first to Brooklyn and then to Lockwood, New York, he finally settled his family on the one-hundred-sixty-five-acre Happy Hollow Farm near Springfield, Massachusetts. The farm was never a commercial success, and following his wife's death, August managed a gas station, which he first owned with Lewis E. Cook and then ran with his sons Paul and Frederick.[14]

Paul's paternal grandparents also had no religious affiliation. Frederick Theodore Bowles was one of four children of Dr. Harvey Edward Bowles, a respected resident of southern New Jersey, where his family had lived for generations.[15] Frederick Bowles and his wife, Ida Berry Robbins Bowles, lived in austere surroundings in a Queen Anne-style house on West Church Street in Elmira, New York, a town of eight thousand on the Chemung River at the foot of Seneca Lake. Stepping into their house was like walking into a forest: "There in the dimness and silence Daddymama and Daddypapa were sitting reading their books, he in his den upstairs and she in her study downstairs" (*WS*:16). To Paul's way of thinking, Grandfather Bowles was the most exotic and therefore most interesting of his four grandparents. A commercial silks merchant and Civil War veteran, he claimed to have been in every state of the Union and had taught himself both French and Spanish to read literature in the original language.[16] More important, he collected artifacts of the Native Americans, whom he called the "Amerind," and studied their history and culture. His example prompted Paul to vow to travel across the country collecting mysterious Indian objects and tales from other places.

Ida Robbins Bowles dabbled in spiritualism and spent her time reading Theosophical texts and comparing notes with her brother Charles Robbins and sister Mary Robbins Mead, a locally famous spiritualist. Their step-father, abolitionist Fox Holden, had built the famous Elmira Water-Cure, which accommodated one hundred ten patients, and Holden Hall, a center for Advanced Thought (an offshoot of spiritualism).[17] After his death in 1890 his wife, Christiana, continued the work at Holden Hall, which her daughter Mary converted into a salon and rest home for troubled souls.[18]

Charles Robbins, Paul's great-uncle, lived about ten miles away in Glenora, on Seneca Lake, so the three Robbins siblings met often. Charles practiced Yoga and later convinced brother-in-law Frederick Bowles the value of proper breathing, which enabled one to inhale *prana* (Sanskrit for breath, life, vitality, or strength). An impressed Frederick then taught Paul "to learn to breathe by stopping and unstopping [his] nostrils with [his] fingers." Paul wrote, "This struck me as arbitrary and wholly absurd, like all the other things invented by the family in order to make my life more unpleasant" (*WS*:17).

The chief inventor of troublesome practices during Paul's childhood, however, was his father, Claude Dietz Bowles. Born in Wisconsin in March of 1878, Claude Bowles grew up in Elmira, New York, in comfortable circumstances, a graduate of the locally prestigious Elmira Free Academy. He worked as a dentist for two years in Elmira before moving to New York City in 1907.[19] Dentistry was a second career choice: he had wanted to be a concert violinist, to the dismay of his parents. After suffering a nervous breakdown, he turned to dentistry, as had his older brother Dwight. As an adult Claude was "nervous and hypochondriacal."[20] He was particularly disagreeable about food. He supervised all household cooking and frequently had temper fits followed by indigestion if he found the food unsatisfactory. With the rages coming like bolts of lightning, family activities seemed to revolve around Claude's hypochondria.

Paul's mother, Rena Frances Winnewisser, was born in October of 1884 in Vermont and attended Robinson Female Seminary in Exeter, New Hampshire, graduating in the class of 1904 at a time when women sought expert coaching to learn how to run their future homes with the same modern efficiency as their husbands would use to run their businesses. In 1907 Rena received a Certificate in Household Economics for the completion of a one-year program from Simmons College in Boston, designed to prepare her "for the intelligent administration of a private home."[21] Her course of study included household arts, sewing, accounts, marketing, household values, and two courses in cooking, along with elementary chemistry, elementary bacteriology, and elementary physiology.[22] Paul remembers a manual on child care constantly at her side throughout his years at home, an essential for child rearing in the modern age.[23]

The Bowleses quietly disapproved of their daughter-in-law, who used cosmetics, drank alcohol, and smoked cigarettes; and during the Prohibition era she hosted parties where they served liquor, played dice, and gambled, though not for high stakes.[24] Rena became so nervous in her mother-in-law's presence that she occasionally took to bed. Ida Bowles was the most suspicious woman she had ever met. Of Paul, his grandmother once said, "It's not natural for a child of his age to have such thick lips." Rena warned Paul, "And your father is just like her. Don't ever let yourself get to be like them. . . . It poisons everything" (*WS*:18).

The contrast between his grandparents was apparent to Paul even as a child. The somber and quiet Bowleses kept two servants, owned three summer houses on Seneca Lake, and traveled to Europe.[25] The Winnewisser money was more volatile, the household more vocally active.

Although Claude came from a family that was older and more established, it was Rena who impressed those who knew her as the more sophisticated of the couple. She had taught school and joined the Delphian Society, for which she wrote poetry.[26] Throughout Paul's teenage years she subscribed to the Theatre Guild productions in New York City. Theater designer Oliver Smith, a close friend of Paul, recalled her as "rather affected, interested in world affairs, travel, and culture. She was outgoing and had great charm. She was very proud of Paul's accomplishments, whereas [Claude Bowles] had a slight disregard for them."[27]

The Lost Childhood

Paul Frederic Bowles was born 30 December 1910 in Jamaica, on New York's Long Island, and was Rena and Claude's only child.[28] Four years after his arrival, which he says was a difficult breech delivery, Rena required surgery, for which his father seems to have held him personally responsible. According to Gramma Winnewisser, when Paul was still an infant, his father carried him to the ledge of an open window and left him there in a wicker basket in the middle of a blizzard. Had she not discovered Paul, he would have been dead within the hour. "Your father's a devil," she insisted (*WS*:26).

For Paul, Claude represented rules, order, discipline, and punishment. Paul's earliest memory, according to friend and artist Buffie Johnson, was of Claude switching his bare legs as he tried to climb stairs that were too tall for him. "Hurry up, hurry up," his father fussed.[29] The words would ring like an anthem, for Claude was ever impatient with his son. Paul was given neither the time nor the right to be a child.

During Paul's early childhood, Claude's office was in their home, a brownstone in Jamaica.[30] The bottom-floor laboratory entrance was "dark and uninviting," and Paul was forbidden to go there. On the second floor of the building were Dr. Bowles's dental office and reception area, and the family's apartment was on the third floor. Each evening at six, Claude entered the living quarters and confiscated any toys Paul had failed to return to the toy chest. Paul could read until dinner, but any other playthings, including his drawings and writings, had to be shut away. Paul observed this arbitrary arrangement strictly; each evening at five, he began tidying up in anticipation of his father's arrival.

In keeping with the then modern regimen for child rearing, for one hour each day Paul exercised outside in the backyard. His parents carefully monitored this hour, apparently with contradictory purposes. If Paul stood still in the yard, his mother rapped on the window upstairs, telling him to move around and play. If, however, he began to run or make any noise, his father admonished from his office window, "Calm down, young man!" From Paul's vantage point of the house, the windows stared back at him like nine huge eyes, one of which held a clock placed there by his mother so that he could tell when his hour of recreation was up and he could come back inside. For the whole hour of playtime Paul felt conspicuous, under constant observation, caught in a double bind.

Another scientific practice of the time was Fletcherism, a process that nutritionist Horace Fletcher introduced and popularized. A former whaler, athlete, painter, marksman, and opera company manager, Fletcher discovered in 1898 that by chewing each mouthful of his food until it lost all flavor, he was able to reduce his weight from two hundred five to one hundred sixty-nine pounds in a five-month period.[31] If properly Fletcherized, food formed a "bolus" and, in effect, "swallowed itself" at the time when the digestive system was most prepared to accept it.[32] Fletcher tested his discovery on a dozen willing subjects and claimed that Fletcherizing cured "obesity and leanness . . . indigestion, bleeding piles, catarrh, pimpled skin and a variety of other ailments."[33]

Fletcher's own phenomenal strength helped to popularize his practices through the first two decades of the twentieth century; at the age of sixty he claimed to best a young "New Havenite" by lifting 840 pounds to the younger man's 420. Fletcherite missionaries took the program to the poor and working classes in Appalachia and, after six months, reported reduced food and alcohol consumption among their converts. Among Fletcher's followers were William and Henry James, John D. Rockefeller, Arthur Conan Doyle, Upton Sinclair, and John Harvey Kellogg. For the first several years of the century, Fletcherism promised a healthier, more efficient, and righteous society.

The Bowleses so strictly enforced Fletcherism that Paul grew to hate mealtimes and remained underweight until after he left home. His father insisted Paul chew each mouthful forty times before swallowing. If he forgot, the elder Bowles swatted him briskly with a linen napkin, shouting, "Fletcherize, young man!" If Paul swallowed too soon too many times in one meal, he was sent to bed without being able to finish his dinner. The only escape from this ordeal was to fall ill and take his supper in bed. Once, having contracted a high fever, he lay in bed as his father stood watching him, hands in pockets, remarking to Rena, "You know, I think he likes to be sick." Paul recalls, "I regularly settled into protracted illnesses with a shiver of voluptuousness at the prospect of the stretches of privacy that lay ahead" (*WS*:25). The connection between illness and voluptuous privacy remained strong, and as an adult Paul suffered from "protracted" illnesses so regularly that his friends considered him a hypochondriac. In his later years, he would take all his meals in bed: "I find it takes longer, and of course, the more slowly you eat the better you digest."[34]

Paul's childhood on Long Island took place during one of the largest shifts in the character of American life in its history, and many felt uneasy with the transition. In 1870, only 25 percent of all Americans lived in towns or cities, but by 1920, that percentage had doubled to 50.[35] Only one year before Paul's birth, in 1909, a planned neighborhood broke ground at Forest Hills Gardens, one suburb west of Jamaica.[36] This garden suburb of one hundred seventy-four acres with its Long Island Railroad connections to Manhattan provided a model for the many "railroad suburbs" that followed on Long Island and in other communities. In 1910, the year Paul was born, entire sections near the main streets of Fulton Avenue and Hillside Avenue stood platted and ready for development.

The 1920s marked a boom in suburban development unequaled by any previous period in history, largely due to the availability of the automobile and a subsequent interest in road building. The huge park system Governor Al Smith and his Long Island State Park Commission president, Robert Moses, created on Long Island made suburban development possible, since thousands of acres of new parkland for New York City residents necessitated new roads to transport them to the island. Moses planned one hundred twenty-four miles of parkway. The population of Nassau County on Long Island tripled in the 1920s.[37]

In 1916, Long Island was just beginning to undergo the series of developments that were to transform it into a suburban area punctuated by parks. On the western sixth of the island were Brooklyn and Queens, jam-packed with two and a half million people in 1920, but east of Queens lay the nearly nine hundred thousand acres of Nassau and Suffolk counties, with a population density of about one person in every four acres. South and west of Jamaica Avenue, which carried miles of lampposts from Brooklyn to

Nassau County, lay vast areas of marshland and grassy meadows, with names such as Sloop Bar Hassock and Duck Creek Marsh.[38] The south shore of the island held sandy beaches lapped by gentle waves where baymen trawled for bluefish. Farmers competed with the wealthy for the northern part of the island. From J. P. Morgan's estate on the northern tip of Glen Cove southward lay the estates of such robber barons as Charles Pratt and Stephen Harkness of Standard Oil; Henry Phipps of Carnegie Steel; Clarence Hungerford Mackay of Postal Telegraph Cable Company (precursor of Western Union); Childs Frick, son of coal and coke baron Henry Clay Frick; Standard Oil heir Payne Whitney; and Cornelius Vanderbilt's grandson Willie. Occupying the north shore were six hundred estates, ranging from about fifty acres to as large as thousands of acres in size.[39]

Sometime around 1916–17, the Bowleses moved from their brownstone on Herriman Avenue, just off Fulton Avenue, to De Grauw Avenue, high on a forested ridge above Jamaica.[40] Few houses had yet been built, and the carefully planned new streets led straight into the woods. Paul enjoyed the nearby trees and birds. Moreover, he was able to spend much more time alone in his new home, whether playing in the surrounding woods or drawing and writing. On walks through the woods, he invented place-names for the trees, rocks, and bushes. In the privacy of his third-floor room, he made lists of the landmarks. He called these lists "timetables," like the railway timetables he knew from the Long Island Railway: "Stations on the Scranton Railroad. Greenport. Scranton. Lack Ave. Taylor. Moosic. Avoca. Pittson. Yatesville," and so on, to "South Transfer Last Stop."[41]

As Paul grew in years, so the neighborhood around him slowly evolved from woods and rolling hills to the orderly and barren arrangements of the suburb. Sometime between 1922 and 1924, the family moved to a large, single-family house on Terrace Avenue.[42] The suburbs around continued to change, now more rapidly than ever. The canopied woods with their dappled light almost completely disappeared, along with the robins, thrushes, and wild violets that Paul had loved, and there were few places left to explore.

The abrupt transformation from a rural to a suburban environment disturbed Paul, and he remarked on the correlation between this disruption and his growing compulsion to label, draw, and write: "I resented the brutal changes, but then I decided that I was too old to think about such things and devoted myself even more intensively to my work" (*WS*:46).

Paul's "work" was an internalization and a re-creation of his suburban neighborhood, a way of "reading" and "writing" the world he knew. In his childhood notebooks are pages and pages of drawings of houses — an endless series of two- and three-story houses with chimneys, some with green shutters, like those of his house, with successive addresses: 608, 610, 612

Mountain Road in Cliffton-Ville, Wen Kroy (backwards for New York), an invented land where several imaginary characters lived. For his favorite characters, like Bluey Laber Dozlen, he drew interiors, down to red-flowered wallpaper.

Paul kept several diaries for the characters he invented, whose lives he chronicled. In the diary dated 1920–21 are various characters who marry, divorce, remarry, have children, fall ill—many succumb to the "Green Horror"—acquire prodigious fortunes and houses, lose them, and take injections to age thirty years at a time. They die of broken necks, influenza, and pneumonia, or their legs fall off. Forest fires devastate their communities. Like Bowles's mature fiction, this early notebook displays a remarkable preoccupation with diseases, catastrophes, and repressed passions, juxtaposed with the ordinary events of everyday life, showing Bowles's conception that domestic life is perilous.

> Tue. It rains awfully hard. Marshelle and Nip go to Mossy Rock it is slippery. They stay over night.
> Wed. Nip dies of Broken Neck. Marshelle faints in a dead faint.
> Thur. Marshelle finds out that Nip slipped and broke his neck. Marshelle swears she will never go to Mossy Rock again.
> Sun. Dukol's sister, Djerkiss, comes to stay. Abbie has her fortune told. She will not live more than a year.
> Mon. Abbie weeps and weeps. Clement says he will kill her if she does not stop weeping.
> Mon. Abbie buys a house and swears she will live for the rest of her life alone.

Paul spent most of his boyhood alone, engaged in his favorite activities: reading, writing, and drawing. He taught himself to read, and by the age of four, he was piecing together small books that he also illustrated. He created an imaginary planet with four continents—Ferncawland, Lanton, Zaganok-world, and Araplaina—of which he drew maps detailing railways, cities, mountain ranges, and rivers.

The young Paul understood the physical properties of books: his books were numbered, indexed, and illustrated. His strong interest in geography and maps shows the importance of landscape in his imagination, and it is easy to see these real estate developments and fantastic diaries as part of a small boy's efforts to bring his world under his control, a response to a world in which adults controlled everything. Through invented worlds, neighborhoods, travel routes, and imaginary characters, Paul established a personal cosmos in which he exerted the kind of power the adults in his life held over him, and he took his work seriously.

By the time he was eight years old, he had established a routine of what he called "daily chores." He issued a four-page daily newspaper in crayon and pencil, which he distributed to family and neighbors. He worked on his imaginary planet, drew houses for his "gigantic real estate development," and kept diaries for his imaginary characters. When he began to study the piano a year or so later, he conscientiously practiced his assigned exercises before going on to improvisation. He then went upstairs to do his home-work and began his chores. The obsessiveness with which he attended to his chores suggests that this regimen kept perfectly natural but unacceptable childhood feelings and energies under control. Together, the chores and the routines indicate a boy who had little of the spontaneity and innocence romantics idealize in children. Paul had become a miniature adult.

Paul was an only child, an increasingly common phenomenon among the middle classes in the first years of the twentieth century. In those days, the distresses of the high-strung and "fanciful" single child peppered conversa-tion and various medical and psychological texts. Such a child was likely to be precocious at best and at worst neurotic, and Paul's family anxiously looked for signs of the single-child syndrome. They were all too aware of his solitude and felt that his precocity was an indicator of the neurosis. He writes, "It seems there was never a time when the Bowles family were not wont to sit discussing my defects. 'It's not natural,' was the commonest introductory phrase. 'It's not natural for a child that age to spend all his time reading.' 'It's not natural for a child to want to be alone.'" Somehow, he says, the Bowleses had completely "overlooked the fact that at the age of five I had never yet even spoken to another child or seen children playing together. My idea of the world was still that of a place inhabited exclusively by adults" (*WS*:17–18, 23). Since Paul's cousins were younger than he, this recollection, strange as it may seem, may well be accurate. Even when older, he spent most of his leisure time alone or with his mother and the housekeeper, reading and playing card games or Mah-Jongg.[43]

Paul's first experiences with other children were far from ideal. "It took me one day [at grammar school] to discover that the world of children was a world of unremitting warfare. But since I had suspected this all along, it did not come as a shock" (*WS*:27). Like most children, Paul did unto others what they had done to him. From hiding places he attacked children walking alone, even going so far as to sharpen the stones he threw to be sure of drawing blood.

Once he invented a boys' club with a special initiation procedure solely to get even with a long-standing enemy whose "babyish quality" infuriated him (*WS*:49). He convinced others to blindfold the unsuspecting boy and dangle him by a rope over an unfinished stairwell. The boy was heavier than they anticipated, and they dropped him onto the ground below. In a reversal of the enforced exercise periods at home, Paul leaned above the helpless ("babyish") boy from three stories up, finding revenge even more satisfying for having been achieved indirectly.

Paul sharpened his skills in passive aggression during the ongoing struggle against his father's corrective measures. "Since I firmly believed that I *had* to win in the struggle between us or I should be hopelessly lost, it seemed to me that it was merely a question of holding out" (*WS*:28). Paul arose early to draw, and one morning his father heard him tiptoe to the bedroom door and lock it first. Lunging up the stairs and pummeling the door, Claude demanded to know what his son was doing behind the locked door. When Paul explained that he was drawing, Claude lost control. A determined Paul held back his tears throughout the ensuing beating, though it caused his father to beat him even harder and longer, asking, "Have you had enough?" Thus began what Paul called "a new stage in the development of hostilities between us. I vowed to devote my life to his destruction, even though it meant my own—an infantile conceit, but one which continued to preoccupy me for many years" (*WS*:43–45).

In contrast to Paul's lonely and monotonous everyday life were glimpses of the rural and urban worlds beyond his suburban neighborhood. He and his mother often spent summer vacations at the Winnewissers' farm in Massachusetts. Paul loved the overgrown landscape of the farm, the old farmhouse and its history, but what he liked best were the "dark and rustic sheds that extended all the way back to the springhouse" (*WS*:11). He luxuriated in the discoveries he made there, the smells of wood, burlap, apples, and earth, all forgotten and lost, encrusted with time. Although the adults forbade him to play in the sheds, he sneaked back to them whenever he could to explore their secret spaces. The dark and the hidden, the mysterious and the forbidden intrigued him. At Seneca Lake, Paul escaped from the adult world by playing in the boathouse, where he spent hours listening to his favorite record, which he remembered as "Down among the Sheltering Palms," a title that he would adapt for his first novel, *The Sheltering Sky*.[44] On woodland trails, in broken-down outbuildings, or in a wooden boathouse, Paul found wonder and history and plunged headlong into it.

An even more exotic world existed in the city. His father's sister, Adelaide Maltby, was a librarian with artistic tastes who lived in a Japanese-style Greenwich Village apartment, "full of strange objects and wonderful smells" (*WS*:26). Paul had long conversations there with Adelaide's friend Anne Carroll Moore, children's librarian at the New York Public Library from 1904 to 1941. "Among the screens and lanterns and flickering candle-light . . . her presence gave the occasion an unmistakable air of celebration, low-keyed and mysterious, the very essence of festivity in its conscious exclusion of the outside world" (*WS*:26). Visits to Aunt Adelaide's were a celebration of the private and the foreign.

Another favorite relative was Uncle Guy, the husband of Rena's sister Emma. As Paul and Jane Bowles were to do during their married life, Emma and Guy Ross lived in separate apartments in the same building. In his apartment, Guy "wore Japanese kimonos and spent a good deal of time keeping incense burning in a variety of bronze dragons and Buddhas" (*WS*:40). Paul felt as if Uncle Guy were "on his side" and considered him a friend. Both Aunt Adelaide and Uncle Guy accepted Paul, and with them he escaped from the discipline with which the rest of his family seems to have been obsessed.

But even the grown-ups he liked and trusted betrayed him. He once visited Uncle Guy when Emma was out of town and was told to stay in the bedroom while his uncle hosted a party "crowded with pretty young men dancing together" in his wife's apartment down the hall (*WS*:41). When Uncle Guy caught his nephew watching, he hustled the boy back to the bedroom and locked him in. "I sat on the bed consumed by fury and frustration," Paul recalls (*WS*:41).

Once Paul came home from school expecting to find his mother and, instead, found an empty house. His father had repeatedly insisted that burglers were an "ever present menace," so the boy felt compelled to search the entire house. Instead of a burglar, he found his mother hiding under a bed in the guest room, because she wanted to play a joke on him. Paul was furious: "I walked out of the room, clenching my fists, climbed upstairs to my own quarters, and shut the door. Fear naturally turns to anger; the anger did not go away for several days" (*WS*:33).

Either or both of these betrayals could be what psychologists call a "screen memory," that is, a memory that remains powerful because it comes to stand for a series of forgotten but related events in one's life. The linking of sexuality and betrayal—his uncle's homosexual party, his mother's hiding under a bed—resonated throughout Paul's life and in his fiction, evidence that Paul felt his family failed to provide him with a foundation for building trust in other people.

Bowles devoted more than a quarter of his autobiography to his childhood, trying to describe the part of his life when its emotional structure was formed. His description is hermetic, full of traumatic memories. This gifted little boy, who lived in a world inhabited exclusively by adults, could scarcely turn out other than unusual, or more likely, highly neurotic. More than once he has attributed his adult sense of isolation to his early years of solitude, to an undeveloped social sensibility.

Yet his upbringing was not uncommon for the early twentieth century, when children in well-to-do homes were to be seen as little as possible and heard from even less. Affluent families had separate wings for their children, complete with nursemaids. When they were old enough, many upper- and middle-class children were sent to preparatory or boarding schools, a fate Paul escaped through his father's veto of Exeter Academy, where his uncle was chaplain.[45] Several similar experiences, bizarre though they seem, can be found in memoirs and autobiographies of other writers of his generation. George Orwell recalled a similar sense of betrayal and isolation: "Not to expose your true feelings to an adult seems to be instinctive from the age of seven or eight onwards."[46] Orwell concluded that the emotional world of the child was one to which most adults have no access. "Treacherous though memory is, it seems to me the chief means we have of discovering how a child's mind works. Only by resurrecting our own memories can we realise how incredibly distorted is the child's vision of the world."[47]

As an adult, Bowles succeeded in the difficult task of reconstructing the world of his childhood from the point of view of the child. Distorted though it may be, the emotional record in his autobiography accords so completely with expression in his fiction that one need not ask whether such memories are objectively true. Subjective experience is the truth where psychological and emotional reality is concerned. The happiest moments of Paul's childhood were those times when he was submerged in experience, magical and mysterious, and unaware of the outside world. The rest of his life constituted a search for this lost, ideal childhood.

A Life of Crime

Like many New England families at the turn of the century, the Bowleses were interested in various kinds of mysticism, which provided Paul with some preparation for his later encounters with the ecstatic religious brotherhoods of North Africa. Paul states that his mother taught him "how to make [his] mind a blank": "I found that very useful. She described her sensations and how she did it—she just lay down in the afternoons on a bed and thought absolutely nothing." This meditation, the spiritual discipline that often serves as preparation for mystical experiences, became the basis for Bowles's writing practice as an adult, as he tried to "cleanse the mind" before he began to receive and record "messages from the subconscious."[48]

Aunt Mary was the true mystic in the family. Quick-stepping, small, and soft-spoken, Mary Robbins Mead ran a retreat at Holden Hall in Watkins, New York (now Watkins Glen), in which she taught "New Thought Philosophy," a cross between spiritualism and theosophy.[49] Spiritualism, the practice of communicating with spirits through human mediums, had become a popular parlor pastime in many nineteenth-century homes.[50] It began in Arcadia, New York, a township fifty miles north of Watkins Glen. There, in the winter of 1848, Katy and Margaretta Fox, ages eleven and thirteen, realized that through cracking the joints in their toes and feet they could create loud rapping noises.[51] Adults around them quickly attributed the "rapping" to spirits and discovered that by going through the alphabet one letter at a time, they could induce the spirits to communicate words and even sentences. The numerous public meetings and exhibitions held to disprove claims of spirit communication served only to further popularize the Fox sisters' discovery and to fan the phenomenon into a movement. By 1870, observers estimated the number of believers at eleven million.[52]

Theosophy, an exotic distillation of spiritualism, Hindu mysticism, Buddhism, Brahmanism, and Kabalistic teachings, was a later and more elegant development of the spiritualist movement. Ex-spiritualist medium Helena Petrovna Blavatsky founded the Theosophical Society in New York in 1881.[53] Blavatsky remained the chief prophet of theosophy and closely guided its growth through her books: *The Secret Doctrine*, *The Key to Theosophy*, *The Voice of the Silence*, and *Isis Unveiled*.

Aunt Mary combined Madame Blavatsky's theosophy with her own insights to offer "Correspondence Lessons in the Fine Art of Living." A brochure on the correspondence courses advertised six books by Mary Robbins Mead, with such titles as *Ideals for Invalids*, *The Mystic Gate*, and *A Soul in the Sunlight*. One book, *Soul Help*, went through at least six editions. The brochure suggested that "pupils who require rest and helpful surroundings" would be received at Holden Hall, "one of the first New Thought homes, established 1887."[54] Guests at Holden Hall paid twenty-five dollars a week for room and board.

Paul spent the summer of his fourteenth year at Holden Hall and found it fascinating. Watkins Glen nestled at the foot of Seneca Lake, next to a tree-lined gorge of the sort that Paul later fictionalized in his story "The Echo," but the house itself, high on a hill, had a sweeping view of the narrow blue lake and the rolling hills surrounding it. The huge thirteen-room, high-ceilinged house was filled with family heirlooms. A stately staircase led up three flights to an observation tower through which, so local children claimed, spirits entered the house at night. Until her death in 1941, Mary used nothing other than oil lamps and candles for illumination. For years memories of Holden Hall stayed with Paul, and when he found a similar vintage house on the island of Taprobane near Ceylon, he listed as one of its greatest charms the tall-ceilinged rooms lit only by oil lamps and candles.

In the tower Meditation Room, with its two sets of heavy draperies, Mary and her guests spent their days practicing the trance like state conducive to spirit communication. To aid their meditations, they burned incense inscribed with Blavatsky's initials (small cubes that Paul thought of as "HPB" incense) and chanted, which, as an adult, Paul likened to Hindu tantric chanting.

Paul considered Aunt Mary one of the most intriguing people he had ever known. But one evening, after he had been sent to bed early, Paul overheard a conversation between his aunt and his seventeen-year-old cousin, Elizabeth, and he found Mary's final remarks to Elizabeth devastating: "Well, I can only say that to me Paul has all the earmarks of a boy who has started on the downward path" (*WS*:64). Paul reviewed his behavior of the past few days and, coming up with nothing that could have prompted Aunt Mary's conclusion, realized that his aunt had judged him not according to what he had done but according to who he was. To Paul, this seemed grossly unfair. Even at fourteen, Paul had embraced the basic doctrine of existentialism: existence precedes essence, or one is the sum of one's actions.

Crime became something of a preoccupation, at least in Paul's creative life. The next summer he began writing a collection of crime stories entitled "The Snake Woman Series":

> In each tale there was a death which, although unexpected, could be reasonably laid to natural causes. However, in each case the reader had to explain away the brief but inexplicable appearance on the scene of a woman named Volga Merna. Since the other characters were not able to remember what she looked like or what she was doing, she was never suspected. Nor was it explicitly stated she had any part in the crimes; the reader could decide. (*WS*:66)

One of his neighbors, Mary Crouch, remembers one of the Volga Merna stories beginning, "Ah yes. There was Madame Volga Merna writing in the dim twilight of her salon."[55] Volga Merna, the Snake Woman, was able to protect herself from suspicion in the crimes through her very anonymity: no one could remember what she looked like. Her alias referred to her ability to change her appearance as much as a snake sheds its skin. Her ability to keep herself above suspicion even while at the scene of a crime was an achievement in which Paul took pride, and in the one story we know anything about, Volga Merna, like Bowles, was a writer.

Paul was working on the Snake Woman series at the senior Bowles's summer cabin in Glenora, New York, when he met the nearby Hoagland sisters, Anna, Jane, and Sue, who wintered in Brooklyn. Through the Hoaglands, Paul met a French teacher, Daniel Burns, who became a close friend. Burns introduced him to a wide range of French literature and encouraged his writing, drawing, and composing.[56] Jane Hoagland also had friends with studios in Greenwich Village, where she occasionally took Paul to observe the bohemian life.

In the early years of the twentieth century, Greenwich Village, or the Latin Quarter as it was then known, had been the place in America where young people went to rebel, to become artists, and to experiment with sex, with the ideas of communism, and with anything that flouted the traditional values of the small towns they fled. It had what writer Floyd Dell called a spirit of "hope, change, and adventure." World War I carried many of these young people away from the Village, along with their high ideals and sense of adventure. The Village disintegrated into a "commercialized peep-show," and postwar Villagers mocked the earnestness and funny clothes of the prewar "Hobohemians."[57] The economic boom of 1923–24 brought to the Village upper-middle-class New Yorkers who had extra income to spend on quaint apartments, old houses, or studios. A few genuine artists profited by the surge of money into the Village, but many were driven out by sky-rocketing real estate prices. The character of the Village of the mid-1920s became self-consciously "artistic" and chic.[58]

There in the mid-1920s, Paul made his first acquaintance with people who considered themselves artists, and he did not admire them. The way artists and intellectuals affected a style to appear "different from ordinary citizens" repelled him. "My own conviction was that the artist, being the enemy of society, for his own good must remain as invisible as possible and certainly should be indistinguishable from the rest of the world. Somewhere in the back of my mind there was the assumption that art and crime were indissolubly linked; the greater the art, the more drastic the punishment for it" (*WS*:67–68).

Such logic suggests that Paul felt his own art was criminal, perhaps even revolutionary. And, indeed, through drawing, writing, and playing the piano, he escaped from his father, which was for him a crime of insubordination and desertion. The antisocial nature of his early artistic impulses allowed Paul to see the possibilities for danger to society in the content of art, as well. Through his Snake Woman stories he explored crime as subject matter for fiction. Then Paul bought André Gide's *Vatican Swindle* (*Les Caves du Vatican*, later retitled *Lafcadio's Adventures*), and like an entire generation of writers and artists, from Ernest Hemingway to William Burroughs, he was "seduced by Lafcadio's *acte gratuit*," the unpremeditated murder of a fellow passenger on a train. His initial encounter with Gide remained so powerful that at the age of sixty he wrote, "I still prefer *Les Caves du Vatican* to Gide's other novels" (*WS*:67).

In his mid-1920s insistence that an artist should remain in anonymity,

Bowles echoed the philosophy of Gide's Protos, who felt "the most impor-tant thing in the world was never to look like what one was." [59] And Bowles felt the artist needed this anonymity, for in the civilized world, the artist was the enemy of society and the artist's work a crime.

The Practice of Secrecy

As a boy, Paul had plenty of opportunity to observe emotional detachment in his daily life. His memories of childhood are dominated by a series of events in which adults told him not to feel anything, deprived him of important information, or simply ignored him. In particular, they refused to discuss the crucial issues of sex, death, and illness, which Paul attributes entirely to their having been New Englanders.

Claude Bowles awoke one morning to discover that a hemorrhage had destroyed his sight in one eye. Because he was a dentist, his livelihood depended upon no one knowing of his impairment. From that day on he guarded his secret viciously. Upon his doctor's orders, Bowles reduced his schedule and took up golf, a prescription that introduced a new ordeal to the family. Three days a week, Claude, Rena, and Paul trooped off together to the Hillcrest Golf Club a few blocks from their house. Paul could not caddy the large golf bag without bumping it along the ground, which gave his father yet another opportunity to criticize his son. Rena feared that the tension caused by having to conceal Claude's blindness combined with the fear of a similar hemorrhage in his good eye might cause a second nervous breakdown. Claude refused to discuss his medical condition with his son but remained constantly alert to at least the first of these possibilities, and his hypochondria became even more pronounced.

Not talking about Claude's condition, while keeping it uppermost in their minds, provided a kind of *continuo* to daily life. Along with this steady drone of the unspoken affliction ran a similar refusal to discuss sexuality in any form. Paul claims he knew less about sex than most of his classmates and therefore perhaps asked more questions, none of which were answered until he took a biology class. When he asked the teacher whether the male and female reproductive systems in humans differed in the same way as they did in mice, she reprimanded him sharply. He later wrote, "I concluded that my suspicion had been correct and that I was on the way to discovering the great secret" (*WS*:58).

Paul found the adults around him equally unwilling to discuss other matters of life and death. He was seven when the influenza epidemic of 1918 struck the family. His mother said to him merely, "Your Aunt Adelaide has gone away. You'll never see her again," and then walked out of the room

(*WS*:31). Six years later, he was playing a game of Mah-Jongg with his mother, father, and housekeeper when the news arrived of his grandmother Etta's death in Florida. His mother read the telegram and dropped it soundlessly into the middle of the Mah-Jongg tiles. "Is she dead?" the housekeeper, Fanny, asked, but there was no reply (*WS*:58). Told to go do his homework, Paul packed away the Mah-Jongg set and left the room. Bowles's description of the scene in his autobiography is one of complete enclosure and containment of emotion. His mother tossed the telegram "into the middle of the game, into the space enclosed by the wall of tiles," where it remained, in Paul's memory, understood but forever undiscussed (*WS*:58).

A visit from Rena's sister Emma later that year initiated a series of denials that made clear his parents' lack of trust in him. He states, "She was really sick, a veritable skeleton that lay in bed moaning most of the time; it went on day and night, week after week. Often the moans became screams, which rose and fell like sirens wailing" (*WS*:59). Emma was withdrawing from morphine, but Paul was told only that she was suffering from headaches. Eventually Emma gained some weight and could move around without help, though she still smoked "three flat fifty tins of Luckies" every day. Years later Bowles wrote, "Imagining that I were given the power to relive my childhood, but under any conditions I chose, I should be content with the same sequence of events all over again, provided my parents made it clear to me that they trusted me" (*WS*:61).

In time, secrecy became more important to Paul than to his parents, especially with his father's family, who "took it for granted that pleasure was destructive, whereas engaging in an unappealing activity aided in character formation" (*WS*:17). Paul felt attention nearly always to be synonymous with discipline. He became an expert of deceit, stage-managing his reactions to convey the opposite of his true feelings. For whatever he enjoyed, he affected disgust, and he feigned enthusiasm for what he disliked. He hid his true self and wore like a cloak the expression least likely to invite criticism or correction.

The development of a "false self" can be the basis of an existential dilemma known as "ontological insecurity," in which one lives but does not feel alive. People in this dilemma feel more unreal than real, more dead than alive, separate or divorced from their bodies, yet so undifferentiated from the rest of the world that they must constantly be strengthening the barriers between themselves and others. They spend their lives adding sandbags to the continually eroding shores of their identity. The ideal of the ontologically insecure person is, in psychologist R. D. Laing's words, "never to give himself away to others."[60]

In the seventh grade Paul devised a code for note taking in class. "After a few months I could write almost as fast in my code as I could in English. The difficulty lay in reading it back, a much slower process. The rumour spread that I took all my notes in a foreign language" (*WS*:54). Coding and decoding required much energy, but like so many of his complicated childhood rituals, the process helped maintain Paul's fragile sense of being in the world. His emphasis was not on the notes but on the secret code, not on the secret but on secrecy itself, a fundamental process in his self-preservation. To keep his true self secret from the world had become an existential necessity.

"You Are Not I": The Art of Detachment

Like André Gide, who suffered unexplained fits of sobbing and "overpowering suffocation" in his youth, Paul weathered various nervous "episodes" of more than one variety in his early adolescence.[61] The first of these states of "nervous excitement" may have been what is now called an anxiety or a panic attack. Bowles explains, "I could not be interested in something without getting excited, and when I was excited, a motor began to buzz in the back of my neck. It made me feel that I was trembling, but this must have been my imagination, for no one ever mentioned it. Daddy, however, often said to me: 'Calm down, young man, calm down'" (*WS*:68).

Bowles endured an inexplicable compulsive episode when he was about thirteen: one torpid June evening, he walked down the hill from his house on Terrace Avenue to Roth's soda fountain. He recalls, after pushing open the swinging screen door, "something happened to me. The best way of describing it is to say that the connection between me and my body was instantaneously severed" (*WS*:59). He turned to his right, walked to the other door, went out onto the street, and came back into the store, moving in a circle until he caught a glimpse of his parents' blue Buick coming down the hill. Released from the compulsion, he ran toward the car and jumped in, telling his parents only that he felt tired.

Although the experience frightened Paul, at least in terms of the childhood he portrays in his autobiography, it was one of several similar events in which there was detachment from reality, a separation between *self* and *body*. Indeed, Bowles opens his autobiography with a description of one such incident. At the age of four, he climbed up on a chair to get a closer look at a pewter cup. "'Mug,' he recalls, "the word sounded so strange that I continued to say it, again and again, until I found myself losing touch with its meaning. This astonished me; it also gave me a vague feeling of unease. How could 'mug' not mean mug?" (*WS*:9). The striking of the clock brought Paul back to "reality." "I was four years old, the clock had struck four, and 'mug' meant mug. Therefore I was I, I was there, and it was that precise moment and no other" (*WS*:9).[62]

Years later, when in his early teens Paul began experimenting with writing poetry, he found that by merely registering his impressions of the world, without letting them filter through his consciousness, he could achieve "poetic definitions." "I received and recorded them; others [other human beings] were people and had 'lives'" (*WS*:53). Two years later, he "found an even more satisfactory way of *not existing as myself* and thus being able to go on functioning: this was a fantasy in which the entire unrolling of events as I experienced them was the invention of a vast telekinetic sending station. . . . This method enabled me to *view, rather than participate in*, my own existence" (*WS*:53; my emphasis). Remarkable in these accounts is the sense of disembodiment, of the true self as something separate from the body (which houses the false self). Equally notable is Bowles's pleasure in having found a way to separate *existing* from *functioning*, a more refined separation of the existing true self from the functioning, physical, false self.

As a writer, Bowles came to rely on a sense of unreality and detachment from the world. He cultivated detachment as part of the writing process, and most of his work articulates various stages of being along the continuum of existential insecurity. As an artist, he became "a registering consciousness and no more" (*WS*:52). It was a mechanism that protected his fragile psyche and allowed him to preserve his secret self, and throughout his life, he was able to use this detachment in the service of poetry and fiction writing.

Apparently, this state of separation came over him at unwelcome and unexpected times. The compulsive incidents he describes in his autobiography fall close to the far end of the psychological continuum, near where neurosis becomes psychosis. Paul's anecdotes could be interpreted as evidence of dissociation or "splitting," a mechanism whereby one defends against unwanted parts of the self or the environment by "splitting-off" the unwanted portion, placing it outside the self (projection) or internally disowning it. Thus several "selves" coexist, each with its own agenda.[63] Splitting is the primary mechanism at work in the schizoid personality disorder and in the psychotic state of schizophrenia. The most extreme clinical examples in which "splitting" has occurred are demoniacal or spirit possession and autoscopy—the illusion or hallucination of one's twin self-image.

In less extreme cases of this rare condition, one feels detached from oneself, as if a spectator observing from a distance, simultaneously actor and observer, a condition that Bowles remembered when he referred to a "second I" who "assumed command" (*WS*:79). His 1948 story "You Are Not I" brilliantly reports autoscopy from the point of view of the split personality:

"The strange thing, now that I think about it, was that no one realized she was not I," says the woman in the story, watching herself.[64] This experience, as Freud described it in "The Uncanny," seems to result from a mysterious ability to disconnect, a "doubling, dividing, and interchanging of the self."[65] In Bowles's case, the experience proceeded one level further, as time and time again the detached "observer" returned to tell the tale of his observations.

Some of Bowles's short stories involve spirit possession or transference, and Gore Vidal, in introducing the 1979 edition of Bowles's short stories, considered that type as one of the three major categories he ascertained in Bowles's stories.[66] Characters transform into other characters, become inhabited by evil spirits, or, in the case of "You Are Not I," change places with each other as if they were twins. In his novels, Bowles dramatizes the split between different aspects of his personality by creating a character for each division: "I needed to clarify an issue for myself, and the only way of doing it was to create a fake psychodrama in which I could be everybody."[67] In this way, writing for him was therapeutic, a way not of healing the divisions but of coming to an understanding and a truce with them.

Even in stories and novels in which such psychological dramas are not initially apparent, Bowles's writing is characterized by the philosophical conviction that to live in the modern world is to be detached from reality by necessity. In this detachment, the conscious expression of an unconscious emotional defense is transformed into a personal philosophy and a technique for survival. Jean-Jacques Rousseau in the eighteenth century declared critical detachment the attitude most conducive to a sense of well-being. Perhaps with Bowles the issue goes even further. Bowles writes about two incidents the year he was twelve—a bus accident and surgery to remove a tumor in his jaw—as events that jarred him out of his fantasies—his fantasies of detachment from experience, fantasies that he could "view, rather than participate in, my own experience" (*WS*:53). The idea of "shock experiences" that force a person from unconscious to conscious awareness was one Freud proposed in *Beyond the Pleasure Principle* (1920).[68] However, another source of this idea seems more likely. In a 1939 essay, "Some Motifs in Baudelaire," German intellectual Walter Benjamin wrote about modern experience as a series of shocks reduced by and filtered through consciousness. Indeed, just prior to discussing his "jarring" experiences in his autobiography, Bowles mentions a family friend named "Walter Benjamin," surely one of Bowles's many games with personal names, a clue dropped for the interested reader.[69]

Bowles's detachment is that of one who has determined to be free from the demands of any cultural authority, the aloofness of one who preserves his personal freedom only by controlling the filter between internal experience and the chaos of modern life. It is the existential detachment of Laing's "divided self," of Benjamin's modern urbanist. It is, in short, the emerging personality type of the twentieth century.

"The Frozen Fields"

In the autumn of 1956, Claude and Rena Bowles visited Paul in Tangier. Following their visit, the author sailed for Ceylon and en route wrote "The Frozen Fields," his most obviously autobiographical short story. It retells the battle he waged against his father throughout his childhood and reveals how he had resolved the matter.[70]

"The Frozen Fields" opens with six-year-old Donald and his parents, Owen and Laura, traveling by train to visit Laura's family farm at Christmastime. Owen forbids Donald to behave spontaneously. Donald is not to draw pictures on the frosted windows of the train, not to show excitement upon arriving at the farm, not to embrace his uncles, and not to allow himself to be kissed. But Donald cannot contain his enthusiasm: "Everything connected with the farm [is] imbued with magic," and his relatives' attention is a happy respite from his parents' "constant watchfulness" (*CS*:262, 264).

As the holidays progress, Donald recognizes a tense undercurrent among the adults. Louisa and Ivor, a married aunt and uncle, are supported financially by the fascinating Mr. Gordon, with whom Ivor lives. One or more of the three may be morphine addicts. When a discussion about these goings-on arises at the dinner table, Donald is sent to bed. There he fantasizes about a wolf on the icy fields who approaches the farmhouse dining room. Smashing through the windowpanes, it attacks Owen, seizes him by the throat, and drags him off across the snow.

On Christmas, Owen and Laura insist that Donald put away his toys and other presents after opening them. Owen explains to the astonished relatives, "Discipline begins in the cradle" (*CS*:270). Owen then takes Donald for his daily exercise and on the walk finds reason to be angry with his son. He begins to rub snow in Donald's face and forces snow down the back of his shirt. Certain his father is trying to kill him, Donald wishes he could die to escape from the torment. "An unfamiliar feeling had come to him: he was not sorry for himself for being wet and cold, or even resentful at having been mistreated. He felt detached; it was an agreeable, almost voluptuous sensation which he accepted without understanding or questioning it" (*CS*:274–75). That night, Donald again dreams of the wolf, "running along paths that no one had ever seen" (*CS*:276). He becomes the wolf's companion; he buries his face in the thick fur of the wolf's neck, and they flee across the frozen fields.

Vengeance, then escape, are the imagined solutions to Donald's problems with his father. Yet there is a third solution to Donald's struggle, the "voluptuous sensation" of detachment, which Bowles himself demonstrated through a life's body of work that chronicles all manner of conflict without comment on its emotional content.

In "The Frozen Fields," Bowles illuminates the connection between his defense of detachment and its infantile origin. "Discipline begins in the cradle," Owen says, and it was from the cradle that Claude Bowles took his son in the middle of a blizzard, carried him to a window ledge, and left him to catch his death of cold.

A hidden solution lies in Donald's identification with the homosexual Mr. Gordon. "He reminds me a little of myself, you know, when I was his age" Mr. Gordon says, and Donald sees in Mr. Gordon another escape from his stifling family (CS:275).

The emotions Bowles would not allow himself to reveal to his father or other adults provided the material and motive for his fiction. Indeed, the main characters in the majority of Bowles's stories and novels share a detachment from their emotions and from other people, which is the source of their dissatisfaction in life. From Port and Kit in *The Sheltering Sky*, to Dyar in *Let It Come Down*, to Stenham in *The Spider's House*, to figures in numerous short stories, characters exist but fail to connect with life and therefore have the feeling that life is always being lived just beyond their grasp. And often, the central image of these stories remains the landscape.

Bowles personally used a variety of mechanisms to survive the contest of wills with his father. He detached himself from the dangerous emotions he felt in his father's presence by going blank, by retreating into emotional numbness. And after many years, he escaped the frozen fields of his father's world for Morocco, where "the sun is always wonderful. And it always shines all day."[71]

Transition

When Paul entered high school in January 1924, he came out of his self-imposed isolation. He enjoyed the "chaos" of the overcrowded Jamaica High School and discovered that school could be an enjoyable experience. He was appointed humor editor of the school magazine, the *Oracle*, and set his sights on the post of poetry editor. When he was fifteen, he read all the works of Arthur Machen, Welsh novelist and essayist whose specialty was supernatural, fantasy, and horror stories, and Gide's *Counterfeiters*, which, he pronounced to the students, "evokes more material for deep thought than any other book we have ever read."[72] Of the several poems Bowles published in the *Oracle*, nearly all are descriptions of landscapes either devoid of characters or through which the narrator wanders alone.

Paul also continued his musical education by attending the Saturday concerts at Carnegie Hall. Igor Stravinsky's *Fire Bird* excited him—"I would not have expected an orchestra to be able to make such sounds" (*WS*:69)—and prompted him to buy a recording—a "truncated version issued by Victor, Stokowski conducting"—that he played "constantly but very softly" to avoid irritating his father. Bowles once wrote, "Stravinsky had the tidiest mind around, besides being the greatest composer since Mozart"; and with Bach and Satie, he remained one of Bowles's three favorite composers.[73]

With several other students, Paul formed the "Fine Arts Society of Queens," an organization "dedicated to advancing the arts."[74] At the age of seventeen, he performed with the Phylo Players, an amateur theatrical company, at the Studio Playhouse, Whitestone Landing.[75] Bowles glossed over these years in his autobiography, explaining that he was too busy living to reflect on his experiences.[76] "Relationships with other people are at best nebulous; their presence keeps us from being aware of the problem of giving form to our life" (*WS*:69). Relationships with other people tend to muddy the waters of one's private reflection pool.

In later high school years, Paul gravitated toward the methods of "unconscious writing" promoted by the surrealists and what spiritualists like Aunt Mary called "automatic writing." In both, the writer tries to eliminate all conscious control. Spiritualists did so to receive messages from another world; the surrealists did so to tap into the resources of the unconscious.[77] After practicing writing poetry "without conscious intervention," Paul progressed to typing "an entire page literally without any knowledge of what [he] had put there" (*WS*:70).

Paul discovered the surrealists in *transition*, a magazine published in Paris, and immediately knew he had found an artistic home. Begun in April 1927 by Emile Jolas, *transition* published works by avant-garde writers such as Gertrude Stein, James Joyce, and Paul Elouard. Its editors dedicated themselves to the exploration of a darker, interior psychic world, declaring, "If there is any real choice to be made, we prefer to skyscraper spirituality the immense lyricism and madness of illogic. . . . Are not the workings of the instincts and the mysteries of the shadows more beautiful than the sterile world of beauty we have known? . . . We believe that there is no hope for poetry unless there be disintegration first."[78] Their mandate was clear: writers must strip the layers of social pretense from the individual and from the larger social structure. This was open defiance of the logic of civilized society.

Bowles saw in it, too, a way to reach the inner parts of himself he had by necessity disguised or masked. It became a lifelong quest that more than forty years later he explained: "The destruction of the ego has always seemed an important thing. I took it for granted that that was what really one was looking for in order to attain knowledge and the ability to live."[79]

Transition was a thoroughly literary magazine, and when Bowles's poem "Spire Song" was in the twelfth issue and his surrealist prose fragment "Entity" in the very next issue, the youth of barely seventeen years felt he had arrived.[80] Encouraged by the success of appearing alongside well-known and established artists, Paul sent out a small stream of works to other journals. He did not pause to ask whether he had "anything to say which could be of interest to someone else. My desire was to impose my personality by any means available; I did not conceive of anything beyond that" (*WS*:72–73). Neither did he pause for critical opinion. A few years later, Gertrude Stein objected to a line in "Spire Song," saying, "What do you mean, *the heated beetle pants*? Beetles don't pant." Bowles replied testily, "It was written without conscious intervention. It's not my fault" (*WS*:122). In the surrealist elevation of the unconscious to the level of the sacred, Paul had found an elegant strategy both for meeting his need for recognition and for self-protection.

Graduating from high school in January 1928, Paul settled on art school—"It was unthinkable, of course, that I should do nothing at all" (*WS*:70)—as an acceptable way of occupying himself until he entered college in September. His father raised few objections, deciding that art school offered training that could be considered vocational.

While attending the School of Design and Liberal Arts in New York City, he discovered that he hated life drawing, having never before seen an "unclothed" human body, and "after the first few weeks of observing the phenomenon [he] had no desire ever to see another" (*WS*:71–72). He found the nude models "repulsive" and painted his images of them blue, a reaction entirely consistent with what became a lifelong distaste for openly sexual or unsolicited physical contact.

In 1928, two unnamed friends critiqued his work, much to Bowles's delight. "The same two discouraging ladies who in 1927 informed me that I am less than an amoeba, this year decided that I am at the end of a civilization, that I epitomize a decayed civilization, in its last feeble flares to resurrect itself in the eyes of other civilizations. They maintained that all my paintings and music merely strengthened the case for them, and were representative of imminent death: the final false energy of the moribund."[81] Bowles received a prize for "greatest output and originality" at the end of his semester at the art school and concluded that the prize had been invented for him because he had no other talents as a painter. He interpreted the prize as meaning that he worked fast and learned slowly, an assessment he rather enjoyed. Originality was "a quality which a happy few succeeded in retain-

ing, in spite of having been forced through the process of education"
(*WS*:73). Bowles preferred to think of himself as an original and an
autodidact: "Did I ever confess to you my passion for Donne? For Blake? For
Coleridge? Probably not! I think it's better that way. I should be thought of
by you as a person springing from contemporaneity, uninterested in even the
Mauve Decade."[82]

Living at home and working a summer job at a bank, Paul saved money for
his first semester of college, and he occasionally visited Greenwich Village.[83]
His aunt Adelaide's co-worker, librarian Anne Carroll Moore, had "managed
to infect me with her enthusiasm" for the University of Virginia, he wrote, as
if enthusiasm were a disease (*WS*:70). His by then long-standing childhood
fascination with the stories of Edgar Allan Poe — "I could not read them
aloud; I had to undergo them" (*WS*:33) — also sparked his interest, for Poe
had been in Virginia, studied, and walked through the mountains, "and
what is good enough for edgar allen [*sic*] poe is good enow [*sic*] for me let me
assure you."[84]

At college, away from the watchful eyes of his parents, Bowles discovered
for the first time in his life that he looked forward to mealtime, and he soon
gained twenty-five pounds. He took long walks in the Blue Ridge Mountains and made expeditions to local stores to find blues and jazz records and
"all manner of rare and limited and autographed editions at remarkably low
prices. and a supply of modern french novels." It took a special request to get
the proprietor to order *transition*.[85] He added daily to a record collection in
which Bach, Haydn, and Palestrina figured "prominently." He also indulged
in a customary college rite of passage, later explaining, "I had done very little
drinking in my life; now I felt called upon to do as much as I could" (*WS*:76).
He confided to Daniel Burns, "I have made literally dozens of friends and
most of them are intelligent and sympathetic. . . . . [Bowles's ellipsis]. And I
am doing all manner of strange things, one of which is to inhale ether until I
am quite drunk," and he later admitted to having experienced "tipsi-
ness . . . but once, and do not need to go through it again, as I can attain the
same effect by staying up until one o'clock."[86]

Paul was happy to pass for nineteen (he was not yet eighteen), though he
facetiously insisted, "I deny it vigorously, look extraordinarily (more than
usual) innocent and say incredulously: but do I *look* nineteen?"[87] He
continued to paint "monochromatic and extremely heavy" works he titled
Sacrifice, *Virgin Mary*, *Nausea*, and *The Poet*.[88] His one musical composition
of that first semester, "Monotonal," bored the few people who heard it, he
reported. Productive and sociable, he made good grades, had plenty of free
time, and, he confided, was not homesick. "Never from one weeks end to the
other do I think of home except through outside pressure."[89] Nonetheless,

this "unaccustomed physical well-being was unfortunately more than offset by a steadily increasing sensation of guilt. . . . 'There will come a day of reckoning,' I told myself."[90]

Sometime after his Christmas vacation, Paul had another compulsive experience. This episode was as inexplicable as the incident in the candy store, but of greater consequence.

> I got back to my room one afternoon at dusk and, upon opening the door, knew at once, although I had no idea of what it was going to be, that I was about to do something explosive and irrevocable. It occurred to me that this meant that I was not the I I thought I was or, rather, that there was a second I in me who had suddenly assumed command. I shut the door and gave a running leap up onto the bed, where I stood, my heart pounding. I took out a quarter and tossed it spinning into the air, so that it landed on my palm. Heads. I cried out with relief and jumped up and down on the mattress several times before landing on the floor. Tails would have meant that I would have had to take a bottle of Allonal [sleeping pills] that night and leave no note. But heads meant that I would leave for Europe as soon as possible. (*WS*:77–78)

The "I [that] was not . . . I" took charge in a situation where Paul could not admit his own emotions. His growing sense of malaise was based on a recognition that he secretly agreed with his father that the university was less a college than a country club. His classmates were not interested in literature and art, only "in talking about those things"; without studying he had made the dean's list and was not required to attend any classes. Boredom, adolescent rebellion, and horror that his father might be right compelled him, but the direction of the act he left to chance, a force beyond his control.

The coin toss fits well the persona Paul Bowles assumed so gracefully. As a surrealist, he had decided that the way to write was to let the unconscious, or the "not I," take over, and the coin toss story demonstrates that at age eighteen he was willing to make this creed a way of life.

The story of the coin toss is so fantastic that one wonders how close it falls to the truth. An autobiographical fragment of writing among his papers illuminates this episode in a slightly different aspect.

> Possibly there was a whole period of transition which prepared the way for my sudden compulsive decision, but if there was I have forgotten the details of it, and remember only the evening when all at once I became aware that there were only two possible choices to make. One was to swallow the contents of a bottle of sleeping-pills, and the other was to disappear, — that is, to go away, leaving no traces. ~~I tossed a quarter~~ When I looked at the little bottle, I knew I had no desire to be dead, so my decision was made.[91]

In the first description he relies on chance; in the second, the passive voice emerges: "the decision was made." But in neither description does Bowles assume responsibility; his course had been decided for him.[92]

Travelogue: 1929

Bowles's arrival in France was accompanied by the familiar feeling of unreality, of not completely being where he was. He sat in his hotel room, "trying to persuade [himself] of the reality of the situation," touching things in his room, repeating, almost chanting, to himself, "They are France. This is France. I am in France" (*WS*:82). As an artist, he believed Paris to be "the center of all existence; I could feel its glow when I faced eastward as a Moslem feels the light from Mecca" (*WS*:70). He sought out artists who were loyal not to society but to ideas, attended concerts (including the *Tsar Soltan*), and went to performances of the Diaghilev Ballet. As John Glassco, a young expatriate Canadian who had arrived in 1927, later recalled, "To be able to live well on very little money is the best basis for an appreciation of beauty anywhere, and I think we admired the city all the more because we could now eat and drink almost as much as we liked."[93]

In Paris Paul began to practice the craft of which he was soon to become a master—that of cultivating useful acquaintances—and to build a kind of social capital on which he later would draw. He met Kay Cowen, recently returned from North Africa, who introduced him to surrealist Tristan Tzara. After finding work as a switchboard operator at the *Herald Tribune*, Bowles presented himself to Madame and General Daniloff, some Russian émigré friends of a New York acquaintance. The Daniloffs undertook to entertain and care for Paul, feeding him elegant meals when he arrived at mealtime, which was often, sending him to their family physician, and going so far as to write his parents for financial assistance on his behalf (his parents had had no idea of his whereabouts). Though the elder Bowleses were glad to hear from him, they sent no money. The Daniloffs persuaded Mary Crouch Oliver, daughter of a mutual friend, to lend Paul enough money so that he could quit his job at the *Herald Tribune*. He began taking small trips into the countryside around Paris, and then he traveled to Switzerland, where he spent ten days exploring the Alps.

After a week in Nice, he returned to meet his benefactor, who had come from England for a visit. Oliver gave him more money and may have persuaded the Daniloffs to contact their friend Sergei Prokofieff about composition lessons for Paul. They arranged an interview with Prokofieff, but Paul decided Prokofieff would find nothing worthwhile in his work. Years later, he reflected, "I was correct in that; my error consisted in imagining that this had anything to do with whether or not I ought to study with him" (*WS*:89). One hour before the meeting, Bowles packed his belongings, took a taxi to the train station, and bought a ticket to Saverne, a city near Strasbourg on the German border, but a name that "meant nothing" to him. "I was not able either at the moment or in retrospect to discover what determined my decision. . . . Clearly I felt that the action precluded the necessity of making a choice, that once I was on the train there would be no question of my having to decide anything one way or the other" (*WS*:89). He refused to acknowledge that by packing, he had in fact decided not to meet Prokofieff. As in the coin toss episode just a few weeks earlier, or earlier still, in his compulsive walking in and out of the candy store in Jamaica, Paul attributed the responsibility to his unconscious mind, the "second I."

Once he had escaped the possibility of embarrassing himself in front of Prokofieff, Paul spent a week walking about the Black Forest and then returned to Paris. With money running low, he took a job in a bank, only to resign two weeks later. From that time on, he explored the city and visited with friends.

One of these friends was a woman named Hermina who gave the sunburned, nettle-stung youth his "initiatory experience" with sex, on an ant bed in a cherry orchard east of Paris. A few weeks later, he met a distant family member, Hubert, who invited Paul to move in with him and gave him a "further sexual initiation, equally cold-blooded and ridiculous" (*WS*:93).[94] While Bowles makes no mention in his autobiography of his feelings about sexuality, except for an admission that in his late teens he felt "any conscious manifestation of sex was necessarily ludicrous" (*WS*:100), he admits that he and Hubert had an extended homosexual relationship. He stayed with his "uncle" for some time, justifying long hours of "boring conversation" with the pleasure he experienced in being made to feel important. Claude Bowles had sent with Hubert a check for two hundred dollars, which Hubert refused to spend, but he did support Paul. Paul could escape only by returning to his family, and after a few weeks longer, in the autumn of 1929, he sailed from Le Havre, France.

The Last Innocent

While Paul Bowles was sailing across the Atlantic to Morocco in 1947, he wrote "Pages from Cold Point," a short story set in a locale very similar to Jamaica, which he had just visited. But Bowles drew "Pages from Cold Point" from a more distant memory, the 1929 liaison with his "Uncle" Hubert.

At the outset of the story, the narrator, Norton, has just lost his wife, aptly named Hope, and to escape the decay of civilization, he has left a university career. He travels to some unspecified islands, where he is happy for the first time since childhood. There he recovers a sense of the unspoiled and beautiful through the landscape and through his son, Racky.

Racky is a "wonderful boy," whose "joyous excitement" and "inexhaustible curiosity" in his explorations of the islands delight Norton immensely. Norton takes vicarious pleasure in Racky's "boldness of manner" and "great purity of spirit." He wonders about Racky's occasional thoughtlessness but decides to remain silent since "lack of confidence on the part of a parent is the one unforgivable sin" (*CS*:88).

On a rare trip into town, Norton ventures into the native quarter, Orange Walk, where a native woman passing in the street warns: "Keep your boy at home, mahn" (*CS*:90). When he writes in the journal that comprises the pages of this story that he is "extremely curious to know what she could have meant" (*CS*:91), Norton has deceived himself: he suspects Racky and therefore already has committed the "one unforgivable sin."

A police officer subsequently calls upon Norton and tells him that Racky "does what he pleases with all the young boys, and the men too, and gives them a shilling so they won't tell about it" (*CS*:94). Norton does not doubt the officer's story, and he knows Racky has lost his innocence. "With the advent of this news," Norton writes, "he had become another person—an adult, mysterious and formidable" (*CS*:94).

Now depravity enters the relationship. That evening, when Norton retires to his room, he finds Racky waiting in his bed, a development in their relationship Norton accepts: "Destiny, when one perceives it clearly from very near, has no qualities at all. The recognition of it and the consciousness of the vision's clarity leave no room on the mind's horizon." He quietly joins Racky in bed, Racky who is "warm and firm, but still as death" (*CS*:98). Racky's and Norton's destinies wrap around each other as darkness and silence envelop them.

The next morning, Racky suggests that his uncle Charles come to the islands for a visit, knowing that Charles will sever ties between Racky and Norton permanently. In the face of such obvious blackmail, Norton feels "the fascination of complete helplessness that comes when one is suddenly a conscious on-looker at the shaping of one's fate" (*CS*:99). As a mere observer of his own life, Norton now can see "the pattern" in process, slowly revealing itself, "like a photographic print becoming constantly clearer in a tray of developing solution" (*CS*:99). Norton falls victim to Racky's "pattern"—incest followed by blackmail—as Racky uses his hold on Norton to obtain an independent life for himself on a separate island.

Tonally, the story is as understated as Racky's insidious behavior. Nothing is overt. Bowles gives no details of the sexual liaison between Racky and Norton, and Norton explains their final separation and financial arrangements as logical and expedient. Just as Norton infers Racky's scheme, the reader must infer the story Norton is telling. Norton is nearly emotionless throughout the story and calmly accepts each turn of events as his fate, leaving the reader to react in his stead to the full import of the situation.

A similarly convoluted relationship between youth and extortion, innocence and the writer unfolds in the later "In Absentia" (1987), a one-sided correspondence from an older man to his friend Pamela and to his young ward Sue. It appears that the correspondent is attempting to maneuver Pamela, who lives in the Hawaiian Islands, into taking over the burden of supporting Sue. When Sue runs away to Fiji with Pamela instead of remaining in school, the correspondent expresses disappointment in the loss of his niece's affection, when in actuality Sue has made it possible for him to withdraw his financial obligation to her. Since he profits by her betrayal, he may have intended this outcome when he first suggested Sue spend her holiday on the islands with Pamela. "She expects me to mind that things didn't work out in the way I thought they would. But that's only because she doesn't know me."[95] The irony of this statement is that no one knows this man, the writer: not Pamela, not Sue, not the reader. Since the writer is physically removed from the scene of action, all suspicions must remain unproved.

At an early age, Paul Bowles became fascinated with stories in which he presented a crime, a victim, and a possible criminal (Volga Merna) but innocently left the reader to decide whether the criminal was guilty. In "Pages from Cold Point," he created a narrator, a writer, who committed a crime but who seems also to be a victim. As was the case with his Snake Woman series, the reader is left to decide, a technique that puts the reader in the position of constructing the crime. Bowles thus created the perfect crime story: one in which the crime itself exists only in the imagination of the reader. Neither the author nor the narrator-writer ever comes in contact with the crime.

In other stories, and in his novels as well, Bowles protects himself, his true self—Bowles the writer—from violence and corruption by writing so compellingly that he lures the reader into imagining horrible acts and perversities he circumnavigates. The combination of Bowles's narrative detachment and bleak subject matter is one of his greatest strengths as a writer. He manages to write of the evils of both European and pre-European societies in the twentieth century with precision, elegance, and even beauty that have eluded his contemporaries. As an existentialist, he has come to terms with the absurdity, alienation, and anxiety of life as well as with the absolute nothingness of death. Yet he shields himself, implicitly preserving the romantic's belief in the purity and innocence of an artist's soul, or at least of the unconscious. Characters throughout Bowles's stories and novels continue a search for innocence and a "lost childhood." In each instance, they learn that the innocence of youth is a sham and that the childhood is always already lost.

Unable to recover his childhood, Bowles recovered his lost innocence by becoming the most innocent of bystanders—the writer who merely records experience. In a fictional world where adults manipulate children, children betray adults, and readers find the worst in every scenario, the writer might indeed be the enemy of society, but he remains the only innocent.

BOOK II

PRETENDING TO BE LIVING, 1929–1933

I wonder if The Young and Evil is really our generation! I
found all the people in it far too serious about being evil.
Or are all the young people serious? I can't keep up with
them any more, and I think I shall just forget about them
and stick to the old ones, as I always have when my good
judgment prevailed. Young people always resent my
pretending to be living instead of living, and older ones
don't notice it.[1]

The Search for a Mentor

FROM 1929 TO 1933, Bowles wandered, traveling through France,
Germany, Spain, and most important, North Africa, meeting the
people and landscapes that would help shape him into an adult. As he
traveled, he adopted a variety of poses, trying out roles as diligently as
any actor. The two that fascinated him most were the naïf and the dandy,
with a range in between.[2] A generation of contemporaneous English writers—Christopher Isherwood and Stephen Spender, among others—per-
fected the role of the naïf, a young man in the process of formation, "all
limpid sensitiveness and generous responsiveness," who established his
identity in "indeterminacy and sheer attractiveness."[3] The naïfs were rebels
at heart, in revolt against the values of their fathers and mothers, in search of
a model by which to form themselves. The more fully evolved dandy was also
a rebel, fundamentally and "heroically" negative.

When Bowles returned to his parents' house from France in the autumn of
1929, he was still answerable to his parents. But, as Paul recalls, his family
seemed impressed with his recent trip to Europe, which they considered an
important cultural experience for an eighteen-year-old, and he found less of
the "New England" demand for accountability than he had expected.

When Paul found a job at Dutton's Bookshop on Fifth Avenue, he rented his own place on Bank Street in Greenwich Village. On the balcony of his apartment, he worked daily on "Without Stopping," a fictionalized account of his recent walking trips in Europe written in stream-of-consciousness style. Afraid if he "consider[ed] the piece critically" he would "stop the flow," he seldom paused to "exercise choice." "And it was the flow above all which preoccupied me, because the writing of 'Without Stopping' was therapeutic. Seeing the number of pages grow gave me the illusion of being on my way somewhere" (*WS*:97). Being on his way somewhere was Bowles's constant preoccupation, and as with his writing, in his life he hoped to allow events to decide his course of action, to allow his life to progress with as little conscious interference as possible.

Although he had spent several months in Europe, the talented eighteen-year-old Bowles was an adolescent who longed "to be assigned a civil status" but most of all to be told what to do. "If a composer said to me: 'You are a composer,' that would be all right. Or if a poet said: 'You are a poet,' that would be acceptable, too. But somebody had to say something," he wrote (*WS*:98). He introduced himself to composers Roy Harris and Henry Cowell, the latter of whom finally gave Paul the sign for which he had been waiting. After hearing some of Paul's original music, Cowell wrote a short and dismissive note to Aaron Copland, concluding, "His music is very French, but it might interest you" (*WS*:98).

At the time, Copland was one of the most influential of all American composers through his work for the League of Composers, his classes at the New School for Social Research in New York (1927–37), his articles for the journal *Modern Music*, and the [Aaron] Copland-[Roger] Sessions Concerts of Contemporary Music, the last of which showcased the talents of young composers. Five weeks before the first concert in the spring of 1928, Sessions received word he had won the Rome Prize and an American Academy in Rome Fellowship, which took him out of the country for the concerts. This meant that Sessions became an adviser, and Copland carried out most of the organizational work for that first season and for subsequent ones. The series opened with concerts on 22 April and 6 May 1928, presenting compositions by eleven Americans: Theodore Chanler, Walter Piston, Carlos Chávez, Virgil Thomson, Copland, Sessions, Robert Delaney, Quincy Porter, Ruth Crawford, Adolph Weiss, and Dane Rudhyar.[4] The series provoked criticism and controversy, which, Paul decided, was a mark of genius. In December 1928, Paul attended the second Copland-Sessions Concerts and decided their organizers had "revolutionary potential."

Following up on the Cowell letter, Bowles found the tall, gently stooped Copland "unusually likable" (*WS*:99), and Copland thought the young man musically gifted and one who, although lacking serious training, had already gelled in his compositional direction. From the start, Copland recalled, "Paul was not a student in the sense of being a beginner. Working with Paul was more like showing things to a professional friend." Although he believed Paul was "born to be a composer," Copland added, "He had an alert, quick mind—a very lively mind. He was knowledgeable about many things—not just music. I can't imagine him ever being dull."[5] Paul became both friend and traveling companion to Copland.

Paul arranged to take daily composition lessons from Copland, and he moved to his parents' house so he could use their piano. During the autumn of 1929 and winter of 1930, Paul studied harmony with Copland nearly every day.[6] At his parents' insistence, Paul returned to the University of Virginia for the spring semester of 1930, so Copland visited him in Charlottesville at Eastertime.

Returning to finish his freshman year, Bowles resumed his standing on the dean's list, which gave him the latitude to skip classes and take long hikes in the mountains nearby. He found most of his fellow students "provincial" and unimaginative but formed friendships with John Widdicombe and, at the University of Richmond, Bruce Morrissette. Bowles worked with Morrissette securing contributions to the University of Richmond literary magazine, the *Messenger*, and with Widdicombe Paul hitchhiked to Philadelphia to the Martha Graham/Philadelphia Orchestra performance of Stravinsky's *Sacre du Printemps*. Paul "listened more than [he] watched," captivated by the pounding rhythmic drive of the piece (*WS*:101).

Attending the Stravinsky performance was no mere college lark. Paul was fiercely interested in modern composition. He wrote to his friend, writer Charles Henri Ford, "If you like real music i should think you would like hindemith and stravinsky in his later spasms and some milhaud and prokofieff. . . . there is a hindemith string quartet on polydor records that is superb and stravinsky's capriccio is swell being made of bits of old stuff stuck on together by means of magic and no matter what anyone says." Bowles was equally enthusiastic about French moderns, especially Arthur Honnegger ("Pacific 231" and "Rugby"), Darius Milhaud ("Le Boeuf sur le Toit"), and Francis Poulenc (Trio for Oboe, Bassoon, and Piano).[7] Small wonder Cowell had found Bowles's music to sound "very French."

Scarcely nineteen, Paul was making friendships that would last many years. At the performance in Philadelphia, Paul met charismatic and handsome Harry Dunham, who became Paul's good friend and traveling companion. Harry introduced him to the editor of the Princeton literary magazine *Argo*, to which Bowles submitted an excerpt from "Without Stopping" as a short story.[8] Although he abandoned the novel version of his walks in Europe, he continued writing and managed to publish poems in *Tambour*

(Paris), *Anthologie du Groupe Moderne d'Art* (Liege), *This Quarter* (Paris), *Messenger* (Richmond), *Palms* (Guadalajara), *transition* (Paris), *Front* (Amsterdam), *Morada* (Albuquerque), *Pagany* (Boston), and *Blues* (New York).

Ten years too young to have been a part of the Lost Generation, Paul had managed to find a place within the next generation of talented people. Charles Henri Ford and Parker Tyler became the spokespersons for this group with *(The Works and Days of) The Young and Evil*, published in 1933. It was Gertrude Stein who gave this novel generational impact when she said, "*The Young and Evil* creates this generation as *This Side of Paradise* by Fitzgerald created his generation."[9] The first half of the title came from a line in "The Love Song of J. Alfred Prufrock," T. S. Eliot's poem about the impotence of Western civilization ("There will be time to murder and create / For all works and days of hands"). Djuna Barnes, who helped Ford find a publisher for the book through her agent William Aspenwall Bradley, suggested the idea of "evil" for the title when she wrote: "Their unresolved acceptance of any happening is both evil and 'pure' in the sense that it is unconscious."[10] In a surreal, picaresque style, Ford and Tyler presented in a loosely autobiographical tale the adventures of two young men in Paris. Ford and Bowles (both surrealists) became friends, and at Ford's request Bowles read some of his own French poetry in Village restaurants during the summer of 1930. Although they remained friends for years, Bowles had occasional misgivings about the "young and evil" Ford. "No for his whole crowd. they don't know a circumflex from a dactyl. they haven't the manners of goldfish being fed. they have no sense of values, of proportion, they are snobs without the slightest excuse. all they have is good taste, good business sense and immense egos," he wrote a friend one year later.[11]

In the summer of 1930, Paul's aunt Mary invited him to stay with her at Holden Hall. Paul could not play the piano at Holden Hall for fear of disturbing meditation with "unharmonious vibrations," so he practiced daily at a neighbor's piano, studying contemporary works by Paul Hindemith (*Übung in drei Stücke*) and Stravinsky (*L'Histoire du Soldat*—he had seen *L'Histoire* in 1928, with Michio Ito dancing the part of the devil).[12] As always, Mary had other guests, including a distant cousin, Nina Smith, and her son, Oliver, who was seven years younger than Bowles. Their time together that summer forged a lifelong friendship between Oliver and Paul, who also became collaborators in the theater, Oliver flourishing as a scenic designer, producer, and codirector of the American Ballet Theatre.

In September, Paul strengthened his commitment to music, joining Copland at the Spencer Trask estate in Saratoga Springs, New York, later known as Yaddo, where Copland was working on his Piano Variations. They took long rides together in the countryside, driving once to meet Carl

Ruggles, whose enthusiasm for the music of Mendelssohn Copland laughed at as truly eccentric. Roger Sessions, on the other hand, whom they also visited, seemed formidable. Copland showed him a piece of Bowles's work, and Bowles remembers the composer finding nothing of interest in it.

Later that autumn, Paul returned to his parents' house to live, where one night in an outburst of temper he threw a butcher knife at his father. He ran from the house, slamming the door behind him and shattering several panes of glass. His father followed and asked him to return home for his mother's sake. An upset Paul, upon reentering the house, shouted, "You can't stand me because every time you look at me you realize what a mess you've made of me! But it's not my fault I'm alive. I didn't ask to be born" (*WS*:105).

Bowles's late 1960s account of this episode uses the passive voice almost exclusively. He had been "subject to" childhood outbursts of temper, but they "had ceased to occur." He had assumed he would no longer "be visited by them." He was "astonished to discover" that he had just thrown the knife. Bowles writes about the episode as an observer. Whether he felt so intellectually separate from his emotional self at the time or simply detached himself from the event in recollection, clearly Bowles preferred to remain aloof from emotions as strong as his anger toward his father, lest their violence invade his defenses. He especially regretted revealing his anger to his father (some friends have suggested his chief disappointment was in having missed his aim with the knife[13]). He rationalized the incident through clinical detachment: "Since nothing was real, it did not matter too much," he told himself (*WS*:105).

With the most adolescent of all complaints, "I didn't ask to be born," Bowles takes leave of his parents' house autobiographically. Having expressed rage at victimization and helplessness, Bowles retreats into passive denial of reality—"since nothing was real." Another writer might have used such an anecdote to suggest how much growing up he still had to do. Instead, Bowles uses the anecdote to reveal mechanisms that set the path of the rest of his life. Withdrawing from forces beyond his control, he chose instead an interior world of music, poetry, and fiction.[14]

Social Capital

During the year after his return from Paris, Paul harbored a desire to go back to Europe. Perhaps the argument with his father strengthened his resolve. By late spring he found he could wait no longer. He borrowed the money from Harry Dunham's parents, who considered Paul a bad influence on their son and were eager to see him leave the country, and left for Paris.

In the spring of 1930 Bowles had begun corresponding with Gertrude Stein on behalf of Bruce Morrissette and the *Messenger*, explaining:

> I cannot overemphasize the fact that I should like your pieces solely because of their literary value which I feel to be immense, and not to exhibit as curios (which I have discovered, alas, to be the motive underlying the printing of your work in one or two, at least, of our American "avant-garde" mags to whose editors I have talked. They are still unable to understand that anyone who writes English today with any degree of mastery owes you an inestimable debt.).[15]

Gertrude Stein donated *Play I* to the *Messenger*, and Bowles continued to write her in a gracious language and tone that led Stein and Alice Toklas to assume he was an older, eccentric gentleman rather than the well-dressed, blond twenty-year-old who looked even younger and who knocked on their door soon after he arrived back in Paris in 1931. Intrigued, they insisted he dine with them when Copland arrived a few weeks later.[16]

In the meantime, Paul was interested in a newly launched magazine called the *New Review*, edited by Richard Thoma (who had been associated with *transition*), Ezra Pound, and Samuel Putnam. Calling at Thoma's house, Paul met American poet Ezra Pound. At tea with Pound, Paul discovered the extent of his own ignorance and Pound's expertise in the areas of opera and sound recording for film. Pound told Bowles that "if he were a young musician he would aim straight at the talking picture without giving a thought to stage music," advice that Bowles remembered but did not strictly follow.[17]

Thoma also introduced Paul to surrealist Jean Cocteau, who hardly sat down during the two hours they spent with him, but instead "pretended he was an orang outang [*sic*], next an usher at the Paramount Theater, and finally he held a dialogue between an aged grandfather and his young grandson which was sidesplitting. I think never have I seen anyone like him in my life. He still smokes opium every day and claims it does him a great deal of good."[18] The young artist pursued such introductions relentlessly.

After giving himself the pleasure of introducing Copland to Stein, Bowles accompanied Copland to Berlin. Copland had an apartment; Bowles found a room in the home of a Baronin von Massenbach. Paul had corresponded with poet Edouard Roditi, beginning, in his faux-naïf style: "I am writing you because there is a chance that we shall meet; and because I have enjoyed your poems in Tambour and other magazines I think it a bit necessary that I see you sometime. There are so many worthless people."[19] Roditi sent him letters of introduction to several friends in Europe, including Jean Ross, with whom he occasionally had tea and who introduced Paul to writer Christopher Isherwood and poet Stephen Spender.[20] A "pretty, dark-eyed girl," Jean Ross became the engaging and flighty Sally Bowles in Isherwood's *Berlin Days* (the novel that was the basis for the musical *Cabaret*). Bowles found no inspiration in Berlin and thought Spender, in his open-necked shirt, too self-consciously "artistic," though they sometimes dined together.[21] Bowles was of the opinion that roles are effective only when disguised as ordinary behavior. Isherwood, however, became one of Bowles's strongest influences; specifically, to Isherwood, Bowles owes his method. "I am a camera," Isherwood wrote in *Berlin Days*, and Bowles grasped the technique, objectively freezing reality as a thing outside himself, separate from his being—a place where others existed and had lives.

Berlin, a cheap place to live in 1931, was overflowing with writers and artists hoping to make meager funds last longer. Young Germans, "who had little money and who [spent] what they had immediately," were living a "life of the senses," in which "roofless houses, expressionist painting, atonal music, bars for homosexuals, nudism, sun-bathing, camping, all were accepted."[22] Yet outside the modernist movement, one out of ten men were unemployed, and wages had plummeted along with the stock market. The middle class was disintegrating into Marxist and Nazi polarities, and Berlin's abundant avant-garde cultural atmosphere was giving way to sentimental theater and film, operettas, and lavish floor shows. Artists who found jobs had little choice but to serve and entertain the conspicuously wealthy. Isherwood gave English lessons to rich Germans who had no interest in studying, and he and Spender became "ever more aware that the care-free personal lives of our friends were façades in front of the immense social chaos."[23]

Within a few weeks, Paul wrote his friend and confidante Daniel Burns. "I have come to the decision that berlin is the least amusing place i have ever seen. it is the synonym for stupidity. i should be quite happy if i never saw the city again after today."[24] Writers could travel free on state railways, and Bowles took advantage of this at every opportunity. Munich was "what I like as a city," he told Roditi.[25] But everywhere Germany was wet and cold, and Paul could not settle down to work. "i have been to bad pyrmont and it rained there, and then i went to hannover and it rained there. i see now why europe is so green. i have written not a poem since march. nor any music. nor drawn a picture. nor learned anything," he reported,[26] Copland's warning hung over him: "If you don't work when you're twenty, nobody's going to love you when you're thirty"(*WS*:166).

Instead, Paul resumed his quest to meet artists he admired. He was less interested in getting to know new people than he was obsessed with adding names to his list. In his letters to Burns in New York, he made a point of name-dropping: "edouard roditi insists i come to london and live with him.

richard thoma had a good time in paris. bernard fay writes from budapest telling how good wine and women are there, and how bad bach and coffee are. gertrude stein writes saying come and visit."[27] The tone is whimsical, but the purpose is still served. In part, Paul was still searching for his "civic status," hoping he could find it in association with other artists; just as important, he was accumulating a bit of social capital, which as a young man of talent but little income, he shrewdly knew he would need.

Paul made the most of his knack for meeting people. His appearance, wit, wide range of interests, and arcane knowledge allowed him to make a first impression that few forgot. Painter Maurice Grosser remembered that in 1931, "Paul was the most extraordinary looking young man you've ever seen in your life. He was very thin, looked like something put together with match sticks. Very thin legs and arms, a flaming mop of bright gold hair, and sunburned to the color of chestnuts." Grosser, a close friend of Virgil Thomson and an artist with a large social circle of his own, found Paul's affinity for acquaintances impressive: "Paul knew absolutely everybody, and he had no hesitancy about presenting himself. He could go up to anybody and make friends with them."[28]

Gertrude Stein

After several weeks in Germany, Paul returned to France and stayed in Bilignin with Stein and Toklas at their country home. It was a memorable visit, and his description of the time he spent with Stein leaps out of an otherwise dispassionate chronicle. Stein babied him, organized his days, and controlled his activities. Each morning she listened outside his door after the maid delivered a pitcher of ice cold water. "Freddy. Are you taking your bath? . . . I don't hear anything" (*WS*:120). She insisted he wear lederhosen, which she called "Faunties," because in them he reminded her of Little Lord Fauntleroy. Then she had him take Basket, a standard poodle, who had also just had his morning bath, outside for exercise. Wearing his Faunties, Paul ran in circles in the garden, and Basket chased him. When Basket caught up, he scratched Paul's legs, while Stein shouted from her second-story window, "Faster, Freddy, faster!" (*WS*:120). She enjoyed his discomfort, while he interpreted her attention as "a sign of the most personal kind of relationship" (*WS*:121).

The scene is uncannily reminiscent of Paul's childhood play period in the yard outside his family's house on Long Island. Like his father, Stein assumed control of Paul's activities, ordered him around, gave him advice, and lectured him on his shortcomings. He, in turn, played a role he knew well— that of the compliant son. In an interview thirty years later, Bowles recalled,

"She'd say, 'Ah, Freddy, Freddy, Freddy.' She would do that all the time and I would just grin and giggle. I was playing a part. She wanted me to be this naughty little boy. . . . I was twenty. No, but she saw me as twelve, that's the point, and that was her whole kick with me."[29]

Paul was happy to be allowed to play a naïf, to be taken care of, to be "naughty," even though it meant undergoing humiliation and personal discomfort. And the naughtiness was imagined, for he obeyed Stein's every command. In this role he was perfectly safe, having no responsibilities other than to fulfill the wishes of his hostess. She was tyrannical, but she was, Paul claims, "such a full person, you didn't mind. Stein was a theater of one, with her on stage and her visitors watching." Paul never minded his role. "She was playing a game. I was too. I could have sat down and said I didn't want to. But I enjoyed the game."[30]

Stein also encouraged his creativity, as had his mother. She was, however, suspicious of "unconscious" writing and of his sincerity as a poet. He remembers her reading his poetry and the discussion that followed:

> "Well, the only trouble with all this is that it isn't poetry."
> "What is it?" I demanded.
> "How should I know what it is? You wrote it. You tell *me* what it is. It's not poetry. . . . It's all false."
> "It was written without conscious intervention," I told her sententiously. It's not my fault. I didn't know what I was writing."
> "Yes, yes, but you knew *afterwards* what you'd written, and you should have known it was false. It was false and you sent it off to *transition*. . . . Unfortunately. Because it's not poetry." (*WS*:121–22)

Bowles felt criticism acutely, especially accusations of falseness, and Gertrude Stein's pronouncement bothered him for a long while. Of the encounter, he wrote, "All my poems are worth a large zero. That is the end of that. And unless I undergo a great metamorphosis, there will never be any more poems."[31] Stein tried to temper her words later, writing him, "My dear Freddy, I am not uninterested in your poems. Bernard Faÿ has just sent them to me. I take back the harsh things I said."[32] This time he sent her a story he had written, and she encouraged him further: "I like your story. I like your writing, go on with them." After suggesting that he send his work to some of the older magazines rather than the "little odd modern" ones he had been pursuing, she closed with, "I always think there is a future in writing."[33]

For his part, Paul discovered that despite her rhythmic gift, Gertrude Stein had little appreciation for music. Her talent was entirely literary, he decided.[34] He also discovered his early theories of her work to be off the mark. "She has set me right, by much labor on her part, and now the fact emerges that there is nothing in her works save the sense. The sound, the sight, the soporific repetitions to which I had attached such great importance, are accidental, she insists, and the one aim of her writing is the superlative *sense*. 'What is the use of writing,' she will shout, 'unless every word makes the utmost sense?'"35

A piece of Bowles's entitled "In the Creuse," bearing the inscription "Cannes 1930," a four-page narrative describing a walk in the country Paul had visited in the summer of 1929, shows the marked influence of Stein on Bowles. It is full of run-on sentences, sentences linked by conjunctions, simplicity of expression, rhythmicity, and repetitiveness. The story begins simply and placidly with a Steinian sense of optimism, as the narrator invites a woman for a walk. "And she agreed and so we started out just as we were, feeling quite happy at trusting the weather which blew at us and blew the clouds across the sun and blew all the leaves of the poplar trees inside out."36 When rain forces the two to take refuge in a little house by the railroad tracks, the story takes on a surreal quality: a woman lies bleeding next to the stove inside the house, and a goat stands outside bleating. As if dictating a dream, the narrator describes the action without commentary. In this work Stein's attention to rhythm and sense in language and Bowles's interest in fables, surrealism, and dream narrative are combined with the famous Bowlesian detachment—all the elements that later became the hallmark of Bowles's mature fiction.

At Paul's invitation, Copland came to Bilignin, and the two musicians began discussing places where they might retreat for August. Stein promoted Tangier by claiming the sun shone there every day. Years later Bowles came to suspect that Stein was curious to see what would happen when he hit the international community of Tangier.37 In any case, the idea was appealing because Tangier was more economical than Paris.38 Furthermore, for Bowles, "The idea suited my overall desire, that of getting as far away as possible from New York" (*WS*:124).

The Magic of Childhood Games

Of all the cities in North Africa, Tangier had the most contact with European and American culture. Located on the far northwestern tip of Africa, since 1923 it had been in the International Zone governed by representatives from eight countries—Great Britain, France, Spain, Italy, the United States, Belgium, Holland, Portugal—and Tangier itself. Cruise ships from London stopped in port regularly, and a car ferry brought tourists from Gibraltar. One resident estimated there were six hundred automobiles in the whole of Morocco, most of them in Tangier. In the early 1930s, Tangier's population of about fifty thousand included nearly twelve thousand non-Moroccans. Tourists, whose numbers nearly equaled the Moroccan population, could play tennis, golf, or polo, visit an English library, and be treated for illness in an English, a French, a Spanish, or an American hospital. The International Zone remained, outside of India, the last bastion of the English sport of pig-sticking. There were balls for the resident socialites, benefits for local charities, and fancy-dress parties for youngsters at country villas. Modern hotels, two three-star French restaurants, and European shops were at the disposal of residents and tourists.

Despite the amenities of the International Zone, the old Arab quarter in the city had no plumbing, and residents there drew water from a communal fountain and emptied sewage into the streets. Outside the city, conditions were similarly primitive. Even the wealthy who lived outside the city in areas such as the hill called "the Mountain," about three kilometers away, or the plain known as "the Marshan" lacked electricity and a reliable source of water. Roads to other parts of the country were questionable at best, and the Tangier-Fez Railway had been in operation only since 1929.

Bowles and Copland settled in a small house on the side of the Mountain. Soon they found a piano and had it moved to their home. While Copland worked on his "Short Symphony," Paul wrote his Sonata for Oboe and Clarinet and took more "harmony lessons" from Copland—working out figured bass exercises and analyzing Mozart sonatas. Copland became increasingly annoyed with all the distractions: roosters crowed, donkeys brayed, plumbing failed, their servant was habitually morose, and worst of all, they had "an African piano which looks like a piano but which sounds like hell!"[39] Stein gleefully counseled the artists, "Yes Chopin had just as much trouble with his piano in the Isles Balearic . . . so cheer up, it is the common lot."[40]

Paul was nearly ecstatic.

The heat here is like that of a Turkish bath. It is utterly delightful, and it is permanent. There is never any objectionable let-up that makes one so conscious of it all when it returns. Steady, hot, dry weather, with a sun that burns a white hole in the ultramarine sky with a moon that is like the sun when it is full. . . . Sometimes there is music being sung from a distant part of the mountain, and often there are complicated drum rhythms that continue hours at a stretch. We live at the top of the cliffs over the Strait of Gibraltar, and Spain is always clearly visible for a stretch of 100 km. along its sandy bluffs, across the blue expanse. The countryside is blotched with cacti of all varieties, and the roads are narrow and fenced in by waving walls of a sort of bamboo that grows fifteen feet or so in height. Our villa is big enough for 10 people, with spacious gardens where palms, figs, flowers, grapes, huge eucalyptus trees and dozens of other things rush about madly in the wind.[41]

Paul was "in love with Tangier" and Morocco; Copland was not. "Up here on the mountain there are drums that beat a lot. That worries Aaron, as he cannot get it out of his head that the Arabs are grieved about something, and are all set to go on the warpath."[42] For Paul, Tangier had the advantage over Europe in climate. "The drums beat all night, in rhythms that keep one awake, make one think of the heat of the sun in its pitiless beating on the hot hills. . . . The waves along the ground [make] everything dance in wriggling arabesques."[43] Enchanted with the mysterious, sometimes sinister aspects of Morocco, Paul thought the country could be the answer to his romantic dreams, a "magic place which in disclosing its secrets would give me wisdom and ecstasy—perhaps even death" (*WS*:125).

Paul saw mystery and secrecy in every aspect of Tangier, from the social life of the Moroccans to the architecture and the twisting streets of the medina. "Will you ever learn the secret, shall I?" he asked Roditi.[44] In Moroccan society the split between public and private was extreme. A man's associates were likely to know little or nothing of his private life. Domestic life also was segregated. A male visitor to a Moroccan household seldom met the women who lived there, nor was he admitted to any of the rooms where they slept, cooked, or visited among themselves. In principle, women did not move beyond their homes. Lower-class women might go to the market to do their own shopping, but among the upper classes the saying held true: a woman leaves her home only three times—when she is born (leaving her mother's womb), when she marries (leaving her father's house), and when she dies (leaving her husband's house).

The architecture of the city reinforced the philosophy of segregation of the public and the private, the professional and the domestic. The exteriors of houses were often blank walls, revealing nothing of the life inside. In wealthier homes, a tiny doorway opened onto a verdant courtyard, flanked by many small rooms used for visiting, for sleeping, or for preparing food. Moroccans lived in a quarter called the medina. There the streets formed by walls with occasional doorways created a maze that was replicated above by the series of interconnected roofs upon which the women conducted their daily activities: they hung their laundry, prepared meals, and discussed the details of their households.

In Tangier, Bowles saw the unconscious come to life. The "dream city" was a surrealist landscape:

Its topography was rich in prototypical dream scenes: covered streets like corridors with doors opening into rooms on each side, hidden terraces high above the sea, streets consisting only of steps, dark impasses, small squares built on sloping terrain so that they looked like ballet sets designed in false perspective, with alleys leading off in several directions; as well as the classical dream equipment of tunnels, ramparts, ruins, dungeons, and cliffs. (*WS*:128)

Tangier also posed an alternative to the Western civilization Bowles hated so much. Moroccans dressed according to tradition: in the city Arab women wore pantaloons and covered their hair and faces with layers of veils over which they draped more fabric—a large shawl, blanket, or *haik*—so that on their few trips outside their homes they resembled walking bundles of laundry. Men slung wool burnouses over their shoulders and shuffled down dusty streets in soft slippers that seemed always on the verge of sliding away. Tangier's narrow winding streets and small cafés brought to reality not only medieval history but also elements of Paul's childhood: the "magic of childhood games"; the incense from Aunt Adelaide's apartment; Uncle Guy's silk robes; the chanting from Holden Hall.

Paul and Aaron Copland remained in Tangier through the summer of 1931, absorbed in their work and each other's company, but taking time for dinners in town and weekly visits with the Dutch surrealist painter Kristians Tonny and Anita Thompson, a couple also in Tangier at Stein's suggestion. Paul had initially balked at meeting Tonny, because he expected a "square-headed Dutchman," and finally went only at Copland's insistence. Eventually Tonny and Paul began a friendship that lasted for years, but at this time, Paul reported to Stein, "Anita is always asleep, and Tonny is quite bored. . . . It seems they gave an extremely successful cocktail-party in Paris last winter. I suppose they are resting on their laurels."[45] Paul began to feel better about Tonny on their second visit, when the painter remarked to Copland, "The young man with you is slightly off his head, isn't he? I noticed it the other night right away. I heard shutters banging in the wind in there somewhere" (*WS*:130).

In late September the two composers sold their furnishings and traveled south to Fez, a holy city that had been open to Europeans for fewer than twelve years. Surrounded by a high stone wall for protection against the infidels, it sat on land so fertile it looked in the distance like "a white jewel set in a field of emeralds."[46] But looks were deceptive, and a week after his arrival, Paul wrote to Stein, "Fez is full of flies and dust, and rats knock everything over on the tables at night. It is quite dirty and *very* beautiful."[47] And he writes in his autobiography, "Tangier had by no means prepared me for the experience of Fez, where everything was ten times stranger and bigger and brighter. I felt that at last I had left the world behind" (*WS*:130). The two composers stayed in the small Hôtel Ariana, where their rooms opened directly onto Fez el Jdid (the "new Fez," established in the thirteenth

century). One could step through the windows onto the rampart wall and
see below the garden of Djenane es Sebir with its willows overhanging the
Oued Fez (Fez River), and to the right, "an ancient waterwheel turned
slowly, dripping and creaking" (*WS*:131). In Tangier the old world existed
side by side with the new, but Fez had isolated itself from more recent
civilization.[48] To Paul, Fez was the most fascinating city in North Africa.

Copland left Fez shortly after their October 1 arrival. Paul remained there
to wait for Harry Dunham, who had cabled from Dresden that he was on his
way to join him.[49] The cable put Paul in a difficult position. Copland was his
mentor and was anxious to return to Berlin, which offered him more
compatible surroundings, but Harry was Paul's financial benefactor as well
as his friend. Furthermore, Paul was in love with Fez, hated Berlin, and
looked forward to having a companion with whom he could explore
Morocco. Bowles and Copland would never again be quite so close.

Dunham had left Princeton to study dance but instead had discovered
photography, which seemed to Paul a great misfortune. As autumn progressed, Paul spent his days surrounded by screaming French and Moroccans, as Harry snapped hundreds of pictures. Given Paul's desire to remain as
invisible as possible, he found traveling with Harry a constant trial: "Harry
thought in terms of confrontation rather than conspiracy" (*WS*:132). As
Paul had already discovered, Moroccans shared the conspiratorial approach
to life and seldom responded favorably to direct confrontation.

Moroccans held great fascination for Paul insofar as he saw in their culture
an extension of the kinds of self-protection he had found useful. He decided
that they hid their true motives or opinions in almost every situation. No less
twisted than the streets of Fez were the interactions in the markets, restaurants, and all other places, public and private. The simplest interaction
required strategic skills, and social situations were based upon intrigue and
diplomacy. Moroccans were "supreme illusionists; they can give a straight
forward action the air of being a conjurer's trick or make the most tortuously
devious behavior seem like naturalness itself."[50] They had mastered the
kinds of mystery and secrecy that excited him. Then too, there was a fatalistic
approach to individual action that appealed to Paul's natural inclinations. In
his view, the Muslims let all decisions rest with Allah. All behavior was
governed according to the Koran. The social behavior he observed repeated
this shifting of personal responsibility as well. He likened visits with
Moroccan friends to "playing a simple, pleasant game in which the hosts lead
the way with regard to the silences to be observed as well as the conversation
to be made, and the guests follow comfortably, happy to have all social
responsibility taken from them."[51]

In this highly structured society, every situation required of its participants a particular role, a specific set of behaviors. "Each Moroccan gave the impression of playing a part in a huge drama; he was involved not only with the others in the dispute, but also with the audience out front. . . . I knew I should never tire of watching Moroccans play their parts" (*WS*:127). Morocco evoked the best parts of Paul's childhood—the mystical and the mysterious. Further, the daily dramas there allowed and required Paul to play the part of voyeur, another role that he was quickly perfecting.

Learning by Doing

Paul and Harry traveled throughout Morocco before returning to Paris. Along the way, Harry acquired a young Moroccan boy, Abdelkader, whom he decided to bring to Paris as a valet but who needed parental permission to leave the country. Harry went on ahead while Paul waited in Marrakech with Abdelkader as the legal arrangements commenced. Each day, Paul and Abdelkader went to the office of notaries, accompanied by Abdelkader's mother and grandmother in a separate carriage. He writes, "It seems to me now that those days consisted largely of endless carriage rides along the dusty alleys, through flickering sunlight and shadow, the other carriage with the two covered figures in it, going on ahead" (*WS*:136). When the legal proceedings dragged, Paul returned to Tangier and stayed with Kristians Tonny and Anita Thompson. He worked on the orchestral parts for his Sonata for Oboe and Clarinet, which Copland had arranged to be performed in London in December. When Abdelkader joined him, he was at last ready to leave Morocco: "It rains all the time here now, and Tonny's house is wet inside."[52]

It was late autumn when Paul arrived in Paris and took Harry with him to call on composer Virgil Thomson, "as a courtesy." The two naïf-dandies stepped into Thomson's studio at 17 Quai Voltaire: "both with yellow hair and wearing yellow overcoats with long, yellow scarves. It was like a double bolt of sunshine."[53] Thomson's studio was across the Seine from the Musée du Louvre, on the Left Bank, a lively European intellectual and artistic community.

Thomson took an interest in Paul's career, and since Copland had moved to Mexico, the two composers argued by mail over the best course of action for their young friend. Copland wanted Bowles to study with Nadia Boulanger; Thomson recommended Paul Dukas, explaining, "Nadia is not the same as when we were there," and adding that Paul's chances of meeting composers of his generation in Paris were better away from Boulanger's studio, which attracted mainly older musicians. "Ive [*sic*] sent Nadia pupils for years and very little good has come of them, none for European purposes. . . . I think it's time to change," Thomson wrote.[54] Copland responded, "There is no matter where or how a pupil learns his stuff just so that he learns it," but he knew Boulanger's method. He concluded, "As soon as I feel the disadvantages outweigh the advantages to be gained from being N.B.'s [*sic*] pupil I'll stop sending pupils, but that time hasn't come yet."[55] In the end, Paul registered for Boulanger's counterpoint class at the Ecole Normale but apparently attended only two classes.

Thomson concluded that Bowles did not continue study with Boulanger because he was "too stingy" to pay for lessons, which flew in the face of correspondence in which Bowles claimed that he had "already paid" for lessons. Bowles apparently had a different philosophy: "I think the advantage of ordinary lessons in general is moral rather than anything else. There is a bit more chance of their being done, with people like me, for instance."[56]

Paul reverted to the behavior pattern that worried Copland. He traveled too much, in Copland's view, and refused to settle down to one course of study or with one teacher, preferring instead to forge ahead, composing as he wished. Yet Thomson disagreed, explaining that although Paul worried a great many of his friends by refusing to "lead the conventional life of a young man of talent," he was instinctively following the right course for himself.

> The force of his own genius is stronger in him than any reason or affection. So with the best will in the world to do as you say and learn the countrapuntal [*sic*] routine, he just cant [*sic*] be bothered. Of course, at bottom, he's right. His musical procedure is far too contrapuntal now. What he is really interested in learning just now is how to write for all the instruments and how to compose in free form. He is learning by doing and all the lesson he needs he gets from you and me and others by showing the finished piece and saying "What's wrong here?" If he ever needs systematic instruction, he'll go get it and pay for it and absorb it quickly. I assure you there is nothing to worry about.[57]

Both composers continued to look out for the welfare of their protégé, even though, as Thomson pointed out, Paul often was unable to follow their advice. Copland came up with a solution: "I play the role of the worrier. You encourage him and I'll worry him and together we'll do very well by him."[58] As Thomson later wrote, Paul's music, "Ravel-like piano improvisations, charmed us all, as it had already charmed Copland." But Thomson doubted whether even Copland's worrying would make much difference: "Copland had tried in New York teaching him harmony but had found him a stubborn pupil."[59] Copland said, "Paul had definite interests and knew exactly what he wanted in his music."[60] As a student in Virginia, Bowles had written Burns, "I should be thought of by you as a person springing from contemporaneity."[61] He seems to have fulfilled this youthful wish for self-origination, for "learning by doing."

Despite his stubbornness as a pupil, or perhaps because of his insistence on retaining his self-taught status, by the age of twenty, Paul had gained a reputation as both a composer with promise and a composer of some accomplishment. In December 1931, his Sonata for Oboe and Clarinet premiered in London, along with Copland's Piano Variations, Thomson's "Capital Capitals," Irving Citkowitz's "Joyce Songs," and Carlos Chávez's Piano Sonatina, in the final Copland-Sessions Concert of New American Music at Aeolian Hall. Although listed among distinguished company, Bowles still enjoyed playing the part of the little boy, as letters to Copland show: "I shall start making the parts, but God knows how right they will be. I wish there were some way of your seeing them before I send them to London. Oh dear, oh dear! I insist on getting them done in time for the rehearsals. In fact I should blow up and die immediately if it could not come off on account of lack of time."[62]

The sonata was the piece on which Bowles had been working while he and Copland were living in Tangier, but he had begun the piece earlier that year after meeting with Kurt Schwitters ("quite mad, but one wonders occasionally if correctly so"),[63] using the rhythms (and vocal inflection) from a Schwitters poem as the basis of the theme in the rondo movement:

> Lanke trr gll.
> Pe pe pe pe pe
> Ooka. Ooka. Ooka. Ooka.
> Lanke trr gll.
> Pi pi pi pi pi
> Tzuuka. Tzuuka. Tzuuka. Tzuuka.
>
> (*WS*:115)

Thus as much as Bowles claimed to rely on the unconscious for the creative energy in his work, he also freely drew ideas from daily life. Indeed, years later the idea for one of his finest extended works, the Concerto for Two Pianos, Winds, and Percussion, began in the falling drops of water from a bathtub tap.

After returning to Paris, Harry Dunham had taken an apartment at the top of 17 Quai Voltaire, the same building where Virgil Thomson lived. Paul had intended to move in with him while attending Boulanger's classes in January 1932, but instead decided to go to the Italian Alps to ski after meeting artist Anne Miracle. "Beautiful and dainty" Anne was "devoted to Paul," Virgil Thomson remembers.[64] Paul became so ill in Italy that he went immediately to the hospital in Turin. While Anne skied, Paul recuperated.

Letters from Paul to Gertrude Stein and Edouard Roditi refer to an "operation" from which he would need "weeks or months" to recuperate.[65] There were rumors that this "operation" was a series of injections for treatment of syphilis, rumors that may have resulted from Harry Dunham's sister Amelia's persistent delusion that Paul was syphilitic. By all accounts, Harry Dunham traveled to Turin after receiving a wire from Miracle; he was furious with Paul and as a result of a quarrel withdrew all financial support. A worried Bowles wrote to Roditi, "Harry has gone off to Ohio with his sister, probably in a rage,"[66] and to Stein:

> So now Boulanger is no more and Harry evidently will be no more and I shall have to study alone. Harry left this morning saying he was on his way to America. So the whole ménage is over. . . . I shall get on all right, as you say, but I think it would be better if I could find things like translations to do. How about your friend whose name you mentioned to me? . . . I am upset, as upset I suppose as I ever shall be, which is not so terribly, but enough to bother me and make me have occasional desperate exciting thoughts.[67]

In his mock-desperate tone and veiled references to suicide, Paul made as strong a case as he could for help from Gertrude Stein. Stein's response came ten days later: "I did not answer sooner because being a little troubled about you I wanted to see Harry first, now I have and as it seems that you are really not well don't you think it would be best to come to Paris where you can be looked after and then we all can decide what you ought to do, you poor boy, its hard to be all alone and I do think that you had better come here don't you."[68]

The tone of this letter pleased Paul. He later wrote a song using it as the text, calling it "Letter to Freddy," and writing to Stein said, "I have made a song out of one of your best letters."[69] The letter from Stein was no better or worse than any other, except that it displayed the grandmotherly quality that Paul cherished in her, but more important, it portrayed him in the naïf role. As Virgil Thomson recalled, "Paul was very good at getting people to feel sorry for him, especially women."[70]

About the same time, Paul had written to Thomson of his plight and from him did get money. Ten days after Bowles had written Stein saying "Boulanger is no more," he assured Thomson that he would begin his counterpoint classes as soon as he returned to Paris. There is no indication that he took more than a couple of classes. Years later he had few regrets: "I found her rather worrying. She was very severe, rather like a crotchety maiden aunt. Everyone says she was a magnificent teacher. I'm sure she was. For me she was a bit formidable."[71]

The events in Italy demonstrated how tenuous Bowles's situation was, and how dependent he was on others. Barely twenty-one years old, Paul had not embarked on a serious course of study nor had he any reliable means of support. Though financially comfortable, the Bowleses were not wealthy—they were decidedly middle class, to Bowles's everlasting embarrassment, and were disinclined to underwrite the freewheeling life Paul had chosen for himself. Nonetheless, Paul had great conviction in his artistic destiny and had convinced a number of people to help him out. "When the world is good to one, what can one do but thank it and work for it?" he wrote Roditi,[72] who recalled: "When Paul and I finally met [in 1931], I was dazzled, like Saint Gregory in the slave-market of ancient Rome, by his angelic Anglo-Saxon physical appearance, but also appalled by his apparent other-worldliness, helplessness and poverty."[73]

Paul's hospitalization and Amelia Dunham's accusations raise other questions about the nature of Paul's relationship with Harry Dunham. According to Roditi, "Everyone went to bed with him [Harry] or tried to, except Paul, I think."[74] To the question, "Were Paul and Harry lovers?" Virgil Thomson replied, "Paul was no good as anybody's lover. Harry was devoted to Paul. Paul liked people being devoted to him. Personally I think he had a low sexual temperament." Early in his stay in Paris, Paul had written Roditi, "Much as I should like to make love too much as you claim you do, I see no way even of beginning. Aaron would say, 'There's nothing to worry about. When you really want to, you will.' I don't think I agree with him."[75] "Paul was almost a 'phony homosexual,'" Thomson said, with the phrase that his generation sometimes used to refer to bisexuals. "He made out in his life as if he were queer. But he was completely and consistently disagreeable with all the men in his life and perfectly wonderful with all the women. Before Janie there was Annie Miracle; before her, a Venetia. There were always women in and out of his life. He was charming and they adored him. But he was quarrelsome with the men."[76]

Certainly, there was an advantage to being homosexual in the 1920s and 1930s; overt homosexuals dominated French high culture—Gide, Proust, Cocteau, and Diaghilev—and homosexuals were prominent in the New York world of music and theater. Then too, there was a certain political chic to being homosexual, a defiance of traditional social norms. Of that time in his life, Bowles himself has stated that he was "militantly anti-heterosexual" and that this was a "gesture of social defiance."[77] Aaron Copland had a reputation for involvement with attractive younger men, yet no one has stated that he and Paul were sexually involved.[78] Their relationship was probably no more than that of mentor/student or, as Copland asserts, professional friends.

Paul was a great believer in allowing others to draw their own conclusions and was no stranger to emotional pretense, but one need not conclude that he feigned sexual interest in order to succeed professionally. Indeed, one might argue that had Paul exploited his sexuality, the nature of these relationships would have been exposed long ago. Perhaps, as Maurice Grosser suggested, by refusing to deny sexual involvement with some, Bowles was able to fend off advances from those who would leave him alone if they believed he were already spoken for. Clearly, he enjoyed attention and being taken care of, whatever the cost, as his history with "Uncle" Hubert and Gertrude Stein attests. It may have been that only when Paul was asked to do more than simply play a part did trouble erupt. For a year after his quarrel with Harry, he wrote to Stein, questioning whether the title of Ford and Tyler's book, *The Young and Evil*, really applied to his generation. If it did, he might have to find another generation: "Young people always resent my pretending to be living instead of living, and older ones don't notice it."[79]

A Dandy in Morocco

The winter of 1931/32 Edouard Roditi introduced Paul to John Trounstine, a literary agent.[80] Trounstine was a "lost soul" in Paris and could afford a traveling companion. Paul, broke and miserable in the Paris weather, soon left with Trounstine for Spain.[81] In southern Spain the oases of date palms set Paul reminiscing about North Africa, and soon he had talked Trounstine into extending the trip to Morocco. The two men argued in Fez and parted company. Paul, with little money and only the hope of a small legacy left to him by his Aunt Adelaide for his twenty-first birthday, stayed and looked up the wealthy merchant Abdallah Drissi, whom he had met the previous year. Drissi locked his guest inside the walls of the house along with the rest of the household each morning when he left for the day, so for a few days Paul spent much of his time watching a "square of sky" visible at the top of the courtyard and marking the passage of time by the changing color of that square, an experience that he later recaptured in his novel *The Spider's House*. Feeling imprisoned at Drissi's, Paul moved to the Hôtel Ariana, where he and Copland had stayed. Soon he caught his first sight of the Moroccan brotherhoods, or religious sects.

The extent of the brotherhoods is unknown. The sects were secret in nature; Moroccans tended to conceal their seemingly "primitive" activities, but Paul estimated almost half the males in Morocco belonged. Reflecting upon that first brotherhood celebration, a slow-moving procession down a street in Fez, Paul wrote, "I had suspected that someday I would stumble onto a scene which would show me the pulse of the place, if not the exposed, beating heart of its magic, but it was a tremendous surprise to find it first in the open street. Yet there they were, several thousand people near Bab

Mahrouk, stamping, heaving, shuddering, gyrating, and chanting, all of them aware only of the overpowering need to achieve ecstasy" (*WS*:150–51).

The deep trances that these worshipers exercised fascinated Paul. He had been practicing the "blank state" since childhood, and his experiments in unconscious writing sprang from an interest in different states of consciousness. Since his conscious life was governed by a welter of self-imposed rules (which were in many ways just as strong as the cultural traditions imposed on the Moroccan Muslims), the trance state provided a great release.

In the brotherhood ritual, Paul found what he identified as the heart of Morocco, and it drew him back again and again to that country. In it Paul found his lost childhood—what he terms the "childhood which never happened." In Morocco, his experiences resonated with his few happy childhood memories and with his strong desire to escape the age to which he had been born. Even more important, he discovered a cultural understanding so strong that simply to observe it, without being a part of it himself, fascinated and satisfied him. The brotherhood ritual made him aware "for the first time . . . that a human being is not an entity and that his interpretation of exterior phenomena is meaningless unless it is shared by the other members of his cultural group" (*WS*:151).

Years later Bowles reflected, "I had decided that the world was too complex for me ever to be able to write fiction; since I failed to understand life, I would not be able to find points of reference which the hypothetical reader might have in common with me" (*WS*:262). When he did return to writing, it was to write of other cultures in a timeless world—cultures so different from his own that readers could not help but find themselves mystified. The points of reference Bowles found to share with his hypothetical readers were exactly these points of mystification, encounters between Western and non-Western peoples in which the Western mind ceases to understand the world into which it has entered.

By May, Paul had returned to Paris and a furnished room in Montmartre, where he was working on his Sonata for Flute and Piano. Although the weather grew warmer daily, Paul continually complained of feeling cold. Finally, poet Carlo Suarès, who was himself from Egypt, suggested the possibility of typhoid. In the American Hospital in Neuilly, Paul finally received the diagnosis: typhoid-A. After two weeks, he was allowed to receive visitors, among them Virgil Thomson, who told Paul that with his "ghastly red" beard, he looked just like Jesus; Abdelkader, who arrived wearing Paul's clothes; and Amelia Dunham, who announced, "At last I've got you where I want you" (*WS*:152). The mails brought a letter from Copland reporting that the performance of Bowles's songs at Yaddo by soprano Ada MacLeish, wife of poet Archibald MacLeish, had been well received. "You're on the map now, and don't you forget it," Copland wrote (*WS*:153).

News that her son had contracted typhoid prompted Rena Bowles to visit; she arrived in early August with Paul's friend Daniel Burns. Paul took his mother to Monte Carlo, the island of Mallorca, and Barcelona. In Barcelona, he suffered a sunstroke after staying too long on his hotel roof. Rena evoked his childhood by reading to him *A High Wind in Jamaica* (1929), Richard Hughes's chilling tale of children captured by pirates. Like the tales of Poe and Hawthorne to which he had listened as a boy, this book left its mark on Bowles's imagination. The primitive nature of the children, the cross-cultural meeting of Jamaican-reared English children with Spanish and Danish pirates, and the senseless murder of a Dutch sea captain by one of the children would have been appropriate in one of Bowles's own stories.

Perhaps Rena's coddling left him wishing for more: after his mother had left Paris, he suffered a second sunstroke while visiting Virgil Thomson and Maurice Grosser on the island of Porquerolles, southeast of Toulon. Some time later he explained that the second "sunstroke" was initially an excuse for ending a one-night affair with a *voyou*, a street-boy of Arabic descent.[82] But Bowles's explanation carries an unfamiliar tone of sexual braggadocio that rings false, as if he were trying to convince Thomson of something. Nonetheless, the tactic of using illness to gain sympathy and yet avoid someone is true to form. Paul had used it for years, beginning with childhood battles with his father.

Gertrude Stein found Paul "delightful and sensible in summer but neither delightful nor sensible in winter," which may explain why Paul was never in Paris during what most composers considered the teaching seasons.[83] He stayed in Monaco during the winter while he worked on a piano sonatina and on *Scènes d'Anabase*, a chamber piece in five sections for tenor and oboe.[84] St. John Perse had renewed in French poetry an interest in the epic with his poem *Anabase* (1924), a tale of a journey across the Gobi desert. Bowles was so inspired by the poem that he used the poem as the conceptual underpinning for his own text, a tribute to Perse.[85] The music ranges from mysterious to jazzy, even raucous, especially in the fifth section, where Bowles concentrated on syncopated ragtime rhythms. Throughout he effectively employed the oboe for a strangely Middle Eastern quality.

George Antheil, a composer known as the "bad boy" of American music, was in Monaco in 1932. Antheil had become an overnight sensation in Paris after the 1925 screening of the Fernand Léger film *Ballet Mécanique*, to which he had composed pulsating, repetitious music for eight player pianos. Like Bowles, he loved the sun and warmth of the Riviera, which he described as "a gorgeous soundproofed paradise, utterly oblivious of the darkening gathering over the rest of Europe. Here a synthetic sun shone on glittering synthetic beaches full of synthetically happy people."[86] Antheil knew many of the same people as Bowles, including Stein, Thomson, and Ezra Pound. Even more important, Antheil knew North Africa, and the two surely discussed his travels there. Given Paul's hatred of cold weather and the topic of his recent work, it is not surprising that in December 1932 he departed again for North Africa, this time leaving from Marseilles for Algiers. From Algiers, he traveled straight south the two hundred miles to Laghouat, and then on for one hundred miles farther into the desert, to Ghardaïa, an ancient oasis in the barren M'Zab region of the Algerian Sahara.

With the help of the French regional commander, he found a small house with a garden near Ghardaïa, "100% primitive," he wrote to Ford. "It's wild, savage, in the middle of miles and miles of chebka—a sort of waste land of broken knifelike stones and rocks that one walks on with difficulty."[87] That winter it rained in Ghardaïa for the first time in seven years, and rain in a country unaccustomed to so much of it can be disastrous. Children who had never before seen standing water tried to walk over a deep pond and drowned. Water cascaded off flat-roofed terraces and balconies, while the edges of mud houses crumbled into pools of paste. Paul nearly asphyxiated himself with the charcoal brazier he used for heat. After his recovery from that disaster, the cold that stayed in any corner untouched by the sun proved too intense, and he returned to Laghouat, an Algerian desert post consisting of a walled town (Old Laghouat) with a new French development on the north side of the wall.[88]

Even in the warmth of the Hôtel Transatlantique, he could not escape the cold. "I work all day covered by a burnous. I think it is colder here than in Paris," he wrote to Stein.[89] Not only was he cold, he was also lonely. Disappointed that he had been unable to convince Charles Henri Ford to join him and perhaps romanticizing his solitary life, he wrote, "I had planned if you came to stay on a while in Africa, but since I am too God damned bored to stay on alone, I think I shall return to New York. You can't imagine how difficult it is to live absolutely alone week in week out, without so much as speaking to a soul from any morning to any night, save to say good morning to the hotel proprietor and to buy stamps at the post-office. I have been trying to keep going by working continually, but it doesn't go."[90]

He found a church harmonium and used it for writing a cantata in French based on his own text, *Par le Détroit*, inspired so much by recurring dreams of *le détroit*—the strait—of Gibraltar that it might have been called "Dream Cantata." He proudly informed Stein, "The harmonium worked wonders. I have a lovely cantata from it."[91]

Toward the beginning of February, when the weather became slightly warmer, he returned to Ghardaïa and there met another traveler—an American near his age—George Turner. Now that he had a companion, Paul decided to prolong his stay in North Africa a bit. This chance meeting began the series of Saharan adventures that Paul incorporated into *The Sheltering Sky*.

In a copy of his novel belonging to John Stuart Groves, Bowles inscribed, "The only 'interesting' thing I can think of to say is that *all* the characters in the book exist, some with the same names used here."[92] Turner's name appears in the novel, changed to "Tunner," and so does the name of the French regional commander of Ghardaïa—Lieutenant d'Armagnac. So too does one of Turner and Bowles's first stops, Bou-Saâda, where they spent a few days. There a young girl danced nude for them, something that was not at all the custom but that found its way into his novel.

Certainly Paul's Saharan travels were the most colorful of his North African adventures. From Bou-Saâda, he wrote Gertrude Stein:

At the moment I am in pain, having just been thrown off the back of a crazy mare into a dry river bed. Which makes various parts hurt very much. . . . I don't know what ailed the mare. She ambled beautifully in the oasis, but the moment she saw the open desert ahead of her, as we came out from between the walls, she was suddenly falling fast horizontally, and the saddle was coming to pieces. My beret flew off and I wondered how long it could go on. Above the dry river she stopped, but I kept going. After that I let her wander here and there, but she remained extremely sulky, and seemed to take no pleasure in anything I did for her. The camels are really nicer, and they can't run more than twenty meters at a time.[93]

Returning to Algiers, where Paul stored his valises and trunk in a hotel, Paul and Turner trekked south to Touggourt, a major stop on a Trans-Saharan caravan route. The streets of Touggourt lay carpeted in red from mountains of grasshoppers, which were sold to natives who discarded the wings and munched the bodies.[94] From Touggourt, they traveled three days across the northern edge of the Great East Erg. Paul rode a camel named Ida, who "had a great deal of character. When it went too slowly, [the driver] would scream 'Hot, Ida!' and Ida would stop altogether."[95] Their destination was El Oued, which Paul described to Ford as "like a city one has dreamt about some time just before waking, and whose sweetness is prolonged into waking."[96] Next they took a two-day ride by caterpillar truck to Nefta, in Tunisia, and then to Kairouan, "where the vermin in the beds was indescribable" and where they were temporarily detained by the authorities (*WS*:162). Paul and Turner took a train and arrived in Tunis at the beginning of Roosevelt's March bank holiday, when American money was worthless.[97]

Paul sent four wires to friends in Europe requesting money. Bruce Morrissette responded with money to buy a ticket back to Algiers. On the train, Paul met a young man named Hassan Ramani who, upon hearing of Paul's financial difficulties, invited him to stay with his family in Constantine until the banks opened again. And during those few days at the Ramanis', "Somehow I was allowed right into the circle, with the women unveiled and so on. Evenings the entertainments were swell."[98]

The city of Constantine lay along a deep gorge. Bowles writes, "A swaying footbridge spanned the abyss. The invisible river that roared far beneath was swollen with the melted snows of the Hodna Mountains; a fine vapor rose constantly from below. Storks stood quietly on the rooftops, and the sad smell of late winter hung in the air." Just outside the city, the Ramanis lived at the edge of this gorge. They ate their meals on "a long terrace overlooking the emptiness below, and the rising mist nearly obscured the cliffs . . . opposite" (*WS*:164). Years later Bowles set his short story "The Echo" (1946) in a house next to a gorge, an "enormous void": "Constant vapor rose from the invisible pool at the bottom, and the distant, indeterminate calling of water was like the sound of sleep itself" (*CS*:55). "The Echo" was set in South America, yet no matter where he traveled, Paul found gorges and abysses, the geography of nothingness.

If Bowles kept any journals of this three-week trip across North Africa, he destroyed them or kept them to himself. Although no notes appear alongside his other papers and notebooks, he preserved in memory the landscape, daily life, and isolated incidents he observed. He had fallen in love with the people, despite what he described to Ford as their "insupportable jealousy," and expressed, "once I shall be away from them I shall immediately regret it, and am sure I shall return and spend all my life somewhere among them." He longed to continue his travels and considered a trip to Mallorca or Menorca, off the northern coast of Spain, where living would be cheaper than in Africa. Financially, by late March he was at the bottom of the barrel, having "exploited all productive mines. Anyway, the trip was wonderful, and quite worth whatever consequences it might entail."[99]

On literary merit alone, Paul was absolutely correct. Although he waited more than a decade to build on it, on this trip he laid the foundation for a career as a writer. His first short stories and his first and most important novel all came directly out of these few months in North Africa. In the spring of 1933, however, his stay was ending. After a few days in Algiers, where he spent his evenings in the Casbah "smoking *kif* and playing dominoes," Paul collected his belongings and returned to Tangier.[100]

Although his unconscious mind was gathering material for a career as a writer, in 1933 Bowles was more intent on perfecting his skills as a composer.

He worked "fanatically," as the number and quality of compositions he produced, despite his wanderings, attest. Back in Tangier he rented a house on the Marshan, across from the Caid MacLean palace, where he worked daily from morning through the afternoon. Because he slept in a hotel in town, using his house only as a studio, after a time Paul was persuaded to share his house with Charles Henri Ford and Djuna Barnes, who was then typing the final draft of *Nightwood*. During the day, when he could get the house back from Barnes and Ford—"Oh, Paul, you come so early," Ford complained—he composed his Piano Sonatina.[101] Aware that his time abroad was coming to an end, he assessed the work he had accomplished during his two years of travel: the Sonata for Flute and Piano, *Scènes d'Anabase*, the Sonatina for Piano, and the cantata *Par le Détroit*. In February he had written Stein, "It is time to show Copland my output. I am sure he will be pleased."[102]

Though Bowles's output was considerable, Copland had been on to something when he worried that Paul seemed unable to settle down and lead the life of a serious student of music. Bowles was as devoted to travel as to composing, and he never did "lead the life" of a student of music. Even as a twenty-one-year-old poet and composer traveling through France, Spain, and North Africa, Bowles rivaled the best of the French literary wanderers: Flaubert, Rimbaud, Roussel, and his own idol, Gide, who first went to North Africa with Paul Laurens in 1893 at the age of twenty-four.

In practical effects, Bowles's travels resemble those of the late nineteenth-century adventurers who traveled heavy and adopted their vocations with missionary fervor. Like them, Paul seldom went anywhere without taking along his extensive wardrobe ("Why does he have so many clothes?" Stein asked Aaron Copland. "He's got enough for six young men" [*WS*:123]). Paul himself recalled his arrival in Morocco in 1931 in these terms: "We disembarked with so much luggage that we needed a small detachment of porters to carry it" (*WS*:126).

He was, in short, a dandy, "a man dedicated solely to his own perfection through a ritual of taste . . . free of all human commitments that conflict with taste: passions, moralities, ambitions, politics, or occupations."[103] He dressed well in expensive clothes, which he bought in quantity to make the most of limited funds. When he found a good tailor in the course of his travels, he would order a half-dozen or more handmade silk shirts or ties for future use. He spent as much time as possible in the sun, which bronzed his skin and bleached his hair. Yet, though he took pride in his appearance, he preferred that admirers keep their distance. Grosser recalled, "He was a great dandy, and a beauty. He always had to live down the fact that he was—not a beauteous young man, but so extraordinarily attractive. And he was always horrified if anybody made an approach to him. He would freeze up immediately." Edouard Roditi recalls Paul fleeing like a "shy nymph pursued by a lustful satyr" the one time a "handsome young Arab" approached Paul in a Turkish bath.[104]

Bowles's dandyism is also consistent with what Gertrude Himmelfarb has called the "moral imagination" of the late nineteenth century, an imagination that sought to "adorn and enhance rather than destroy the decent drapery of life," to dignify and civilize and cover humanity's "naked shivering nature."[105] Every mention of the human body in Bowles's autobiography is connected with shame and revulsion. His obsession with proper clothing was the conscious attempt of an antimodern to "recover" a self that civilization was stripping.

Part of Bowles's dandyism was a sense of artistic duty: "If my insistence upon prolonging the wanderings was compulsive," so too was "the fanatical manner in which I forced myself to work regularly each day" (*WS*:166). Stein's and Copland's continuing admonishments, his growing sense of himself as an artist, and his childhood experiences combined to compel him to work, to produce, and to maintain his independence.

By 1933 Bowles had outgrown his role as naïf as well as his youthful need for a mentor. He had become a dandy and a cynic, committed to rebellion against Western values. He had begun an independent artistic apprenticeship. For several years he remained unaware that he had apprenticed himself not to music but to the word.

BOOK III

A NOMAD IN NEW YORK, 1933–1947

I looked for home elsewhere, and was confident of
finding none which I should relish less than the one
which I was leaving.[1]

A Composer and a Dandy

PAUL SPENT the next fifteen years based in New York, successfully supporting himself composing music for the theater, escaping the city at every opportunity, and settling down as little as he had in Europe. Being a composer tied him to the city, a fact to which he never completely adjusted.

Paul returned to New York via San Juan, Puerto Rico, dragging his feet all the way. From San Juan he wrote Gertrude Stein, "I had no desire to come to America and have no idea why I did now that I am here. I think it was my mother."[2] From New York he wrote Virgil Thomson, "Certainly nobody hates N.Y. as much as I do. . . . Why the Hell Aaron advised me to return is more than I know."[3] After three weeks in June with his parents, which he spent nursing an ulcer, he headed to Northampton, Massachusetts, to stay with his aunt Emma, who had divorced her husband Guy and was now Mrs. Orville Flint. He wrote to Stein, "I am staying in desolate country with an aunt for the summer, working; I must always tell you that, because you never believe it. This was the wrong year to come home. Copland has a new pet [violinist Victor Kraft]. . . . And since he was the only reason for returning, I feel deceived."[4]

In New England, Paul found himself again in the "accustomed mist" of theosophy, Madame Blavatsky, and her many disciples. When his relatives asked him to speak on his spiritual awakening, he read to them from the Koran and talked about theosophy's new Messiah Krishnamurti, whom he had visited while in Europe. They had had "no long conversations," but

Bowles had been convinced of the "limpidity of his mind" and told his listeners that with Krishnamurti's mind, he "could be happy and *know why*."[5] Beyond this flurry of attention, he felt completely alone in "utter silence, utter country" and complained to Thomson about the chastity he had suffered since leaving Morocco.[6]

By summer's end, Paul had repaired his relationship with Copland and made plans to stay a few days with the composer at Lake George before returning to New York to live with Harry Dunham, "as usual," for the winter. Admitting this arrangement had not always worked smoothly in the past, Bowles concluded that with Amelia Dunham not around, "there is no reason that I can see why everything won't be bearable."[7] He had declined an invitation to live with his parents and parodied his father's tone: "I cordially *invite* you! And even then you won't! Very well, it's quite all right."[8] Although Paul did move into Harry's East Thirty-eighth Street apartment, he soon moved out, this time to an apartment on West Fifty-eighth Street. Copland agreed to pay half the rent for the apartment, in exchange for his use of it as a studio and for meetings of his Young Composers Group.

Copland convened the Young Composers Group in 1932 to encourage American music through informal meetings among artists living in New York. The group soon established an age limit (twenty-five) and on 15 January 1933 presented its first concert at the New School for Social Research. Regular members included Henry Brant, Israel Citkowitz, Lehman Engel, Vivian Fine, Bernard Herrmann, Jerome Moross, and Elie Siegmeister, "a representative body of the future guardians of American musical progress."[9] Irregulars included George Antheil, Marc Blitzstein, Carlos Chávez, John Kirkpatrick, and Irwin Heilner.[10] During the weekly meetings, Herrmann, Citkowitz, and Brant engaged in vociferous and even combative discussions that Paul found depressing and futile. (Another acquaintance of the group, Oscar Levant, found Herrmann and Moross "remarkably unpleasant young men, truly possessed of a talent for inimicality."[11]) Exacerbating matters for Paul was a denigration of the works produced by cosmopolitans. Bowles did not remain with the group when they went to Roger Sessions's harmony classes—he found Sessions, like Boulanger, "formidable" and attended only a couple of classes.[12] Composing a short piano piece, he borrowed Thomson's technique of creating musical impressions of his colleagues. Bowles's "Portrait of Five" has subtitles that offer verbal impressions of his colleagues: "Virgil Thomson (smiling)"; "Aaron Copland (remembering the world)"; "Roger Sessions (looking careful & honest)"; "George Antheil (in a hurry to go)"; and "Israel Citkowitz (practicing being pleasant)."[13] The music itself consisted of "semi-parodies of the styles of the various composers."[14]

Paul's first public presentation of another composition brought him up against another unwritten rule of the period: art must have socially relevant content. As a dandy, Bowles remained aloof from a political agenda in his art. Upon first arriving in New York, Paul had taken a few pieces to John Kirkpatrick, a friend of Copland and a pianist who specialized in playing new music. Kirkpatrick played Bowles's Piano Sonatina for Claire Reis, director of the League of Composers concerts, and Reis scheduled the work for a concert late in 1933. Reviewing it in *Modern Music*, composer Marc Blitzstein described the sonatina as "what is called damned clever. Whiter than even the White Russians dispense it." To Bowles personally, Blitzstein remarked, "I didn't know you had it in you."[15] Paul could not decipher from either of these remarks whether Blitzstein was praising the work or denigrating its composer. Later Bowles facetiously wrote another pianist who was to perform the work, "I can't imagine which 'White Russians' he was thinking of."[16]

At the League of Composers concert, Paul met John Latouche, a young poet and lyricist who was still a student at Columbia University. Small, with an abundance of black hair, he had a precocious talent for words and sharp wit. When not a target of his wit, acquaintances agreed that Latouche, like Bowles, could be "vastly entertaining." The two men became close friends and collaborators.

In 1934, however, Paul had not begun the type of composing that was to provide the bulk of his income throughout the next decade and a half. Paul soon found himself in serious financial trouble. Copland no longer needed the studio on Fifty-eighth Street, and three months later, Paul decided that he could not afford to pay the rent and skipped out on the lease. Later Paul was successfully sued for the entire amount. Meanwhile, he found a more economical place on West Fifty-fifth Street, an apartment next to a Decca record factory. The scene outside his window epitomized New York: "noise, grime, and gloom." He tried to concentrate on his work—composing and attending the vocal and instrumental rehearsals for the Virgil Thomson-Gertrude Stein opera, *Four Saints in Three Acts*—but found memories of North African air and light interfering with increasing frequency. Sooner or later, he knew, the opportunity to return would present itself.

That spring Paul completed his six-song cycle "Memnon," on a text by Cocteau. Following Thomson's example, he also composed two songs using words from Stein's *Useful Knowledge* and called them "Scenes from the Door." Pleased that his compositions were "as different from Virgil's settings as anything could be," he decided to publish them himself, on his own label, Éditions de la Vipère.[17] Other works published under the Vipère label, a label he used in 1934 and 1935, included compositions by David Diamond and Eric Satie, with art by Anne Miracle, Kristians Tonny, and the Russian painter and scene designer Eugene Berman.

Diamond never "took a shine to Paul," and working together seriously strained their relationship.[18] Diamond blamed the tension on Paul's penuriousness and his unrealistic hope that publishing music was a way to make money. Bowles's letter to Diamond does little to refute Diamond's claim:

> I have been looking each morning for a letter from you, and it is perfectly true that I am put out at not finding it. In case you are procrastinating in any way about sending it, because it is too much bother to find a post-office where you can make a money-order, I recommend your making a special effort, because I need the money badly, and I should not like to think that it is lying idle on your mantelpiece in an envelope marked PAUL merely awaiting the day when you will have sufficient energy to send it off. You must remember that so far I have not received a penny for my labor; more than that, I have even spent a little of my own. . . . You must also send me a copy of the Sonatina if a letter is too trying.[19]

A second letter from Bowles took a more fanciful tone in enumerating a host of dandy essentials:

> The money-order just arrived, and I thank you immeasurably. I hope it wasn't too much effort. . . . Now I shall be able to buy stamps, a haircut, stationery, glue and toothpaste, besides a fine collection of useful and fancy articles such as Birthday cards, carpets, baskets, travelling bags, portmanteaux thermos, artificial flowers, ladies' articles, haberdashery, hosiery, jerseys, umbrellas, sticks, razors, scissors, Japanese and Indian articles, Field and opera glasses, electrical apparatuses, bells, guns, boots, fishing rods, hemp shoes, toilet requisites, waterproofs, kodaks, straw hats, perfumery, cartridges, leggings, inks, gunpowder, and wax.[20]

Diamond assumed that Paul had money and found Paul's insistence on being repaid promptly for typesetting and printing charges perplexing. "I liked him," Diamond said years later, "but I was very wary. I said to Aaron, 'I do like him, but there is something about the way he's dressed.' I was surprised when I read his autobiography and found out where he came from."

Paul's self-presentation was at odds with the behavior Diamond witnessed: "In spite of his elegant appearance, I can't say that I ever remember Paul being generous, picking up a tab or offering a person a drink. Maybe he just did not have enough money. Or maybe the money went into fine clothes and keeping up this exterior that he created." For his own part, Paul found Diamond's label of "elegant" vexing. He argued, "It would have taken a lot more money than I ever had for me to have achieved elegance."[21] As much as

Paul affected the style of the well heeled, he lacked the wherewithal; he could dress the role but could act it only within limits.

Apart from the issue of money, Paul also made Diamond uncomfortable in other ways. "He created an artificial persona," Diamond said. "Paul was an anachronism with his affectations. In those days, none of us had money, but there would be Paul, with his silk shirts and panoply of gold-tipped Turkish cigarettes, always perfumed. He would mix perfume for people, matching the scent to the personality." But Diamond found redeeming features, too: "In no way did I find Paul rebellious, except in that he was interested in the arts. He was a transplanted American who retained his Americanness. He had superb French. Yet as a personality, he did not take on any of the bohemian characteristics. He always kept his Wallace Stevens persona—and this in the middle of the Depression."

Both Diamond—unwittingly—and composer Ned Rorem suggested that at some point after his 1933 return from Morocco, Paul passed beyond his youthful dandy role into a more complicated one, that of the rogue, a "young man who dressed up as a professor, a prime minister, an admiral, a millionaire, who can talk and act just like the real thing."[22] Rorem explained, "Paul played the role, physically, of a businessman, a very handsome businessman. His manner of wearing expensive, very conventional clothes contradicted his unconventional conversation. You would come over and he would have a book on, say, sadism in the seventeenth century conspicuously out where you would see it, with a dead body on the cover. Or a book on midgets in China. All of this in contradiction to his conventional appeal."[23]

The Nadir

While in Fez in 1931, Bowles had met Charles Brown, a Swiss and the administrator of the American Fondouk, an organization formed to care for mistreated animals and to educate their owners. When Paul heard that a member of the American Fondouk in Fez was visiting New York, he quickly paid him a visit. This man, a Colonel Williams, was planning a trip to Morocco to check on Brown, and Paul convinced the colonel to hire him as a personal secretary, agreeing to meet him later that summer. Bowles left in June 1934 and after three weeks in Andalusia, crossed to Tangier. Until October, Bowles traveled throughout Morocco, from Tangier to the High Atlas Mountains, from Fez to Tafilelt, Ksar-es-Souk, and Erfoud in the southeast, and back to Tangier. Having made the most of his position with Williams, he then tried to contact his friend Ramani in Algeria, hoping for an invitation to visit. When one of his unanswered letters was finally returned, Paul knew he could no longer put off his journey home.

The only ship he could book passage on was the *Juan Sebastian Elcano*, on which he had returned to the United States a year earlier. It stank of fish, and he spent most of the voyage in the infirmary conversing in Spanish with officers and crew and listening to *cante jondo* and *flamenco* records he had brought along. At San Juan, a teenager with a cigarette case of *grifas* boarded, headed for Venezuela. On the island of Curaçao in the Netherlands Antilles, Paul first smoked marijuana. He felt "irretrievably *there* in that place, drowned in the noise of the ubiquitous frogs and insects," but it also made his heart beat violently and rapidly (*WS*:179). He soon after wrote to Burns from Barranquilla, on the coast of Colombia, where Paul had settled into a hotel to enjoy the "magnificent violence" of the weather: "I have decided [marijuana] is not quite healthy to use. Thus I have sold all I had, and profited thereby pleasantly, (inasmuch as all I had was given me by a frightened person who was carrying pounds!) The only souvenir is the very strong odor in my luggage, which will probably intrigue some customs officials who sniff it out."[24]

Throughout his 1934 trip Paul gathered images that returned years later in different forms in his writing. In the Moroccan marketplace of the Djemaa el Fna—a combination grocers' market, jumble sale, and carnival sideshow in Marrakech—he witnessed a deformed man contort himself. "I'm turning into a goat," Paul remembered the man announcing: "and damned if he didn't!"[25] A similar transformation occurs in his 1945 story "By the Water." In Colombia he spent time recuperating on a *finca*—a ranch—halfway up the side of a mountain near Jamonocal, and images of it appear in *Up above the World* and "The Echo." A brief glimpse of a naked man running through the mangrove swamp near Ciénaga inspired the ending to his story "Call at Corazón": a disillusioned husband boards a train alone at Ciénaga and departs, leaving behind a "figure in white," presumably his wife, running toward the train station.

From Colombia Paul crossed into the Pacific and traveled on to Los Angeles, where he wrote a series of piano preludes and set to music a letter from Gertrude Stein ("Letter to Freddy"). But the most important outcome of Paul's two months in California—one in Los Angeles and the second with relatives in San Francisco—was a visit to Henry Cowell. Born in California in 1897, Cowell had made his name as a pianist in concerts throughout Europe and then in New York by performing his own works, complete with tone clusters that he played with his forearms and harp-sounding passages achieved by reaching into the piano and playing on the strings. Like Bowles, Cowell had educated himself and then, after having composed extensively, decided to take on some formal training with Charles Seeger, who described him as "a very good example of autodidacts all through his life: he never learned anything from anybody else; he appropriated what he liked and paid no attention to what he didn't like."[26] In their approach to training, if not to music, Bowles and Cowell were kindred souls.

As a controversial young composer in the 1920s, Cowell had encountered firsthand the problem of getting music published. Even well-established firms, such as G. Schirmer, or publishers that specialized in American music, such as the Arthur P. Schmidt Company of Boston or the Society for the Publication of American Music, preferred more conventional composers. Arthur Foote, Edward MacDowell, Howard Hanson, and Daniel Gregory Mason represented "new music" in their eyes. So Cowell decided to publish a magazine, *New Music*, and announcing it in the summer of 1927, he proclaimed it "the only magazine in the world devoted to the publication of modern music."[27] His first issue featured Carl Ruggles's mammoth *Men and Mountains*. *New Music* also was the first to publish music of Charles Ives; it followed with other experimental composers, both American and European, including Dane Rudhyar, Wallingford Reigger, Colin McPhee, Lou Harrison, Edgard Varèse, Nicholas Slonimsky, Carlos Chávez, Anton von Webern, and Arnold Schönberg. The magazine became a forum for the avant-garde, and Henry Cowell the lightning rod and "central information booth" for the younger generation of American composers.

Cowell inspired Bowles and was interested in Bowles's compositions as well as his travels. Bowles sat in on Cowell's rhythm class at Stanford and demonstrated the *claves* he had brought back from his trip. Cowell responded by devoting his April 1935 *New Music* issue to works of Paul Bowles and Carlos Chávez. Bowles's new piece, "Letter to Freddy," appeared along with three other Bowles compositions: "Café Sin Nombre," Parts IV and VI from "Danger de Mort," and Part III from *Scènes d'Anabase*. Later, when Cowell was teaching at the New School for Social Research in New York, he remembered Bowles's records of Moroccan Chleuh songs (popular music derived from the folk music of the Souss) and dances. He and Bowles made copies, some of which Cowell sent to Béla Bartók. In the mid-1940s, Paul was surprised to hear a strain from one of the records, a Chaabiya Souassa song, in the opening theme to the fourth movement of Bartók's Concerto for Orchestra.[28]

Paul decided to leave California and on 1 February 1935 boarded a bus to New York, pausing in Chicago to see his traveling companion from Morocco, George Turner, with whom he planned to stay for nearly a month.[29] He subsequently reported to Stein, "I think my welcome was worn out quite a while before that and so I moved on to see [Bruce] Morrissette in Baltimore."[30] Morrissette introduced him to Mr. Fuhrman, an invalid suffering from encephalitis, and after a short stay in New York, Paul returned to

Baltimore to work for Fuhrman. He read daily to the invalid. Although he continued working on other plans, which he hoped would allow an escape from his exile in Baltimore, and visited New York often, he must have stayed in Baltimore for several months.[31]

When in New York, Paul visited the Russian émigré painter Eugene (Genia) Berman, and the two had soon hatched a plan to write a ballet together. Back in Baltimore, Bowles used his free time to work on the score to the ballet and to sell what he could of Berman's drawings to Gertrude Stein's friends Etta and Claribel Cone, who had a collection of modern art (particularly that of Matisse), and to the Baltimore Museum. The diminutive and cherubic Berman had been raised in St. Petersburg in luxurious and aristocratic circumstances. He wore hand-tailored suits, striped shirts, and expensive shoes and was typical of the rarefied group with which Paul associated—wealthy, titled, aristocratic, foreign, or famous, but seldom bohemian.

In Baltimore Paul visited Communist party headquarters; later in New York he studied pamphlets and periodicals at the Worker's Bookshop and concluded that in the United States the Communist party would never be effective and "could serve only as a harassing instrument."[32] Although this realization convinced him of the futility of the party's future in this country, in 1938 he joined the party, a roguish action that all who know him attribute to whimsy rather than deep-seated political conviction. The harassing potential of the party, along with Paul's conviction that it could not succeed in this country, invested "joining" it with a kind of romantic absurdity that Paul found irresistible.[33]

In 1937, on a trip to Mexico, he took it upon himself to print and distribute anti-Trotsky posters as he traveled the country, actions that caused earnest peasants to surround him, begging his help in learning more about communism. He was reprimanded for taking individual action without party approval, and no doubt he relished the absurdity in his self-propelled leap into the role of rogue missionary. Several years later, he wrote, "I must confess that the irrational part of me still hopes to witness total destruction and total hopelessness, even though I personally feel otherwise. There's no doubt that the appeal of the Party to me was a strictly emotional one, an attempt to feel instrumental in causing the downfall of the hated species and not an error in placing my faith."[34]

Paul called 1935 the "nadir" of his life, yet Cowell's April publication of his works marked the beginning of a slow rise in fortune. In January 1936, Ida Bowles died, leaving a bequest of one thousand dollars in the care of her sister Mary, who passed it on to Paul. Paul "salted [it] away in the bank for future use" (WS:187).[35] Late in 1935 Thomson requested Bowles provide music for a concert of contemporary music by the Friends and Enemies of Modern Music, an adjunct group to the Hartford Museum, in Hartford, Connecticut. Both the museum and the Friends and Enemies were directed by A. Everett "Chick" Austin, Jr., a Harvard classmate of Thomson and the energy behind the original 1934 production of Thomson's *Four Saints in Three Acts*. Bowles accepted, but a disagreement ensued that prompted Bowles to write Thomson, "I am *very* much disappointed that you should so summarily reject the idea of my participation at H! But its your party I realize."[36] Bowles went on to perform his music at least twice that year in Hartford.

In spring 1935, Bowles moved back to New York City, arriving with more than half the score for the ballet collaboration with Berman complete. He and Berman took long walks together along the waterfront discussing the project. At that time, zoning laws required New York buildings above a certain height to recede in order to leave more open sky.[37] Most architecture was moderne or art deco, and the jagged skyline of Manhattan sprouted minarets, spires, cupolas, domes, and pyramids, all in a cubist angular disarray. Berman's enthusiasm quickly shifted from the ballet to the views of Manhattan he and Paul saw from the water's edge, and he was soon immersed in a series of paintings that showed the city in ruins. Recognizing they would never finish the ballet, Paul used much of the music for a 1936 theater production.

Soon he was involved in another project when Lincoln Kirstein asked him to write a new ballet score to be called *Yankee Clipper*, based on Bowles's interest in travel, and to be choreographed by dancer Eugene Loring. Paul composed a score drawn from his travels, using "authentic rhythms characteristic of the foreign parts" to be visited by the "New England sailor" in the ballet.[38] Percussion instruments included two African drums, tuned a minor third apart, a bass drum, *tambour de provence*, a xylophone, timbals, *guiros*, and *claves*.[39]

Indigenous music of all countries intrigued the young composer, particularly rhythmically complicated music. Bowles was obsessed with rhythm, in a nearly clinical sense. According to more than one acquaintance, he was "always drumming patterns on the table-top or arm of a chair. He was never still." He had been interested in African American music since high school, when he had begun a correspondence with ethnographer John Hammond, and he had collected "race" records (sold in secondhand furniture stores, alongside Victrolas) while a student in Virginia. In 1936, he often visited Hammond in his apartment on Sullivan Street, where he spent many evenings listening to Hammond's extensive blues and jazz record collection. With Hammond, Bowles went to Harlem to meet young pianist Teddy

Wilson; and Bowles returned to Harlem often to listen to music and on occasion to smoke the "reefers" available there. Bowles's extensive knowledge and application of jazz gave what was then called an "American" flavor to much of his music.[40] He was one of the first Americans to review the music of African American jazz artists in serious publications on a regular basis, and his reviews show an astute ear and a shrewd understanding of the uniqueness of African American music. In a 1939 review of the American Society of Composers and Publishers (ASCAP) Festival of American Music, Bowles lamented, "The program 'devoted to compositions by our Negro Composer-Members' was excellent evidence of the effect chauvinism can have upon musical culture. The music was considered a thing apart because Negroes had written it, which would have been valid if the material had shown any connection with Negro music." Conversely, he praised the James Weldon Johnson composition, "Go Down, Death," which in form and content sprang "directly from a Negro religious service" and contained blues shouting, solo and group call-and-response singing, and improvisation. Finally, Bowles loved an ensemble with Louis Armstrong, Fletcher Henderson, and Lionel Hampton and marveled that the audience could not keep time to the music. "It was astonishing that never once was there a unanimity of opinion about the rhythm. . . . Said one Negro, 'This could never happen at the Apollo.'"[41]

Bowles found occasional support from the New Deal's Works Progress Administration, which had formed several subagencies to provide employment for artists. On 2 April, the Federal Music Project presented an all-Bowles concert, which included his Sonata for Flute and Piano; Trio for Violin, Violincello, and Piano; Suite for Violin and Piano; *Scènes d'Anabase*; and several piano pieces, as well as a presentation of Harry Dunham's film *Venus and Adonis*, with music by Bowles (Harry censored the film's nude scenes by holding his hands in front of the projector). The public forum with questions from the audience was "strictly a heckling session," in which leftists criticized Bowles for writing music that depended on style rather than socially relevant content. Paul's parents attended the concert, Claude's reaction to the film and the music a despairing: "And this is where our tax money goes now. My God!" (*WS*:192). Still not all the comments it provoked were negative. Reviewer (and composer) Colin McPhee agreed with the Bowleses that the film was "incredibly stupid" but added that "the music carried it along in its allure and melodic individuality."[42]

The same issue of *Modern Music* that carried McPhee's review held an essay by Aaron Copland on the promising young composers of the day. Answering anticipated criticism, and perhaps countering his own hesitations, he wrote, "There are those who refuse to see in Bowles anything more than a dilettante. Bowles himself persists in adopting a militantly non-professional air in relation to all music, including his own. If you take this attitude at its face value, you will lose sight of the considerable merit of a large amount of music Bowles has already written. It is music that comes from a fresh personality, music full of charm and melodic invention, at times surprisingly well made in an instinctive and non-academic fashion. Personally I much prefer an 'amateur' like Bowles to your 'well-trained' conservatory product."[43] Bowles had now published in Cowell's *New Music*, had an entire Federal Music Project devoted to his work, and despite being first an "amateur" dandy and then a rebel rogue, had won the support of McPhee and, more important, Copland in *Modern Music*.

In July 1936, Paul joined in the outpouring of sympathy for the republican government fighting Franco in Spain by helping to form the Committee of Republican Spain, which raised two thousand dollars for the Madrid government through their production *Who Fights This Battle?* Paul wrote the score for Kenneth White's script, which was directed by Joseph Losey, with Earl Robinson serving as music director.

Even though he was increasingly active as a composer, Paul still had little in the way of regular income. Then Virgil Thomson stepped in and gave Paul a useful introduction to Orson Welles. Along with John Houseman, Welles had gone to work for Project 891, or the Classical Theatre, one of half a dozen theatrical units of the Federal Theater Project, which Hallie Flanagan administered under the Works Progress Administration. Flanagan, who had been head of Vassar's Experimental Theater since 1925, had been assigned the task of employing talented actors and writers during the Depression. By 1935 she had formulated a plan to form an experimental theater, create rotating companies in the New York boroughs, and produce works in many other cities. Her boldest move was to establish the Negro Theater Project in Harlem, which opened in the previously abandoned rat- and cockroach-infested Lafayette Theater on Seventh Avenue. By the time Bowles met Welles, the director had concluded his second triumphant production there, an all-black *Macbeth*, with Virgil Thomson and Asadata Dafora Horton conducting and coordinating African and African American dancers and drummers led by a "witch doctor" named Abdul, whom the twenty-year-old Welles insisted on calling "Jazbo."

Welles and Houseman had now decided on a French play, *The Italian Straw Hat*, which had been made into a silent film by one of Welles's favorite directors, René Clair. Edwin Denby translated the 1851 Eugène Labiche work, and Welles and Houseman transformed it into a surrealist farce. Actors included Sarah Burton, Joseph Cotten, Edwin Denby, Arlene Francis, Paula Laurence, Hiram Sherman, and Virginia Welles. Bowles's music helped establish a frantic pace similar to that of Keystone Kops silent films.

Paul worked on the music in the spectacular apartment of Alfred Barr, curator of the newly founded Museum of Modern Art, who, for the summer, had lent his apartment above the East River to Thomson and John Latouche. Bowles had no experience in orchestral music, so Thomson helped him assemble and then orchestrate an elaborate score—"overtures, intermezzos, meditations, marches, even a song or two"—from works Bowles had already written, including the abandoned Berman ballet.[44] As Thomson recalls, "There were lots of musicians available. There was an orchestra of 35 in the pit, including a gypsy waltz violinist and a Turkish lady trumpeter," in addition to two dance bands ("a five-man group dressed in red coats and playing Hungarian gypsy music and another band playing turkey trots") and a mechanical piano on stage.[45] The trumpeter, a woman dressed in a Hussar's uniform, stood in one of the upper boxes playing selections from *The Carnival of Venice* and "similar brilliant selections," alternating with the player piano in the other upper box. The play, called *Horse Eats Hat*, opened at the Maxine Elliott Theater in October, and one critic declared the production a "demented piece of surrealism perilously close to being a genuine work of art."[46] Brooks Atkinson, whose reviews for the *New York Times* created or destroyed theatrical reputations, proclaimed, "It was as though Gertrude Stein had dreamed a dream after a late supper of pickles and ice cream, the ensuing revelations being crisply acted by giants and midgets, caricatures, lunatics and a prop nag."[47]

Horse Eats Hat led to a Project 891–Welles production, also staged at the Maxine Elliot Theater: Christopher Marlowe's *Tragicall History of Doctor Faustus*. This vehicle for Welles's genius and his fascination with magic demanded a total of seventy-six lighting cues and sound effects, including a scene in which a pig, a side of beef, two chickens, and a pudding fly off the dinner table and pirouette and then disappear into black velvet drapes.[48] Bowles alone wrote the music for the production, Thomson being in France, and the play enjoyed huge success. The *New York Times* estimated that in the first five months following its 18 January 1937 opening, more than eighty thousand people saw the standing-room-only show. In the theater, Paul found both a new and an unexpected source of income and an outlet for expression in which he was particularly talented.

In the winter of 1937, Paul resumed his friendship with Kristians Tonny and his wife Marie-Claire Ivanoff. One evening, at the Patchin Place apartment of E. E. and Marion Cummings, the conversation turned to Mexico. Bowles, Tonny, and Ivanoff formed a plan to go there, and a fourth guest, Jane Auer, declared her intention to accompany them. A friend of Thomas Mann's daughter Erika (whom W. H. Auden had helped escape from Germany by marrying), Auer had come to this circle by way of John Latouche.

Paul announced his intention of resigning from the Federal Theater Project and traveling to Mexico. Berman accused him of being irresponsible, a criticism that had never dissuaded Paul in the past. After printing fifteen thousand anti-Trotsky stickers to take along, Paul set out. Determined that Tonny not arrive in Mexico penniless, Paul insisted that the quartet stop first in Baltimore, where after contacting the Cone sisters and the Baltimore Museum, they sold several of his drawings.

The four spent two weeks on a Greyhound bus journeying to New Orleans and then another week traveling to Monterrey. From there it was a two-day bus ride to Mexico City, during which Jane became ill. Once they arrived in Mexico City, Jane left the group to go first to the Ritz Hotel and then to San Antonio and back to New York. Paul used a note of introduction from Copland to meet the composer Silvestre Revueltas and heard for the first time Revueltas's *Homenaje a García Lorca*. He spent some time with Revueltas and through him met the Mexican composers called the Grupo de los Cuatro: Daniel Ayala, Pablo Moncayo, Salvador Contreras, and Blas Galindo. Revueltas, "hedonistic and gregarious," served as Bowles's guide to the world of Mexican music and composers.[49]

Then Bowles left for a tour of the wilderness of Tehuantepec in southern Mexico, which he found even more beautiful and hostile than the Sahara, and he celebrated May Day with Zapotecans who asked him to teach them about communism. Back in Mexico City, where Tonny was hard at work on a new style of "Mexican" painting, Bowles received a wire from Lincoln Kirstein saying that the ballet *Yankee Clipper* was being presented in Philadelphia and that Bowles was needed to orchestrate the score.

Trouble with orchestration plagued Bowles. He managed to pull together an orchestral version of *Yankee Clipper* by having Harry Brant concentrate on the ship scenes while Paul did the ports of call. The method worked, but Paul suspected that Brant had sabotaged him on the orchestration. Rena Bowles, John Latouche, Marian Chase, and Jane Auer accompanied Paul on the trip to Philadelphia, where Alexander Smallens conducted the piece on a program that included *Filling Station* by Virgil Thomson and *Pocahontas* by Elliot Carter, who called the "tuneful" sailor dances Bowles's "best music . . . pastiches of the exotica."[50] Critic Rosenfeld asserted, "It is music of a kind that no civilized community can do without. It is hard of edge and light in content, music in kid gloves, the music of a dandy."[51]

Disorder and *Denmark Vesey*

For the next several months, Paul was as peripatetic in New York as he had been in North Africa and Mexico. During the summer he spent some time with Tonny and Ivanoff and Chase, staying at his uncle Charles's lake house at Glenora. He was working on a new piece: *Denmark Vesey*, an opera with a libretto by Charles Henri Ford for an all-black cast, concerning the 1822 Charleston slave conspiracy led by a former slave named Denmark Vesey. He tried to entice Ford to join them: "Room all yours, canoe, row-boat, lake swimming, pool swimming, complete isolation, tout confort moderne, quiet, squirrels, katydids, woodfires."[52] Although Ford declined, Bowles stayed in the country through October.[53] Returning to New York, Paul took up residence in the Chelsea Hotel and worked on the opera in Edwin Denby's loft on Twenty-first Street. The opera's theme — an uprising of the oppressed against their oppressors — was a natural for Paul, traumatized into an unshakable identification with the subjugated and enslaved. He devoted prodigious effort to *Vesey*, which in letters to Ford he often called his "baby." By January, the first act of *Denmark Vesey* was ready for the Juanita Hall Choir to perform at a benefit for *New Masses*.[54]

Even unfinished, the opera was impressive enough for Virgil Thomson to call it one of the three best "unperformed" American operas, a status above which, sadly, it never rose.[55] In 1939, the Juanita Hall singers again presented the first act, along with part of act 2, giving Paul "a chance to show my teeth above a white tie and hang my head before applause," but meanwhile, Paul reported to Ford that Du Bose Heyward had stolen the idea of Denmark Vesey for an opera of his own, called "Don't You Want to Be Free?"[56] Heyward did not write an opera, but his wife, Dorothy Heyward, did write a play called *Set My People Free,* and when it finally premiered in November 1948, critic Brooks Atkinson called it one of the season's "best theater experiences."[57]

As a result, Bowles resolved not to give the script to any more "Broadway people"; then, inexplicably in 1945, he gave his only copy of the score to tenor Romolo Spirito for a recording by Disc.[58] Two years later Ford hoped to finish it and wrote to Bowles asking whether he could write a final act. He sent Bowles the script, but Bowles responded, "Of course it's a wonderful scenario, but what good does it do me, when my score appears to have been completely lost by [Romolo] De Spirito? . . . Anyway, I am depressed about it, because it represents two years' work, and naturally I shall never start it again. It's my own fault and I'm crazy to be so careless. But of course I always act as though I had twenty more lives to live. Not only that, but as if all twenty were to be exactly alike . . . the same one over and over."[59] Ford persisted, and three months later, Paul testily replied, "You don't appear to understand that *Denmark Vesey* is still lost; it is as if it had never existed, — at least, until someone finds it. Thus the question is not that of finishing it, but of finding it. Romolo never gave me back the score after making the records for the album issued by Disc. Naturally he swears he did, now that nearly two years have elapsed."[60]

Part of the problem was Paul's constant moving about, making any kind of continuous contact difficult. A year after he had begun *Denmark Vesey*, he had taken a trip through Central America, stayed in upstate New York, moved to New York City, and then traveled to France, where, he reported, "Denmark fills out sometimes, but i don't really know how i like it. by now i repudiate the first act, but i suppose it is always that way. guatemala and costa rica were too thick to come in between for so long."[61] Because he moved so often, taking only clothing and books with him, he frequently lost track of items stored, packed, or otherwise uprooted. Meticulous as he was about his own appearance, he seems to have taken a cavalier attitude toward his belongings. Years later he once spent days correcting manuscripts of six piano pieces for recording, only to misplace them. He wrote the pianist who was to record them, "I don't know why my flat is so disorganized, does it mean that I myself am disorganized? I lose papers, and then months later they turn up. The Manila envelopes are piled up everywhere—on tables, in bookcases, in the one closet I have, and in fifteen or twenty suitcases, most of which are too heavy for me to lift, in order to find out what's in the valises underneath."[62]

An attempt in 1976 to revive the Denby *Horse Eats Hat* met with results similar to Ford's attempt to get *Vesey* going again. As Bowles explained to Thomson, "What happened is that Andreas Brown, at some point in 1969, having the keys to the closet at Libby Holman's on 61st Street, removed all my music, both published and manuscript (and even recordings). . . . A certain amount of the material turns out to be in the archives at Austin; the rest—quíen sabe? . . . When I incorporated something in the score, I discarded the first version. In that way I lost everything."[63]

Many of Bowles's theater scores were lost because companies kept the scores themselves rather than return them to the composer. "It wasn't only the Federal Works Projects that kept scores after productions had closed; Broadway did it, too. And of course at that time one had to have music photostated in order to keep a copy, and it cost 75 cents a page for negative and positive, and that was too much, or so I thought. In any case, now I have nothing."[64]

Bowles's film scores, as well, disappeared. French surrealists were among the most artistic in creating a union of film and music, and Bowles followed their work with enthusiasm. Eric Satie's music for the Francis Picabia and René Clair film *Entre'acte* and Georges Auric's music to Cocteau's *La Vie d'un Poete* provided contemporary composers with examples for the relatively new medium. In the late 1930s, several American composers began experimenting with writing for the new media—film and radio—in order to gain new listeners for American music. The documentary film was a new genre that lent itself particularly well to serious music. Thomson wrote music for three documentary film scores: *The Plow That Broke the Plains* (1936); *The River* (1937); and *The Louisiana Story*, for which he won the 1948 Pulitzer Prize. Copland composed the score to *The City*, a film produced for the 1939 World's Fair and originally conceived by Pare Lorentz, who had directed Thomson's first two films. Copland also wrote music for *Of Mice and Men* (1939) and *Our Town* (1940); and in 1943, Copland created a suite in five movements called *Music for Movies*, based on the three films, and dedicated it to Darius Milhaud, the French composer whom he considered a pioneer in the field of film music.

As a composer, Bowles monitored the state of film music in the United States and abroad.[65] He began his own work for film in 1933 with the score for Harry Dunham's short and what Bowles called "lurid" film, *Bride of Samoa*. *Venus and Adonis* (1935) was their second film. Bowles worked with Swiss-born experimental filmmaker Rudy Burckhardt on two films in 1936: *Seeing the World* and *145 West 21*, the second of which referred to Edwin Denby's address and captured the acting talents of John Latouche and of Aaron Copland as a roofer. Two years later Paul scored two more Burckhardt films: *Chelsea through the Magnifying Glass*, which Paul, a Lewis Carroll fan, called "Through the Looking Glass," and *How to Become a Citizen of the U.S.*, which Burckhardt remembers being screened "somewhere in Brooklyn in a room that couldn't be made dark in the daytime" and afterward hearing "one Brooklyn woman saying: 'I can't see a thing but I'm sure it's subversive.'"[66]

In 1936, Bowles suggested to Stein that they collaborate on a film, along with Thomson, Grosser, and Dunham: "I am still to do the music, which I think will be grisly, because the film will need it that way. Have you any preferences in music?"[67] This project never got off the ground.

The following winter, Bowles scored *America's Disinherited*, a Southern Tenant Farmers' Union film. The entire project was suspect in New York, because the STFU leadership was supposedly Trotskyite. Bowles created musical motifs from tunes sung by the tenant farmers. "They were strange people who huddled together and whispered," he remembered (*WS*:195). He wrote music for *Roots in the Soil*, made for the Soil Conservation Service of the United States Department of Agriculture (1940);[68] for *Congo*, a 1944 film with Latouche and André Cauvin; and, in 1947, on the recommendation of Latouche, *Dreams That Money Can Buy*, for experimental filmmaker Hans Richter.

Sadly, most of his music was recorded on acetate records instead of being added to the films as a soundtrack. By the 1960s these had disintegrated, and

Bowles had kept neither written nor mental notes of the specific scores.[69] This kind of casualness with regard to his own work contrasts dramatically with the otherwise near-compulsive habits of someone who, by his own admission, "lived by immutable self-imposed rules" (*WS*:191).

Youth, inexperience, thrift, or failure to consider the future may explain Paul's failing to hold onto originals or to make copies of his musical scores, but it cannot explain why Bowles did not have this problem with his literary manuscripts. His music manuscripts contain numerous careless errors as well, and he even admitted, "mistakes seem to be an integral part of all my scores."[70]

To a certain extent Paul's musical career preceded his literary one, and he may have learned from his mistakes. Additionally, he did not write his music with the idea of publication in mind, so it stands to reason that he might not have been as careful with music manuscripts. Yet in general, Paul did not have disciplined habits where his music was concerned, and as a consequence his music remains much less available than his writing. From the point of view of a perfectionist who always felt insecure in the field of music, worse things could have happened.

Breaking into Theater

New York in 1936 was an expensive place to live, and finding an apartment with a private bath was difficult.[71] Paul coped by moving frequently, staying in vacant apartments of friends, and renting cheap studios in which to work. One studio was at the corner of Washington Street and Battery Place above an Arab café. There he found a room to which he was able to summon Turkish coffee and honey cakes with a clap of his hands. He kept an accordion for his composing and worked on a table surrounded by Islamic chromo-lithographs, although he refused to sleep there because of the possibility of bedbugs.

Paul had a second studio, on the East River at 2 Water Street in Brooklyn, which had two rooms and a piano and served as "general headquarters." The space was heated, so Paul was able to spend more time there, even holding rehearsals of the Juanita Hall Choir for the *Denmark Vesey* performance. The neighborhood surrounding Water Street was known as Brooklyn Heights—New York's first "ferry suburb"—and had been home to a score of notables, from Thomas Paine and Henry Ward Beecher to Alfred Kazin, Hart Crane, Thomas Wolfe, John Dos Passos, and Marianne Moore. Oliver Smith settled in Brooklyn Heights for life. Paul's Water Street studio, however, belonged more to the waterfront itself than to the literary neighborhood. From it one could taste the salt in the air, feel the winds of the sea, and remember that

Manhattan was still an island. Close to "silent miles of warehouses with shuttered wooden windows, docks resting on the water like sea spiders,"[72] the studio brought Paul to a watery wasteland, a New York equivalent of the desolation of North Africa.

The writer Truman Capote lived in a hotel at 1 Water Street in the 1950s and wrote, "Daytime the location, a dead-end Chiricoesque piazza facing the river, is little disturbed; at night, not at all; not a sound, except foghorns and a distant traffic whisper from the bridge which bulks above. Peace, and the shivering glow of gliding-by tugs and ferries."[73] When inhabited, the dockside tended toward an exoticism that thrilled Bowles. As Capote described it, "Every kind of sailor is common enough here, even saronged East Indians, even the giant Senegalese, their onyx arms afire with blue, with yellow tattooed flowers, with saucy torsos and garish graffiti . . . Runty Russians, too—one sees them flapping in the pajama-like costumes."[74] Charles Henri Ford, present for a rehearsal of *Denmark Vesey*, was less impressed when he glanced out the window. He turned with disgust: "Paul, you're so *romantic!*" (*WS*:207).

The nine months or so following the trip to Mexico were marred by a quarrel with Tonny that soon extended to Thomson. The very thing Paul had hoped to forestall by selling some of Tonny's drawings before leaving for Mexico had come to pass. Paul had to lend Tonny money to make it through the trip. On returning, Tonny borrowed money from Thomson. Paul then asked Thomson to join forces with him in collecting, and Thomson refused. Then Thomson collected some of his money, and Paul got nothing. Paul fumed about the matter in public, and one evening at Kirk and Constance Askew's, Thomson announced that he was bored with the whole affair and wanted to hear nothing more about it.

Annoyed, Paul responded with a letter to Thomson, complaining that Tonny might have repaid Paul before he left for Europe had Virgil not interfered. He added that he saw no explanation for Thomson's behavior other than that of "unparalleled malice."[75] Thomson penned an eight-page letter to Paul, in which he claimed to have done all he could to see the money returned and suggested Tonny might have repaid the debt had Paul been more frank and less vocal. Stingingly, he added, "I've heard too much about Paul's poverty. You could hardly have less cash in hand than I." Thomson put forth that Paul had been unhappy since their collaboration on *Horse Eats Hat* for reasons that Thomson could not fathom and that he was tired of trying to understand the reason behind Paul's "hymns of hate" and "deliberate mis-quotation (usually known as lies)." Thomson concluded with the deepest cut possible: "Already you have paid for your bad blood and your hateful thoughts by a considerable stoppage in your musical inspiration. That also is none of my business, except that I regret all time of non-functioning in a composer's life which might mean a loss to art."[76]

The "Bowles-Thomson War" (Thomson's phrase) underscores Paul's financial insecurity, as had his disagreement with David Diamond a year earlier. Although he had begun to support himself as a composer, music was a financially uncertain proposition, and Paul was less comfortable with this uncertainty than other artists. Maurice Grosser believed, "Paul is what the French call *regardant*. He's not stingy, but he's careful. It's not that he has less money than he needs. I think it's just a habit of mind."

While Thomson had been on the mark in his assessment of Paul's "stoppage of musical inspiration," at least Paul was not inactive on the concert scene. In addition to the Juanita Hall performance of the first act of *Denmark Vesey*, Paul was also involved in a series of programs called the High-Low Concerts. Through Latouche, Paul had met Vladimir Dukelsky, otherwise known as Vernon Duke. Duke hired him to copy music and later to write a brochure for his High-Low Concerts in which Duke programmed modern chamber music alongside jazz in hopes of stimulating interest in contemporary music. He included one of Bowles's pieces, *Mediodía*, in a concert that also included Duke Ellington and his band.

Paul's growing friendship at this time with Jane Auer may have limited the time he spent composing. In the summer of 1937 they began "to spin fantasies about how amusing it would be to get married and horrify everyone, above all, [their] respective families" (*WS*:207). On 22 February 1938, they did so in a Dutch Reformed church in New York and left shortly afterward on a honeymoon trip to Central America and Europe. From Guatemala, Paul wrote Gertrude Stein: "I am married to a girl who hates nature, and so here we are here with volcanoes, earthquakes and monkeys."[77] After several weeks traveling through Panama, Costa Rica, and Guatemala, the Bowleses sailed for Paris.

Jane had felt uncomfortable with the excesses of nature in Central America; going to Paris was like a homecoming for her. She renewed her penchant for staying out late in bars, talking with strangers. Her absences left Paul irritated and restless. After a "heated" argument in their hotel room, he left for Saint-Tropez but met up with Jane in Cannes. They decided to settle in the village of Èze, through which passed an assortment of interesting company, including New York heiress Kay Cowen, Brazilian folk singer Elsie Houston, and composer Samuel L. M. Barlow, who helped Paul and Jane find their house. Paul, busy with *Denmark Vesey*, wrote to Ford that he had no time to socialize. On the other hand, he wrote, "Jane won't even work, and I think it's because cooking interests her more for the time being."[78]

Not long after the couple had settled in Èze, Paul received a wire saying

Welles needed him in New York to score a production of *Too Much Johnson* at the Mercury Theatre. Paul and Jane moved their considerable collection of luggage back to New York, and Paul began work on the score, for which, as he informed Ford, "there is a hell of a lot of music."[79] Then Welles changed his mind and decided instead to present another play, *Danton's Death*. The decision left Paul with a one-hundred-dollar honorarium and his music. The latter he converted to a chamber piece titled "Music for a Farce." Welles continued to experiment with *Too Much Johnson*. He had Harry Dunham film a twenty-minute prologue and two ten-minute introductions to the second and third acts, in the Keystone Kops tradition. He opened the play in Stony Creek, Connecticut, where fire laws forbade the use of flammable nitrate film. Without the film sequences, the play bombed.[80] Bowles, too, continued work on the score, which he converted to the chamber work "Music for a Farce." Nearly half a century later Bowles bitterly remembered the uprooting from Èze as "the most expensive trip I ever took."[81]

Paul and Jane settled in the Chelsea Hotel, and Paul took up work in Friedrich Kiesler's studio at 57 Seventh Avenue (Kiesler was an Austrian architect and stage designer). They had spent all their money on their lease in France, the theater commission had evaporated, and the cost of living was much higher in New York than in Èze. Paul needed a steady income and with the help of a sympathetic investigator, he was able to get on the WPA rolls as a composer, for which he wrote pieces on demand and was paid $23.86 a week. Eventually, since Paul still had his Water Street studio, they were able to get food once a week from the Brooklyn relief board.

In the spring of 1939, Paul's fortune changed for the better. He received an offer from Robert Lewis of the Group Theatre to write the score for William Saroyan's *My Heart's in the Highlands*. The Group Theatre was a true artistic collective, formed in 1928 out of a series of discussions between Lee Strasberg and Harold Clurman, in which they proposed an alternative to the staid, one-dimensional academic theater then prominent. The Group Theatre was to be a permanent institution, integrated and unified. In it, there were no stars; all actors were listed alphabetically, and salaries were computed on a sliding scale according to other income. True to its founders' populist beliefs, the Group Theatre encouraged audience participation to contribute to its development; along with a theater company, they were building an audience. Saroyan's play in 1939 was to be the Group Theatre's first big success.

Bowles completed the score for *My Heart's in the Highlands* in six weeks, sitting at the Hammond organ in playwright Clifford Odets's apartment, which Lewis had given him to use while Odets was out of town. To the somewhat standard chamber instrumentation of cornet, oboe and English horn, drums, and percussion, Paul added a Hammond organ, no doubt inspired by his use of the organ in Odets's apartment. Critics gave the music as much notice as incidental music usually receives, their comments ranging from the noncommittal—"the music by Paul Bowles was probably good too, being a little weird"—to the positive: "the music by Paul Bowles is evocative and effective."[82] One piece that survives from this score is a song with lyrics by Saroyan, "A Little Closer, Please (The Pitchman's Song)." From a pleading, lyrical beginning, the piece launches into a raucous, burlesque hall chorus of "Come a little closer please," with stride piano punctuating the words perfectly and humorously. The song enjoyed a modest success on its own outside the theater.

My Heart's in the Highlands continued on Broadway under Theatre Guild production, and with the money from his commission for the music, Paul paid five months rent on a farmhouse near Prince's Bay, Staten Island. Paul went into New York once a week to collect his relief checks and to write his WPA music.

In the autumn he moved to a room in Columbia Heights in Brooklyn, while Jane stayed a while longer at the farmhouse. About this time, Paul was asked to collaborate on *Love's Old Sweet Song*, another Saroyan play. It was also produced by the powerful Theatre Guild, a firm of Broadway producers that commanded theater leases and subscription audiences on Broadway from the 1920s through the 1940s.

His next employer was a New Deal agency, the Soil Erosion Service, which was making a film on problems related to soil erosion in the Rio Grande Valley. In New Mexico Bowles researched the area and made notes for scoring *Roots in the Soil*, while working with the filmmaker Richard Boke. He settled in Old Albuquerque. On long walks in the desert north of the town he planned the score for the movie, carrying a stopwatch and the scene sequence. By the spring he had finished the score, and then he and Jane left for Mexico, where he planned to remain for some time.

The Theatre Guild interrupted his respite in late summer, asking him to return to New York to compose the incidental music for a production of Shakespeare's *Twelfth Night*, in which Helen Hayes played Viola and Maurice Evans played Malvolio. Bowles chose an idiom "meant to sound like antique and intricate chamber music," and the score was his greatest success to date (*WS*:230). *New York Times* critic Brooks Atkinson wrote, "Paul Bowles has composed music without Elizabethan affectation, more in a spirit of liveliness than of innocence."[83] Thomson exuded enthusiasm in an entire column devoted to the music: "If Miss Hayes, Mr. Evans and Mr. Shakespeare did not each have such a faithful and absorbed public, Mr. Bowles might easily have walked away with 'Twelfth Night.'" Bowles's instrumentation for *Twelfth Night* was sparse, in what Thomson called "The Bowles Formula": sharp timbred instruments—flute, oboe, harp, harpsichord, percussion, and muted trumpet—playing melodic parts in a carefully equilibrated sonority. "All of his emphasis comes from contrast of tune and timbre, from structure and harmonic progress, never from weight. . . . Every member of the 'Twelfth Night' cast and every scene of Shakespeare's play was aided and enhanced by the presence of this sumptuous and suitable music, every measure of it embroidered by hand. No one writing in the Broadway theater makes a song within a play so charmingly as Bowles does."[84]

Twelfth Night had just opened when Theresa Helburn of the Theatre Guild gave Bowles the manuscript to Philip Barry's *Liberty Jones*, an "extravaganza" with one hundred fifty-eight musical cues in the score. To support this, Bowles's instrumentation included two clarinets (alternate bass clarinet), two trumpets (alternate trombone), one electric violin, one electric guitar, one bass, one harp, two pianos (alternate Hammond organ and celesta), and drums. Samuel L. M. Barlow, whom the Bowleses had met in France, devoted an unusual amount of space in an article praising Bowles's music for this production, beginning, "As usual with Paul Bowles' music there is the amazing contrivance of original and appropriate sound. . . . Where a sound effect is called for, Bowles creates and sustains a scene with hair-raising unobtrusiveness." Barlow's greatest criticism was of Bowles's violation of his usual "unobtrusiveness" with "unaccustomed indiscretions" at the finale: "And as the music had no power of growth in itself, no *phusis*, the climaxes could only be achieved by making things louder. . . . Mere orchestronomy won't hold."[85]

Bowles had planned to return to Mexico within six weeks, but the Theatre Guild asked him to write the music to yet another play, Lillian Hellman's *Watch on the Rhine* (a work that eventually won the 1941 Drama Critics Circle award over Saroyan's *Beautiful People*). Bowles worked on *Watch on the Rhine* through the winter of 1940/41 and then, engaged for a ballet by Lincoln Kirstein, moved with Jane to 7 Middagh Street, "a strange house in Brooklyn Heights, a kind of artists' commune."[86]

This "ram-shackle, remodeled four-story brownstone," which was said to resemble a Swiss chalet, became home to a number of literary figures indulging in a successful experiment in communal living. Bowles and his wife, newly returned from Mexico, moved into rooms vacated by Gypsy Rose Lee. They shared the second floor with Oliver Smith and the house itself with W. H. Auden, Benjamin Britten, and Peter Pears, who lived on the third floor, and Thomas Mann's younger son Golo, who lived in the attic. (When the Bowleses moved out, Carson McCullers took their rooms, and Richard Wright and his wife and child moved in. The Wrights did not stay long because of troubles with the neighbors and because the black superintendent refused to tend the furnace for another black man.[87]) The lease on the house was held by George Davis, talented fiction editor of *Harper's Bazaar*, who had been given the opportunity to rent it through the generosity of Lincoln Kirstein. Kirstein's idea was to provide living quarters for working artists at reasonable prices. Davis claimed the house appeared to him in a dream, and he found it the next day, exact in every detail, whereupon he rented it. Auden, who presided at dinners and handled household bookkeeping, collected the twenty-five-dollar monthly rent. Auden was adept at getting money when it was due and kept a short rein on dinner conversation, prefacing meals with: "We've got a roast and two veg, salad and savory, and there will be no political discussion" (*WS*:233).

Anaïs Nin called the house "amazing . . . like some of the houses in Belgium, the north of France or Austria . . . filled with old American furniture, oil lamps, brass beds, little coffee tables, old drapes, copper lamps, old cupboards, heavy dining tables of oak, lace doilies, grandfather clocks . . . a museum of Americana."[88] Amid secondhand furniture that he labeled "nineteenth-century American Ugly," Bowles worked on his ballet *Pastorela* for Kirstein's American Ballet Caravan, writing music inspired by the Christmas *posadas* he had heard sung by Mexicans. Bowles placed vocal sequences, using "actual words and melodies" of the *posadas,* throughout the score, composing on an upright piano he installed behind a furnace in the "freezing and airless" cellar. Benjamin Britten monopolized the Steinway he had installed in the first-floor salon.[89]

If Bowles felt like a second-class citizen in his basement studio, Auden's announcement provided confirmation: "I shall be requiring your room over the weekend. I have a friend coming from Michigan, and he will go into your room." Having just recovered from the measles and the flu, Bowles had no intention of spending the weekend in his nearby Columbia Heights studio or of giving up his room "to anybody for any reason." Auden left, "slamming the front door violently." From then on Paul made a point of roguishly taking a Stalinist position on any subject mentioned at the dinner table, simply because he knew this would annoy Auden, his "antagonist."[90]

The Wind Remains

In the spring of 1940, Paul applied to the Guggenheim Foundation for a fellowship in music. It was his third application. He had been encouraged this time to specify the category of "creative music," and he proposed an opera with a libretto by William Saroyan. Saroyan, who claimed never to have been to the opera, had written and mailed Bowles his script, entitled "Opera, Opera!" while Bowles was in Albuquerque working on *Roots in the*

Soil. Although Paul looked through the libretto, he made little progress with it over the next year, turning instead to commissioned work: *Twelfth Night*, *Liberty Jones*, and *Watch on the Rhine*.

Paul received one of six Guggenheims in music awarded in March 1941.[91] The money from this award, added to weekly royalties from *Twelfth Night* and *Watch on the Rhine* and a few other commissions, meant he could afford to concentrate solely on the opera. He and Jane returned to Taxco in Mexico.

The opera, however, did not initially receive his attention. Shortly before he left, Katharine Hepburn had asked Paul whether he would be interested in writing music for a play her brother, Richard, was writing. The script, "Love Like Wildfire," was waiting for him in Taxco. The rest of the spring he worked on songs for Hepburn's lyrics. In his autobiography Bowles writes at some length about the difficulties of composing this work, giving insight into his approach: "Inasmuch as harmony rather than melody was the pivotal element in my musical thinking, I was unable to compose without having access to a keyboard instrument. I can hear clearly only up to five simultaneous tones on my mental keyboard; after that I falter" (*WS*:235–36).

Paul rented a piano and then found that although the actual composition went well, the "many more hours" he had to spend orchestrating and copying parts were difficult, because for these tasks he required "absolute privacy." An hour's horseback ride away from town he found what he needed "near the top of a cliff" that "faced the nothingness to the south" (*WS*:236). "I have a mud hut and a jungle down in a valley some thousand feet below Taxco. Plus a . . . waterfall that looks like Yosemite. And no one else in the whole valley as far as one can see, save the guardian of a ruined hacienda another five hundred feet directly beneath me, who said to me one day when I went down to see if the place was really abandoned, (he was sitting on his haunches, musing over his pickaxe when I approached,): 'You see how cruel life in Mexico is?' and nothing else."[92]

In addition to completing "Love Like Wildfire," during the summer Bowles negotiated with Kirstein over his ballet *Pastorela*, which Bowles asked Thomson to check on, to see whether it was as "lousy, terrible" as Kirstein claimed. (Paul was not to see it produced for another five years but then was "favorably impressed" [*WS*:272].) The antiphonal reed and brass sections and luscious flute parts were infused with polyrhythmic interest that must have been wonderfully inspiring to dancers, rhythm being one of Bowles's particular strengths.[93]

By the autumn, Bowles had begun work on the opera, first with Saroyan's libretto.[94] By December he had switched to sections from García Lorca's *Así que Pasen Cinco Años*, in an effort to construct a *zarzuela*, a Spanish form of musical theater consisting of loosely connected songs and dances. Throughout the winter and spring Bowles worked on the *zarzuela*, which he had decided to call *The Wind Remains*.

Bowles returned to the United States in the summer of 1942, going first to his aunt Mary's Holden Hall before moving to the Chelsea Hotel in autumn and again turning to his opera. The Museum of Modern Art presented the opera on 30 March 1943, one of a series of "Serenades" of rare music, ancient and modern, which Yvonne de Casa Fuerte had organized. Paul asked young Leonard Bernstein to conduct the work.[95] The producer and director of the opera was Schuyler Watts. Oliver Smith designed the set, and Merce Cunningham provided choreography and danced a solo part. Bowles privately described his creation in a notebook:

> The text of *The Wind Remains* is a contraction of García Lorca's most personal and incidentally controversial play . . . its Surrealist technique fitted it for the fragmentary kind of treatment I wanted to give it. I wanted to make of it an intensified and prototypical zarzuela, where the thread of dramatic action motivated by dream logic on which the songs and dances are strung becomes scarcely discernible. I translated into English what was not to be sung, leaving the songs in the original Spanish. In the writing of the score I was intent on transferring into musical terms the essence of García Lorca's poetic language — its textural delicacy, the freshness of its imagery and sound, the subtlety with which it attains an effect of naturalness. It was not part of my desire to write music that sounded Spanish; it seemed to me that if the music were like the text it would end up by being Spanish in the way I wanted it to be. The electric violin [used previously in *Twelfth Night* and *Liberty Jones*] and the wind-machine are the two important sound-makers, dramatically speaking, as the final lines of the play suggest "Queda el viento / Y la música de tu violín." (The wind remains / And the music from your violin).[96]

Thomson was more pleased with the work than Bowles: It was "partly in prose and partly in verse, partly spoken and partly sung, partly in English and partly (the verse parts) left in Spanish. It was also partly acted and partly danced. The whole thing was quite beautiful but in an artistic sense only partly successful; largely, I think, because the free form of the *zarzuela* is unacceptable to English-speaking audiences."[97]

Howard Taubman, a reviewer for the *New York Times*, agreed with Thomson, writing, "to those unfamiliar with the tradition of the *zarzuela*, it made little or no sense. The spoken lines were filled with strange symbols, often apparently unrelated." He labeled it a "sensitive plant that could scarcely withstand transplanting. It was precious more often than exotic. But that does not detract from the quality of Mr. Bowles's music. It had atmosphere; his writing for tenor and soprano voice was sensitive and congenial; his scoring for small orchestra was adroit. He is a gifted theatre composer."[98]

Years later composer Ned Rorem recalled, "I remember Paul once played a record of an extract from his opera that had been broadcast by one of the radio orchestras in Spanish, an aria called 'Queda el viento,' and I'd never heard anything so beautiful in my entire life. A breakthrough. It's about a five-minute aria from *The Wind Remains*. I'd say it's one of seven pieces important to me. It's very unexperimental music, at most sounds a little like De Falla, but there is a descending minor third I found very haunting, and I've never gotten it out of my mind."[99] The "Carnival Night Overture" from this radio broadcast is still available, distinguished by a delicate texture, clarity of parts, and complex rhythm and meter supported by interesting percussion. Through it all is a vaudevillian tone that is reminiscent of the Keystone Kops effect Bowles used in previous pieces.[100]

Bowles, however, was not happy with his *zarzuela*. "The trouble with the opera," he writes in his autobiography, "was that its text was an excerpt from a Surrealist play. It meant nothing and went nowhere; nor was it an opera, but rather a zarzuela with solo songs, spoken dialogue, instrumental sections, dances and choruses" (*WS*:249). He had received a Guggenheim, written his opera, and seen it premiered in New York. Reviews were good. But Paul felt dissatisfied and began to wonder whether he wanted to continue this way in music and in New York.

Friends and the Economics of Music

Thomson had dubbed Paul's immediate circle the "'Little Friends,' all young and a quarter mad." Bowles and Dunham constituted the "founding fathers," along with Latouche; Marian Chase, who married Harry Dunham; Marian's friend, the wealthy Theodora Griffis, who later married John Latouche; Jane Bowles; and Kristians Tonny. A strange fatality pursued the Little Friends: Dunham was shot down in Borneo in 1943; Griffis died young of cancer; Latouche died of a heart attack at the age of forty; Marian died of polio; and Jane Bowles suffered a debilitating stroke at forty. According to Thomson, the group broke up in 1938 with the Tonnys' departure for Europe, Harry's leaving to photograph the Spanish Civil War, and Jane and Paul's departure for Panama.[101] The disintegration of this group seemed to mark the end of an era for Thomson, and he, too, decided to leave New York.

After their unrewarded return from France in 1938, the Bowleses continued to spend time with the Little Friends, but their circle gradually widened to cut across the disciplines of theater, dance, music, and literature, touching many influential and significant figures of the period. Thomson, Latouche, the theatrical designer Oliver Smith, dance critic and poet Edwin Denby, playwrights Tennessee Williams and William Saroyan, and young conductor and composer Leonard Bernstein were Paul's professional associates and his close and valued friends. They regularly met with other artists at the home of Kirk and Constance Askew. In 1943, they spent several weekends with composers Samuel Barber and Gian-Carlo Menotti at their home, Capricorn, in Mount Kisco, New York, where a number of artists passed through. In Manhattan, Paul and Jane dined occasionally with Xenia and John Cage, and Paul remembers Cage as one of the true innocents he has known in his life. "I remember him rolling on the floor in delight at his own music."[102] Paul met Bernstein at a birthday party for Aaron Copland in 1937, and the two struck a friendship. Paul asked Bernstein to conduct the premiere performance of *The Wind Remains*, and Bernstein dedicated to Paul the fourth of his *Seven Anniversaries*, a suite of piano pieces for seven people whom he loved.[103]

Peggy Glanville-Hicks, an Australian composer whom Ned Rorem described as "90 pounds of very intense opinion," became one of Paul's closest friends in the midforties. From 1945 until Paul left for Morocco, they were "almost constant" companions (*WS*:259). Artists often find their friends among supporters of their work, and Peggy was particularly supportive of Paul, who said that one reason for their friendship was that they had "much the same musical tastes" (*WS*:259). Glanville-Hicks was unusual in that not only was she a composer but she served as an organizer for contemporary music in New York in the 1940s and 1950s. She coordinated concerts, arranged financial support, and wrote criticism, including several articles praising Paul's music. As a passionate and tireless worker for whatever cause she embraced, Glanville-Hicks kept Bowles's name in circulation in New York even after he had left that city. She also supervised the recording of his Concerto for Two Pianos while he was in Morocco. Rorem, among others, says of Glanville-Hicks's composing: "She was influenced by the fact of Paul," while Paul, Rorem continued, "has a way of being quite passive." Rorem said, "He'll do the worst part, the heavy work of writing down music, but he'll sort of use his charm to get people to do the rest. Peggy was very useful in that way."[104]

In New York visibility was a key to success. Consequently, in November 1942, Paul accepted Virgil Thomson's offer to join the staff of the *Herald Tribune* as music critic, where he and Arthur Berger replaced staff gone for military service. Thomson's advice was succinct: "Just tell 'em what happened, baby. That's all they want to know. Nobody cares about your opinion. Who are you?"[105] The work gave Bowles invaluable experience in producing a straightforward narration of events and in putting nonverbal experiences into verbal expression. Years later, Bowles's prose continued to "tell 'em what happened."

At first the job taxed Bowles enormously; a pianist recalls seeing Paul in the lobby during the intermission of a performance, pacing back and forth. When the musician greeted him, Bowles looked up in terror and implored, "What am I going to say? What am I going to say?" The initial tension and headaches over having to complete his daily reviews in forty-five minutes or less gradually lessened; over the next three and one-half years he wrote nearly four hundred articles. In addition to his reviews of classical and chamber music concerts, Bowles instituted a Sunday jazz column and wrote about folk music.

Years later Bowles professed to "have forgotten why [he] thought it necessary for [his] name to be constantly in print"; "I certainly believed that if the public got to know the name, regardless of whether there were any particular concept associated with it, the name would remain" (*WS*:247). The job provided Paul with a small but steady monthly income and gave him perhaps his first confirmation that he could earn money through writing. Whatever the reasoning, taking the job at the *Herald Tribune* accounted more than any other single factor for the music that Bowles composed during the decade. "It was a constructive step, inasmuch as it obliged me to remain in New York for the next several years and thus to lead a life which was largely musical."[106]

While he was writing for the *Tribune*, Bowles immersed himself in New York, which he called "the most extraordinary city of them all" (*WS*:247). He bought a bicycle, and at night, when the lights of the wartime city were blacked out, he rode streets that lay like "gorges" between the chalky cliffs reflecting moonlight high above. In the winter, clouds hid the tops of the skyscrapers, creating a maze of the streets below. Mystical beauty awaited his romantic eye even in New York. Other than Tangier, it is the only city in which Bowles stayed longer than a year or two.

Bowles rode his bicycle at night, because he spent nearly all his time either attending concerts to review, reviewing them, or writing incidental music for the theater. Between 1943 and 1947, Paul wrote music for twelve plays, beginning with two in 1943: Dorothy Heyward's premusical *South Pacific* and John Ford's *'Tis Pity She's a Whore*. During three days in 1944 Bowles wrote and orchestrated the music to Tennessee Williams's new play, *The Glass Menagerie*, one of his most successful theater scores, which composer Rorem terms "delicious" in the use of the celesta to mimic the sound of tinkling glass.[107]

It is difficult to judge Bowles's theater music, because it was so ephemeral. One must accept the word of one of America's most astute critics, Thomson, and believe that Bowles's gift for the theater was every bit as rich as his talent in the American song. Thomson claimed "Paul had a unique gift for the theater. It's something you either have or you don't, and Paul did."[108] In 1946 alone, he wrote music for six different plays. One of his last works of the forties was for Tennessee Williams's *Summer and Smoke* for which he used the Hammond Novachord (a forerunner of the synthesizer), along with violin, harp, cello, bass clarinet, Chinese drum, cymbals, gong, and snare. Bowles actually returned to New York from Morocco to work on the score, having just finished his first novel. Musician Arthur Hartmann publicly praised Bowles for a score that "created exactly that haunting, recurring, eerie fixation which is truly tremulous with beauty and which, with my deep admiration, I put on a par with the original creation of Tennessee Williams' fabulously poignant work."[109]

In addition to his collaborations with Williams for the theater, Bowles wrote several songs to lyrics by the playwright, among them *Blue Mountain Ballads* (1946), a suite containing some of Bowles's most natural sounding music, which exemplifies in miniature Bowles's skill in matching the actual rhythm of the spoken word as in "Heavenly Grass." The 5/4 meter forces the singer to pause between thoughts, giving a conversational quality to the piece. In the bluesy and occasionally dissonant "Sugar in the Cane," phrases such as "I'm red pepper in a shaker" descend in a manner so close to speech that they seem chanted rather than sung. The song "Lonesome Man" is sung to a cakewalk rhythm, while "Cabin," to which the composer's note reads "like a ballad," gently rocks between 6/8 and 9/8 meter.

Bowles wrote some of his best music for the voice, including his *Scènes d'Anabase*, *Picnic Cantata* the songs to Stein, to García Lorca, Charles I, Frances Frost, C. H. Ford, Seamus O'Sullivan, Richard Thoma, and the *zarzuela The Wind Remains*. Yet, with the exception of the Lorca songs, it is the songs with American texts that stand out among his vocal repertoire. Although he expressed many reservations about American civilization, his music shows that he was most at home composing in the American idiom.

Like many composers in the 1930s, Bowles had participated in several government-assisted projects. In the 1940s, as the nation moved out of the Great Depression, the source of funds shifted from public to private support from commissions and foundations. In addition to the income he earned from theater work and the Guggenheim grant, Bowles found several individual patrons for his works. One such patron was the Marqués de Cuevas, who "suddenly had access to a vast sum of money and intended to found a ballet company" (*WS*:252). At a party at his home, the marqués revealed to Bowles his idea for a collaboration between Bowles and Salvador Dali. They continued to discuss the idea over lunches, which the marqués prepared himself, while Bowles played his music on the piano or phonograph. The subject for the envisioned ballet was a poem by Paul Verlaine, "Dans un vieux parc solitaire et glace. . . ." After signing a contract, Bowles worked out the music and its orchestration, then flew to Mexico for a month's vacation. When he returned, orchestra rehearsals for the ballet *Colloque Sentimental* had begun.

Reviewing other performances for the *Herald Tribune* kept Bowles so busy that he was unable to attend any of the dance rehearsals prior to the dress rehearsal. What he saw that night caused his heart to sink. The eccentricities of Dali's stage design were exceeded only by the costumes: the two "lovers" of Verlaine's poem wore underarm hair reaching to the ground, and other performers were attached to yard-long beards and rode bicycles across the stage at will. A huge mechanical tortoise with colored lights on his back lurched randomly through the chaos. The play was performed in the autumn of 1944 to "catcalls, boos, shouts, and whistles." Bowles lamented, "I was desperate because my music might as well not have been being played for all it was heard. At the party afterward, Dali was gleeful; he considered the noisy reception a triumph" (*WS*:255–56). One of the musicians who did hear the score, the pianist for the production, well remembers that the "insanities" of "the manic Salvadore Dali," obscured a "lovely and atmospheric" score.[110]

Bowles found financial backing from such divergent sources as Peggy Guggenheim, Libby Holman, and the exiled Belgian government of the Congo. In the spring of 1943, Guggenheim's *Art of This Century* record series recorded Bowles's Sonata for Flute. That summer, Bowles helped Guggenheim acquire a summer home in Connecticut by leasing a home in his name in an area that tacitly refused to lease to Jews. The film *Congo* (1944), for which Bowles wrote the score, was a joint effort among Bowles, Latouche, and filmmaker André Cauvin, with Bowles salving his conscience for support of colonialism by reminding himself that Paul Robeson had agreed to provide narration. Those who remember the film suggest that Bowles's soundtrack undermined the Belgian government's plan to portray the Congo as better under colonial protection through his skillful thematic use of the Belgian national anthem. What begins in the film as a tuneful allusion to the anthem overtakes itself as a strident conqueror's march.[111]

Another patron was Paul and Jane's good friend Libby Holman, the original torch singer made famous by the song "Body and Soul" in the 1930 play *Three's a Crowd*. At the height of her popularity the National Silk Manufacturers Association named a shade of pastel silk in her honor—Libby Holman blue. Holman passed from popularity into disrepute when she was tried for the murder of her husband, Smith Reynolds, heir to the R. J.

Reynolds fortune. Paul met Holman through Latouche in 1946 after auditions for the Latouche/Duke Ellington *Beggar's Holiday*. They became friends, and Holman talked about an opera she wanted Paul to write for her. Later, when Libby visited Paul in Morocco, they decided on García Lorca's three-act poem *Yerma*. Bowles did not finish the opera until 1958, by which time he had lost enthusiasm, and the moment had passed for the match between Libby and Yerma.

Some of Bowles's most successful music came about through the patronage of duopianists Robert Gold and Arthur Fizdale. After hearing Bowles's *Nocturne* for two pianos in the 1930s, they asked him whether he would be interested in writing a piece for them. Over time they commissioned three major works: Sonata for Two Pianos (1946), Concerto for Two Pianos, Winds and Percussion (1947–48), and *A Picnic Cantata* (1953).[112]

The Sonata for Two Pianos turned out to be one of the showiest works for piano that Bowles wrote. Its first movement is nonmelodic, jazzy, and percussive, with the Debussy-like repetitive phrasing that is characteristic of Bowles's music. The second movement is impressionistic, at times bluesy, and illustrates a quality in Bowles's music that composer Glanville-Hicks described as "an emotional-mystical quality, a passion of the mind which hovers often near to eloquence, but always manages to remain as an undercurrent beneath the natural austerities and restraints of his style. It is at once personal and remote."[113] Although certain phrases in the movement have a folk quality similar to the *Blue Mountain Ballads*, they fit nicely with the lazy feel of the rest of the movement and do not seem out of place in this otherwise abstract work. The third movement (with a repeating rhythmic figure borrowed from his ballet *Yankee Clipper*) features the pianos as percussion instruments at a length that is unique in Bowles's scores. Although Bowles wrote that he was "rather ashamed of it" because "the style seemed wrong," this movement is among Bowles's most progressive work, improving upon Cowell's piano-percussion experiments and predating minimalists such as Steve Reich and John Addams by two decades.[114]

Bowles began his second Gold and Fizdale commission, the Concerto for Two Pianos, Winds and Percussion, during the summer of 1946 in a beach house in Southampton, where he and Jane were guests of John Uihlein, a friend of Jane's. Away from New York City, the calm of these surroundings gave Bowles the proper setting in which to compose a long, serious work. He writes, "Only in such serenity could I have found the theme I was looking for with which to open my Concerto. It came one morning after I had drawn a bath and shut the water off. The taps continued to drip, and the theme was in the succession of drops of water as they fell into the tub" (*WS*:266).

Gold and Fizdale premiered the concerto in November 1948, with an ensemble conducted by Lukas Foss and composed of Mitchell Miller, oboe; David Weaver, clarinet; Harry Freidstadt, trumpet; and Eldon Bailey and Robert Matson, percussion. Percussion instruments included marimba, cigar box, and milk bottle, combining to produce an effect one listener compared to a gamelan. Critics noted the "complicated African rhythms, and bizarre instrumental combinations of the opening Allegro movement."[115] Arthur Berger preferred the "languorous" quality of the concerto, an effect he thought Bowles actually achieved more successfully in his two-piano sonata, yet decided that "the very choice sonorities, the montage and timing in the sequence of the primitive and jazzy ideas in the other movements he has never surpassed."[116]

Bowles may have created the first movement as a satirical comment on New York cocktail parties. Throughout it, and the concerto as a whole, there are shifts in mood achieved through sudden variations in his instrumental combinations, as if moving from one conversation to the next at a party. The first movement begins with marimba and pianos, providing the "gamelan" sound (no doubt influenced by friend/composer Colin McPhee's work of eight years in Bali). The whole-tone passages on the oboe sound Middle Eastern, but switching the melody part to the trumpet over different percussion transforms the passage to a Latin American sound. In the second section of the first movement, the pianos drop out entirely while the clarinet takes over the melancholy melody. The third section returns to the piano-marimba combination of the first and finishes with a final snare flourish.

The distinguishing characteristic of the fast and breezy second movement is its rapidly changing meter. The somber third movement seems to make use of the Bowles Formula, with the sharp-timbred woodwinds playing in counterpoint. Parallel chords in the ensemble and the sumptuous chordal piano parts combine to produce an impressionistic effect, which the repeated use of the gong emphasizes. At some of its loveliest moments the movement suddenly shifts mood, as if unwilling to take itself too seriously.

The boisterous fourth movement is the jazziest of the four and contains examples of nearly all jazz styles, from blues to ragtime to swing. An extended "Middle Eastern" section, marked by oboe, a garish muted trumpet, and raucous tympani burlesques the mock-Moroccan craze of the forties. It playfully demonstrates most obviously the strength and the difficulty of the concerto: the quick movement from one idea to the next. Bowles introduces ideas and then moves on rapidly, so that a listener must be willing to let go of each new line quickly, sometimes before one is ready. The result is a musical montage ideally suited to and probably derived from the film and incidental music at which Bowles excelled, but sometimes disconcerting to the listener with no visual program to guide the attention. In the end, it signifies an equal valuation of art, popular, and indigenous traditions unusual for the times.

People who know Bowles through only his music or only his writing often are surprised to learn of his accomplishments in the other field and wonder what his work in the two areas can possibly have in common. His music is charming, sophisticated, and always entertaining, while his fiction can be horrifying and grim. Yet in both art forms, Bowles used the same economy of style. He chose his notes as carefully as he did his words and seldom repeated phrases in order to develop his musical ideas. What interested him most in writing music was just what he would strive for in his prose: to evoke in the listener or reader a particular emotional state through his art, to entrance his audience and bring it to the subconscious state of being in which his art could have its most powerful effect.

In the late 1940s Bowles wrote an autobiographical sketch explaining some of his interests as a composer. His first interest in music "came from a purely hypnotic reaction that musical sounds always had on me—not music itself, for it always had formal patterns."[117] Music followed rules of form and structure; it belonged to the "adult world." Sounds, however, were another matter: "I refer to the musical sounds I could produce myself by spinning a large musical top or by sliding a metal object up and down the strings of a German zither my grandfather had given me, or the creaking of a rusty door hinge: these sounds . . . always put me promptly into a non-thinking state which lasted as long as I repeated the sounds. I confess that these basic infantile criteria still seem perfectly valid to me."[118] Musical sounds, as opposed to formal music, belonged to the world of the child and to free imagination. They led away from rules and structure into a hypnotic state. In these childhood sounds and in the music of the Moroccan brotherhood rituals—the music of "savages," as many Moroccans labeled it—Bowles happily found release from the thinking state of everyday consciousness.

During his years in New York Bowles discovered that incidental music for theater provided "the perfect medium for carrying out some of the ideas [he] had subconsciously been trying to express. . . . Here, and in writing for the films too, one can with immunity write climaxless music, hypnotic music in one of the exact senses of the word, in that it makes its effect without the spectator's being aware of it."[119] With incidental music Bowles was free to create a mood without any pressure to develop the music formally beyond its evocative ability.

Yet Bowles was unsatisfied with writing incidental music even though, economically, it suited him. He managed to write a substantial amount of chamber music and nonincidental theater music, such as opera and ballets, but he wrote most of it on commission. More than one acquaintance recalls that Bowles wrote only music for which he had been commissioned and, therefore, paid.[120] This allowed Bowles to support himself as a composer, but it also fettered him. It eliminated the possibility of experimenting or launching out on his own. As he expressed it: the "obvious remedy" to the problem of always being tied to the apron strings of someone else's ideas "was to seek refuge in the writing of one's own music. I did; the works were two commissions from Gold and Fizdale. It was great fun composing them and, of course, even more listening to them when they were played. But when I had finished them, I did not go on working on my own music. On the contrary, I accepted more theatrical commissions and consequently never attained the state of freedom I sought" (*WS*:273).

By 1947 Paul had lost his taste for writing the one form of music that he knew he could depend on for income. Looking back on the decade, he reflected: "It is true that I 'produced' during those years, but in such a way that I always seemed to find myself doing what someone else wanted done. I furnished music which would embellish or interpret the ideas of others. . . . To my way of thinking I was only marking time. The malign effects of writing too much *Gebrauchsmusik* gradually became apparent during the spring. I was made aware of a slowly increasing desire to step outside the dance in which inadvertently I had become involved" (*WS*:273–74).

Given Paul's earliest artistic efforts — a real estate development, an imaginary planet, a series of diaries for invented characters — his discouragement at working behind the ideas of other artists seems inevitable. From the beginning he was an artist whose joy derived from the creation of entire worlds with characters to inhabit them. He gained no pleasure from filling in the contours of someone else's design.

Paul had achieved success as a theater composer, both financially and critically, and it was hard for him to turn away steady work. In a brief and otherwise very general autobiographical sketch for *Anteus* in 1985, Bowles made a point of noting the amount of money Tennessee Williams paid in taxes in 1948, the year his play *Summer and Smoke* opened: "It was a rainy winter, and he was busy much of the time trying to make out his federal income tax; I recall being appalled when I saw that he was having to pay $111,000 tax that year. 'Baby, they take everything,' he said."[121] In 1946, when Bowles was at the height of his composing career, he paid $738.58 in taxes and earned $4,500 in commissions for six theater works, the most he had ever written in a single year.[122] As a composer for the theater, Bowles worked side by side with artists whose earnings far outstripped his; this inequity must have influenced the direction of his career.

Another factor in Bowles's gradual disillusionment with composing was his discomfort with his skills as a composer. When Thomson left his post as senior critic for the *Herald Tribune* in 1954, he entertained a fantasy of turning the position over to Bowles. Paul later told Thomson, "I don't think I could have handled it, any more than I could have followed a career in composition. I lacked the musical training that you and Aaron had."[123]

The lack of training may have been a convenient excuse. Bowles taught himself French, Spanish, and Arabic through hours of copying out the conjugations of verbs. He trained himself to write, using a method that began with surrealist automatic writing, continued with translating works from several different languages, and culminated with mythopoesis, through which he discovered how to invent his own myths and stories. As a young composer he had the chance to study with two of the greatest American composers of the twentieth century, and as a working composer he had no lack of situations in which to perfect his skills. As mystery writers like to say, Bowles had both means and opportunity to become a composer of the first rank. He lacked only the motivation.

Creeping Back to Fiction

By 1946, the man who had once gone out of his way to introduce himself to any and all artists whom he wanted to meet was bored. In 1947, a few years after leaving New York City, he wrote to Charles Henri Ford, "I can't say that your description . . . made me want to be there, because I have never known it to be anything but unbearable no matter who gave dinner parties. (Perhaps I got invited to the wrong ones always, but my suspicion is that I was the wrong person instead.) As you know perfectly well, I've never yet felt a part of any place I've been, and I never expect to."[124]

One of the by-products of Bowles's musical talent was an acute sensitivity to sound. In New York City, this was a handicap. Indeed, in a column Paul wrote in 1943, he commented, "One would never wish to be blind, yet not a day passes in the city that one does not tickle one's imagination with the idea that total deafness might be a delight."[125] Late in 1944, Paul heard crickets, church bells, and a fluttering in his ears; sounds at high registers were painfully distorted. His colleagues do not recall his mentioning these difficulties, but when asked about it, Thomson found it not at all surprising: "Jesus, what a hypochondriac. He spent his life in and out of hospitals. He was turned down by the draft board because he had a history of so many diseases."[126]

By the age of thirty-four, Paul had run through a variety of exotic illnesses. He had nearly died from carbon monoxide poisoning; had contracted typhoid fever; had incurred an attack of a mysterious flu (or syphilis), two severe cases of sunstroke, dysentery, an ulcer, measles, at least three, probably four, attacks of hepatitis; and had had a tumor removed from his jaw twice.

Since the age of twenty, he had suffered migraine headaches so severe that "fluorescent zigzags" flashed across his field of vision.[127] In 1944, a doctor diagnosed Bowles's hearing problem as a side effect of tonsillitis and performed a tonsillectomy, which failed to relieve his symptoms.

Bowles himself says he can hardly be called hypochondriacal, since the diseases were real. The army psychiatrist who interviewed him in 1942 was interested in the fact that he wore wax stoppers in his ears to sleep (he also wore a nightshade over his eyes, the result of "photophobia" lingering after his bout with typhoid) and rejected him for service, writing on his report: "Not Acceptable. Psychoneurotic Personality." A story that made the rounds of Bowles's friends was about Bowles's session with a psychiatrist. After talking with Bowles for half an hour, the psychiatrist told him that he had built a "strange and complicated super-structure that was quite unreasonable and crazy." But, the psychiatrist added, tearing it down would not make sense, since Bowles seemed to function quite well within it, in his own peculiar way.[128]

During his recuperation from the unnecessary tonsillectomy, Bowles happened upon a notice of a London production of Jean-Paul Sartre's *Huis Clos*. When he mentioned the article to Oliver Smith, Smith enthusiastically suggested they contact Sartre, then on a government-sponsored tour of the United States, regarding American rights to the play. The three met in Washington and signed a contract only two days before Theatre Guild directors Theresa Helburn and Lawrence Langner called on Sartre for the same purpose. Bowles worked on his translation, which he called an adaptation, for two years; it culminated in a production directed by John Huston that won the Drama Critics Award for the best foreign play of the year.

Bowles found many faults with the production, such as being forced to divide the tightly woven play into two acts, to introduce an intermission, and to add current political themes to the story line. As the adapter of the play, he knew he would be held responsible for such changes. Further, he was amazed to discover that his title for the play, which had taken him weeks to determine, was to be retained in future literary translations with which he had nothing to do. The title, *No Exit*, which he had taken from a sign in a subway turnstile, stayed with the play.

At the opening Thornton Wilder advised, "You stick to your music and you'll be better off" (*WS*:271). But Bowles went on to translate a second play, *La Folle de Chaillot*, by Jean Giraudoux, a job he completed in six weeks by working in a nearly empty hotel in Ocho Rios, Jamaica. After so many years of writing incidental music, turning his attention so intensely to the literary side of the theater put Bowles a step or two up the ladder in his gradual climb back to the literary world.

Many people, including Paul himself, credit Jane's publication of her novel *Two Serious Ladies* in 1943 with stimulating his return to writing. Yet Paul had been experimenting with fiction for many years, including one published story, "Tea on the Mountain," which he wrote as early as 1939. He and Jane discussed his return to writing "very solemnly" when they lived at the Chelsea.[129] The process of return was incremental, beginning with Paul's contributions to Ford's art and literary publication *View*.

In many ways, *View* was a 1940s American version of the earlier Paris *transition*, taking advantage of the European artists who had immigrated to the States. In the 1930s, Charles Henri Ford and Parker Tyler had published the magazine *blues*, subtitled *a magazine of new rhythms*, attracting essays from former *transition* contributors such as Kay Boyle, Gertrude Stein, Bravig Imbs, Eugene Jolas, and, of course, Paul Bowles. With *View: The Modern Magazine*, they continued to explore surrealism, but added modernism and primitivism, with art and literature by Man Ray, Max Ernst, de Chirico, André Breton, Yves Tanguy, Henry Miller, Alexander Calder, Florine Stettheimer, and Isamu Noguchi.[130]

Poet William Carlos Williams, a frequent contributor to *blues*, suggested in a 1942 letter to *View* that "surrealism is to disclose without trying."[131] Poet Randall Jarrell was less committed, writing to tell the editors that *View* was "almost the weirdest magazine I've ever seen."[132]

Although he was already writing music criticism for the *New York Herald Tribune*, in the pages of *View* Bowles made the transition from music critic to fiction writer. His first contribution, in April 1943, was a column on jazz called "The Jazz Ear," but that same year he also published a section from one of his childhood diaries entitled "Bluey," accompanied by an editorial note: "This *Chef-d'oeuvre* of the primitive style was created by its author at the age of nine. For pure comedy, dramatic tension, and harmonic development of theme, it seems unequaled by any other work by a writer of the same age, and needless to say, is far more persuasive than the writing of most adults."[133] (Actually, the published version differs substantially from the childhood notebook.) In 1944 he published a translation from Italian surrealist de Chirico's work *Hebdomeros*, followed by a second installment of the same work in December of 1944.

In May 1945, Bowles edited a special "Tropical Americana" issue, comprising his translations, texts, and photographs of Central and South America. This issue also included translations of stories and articles by Ramón Beteta, Bertrand Flornoy, Ramón Sender, and Paul Rivet; a Tarahumara story; and two selections from the *Popol Vuh*, a Mayan mystical work. Bowles also included two "documents," purportedly from Mexican sources, one of which he had invented. This use of "documentary" material helped spur his interest in writing fiction, and he returned to this technique at many points in his career, most notably with his late work *Points in Time*, a collection of episodes in the history of Tangier. The indigenous material stimulated his imagination and suggested not only the documentary technique but also one he called "mythic," which truly launched him into a new use of the imagination.

Bowles published four more translations in the 1945 November and December *View* before submitting a story of his own. His ethnographic reading got him interested in myths, and he began to wonder whether he could invent some. Returning to the surrealist method of automatic writing, which he had used with his poetry, he experimented with the method in prose, by clearing his mind of all distractions and allowing an image or character to come to mind from his mythic, subconscious mind. Then as he *passively* meditated on the image, he allowed the myth to develop and wrote it all down as it happened in his imagination.

View published "The Scorpion" in December of 1945, the same month in which Bowles resigned from the *Herald Tribune*, and he "went on inventing myths." "The subject matter of the myths soon turned from 'primitive' to contemporary, but the objectives and behavior of the protagonists remained the same as in the beast legends. It was through this unexpected little gate that I crept back into the land of fiction writing" (*WS*:262).

"The Scorpion" was Bowles's first published fiction attempt since Gertrude Stein had told him he could not write, and in it he provided clues to the course his fiction would take from that point.[134] Reputedly an experiment in writing myths, it was the writer's mythic return from "exile" as a composer in New York. The subject of the story, an old woman cave dweller, dreams about being a little girl again and then of swallowing a scorpion, which she harbors inside. When Bowles picked up his pen for writing stories instead of musical scores, he returned to a kind of fantasy in which he had spent much of his childhood. Writing was revenge for that lost childhood; writing was a scorpion he could control, and he would take its sting with him as he emerged from his cave and ventured into the world of fiction.

Nine months later, in September 1946, *Harper's Bazaar* came out with Bowles's "The Echo," and in October *View* published "By the Water." But it was when *Partisan Review* accepted "A Distant Episode" for the January–February 1947 issue that Paul felt he had achieved literary acceptance sufficient to merit a career as a writer. Although both *Harper's Bazaar* and *Mademoiselle*, for which Bowles had written articles on contemporary music, carried some of the most daring and exciting new fiction of the 1940s, including articles and poems by Virginia Woolf, Colette, Christopher Isherwood, W. H. Auden, Carson McCullers, and Truman Capote—due largely to the discerning eye of George Davis, fiction editor of *Harper's Bazaar* from 1936 to 1941 and of *Mademoiselle* until the end of the decade—*Partisan Review* had a higher threshold, and Bowles had crossed it.

Until 1947, Bowles had made his way in New York as most did, through a combination of hard work, personal connections, and luck. Perhaps because he had been so well connected, he never entirely accepted his success as a comment on his abilities. When *Partisan Review* published "A Distant Episode," which remains one of his finest pieces, it was as if somebody had finally said the something Paul needed to find the "civil status" he began looking for eighteen years earlier.

If sustaining an active composing career had depended on remaining in New York, writing did not. In the summer of 1945, Bowles traveled to Central America with Oliver Smith. They visited Cuba, Jamaica, Guatemala, El Salvador, and the Gulf of Honduras. "The big number however," Paul wrote, "was a river trip through Guatemala which in spite of certain discomforts Oliver enjoyed very much. I don't need to add that I did too, as I'm such a masochist when it comes to the tropics and their curses that I enjoy everything as soon as the first horror has either worn off or become a habit."[135] Not since his honeymoon in 1937 had Paul traveled in such remote country, and he could not help comparing the jungle wilderness with the dinner and cocktail parties of New York. For Paul, writing meant bringing the unconscious to conscious expression. For this activity to flourish, he needed the rotting fermentation of the jungle around him or the arid, picked-clean beauty of the desert. In New York he had occasionally found an artist's haven, overlooking the Hudson River in Brooklyn or in a single room above a Turkish café. But these retreats provided only temporary relief from the people and parties that constituted the artist's life in New York. Paul knew he could not remain there if he were to write as he wanted.

"Pastor Dowe at Tacaté," written in New York in 1946 and set in Guatemala, was inspired both by this trip and by his honeymoon trip, when, in Chichicastenango, Guatemala, he met a legendary priest named Father Rossbach, an authority on the Mayan *Popol Vuh*, who had incorporated Mayan practices into his Christian worship services for the Quiché Mayan people. The name for Bowles's fictional pastor came from a church pastor he and Jane had known in 1939 when they lived on Staten Island.

In the story, Pastor Dowe has gone to live with the Indians at Tacaté, who will not listen to his sermons unless he plays music on his Victrola, preferring above all "Crazy Rhythm." In talking to Nicolás, the town leader, the pastor discovers that the Indians have an elaborate worship system of their own, much of which is entirely unknown to him. In addition to Hachakyum, whom he has always known as God, the Indians worship Metzabok, who made "all the things that do not belong here" (*CS*:139). The pastor feels strangely alone; he consoles himself "by recalling that it is only in each man's own consciousness that the isolation exists; objectively man is always a part of something" (*CS*:140).

The pastor begins to realize that all he tries to tell the Indians is "transformed on the way to them into something else" (*CS*:145). To calm his agitation, the pastor goes for a walk and soon arrives in the forest, which smells of "living and dead vegetation in a world where slow growth and slow death are simultaneous and inseparable" (*CS*:146). He follows two Indians down to the river's edge, and they instruct him to come with them in their raft. The pastor travels farther from any world familiar to him and "outside God's jurisdiction. . . . The journey downstream was a monstrous letting go, and he fought against it with all his power" (*CS*:148).

Passing through the jungle into a lagoon, the pastor passes from a rational into an emotional state, "sunk within himself, feeling, rather than thinking, 'Now it is done. I have passed over into the other land'" (*CS*:149). When the Indians ask him to pray at an altar for Metzabok, Pastor Dowe feels "strong and happy." He experiences this not in "mental terms" but rather viscerally: "His spiritual condition was a physical fact" (*CS*:150).

When the Indians take him back to the village, he stays overnight with Nicolás and has to be reminded the next morning of the church services, at which he allows the Indians to play "Crazy Rhythm" twice, and he substitutes local names for the characters and deity in the psalm. The Indians are "electrified." "He realized that what he was saying doubtless made no sense in terms of his listeners' religion, but it was a story of the unleashing of divine displeasure upon an unholy people, and they were enjoying it vastly" (*CS*:152).

As he reads, a baby alligator crawls near him; the people pile up bars of salt, which they have demanded the pastor provide, and begin to lick them rhythmically. As this obscene spectacle continues, the pastor signals for "Crazy Rhythm" to be played once more. Nicolás shatters the pastor's new-found equilibrium by announcing his intention to give his child Marta to the pastor as a bride. To refuse would be to alienate himself forever, but Pastor Dowe cannot take this final step. He packs his small valise with his Bible, notebooks, toothbrush, and Atabrine tablets and runs through the village into the night.

The pastor has taken a journey into the jungle and gained an understanding of what it is to belong there: to feel rather than to think, to participate unselfconsciously in the world around. He loses all the appurtenances, the crazy rhythm, of European civilization and steps into the jungle, but he cannot relinquish a moral code that forbids him from taking a child as a wife. He must return or be forever lost. In the jungle, as in New York City, there is no halfway. The indigenous people of Bowles's story would not be annexed by civilization; ultimately, neither would Bowles.

Escape from New York

Paul took a familiar route on his return to Tangier, one that led from his daily life through the unconscious and back again without much conscious intervention.

> One balmy night in May [1947], asleep in my quiet bedroom, I had a dream. . . . In the late afternoon sunlight I walked slowly through complex and tunneled streets. As I reviewed it, lying there, sorry to have left the place behind, I realized with a jolt that the magic city really existed. It was Tangier. . . . The town was still present the following morning, fresh and invigorating to recall, and vivid memory of it persisted day after day, along with the inexplicable sensation of serene happiness which, being of the dream's very essence, inevitably accompanied it. It did not take me long to come to the conclusion that Tangier must be the place I wanted to be more than anywhere else. (*WS*:274)

Paul did not plan to leave New York permanently but only to travel for a while in Morocco while he wrote his novel, and he had no conscious intention of abandoning composing. In an interview in 1952, conducted by mail shortly after publication of his second novel, *Let It Come Down*, Bowles explained the two aspects of his career: "I had always felt extremely circumscribed in music. It seemed to me there were a great many things I wanted to say that were too precise to express in musical terms. Writing music was not enough of a cathartic. Nor, perhaps, would writing words be if I should do it exclusively. The two together work very well."[136]

Yet as Paul drifted farther from the island of Manhattan, he found himself drifting away from composing as well. Jane, who stayed in New York while he worked on *The Sheltering Sky* in North Africa, wrote him of her fear that he might not continue to compose: "Perhaps writing will be a means to nomadic life for you, but I hope you won't slowly stop writing music, altogether, I think you will do both."[137] Her fears were well grounded. Theater music, which had constituted the bulk of Paul's work, demanded collaboration, which was all but impossible from Tangier. His work as a composer depended on commissions. As he wrote less and less music, he received fewer commissions. "I never really left music," he told an interviewer. "It was a very slow melding so that at any one time I might be writing both music and a novel on the same day. That seemed the natural state of affairs but, eventually I was writing more words than notes."[138]

If writing notes had moored him to New York, writing words cut him free. A typewriter was infinitely more portable than a piano, and Paul found he could live more cheaply abroad than in New York. Tangier was cheaper even than Mexico. Though some friends expressed surprise at the polish of Bowles's first published stories and novel, few were genuinely shocked at his shift in vocation. To those who knew him well, Paul's move to Tangier to write a novel seemed logical and even practical. Jane wrote him, "I think it is very important that you have this extra source of income if you can really develop it substantially, because it will permit you to do much more work out of the country than your music does which is after all what you want."[139] Gordon Sager, a writer who accompanied Paul on the 1947 journey to Tangier aboard the *Fern Cape* freighter, said: "Many people were breathing a sigh of relief that the war was over at last; oceans were once again open to peacetime navigation. So I don't really think that Paul's decision to leave New York in '47 was at all remarkable; and as for Tangier, well, he had known it and liked it in the past."[140] It was not a remarkable decision to someone who knew Bowles for the expatriate he really was, a nomad on Manhattan Island, biding his time until he could make his escape at last.

BOOK IV

THE SHELTERING RELATIONSHIP, 1938-1951

During the years of being married to him she had examined him from so many angles and at such close range that now all she could see was a mass of contradictions. He was a savage fanatic, a sentimental cynic, hedonistic in his practice of asceticism; he always hoped for the worst, and when the worst actually happened, he went to pieces. . . .When a decisive moment arrived, his entire personality seemed to melt, to liquefy; she could see him disintegrate before her eyes; where there had been someone there was no one, and she was both ashamed for him and terrified by the phenomenon. He however, could undergo it, come out the other side, and discuss it with bland objectivity, as though it had happened to someone in a book, not to him at all, and he could never understand why she was furious with him at such moments.[1]

Jane

JANE AND PAUL met in February 1937 through John Latouche, who had brought both Jane and Erika Mann, the daughter of Thomas Mann, for an evening in Harlem, where Bowles often went to hear jazz and, occasionally, to smoke reefers. Paul remembered the evening and Jane: "The redhead's name was Jane, and she was not communicative" (*WS*:196). Several days later he saw her again with "Touche" at Patchin Place, a small enclave of cottages in Greenwich Village and the home of Marion and E.E. Cummings. Kristians Tonny and his wife Marie-Claire Ivanoff were also there, and they enjoyed talking with Jane, who spoke French beautifully. With Paul they began to discuss taking a long trip to Mexico.

Paul and Jane spent hours in conversation on the bus from New York to Mexico. Jane had cut her hair short for the trip. She wore Paul's fedora hat on the bus and smoked a corncob pipe that she had bought in Tennessee.[2] Paul never forgot the image of her next to him on the bus. The last part of the trip was a disaster for Jane: "For two days going through the mountains [of Mexico] she crouched, frightened and sick, on the floor at the back of the bus" (*WS*:198). As soon as they arrived in Mexico City, Jane left for the Ritz Hotel. She ended up at the Hotel Guardiola, where Paul, Tonny, and Marie-Claire found her three days later, ill. She left for the United States the next day without saying goodbye. When Paul returned to the United States several months later, they began to see each other again.

Before meeting Paul, Jane had not demonstrated any romantic interest in men, although she openly pursued women. She still considered herself a virgin and "intended to remain in that category until she married" (*WS*:199). In contrast to Paul, who was nearly seven years older and had traveled widely, Jane had lived in the States except for two years in Switzerland and was then living with her mother in the Hotel Meurice. She and Paul shared similar interests and many of the same friends. When they met, Jane recognized Paul's name from a poem she had read in *transition* in 1929, remembering only that it began with the line, "It was a long trip back."[3]

Jane had grown up in an upper-middle-class family in Woodmere, Long Island. Her mother, Claire Stajer, had been born in New York City; her father, Sidney Major Auer, in Cincinnati, to Austrian immigrants. Like Paul, Jane was a precocious only child in a large circle of adults. Her family were not practicing Jews, but they clung to their cultural heritage "like a tribe," and while Jane's grandmother was alive, they still went to temple on holidays.[4] Jane's father died in 1930, when Jane was thirteen. His widow moved herself and Jane back to New York City. After one semester of public school, Jane was sent to Stoneleigh, a girls' school in Greenfield, Massachusetts, where a horseback-riding accident precipitated a series of operations in a futile attempt to reverse the damage to her right leg. When tuberculosis developed in Jane's knee, Claire checked her into a special clinic in Leysin, Switzerland.[5] She was there from 1932 to 1934; her mother lived in Paris. When she and her mother returned to the United States, Jane endured yet another operation on her knee. At this time, doctors decided to freeze the knee joint. She was unable to bend her knee for the rest of her life, but she was free of pain.

During her recovery, Jane started writing her first novel, *Le Pháeton Hypocrite*.[6] Back in New York she began spending evenings with friends in Greenwich Village clubs. One of her favorite hangouts was Spivy's Roof, where the cabaret singer Spivy Levoe sang John Latouche songs. Jane's Jewishness, the loss of her father, her mother's overprotectiveness, her stiff leg, and her sexuality remained difficult issues for her. For several years, she laughingly referred to herself as "Janie, the Crippie Kyke Dyke."

The attraction between Jane and Paul was mutual. Each held for the other the promise of intellectual compatibility, similar artistic interests, and an understanding of what it was like to feel alien to one's own culture. Maurice Grosser, who knew them both well, said, "They were very much alike, you know. There was a sort of fastidiousness about both of them." There was also a strong bond of affection. As they continued their friendship through the winter of 1937, they began to fantasize about marrying. "From fantasy to actuality is often a much shorter distance than one imagines," Paul said (*WS*:207). They were married on 21 Feburary 1938, the day before Jane's twenty-first birthday and almost two months after Paul turned twenty-seven. Paul writes of the event, "No one was present but my parents and her mother, and no one seemed horrified, which made things much easier, if less dramatic" (*WS*:207).

In marrying, Jane and Paul were defying one convention by confirming to another. An unusual couple such as Jane and Paul were expected not to marry. Jane's lesbian relationships were well known in the circles in which she and Paul traveled. Paul himself was "militantly anti-heterosexual," and many of his friends were homosexual. Thus the only people in Paul's world that marriage was likely to appease were his parents, and they disliked his bride.[7] The wedding gave his parents something to be unhappy about in the shape of an event they could not help but bless. It was a masterstroke of passive aggression.

With two wardrobe trunks, twenty-seven suitcases, typewriter, and record player, Paul and Jane embarked upon a six-week honeymoon trip through Panama, Costa Rica, and Guatemala, acquiring and losing their first parrot, taking ferryboats through inland lagoons, and riding horseback through jungles. Paul later wrote, "In Central America life had gone smoothly; Jane and I never argued, never grew tired of being together" (*WS*:210). Yet both Paul and Jane later wrote stories set in Central America, and the stories were about estranged couples.

Given their itinerary, it was no wonder that Jane, who "hated nature," cut herself loose in Paris, which offered the city life she loved. She visited the cafés until late at night, leaving Paul to wait for her at their hotel. As he put it, "In Paris she had friends, and I was suspicious of them" (*WS*:210). Like Paul, Jane had a gift for meeting interesting people everywhere. In Paris, she spent several evenings drinking with writer Henry Miller and also met surrealist painter and writer Brion Gysin and Denham Fouts, the beautiful young man whom writers from Truman Capote to Christopher Isherwood immortalized as the most expensive male prostitute in the world. Fouts had just returned from Tibet with a crossbow and horrified Jane by shooting flaming arrows out of his hotel window over the trees on the Champs Élysées.[8] Paul and Jane quarreled over her late-night adventures and drinking, and finally Paul left for Germany, suggesting that Jane join him later.

Paul's plan to do something shocking had somehow backfired; he found he preferred a more conventional marriage arrangement, perhaps even a monogamous one. Jane continued to pursue extramarital affairs, apparently all lesbian. Years later, Paul's preferred description of their sexual relationship was that they had "frequently separate sexual lives."9 Maurice Grosser characterized it as "a very intense relationship." He added, "How much they actually slept together, I don't know. I suspect very little. But they were terribly fond of one another. And they were all entwined with one another. They were very dependent upon one another." Jane's drinking partners and lovers gradually became a part of her life with Paul, and when he grew weary of or exasperated with the situation, they would separate. In this way, parting and reuniting, Jane and Paul continued for the rest of their life together. It was one way they had of reconciling irreconcilable differences.

The contrasts between the Bowleses ranged from physical to psychological. Although Paul was of medium height (five feet eight inches), people often termed him tall. He was slender and blond, an impeccable dresser, with a wry expression that gave the impression of being slightly aloof. Jane was small—Truman Capote called her "elfin." Her short, curly hair was dark but tinted with henna and slightly tousled around her face. She cared little about clothes and often lost the expensive items her mother purchased for her. She had a warmth and openness of manner that drew people to her immediately and made them want to care for her as much as she seemed to care for them. At parties, she was fond of sitting on people's laps; she called her friends "honey," and they remember her as cuddly.

Whereas Paul preferred to stand back and watch in social situations, Jane enjoyed performing. She was intensely funny, odd, piquant: she had a peculiar way of expressing herself that invariably made people laugh, whether what she was saying was humorous or not. Her syntax was different from what one expected; she stressed unlikely words and syllables in ways that others found amusing. There often seemed to be something missing in her phrasing. "There's no security in alligators," she philosophized, and though friends agreed, they were not always sure why.10 She worried constantly and made no attempts to hide her many irrational fears. To ask Jane out for dinner was to invite hours of delay while she debated what to wear, whether it would rain, who should accompany or meet them, the best way to travel, where they should go, and what she should order once they arrived. She invented roles for people and seemed to collect friends in order to turn them into characters in the plays only she knew were being performed. Christopher Wanklyn, a Canadian writer and friend of the Bowleses in Morocco, said, "Sometimes these comedies, while amusing in retrospect, were torture for the captive audience who might find himself swept into the drama. One such was a kind of game that she and Charles Gallagher [a historian] would play in Tangier restaurants, trying to outdo each other in being difficult about the food and the service. 'You know,' Jane once furiously exclaimed to a waiter she had never seen before, 'You *know* I can't stand sauces!'"[11]

Joe McPhillips, head of the American School in Tangier, said, "One thought one was in a play when one was with Janie. She had the ability to invest the ordinary with something beyond ordinary. Everything was an event, an occasion, even if it was just a ride in the car. She saw the world differently."[12] Grosser declared her "one of the most charming, one of the funniest people I have ever encountered. She had a very strange wit, like nobody else's. She was quite a wonderful character. Of course, she was a terribly worried girl, but her worries were always funny."

Jane made a great show of her weaknesses and her vulnerability. Her vulnerability was one of the drawing cards of her personality. She used it to gather attention and elicit sympathy, and it worked. Yet while she carefully managed her weaknesses to her own best advantage, she did not create them. And to expose herself constantly to public display was to take a great risk. Others could just as easily have rejected her. But because she presented herself so expertly, they did not.

In emotional makeup, the Bowleses seemed to dovetail, creating a complementarity that enabled them to balance their excesses, each against the extremes of the other. Jane was unpredictable and excitable to the point of hysteria; Paul was ever disciplined and reserved. Where Paul was analytical, Jane was unabashedly emotional. Perhaps this was the quality in her that most drew Paul to her. As much as anyone else, he loved watching Jane perform: "She was even more mischievous when I was around because I doted on her mischievousness, on her uniquely amusing quality that no one else could ever come near."[13] It was as if she acted out for him the extravagances of personality that he could not allow himself to express. In turn, Paul reassured Jane; his fussiness distracted her from her own fears.

Jane was obsessed by the idea that every decision was a moral one "and that was so even if the choice was between string beans and peas," said Paul.[14] This need to make the right choice often resulted in paralysis, an inability to make any decision at all. Jane relied on an elaborate system of omens and signs to help her, for each decision was a terrible responsibility.

By the end of their second year of marriage, Paul stated, Jane had told him that his view of life "depressed her so deeply that when she was with me, everything seemed hopeless. The result was, she said, that she could be with me alone for short periods, and then she had to escape the overwhelming gloom I created."[15] Jane called Paul "gloompot," probably because in him she found the manifestation of her own deepest fears—fears that were too deep for both to share at the same time. In a work Jane wrote later in life but never finished, the narrator concluded, as Jane must have concluded about her own marriage: "It would happen some day, surely. A serious grief would silence their argument. They would share it and not be able to look into each other's eyes. But as long as she could she would hold off this moment."[16]

Jane's marriage to Paul allowed her both to hold off the moment of danger and to stay very close to it. She would withdraw from Paul into her own circle of friends or into another relationship, and when he left or found another close relationship, she soon found a way to join him. Jane was not fond of travel and was terrified of the "forces of nature." As Paul put it, "She was afraid of anything unknown, of the jungle or the mountains. Nature in general horrified her. Her idea of a beautiful landscape was a meadow with cows grazing, no mountains in the distance, nothing else. The sea or storms frightened her. She'd say, 'yes, yes, they're beautiful, but it's terrible. I don't want to look at it, thank you. Let's go inside. It's almost the cocktail hour.'"[17] Even so, Jane traveled with Paul over three continents and lived in several different countries and, once, on a small island. They shared illnesses, execrable food, and a deep sense of loneliness and separateness from each other even in their moments of togetherness. Although Jane's insistence on following her husband seems self-destructive, because living with him demanded continual self-confrontation, Paul provided a sense of security Jane could not establish on her own.

Living with Jane brought Paul close to the kind of personal conflict he preferred to ignore and provided him with daily emotional upheaval. Jane, who tended toward total emotional immersion, must have seemed at times a living manifestation of the detached part of himself and the emotional equivalent of the primitivism Paul sought through his travels.

New York and Mexico

When the Bowleses first returned to New York from France in 1938, life was far from exotic. When *Too Much Johnson* was canceled and Paul and Jane were left with one hundred dollars, they moved into a dilapidated but cheap apartment at 201 West Eighteenth Street. When a fire in their fireplace spread to the floor of their apartment, they moved in temporarily with their friend John Becker. In spring 1939, Paul received his check for *My Heart's in the Highlands*, and they moved to Staten Island.

Many New York friends came for weekend visits on Staten Island: Latouche, Colin McPhee, Leonard Bernstein, Elsie Houston, Harry Dunham, and Marian Chase. When the Bowleses' lease was up in November, Dunham paid a couple more months rent just to "keep the house in the family."

Paul's former benefactor Mary Oliver invited herself (and her German maid) for a visit, and she and Jane got along so well that she stayed. With Mary there, "the quantity of alcohol consumed at the farmhouse increased by the week" (*WS*:217). About October 1939 Paul decided to leave the farmhouse altogether for an apartment in Columbia Heights, Brooklyn. Jane came to lunch with him almost daily and often spent the night with him in Brooklyn, but she continued to live with Mary, at first on Staten Island, later in a West Thirteenth Street apartment.

Despite living separately, Jane and Paul were very much a couple when they socialized. They regularly attended gatherings at the home of art dealer Kirk Askew and his wife, Constance, who held what Paul called "the only regular salon in New York worthy of the name" (*WS*:220). There Paul played the piano and sang his own songs, while Jane visited, sitting first on one man's lap and then in another's. Composers Virgil Thomson, Aaron Copland, Elliot Carter, and Marc Blitzstein could be counted on to be there, as could Lincoln Kirstein and George Balanchine and their dancers. Several connected with the Museum of Modern Art attended: curator Alfred Barr, architect Philip Johnson, artists Eugene Berman and Tchelitchew, and historian Russell Hitchcock. Poet E. E. Cummings and director John Houseman were often there as well. As Europe headed toward war, artists immigrated to New York and to the Askew salon. Among them were surrealists — Marcel Duchamp, Yves Tanguy, and Salvador Dali — who dominated the intellectual tone of the Askew salon from 1940 on; Paul felt at home with them, but Jane did not.

Separately entertaining though each was, as a couple Paul and Jane amused each other and their friends with witticisms and stories that bounced back and forth so quickly they seemed to be coming from one person. The couple elaborated long-running fantasy games built on incidents from their travels or on people they knew. Using material from their honeymoon in Central America, Paul and Jane played a private game in which he was a stubborn parrot and she was the master who would tell him, when he was obstreperous, "Get back in your cage Bupple." Jane's character was Teresa Braun, keeper of the giant parrot.[18]

Jane had an astounding gift of mimicry and could imitate singers from Helen Morgan to Libby Holman with such accuracy that people would come running from the next room thinking the famous singer had just appeared. Paul's wit and abilities as a storyteller made him fascinating company. He was also a good mimic and physically acted out the parts of people in the stories he told. Artist Don Bachardy said, "His stories often made fun of himself. He was very low-key and soft spoken, not the least bit aggressive, and then had this surprising ability to imitate people."[19]

Ned Rorem, a generation younger than Paul, remembers Jane and Paul with some awe as "pace-setters" in New York in the early 1940s. David Diamond recalls Paul as "pseudo-elegant, never relaxed." Publicly it appeared that Paul and Jane Bowles were the quintessential artistic couple, "New York sophisticates." Their friends and acquaintances spanned the worlds of modern art, surrealism, theater, music, and literature, and as the forties continued, both Paul and Jane began to produce the kind of work their wit and genius had promised. They were attractive, their conversation intrigued, and they complemented each other in ways that made them prized dinner and cocktail guests.

Privately there were many problems. Much more than Paul, Jane required the company of other people, parties, and alcohol; Paul preferred privacy and a regular working schedule. And there were fundamental incompatibilities; although they shared a negative outlook for civilization, Jane preferred to escape from her own pessimism whenever possible, while Paul detached from his with cynicism.

Briefly in 1940, Paul and Jane lived together again at the Chelsea Hotel. When Paul accepted the commission for *Roots in the Soil*, Jane agreed to go along to New Mexico only if she could take Robert "Bu" Faulkner, a young New Englander and former Patchin Place resident working at the *New Yorker*. It was then that Jane told Paul that he was so gloomy she could be alone with him only for a short while.

Faulkner stayed with Paul and Jane throughout the spring in Albuquerque and accompanied them to Mexico. The trio settled in what Paul called a "melancholy" hacienda ten thousand feet up in Jajalpa, near Toluca and Mexico City. Mountains surrounded the house. As Paul sat upstairs in an abandoned room and looked out across the valley at the volcano of Toluca, he "remembered Thomas Mann's observation that being in the presence of a great natural spectacle impedes the desire to create" (*WS*:226).

Claiming the altitude in Jajalpa was making him sick, Paul left for Mexico City, where he met friends Lou and Peggy Reille (now Rosamond Bernier) and accompanied them to architect William Spratling's cliff-top beach house in Acapulco. After two weeks, Jane wired Paul that she and Faulkner planned to join him, so Paul rented a separate house, with a patio one hundred fifty feet long, shaded by avocado and lemon trees. A young Tennessee Williams, round-faced, sunburned, and wearing a floppy sombrero and a striped sailor sweater, "came around and knocked on the door one day, introduced himself, handed me a little letter from Lawrence Langner, and said he had done a play,

'The Battle of Angels.' I was sort of impressed, but I didn't get to know him at all." The Bowleses and Williams went to the beach and got drunk together. Then Williams left.[20] Williams recalled, "The one evening we spent together was given over almost entirely to the question of what he could eat in Acapulco that he could digest, and poor little Janie kept saying, 'Oh, Bubbles, if you'd just stick to cornflakes and fresh fruit!' and so on and so on. None of her suggestions relieved his dyspeptic humor."[21]

Jane decided she could not write in Acapulco. She caught a ride to Taxco with Gordon Sager and Morris Golde and there decided to rent a house, much to the annoyance of Paul, who had declared Taxco the one place in Mexico where he did not want to live. Relenting, he moved their furnishings, plus their newly acquired cat, duck, parrot, macaw, parakeet, armadillo, and two coatimundis from Acapulco to the mountain town.

Taxco was one of the better-known attractions in Mexico. Mexico itself in the 1930s had become a cheap vacation spot or a place to seek relief from economic distress in the United States, especially after leftist social criticism and the popularization of anthropology inspired enthusiasm for indigenous art and cultures. American historian Stuart Chase traveled to Mexico in 1931 after several years of studying and writing about waste and inefficiency in America's consumer culture and the machine age. He was attracted to Mexico by the murals of Diego Rivera and the opportunity to observe a handicraft economy unchanged since the Middle Ages. His *Mexico: A Study of Two Americas*, first published in August 1931, became so popular that it was reprinted twice that same month and again in October. American architect William Spratling was drawn by the certainty of undiscovered ruins. He settled first in Taxco, where he tried to revive interest in its ancient silver mines. Charles Flandrau had written about his travels in *Viva Mexico!*, which Paul read several times.

A town of fewer than fifteen thousand, Taxco lay south of Mexico City on the edge of the Sierra del Sur. There the artist Diego Rivera held Marxist discussions of the folk heritage of Mexico. American Hart Crane had written epic poetry in Taxco; Mexican artists Carlos Mérida, Miguel Covarrubias, David Siqueiros, Rufino Tamayo, María Izquierdo, and Juan O'Gorman and songwriter Gudy Cárdenas all lived and worked there. Folklorist Frances "Paca" Toor lived in Taxco and edited the bilingual journal *Mexican Folkways*, in which one could read articles on the women of Tehuantepec, the Tarahumara Indians, a regional dance called the *"Huapango,"* or transcriptions of *posadas*, accompanied by illustrations by Diego Rivera. *Folkways* extensively inspired Paul in his trip to Tehuantepec; in his translations in *View* of Tarahumara myths; in two delightful piano compositions he called *Huapangos*; and in the ballet *Pastorela*, which used *posadas* tunes as motival material.

Gordon Sager was an aspiring writer at the *New Yorker* when he met Faulkner in 1937.[22] In the summer of 1940, he ran into his friend by chance in Mexico City. Either at that point or several weeks later—in Acapulco—he joined Faulkner and Jane. As he describes it, "Taxco was of course an obvious mecca at that time for expatriates. . . . In any case, Europe was of course out, and would-be expatriates like myself had no great choice. Besides, Taxco was beautiful, relatively unspoiled despite the silversmithing, and eager to extend a welcome to foreigners. The climate was magnificent, and Mexico was astonishingly cheap. It was a potent combination. We did find a house and our life was quite unremarkable and not at all admirable, as expatriate lives in such places tend to be. Most of us tried to sandwich some work in, but few succeeded. We were all quite young."[23]

From his experiences that summer in Taxco, Sager wrote his first novel, *Run Sheep Run*. Sager denied that the characters were based on Jane, Paul, and Faulkner, yet it is difficult to read the novel without seeing Jane and Paul in protagonists Gillian and Andrew Greenfeather ("Greenfeather" being a good description of Paul's alter ego, the parrot). Andrew was "neat, immaculate, precise. He dressed, always, with absolute nicety; all his possessions had been carefully purchased: his snakeskin ties, his alligator shoes, his silk shirts, and handkerchiefs and linen. . . . He had brought with him his diverse collection of perfumes, his cuff-links and his four wristwatches, his Turkish cigarettes as well as the solid ambergris with which he scented them, and a faultless group of books."[24] The publisher, Simon and Schuster, asked for a statement from Jane and Paul saying that they did not object to its publication. Sager recalls, "It seemed to me that the only character in the book that attempted to be a portrait of a real person was Gillian; the others were all composites; I never saw the book as a roman à clef; but of course I gave Jane and Paul a copy, and they gravely informed Messrs S&S in writing that they had no objection."[25] Elsewhere, Sager reiterated that Kevin, the third character in the triangle, was not based on his friend Bob Faulkner, adding, "The only point of similarity was that Bob did indeed go to Mexico with Paul and Jane, and one of the things I was trying to describe was the astonishing impact someone like Jane could make."[26]

Bowles too has denied the novel's resemblance to reality. When responding to the suggestion that the book was unflattering, he replied, "Jane thought so, too. But that's true only if you assume it was true to life, which of course, it wasn't."[27] Yet when he first read it, "I rather objected to it, as every character in it had an actual counterpart, and for anyone who had lived in Taxco they were not hard to identify. So that in that sense it was a *roman à clef*. But then the author, having introduced his protagonists, embarks on a series of malicious inventions in the action, some of them (at least at that time) bordering on libel."[28]

The period Sager captured in *Run Sheep Run* saw Paul and Jane poised before hitting stride in each of their fields. Jane was working on her first novel; Paul was just about to launch into a period of active theater composing. Sager caught the brilliance of Andrew and Gillian, who were "witty, imaginative, highly—perhaps excessively? civilized. They were perceptive, they were articulate; they had odd theories on a number of exotic subjects. Beside them Kevin felt occasionally gauche, like a St. Bernard with two exquisite, thoroughly confident Persian cats." Kevin observed that "they loved each other very deeply (that fact was inescapable), although there would of course be no question of a conventional marriage."[29]

Paul found the mountain air of Taxco oppressive. In September 1940, he returned to New York for the first of several commissions that kept him there until he received his Guggenheim Fellowship in March 1941. He returned to Mexico that summer, and though he said he preferred the beach to the mountains, he and Jane settled once again in Taxco.

Initially Paul described Taxco as being "like the Riviera and a little like Morocco and a great deal like Andalusia and . . . very gay after all. We eat at the Comtesse de Charantenay's house and then she eats at ours."[30] Later, he wrote less cheerfully: "The foreign colony is made up still of about the same proportion of dopes, drunks and nice individuals. Then there are the hordes of Californian, Middle Western and Texan tourists who come afresh each day with guides from Mexico, have lunch and go back again. And a certain number of wealthier New York and Connecticut people who stop on their way down to Acapulco in their cars. But unless you seek them out, all these people, you never see them."[31]

Far from seeking people out, Paul went to great lengths to avoid them. Paul found it impossible to orchestrate and copy his music in the house with Jane, Faulkner, and Helvetia Perkins, an American woman to whom Jane was growing more and more attached. Perkins was born in Switzerland, raised in Illinois, and schooled in Connecticut. In 1940, she was forty-five and divorced with a daughter who was twenty-one. According to Maurice Grosser, Perkins "looked exactly like a Pekinese dog. She had bangs, round eyes, slightly bugged, couldn't have been nicer. She was bright and rich, a cultivated woman with marvelous French."

By June, Paul had found a remote studio below Taxco in which he was seized by the "old, accustomed paralysis." As he told Thomson, "The place in itself is nonexistent, and some days are so completely empty, the hours of events and the air of any suggestion of an idea, that one is tempted to look down at one's toes and think of life and death. Which is a very bad sign, as you know. At any rate, I can always truthfully say that nothing has happened, because no matter what did happen, nothing would really have happened at all."[32]

Paul was also having trouble writing some articles that he had promised *Modern Music.* "Whatever articles that were to exist should have been written . . . when I first arrived. Now I haven't an idea in my head, nor probably the power of concentration necessary for writing one. It's a period of muscular relaxation."[33] Whether he called it "muscular relaxation" or "paralysis," the feeling had appeared from the beginning of his visit. A poem dated "September 1940" obsesses on this sensation:

> Wait until the day
> When time's paralysis overtakes this house:
> . . . .
> Which year did motion cease?
> What was the breath? Explain the use of tears.
> If sound existed, would you cry for help?
> Tell in one word how long you will stand thus
> Maimed with fear of an end already come.[34]

Although Jane complained of being dragged away from civilization, in Taxco she wrote seriously each day when Paul had left for his studio. It was a slow process. She stood at the window for long stretches of time, sat down at a desk to write a few lines, scratched them out, and then returned to the window. Sometimes she showed Paul her work, sometimes not. For a while she took benzedrine to help her write, but she later threw away all that she had written under its influence. And when she was not writing, she was drinking.

At the first of August, Paul, Jane, Oliver Smith, Faulkner, and Helvetia Perkins left for three weeks in Acapulco, where they rented Bill Spratling's largely glass house, which "hung out over the ocean with the waves breaking below, and the whole sea, incadescent [*sic*], like molten metal."[35] In Brooklyn, Charles Henri Ford had decided that Paul was a hopeless romantic, and Oliver Smith reached much the same conclusion in Acapulco.

Back in Taxco, Paul became ill, suffering first from a general malaise and then three separate times from jaundice. In December a doctor sent Paul to a sanatorium in Cuernavaca, and while he was there, Jane brought him the completed manuscript to her first (and the only one to be published) novel, *Two Serious Ladies.* Although many people had heard Jane read aloud from the book, Paul was the first to read it from beginning to end. In his autobiography Paul writes, "I doubt that I told her how much I admired it, but perhaps I did. I hope so, as I know I found great fault with it for its orthography, grammar, and rhetoric" (*WS*:240). Jane disagreed with Paul when he told her it was a wonderful book. When he shouted at her about the "abject" state of the manuscript, she dismissively replied: "If there's a publisher, he'll take care of those things. They don't publish a book because it has perfect spelling, Gloompot."[36] Paul made several structural suggestions, advising her to omit one long section entirely. Jane accepted Paul's help along these lines without question, but the criticisms fueled feelings of competitiveness and unworthiness that shadowed the Bowleses' professional and personal relationship. Jane became convinced that Paul would never be satisfied with her work, no matter what he said to the contrary, nor was she happy with her work when she compared it to his. Years later, after publishing her long story, "Camp Cataract," she wrote to him, "Now that it has been fixed up, I *know* that it's the best thing I've ever done—and always was latently. But I don't think it would ever have been if you hadn't helped. I wish though that you had liked it more."[37]

Although Jane drew upon her Mexican and Central American experiences in *Two Serious Ladies*, for the most part the book explores Jane's childhood, her significant adult relationships, and herself. Each of its peculiar women characters is a magnification of a different aspect of her own personality. The characters of Mr. and Mrs. Copperfield embody the outer, visible sides of Jane and Paul. They are tourists, and though Mrs. Copperfield does not enjoy traveling as much as her husband, she wants to be near him.

> "I don't have winged feet like you," she said to him. "You must forgive me. I can't move about so easily. At thirty-three I have certain habits."
>
> "That's bad," he answered. "Of course, I have certain habits too—habits of eating, habits of sleeping, habits of working—but I don't think that is what you meant, was it?"
>
> "Let's not talk about it. That isn't what I meant, no."[38]

Mr. Copperfield has definite habits of working, eating, and sleeping and likes a daily routine regardless of where his "winged feet" take him. When Mrs. Copperfield deserts him, he writes her: "You . . . spend your life fleeing from your first fear toward your first hope. Be careful that you do not, through your own wiliness, end up always in the same position in which you began. . . . For God's sake, a ship leaving port is still a wonderful thing to see."[39]

Paul and Jane remained in Mexico until the spring of 1942, when Jane decided to return to New York with Perkins. Paul had a relapse of jaundice and again returned to the sanatorium in Cuernavaca, where he also had surgery to remove a tumor from his jaw. He wrote to Thomson:

> I have been ill so often lately that I am completely fed-up with this republic. . . . This is a charming country if one is full of vigor. Otherwise it turns easily into an almost perpetual nightmare. If I hadn't had previous years of Morocco and other hostile spots to prepare me more or less, by this time I think I should be completely mad. The way of staying sane is simply

that of accepting, accepting, one horror after another, and being thankful to be still alive. I suppose war is like that, but perhaps not, since one doesn't undergo it alone. Here there are no horrors unless one is alone. But I generally *am* alone.[40]

After his recovery, Paul traveled a bit more through central Mexico and then left for Holden Hall in Watkins Glen, bringing with him Antonio Álvarez, a young bullfighter, tall and handsome, who had been a friend of Oliver Smith and who had also appeared as a character in *Run Sheep Run*. Joining Jane and Helvetia Perkins, they stayed at Aunt Mary's throughout the summer, with Antonio occasionally being mistaken for a Japanese spy and Paul being arrested twice for "suspicious activity," which seems to have consisted mainly of speaking in a foreign language. Thus did the war intrude itself on his restful country retreat.

That autumn they left Holden Hall. When Marcel Duchamp moved out of architect Friedrich Kiesler's penthouse on Fourteenth Street, Paul was happy to move in with his piano and take advantage of the view of the city and the harbor. Still, he spent most of his free time with Jane and Helvetia at Helvetia's home on Waverly Place. Jane's book was published in the spring of 1943, and although reviews were generally negative, her friends and a few critics pronounced it brilliant. Jane continued in her agonizing way to write.

Jane and Helvetia entertained often, sometimes at Helvetia's Vermont farmhouse, and many friends from New York came to visit, along with Paul. Grosser, who spent a great deal of time with them in Vermont, remembers, "The only thing that was difficult was that for Jane the cocktail hour was sacred, and one had to respect it, which meant that you'd never know quite when it was going to end. Then at dinner they'd produce a rare steak, whenever Jane thought the cocktail hour was over. By that time, Jane had usually drunk so much she couldn't eat. Jane was a very heavy drinker."

Paul had not yet found his way out from under the feelings of malaise and paralysis that had plagued him in Mexico, and his increasing estrangement from Jane left him beleaguered. In September 1942, he paid a visit to Paul Peters, a staffer for *Life* Magazine, which had done a piece on the Bowleses in Mexico. Bowles spent from ten in the evening until four the next morning talking with Peters, who found him: "Sick, he's very, very sick. You know that awful sickness that goes with: 'Yes, I know I'm all tangled up. But I don't really need analysis. I know what's the matter with me. I ought to be able to help myself' . . . so many secret fears, and so sick. Quietly crazy, really: under a charming, gay, extroverted outside, really crazy."[41]

Then early in 1945, Oliver Smith discovered a building on West Tenth Street and persuaded Paul, Jane, and Helvetia to lease it with him. Helvetia took the lease for the second floor for herself and Jane, Oliver the third, and Paul, in repetition of childhood, took the top floor, where he lived alone, along with a Steinway piano and a skylight. As Paul described it, "Work and sleep were private, while eating and entertaining were largely communal" (*WS*:259). Jane finished her play *In the Summer House* there, and Paul went through a phenomenally productive period as a theater composer, music critic, and translator and began to write short stories. The individual but communal living arrangement turned out so happily for Paul and Jane that they maintained it for nearly three years and resumed it later in Tangier. Detached apartments offered a way to enjoy each other's company, to gossip, to share their work with each other, and yet to protect one another from the complications of their separate lives. It was the physical expression of the complicated emotional bond Paul and Jane both addressed in their fiction.

In the mid-1940s, Paul became close friends with composer Peggy Glanville-Hicks. Peggy's husband, Stanley Bate, was also a composer, but according to Paul, he was a brute who regularly beat Peggy, "tossing her around the apartment" (*WS*:259). Paul explained the relationship by their very similar musical tastes. Yet "I Heard the Sea," a piece of music bearing the inscription "for Peggy Bate" in Bowles's handwriting but not published until 1984 as "Secret Words," suggests a deeper affection for Peggy.[42] The song in 3/4 time moves gently with arpeggiated chords in both hands and beautifully illustrates Bowles's talent for fitting lyrics to music while retaining the natural rhythm of speech, particularly in such swiftly moving passages as "Oh, sing a song of isles where we might have wandered." The lyrics, which Bowles also wrote, explore a romantic theme. They also continue Bowles's romantic fixation on an earlier, simpler time — the mythical lost childhood. They hint, as well, at the restlessness that was to take him across the ocean to Morocco:

> Far within your face I saw the night
> And in the night I saw the stars
> And then the stars became your eyes
> Entreating tender things of me
> But that can never, never be
> Because I saw the night within your face.
>
> Oh, sing a song of isles where we might have wandered.
> So long ago.
> Sing a song of years when the earth was younger.
> Days we'll never know.
>
> Far beyond your words I heard the sea.
> And on the sea I heard the wind.

And then the wind became your voice
Repeating tender things to me.
But that shall never, never be
Because beyond your words I heard the sea.

The Sheltering Sky

In the 1940s, the crest of a wave of interest in primitivism that had begun at the turn of the century rolled over Manhattan and submerged it in a flood of exoticism. The unique situation of Morocco's International Zone in World War II made it a focus of public thirst for intrigue. The most stylish of New York's café society, people who still dressed for dinner, crowded into El Morocco's zebra-skin booths and sat on leather and rosewood benches. Errol Flynn, Gary Cooper, Clark Gable, Cary Grant, Libby Holman, Mrs. William Randolph Hurst, James Russell Lowell, and Elsa Maxwell all were photographed among El Morocco's cacti and palm trees. At the same time, many jazz artists were exploring the North African roots of their heritage through such pieces as Dizzy Gillespie's "Night in Tunisia." At the height of an American obsession with primitive societies, Paul had an advantage. His apartment was full of Moroccan rugs, snakeskins, musical instruments, recordings, paintings, and objets d'art he had collected on his travels. A concert pianist who premiered some of Bowles's Latin American pieces once visited his apartment after a concert. "I remember his guests, all men, sitting on low cushions in a kind of tropical decorated room."[43] Yet Paul's enthusiasm was serious and most of his knowledge firsthand. What distinguished him from most of his countrymen was the extreme to which he had carried his fascination with other cultures.

After several years of experimenting with short stories while living in New York, Paul began to dream again of Morocco and knew he must return. By 1947, he had completed nearly a dozen short stories and hoped to publish them in a collection but discovered that publishers were unwilling to take on such a project from an author who had not yet written a novel. Through acquaintances at Dial Press, he met Helen Strauss of the William Morris Agency, who late in May secured for him a contract for Doubleday for a novel. Contract in hand, Bowles planned his return to Morocco to write. Memories of North Africa engulfed his consciousness. On a Fifth Avenue bus, he formed these visions into a scenario. Bowles believed his book "would write itself" once he had "established the characters and spilled them out onto the North African scene" (*WS*:275), and by the time he reached midtown Manhattan, he "had made all the most important decisions about the novel" (*WS*:275). The most important of these decisions was that the novel would write itself.

Bowles thought his novel would be similar to "A Distant Episode," the story he had just published in *Partisan Review*. Like *The Sheltering Sky*, this story had been conceived "on the road" — more precisely, on the subway.[44] In this tale, as in many others, he created a confrontation between rationality and sensualism, using the stark and savage setting of North Africa to arouse sensations: as readers we smell the rotting fruit and burning olive oil in the desert town; we hear the desert flute; we feel the slice of the knife blade. In both the story he had completed and the novel he was about to write, Bowles placed intellectuals among savages and then followed their transformation from intellectual to sensual awareness. Thus in his own way, Bowles transported the classic American confrontation between "civilization" and "savagery" across the globe, replacing a geographical frontier with a nomadic intersection of Western and Eastern cultures.

In "A Distant Episode," a linguist returns to Aïn Tadouirt after a ten-year absence. Having learned the Moghrebi dialect, he plans to study its variations. He hopes to renew his friendship with a café keeper, Hassan Ramani (named for Bowles's friend in Algiers), but on his first night in town, he is told that Ramani is deceased. A local resident leads him out of the village into the desert, and there the linguist is accosted by a group of Reguibat, the fiercest of all the desert tribes. Even the professor has heard the sayings: "The Reguiba is a cloud across the face of the sun"; "When the Reguiba appears the righteous man turns away" (*CS*:44). The Reguibat capture the professor, beat him, and tie him up. The next morning before he is fully conscious, a Reguiba squeezes the professor's nostrils together, pulls out his tongue, and cuts it off. The Reguibat dress him in strings of tin cans tied together and train him to dance for their amusement.

After his mutilation, the professor exists in a "state permitting no thought." He knows no language, no words. He eats, defecates, and dances. Only when the Reguibat sell him into a household where he happens to see a calendar written in French does he begin to hear the sound of words inside his head again and to think of time's passing. When the Reguiba severed the professor's use of language, he ceased to function as an intellectual being; his stay in the desert was timeless, with one day much as the one before it. The return to language, to time, and to intellectual effort brings the pain of self-consciousness. "A Distant Episode" concludes with the professor's escape from consciousness. He runs into the desert, jumping wildly in what Bowles calls "an access of terror."

Bowles, too, was fleeing civilization as he prepared to leave New York. Yet contrary to the story, in which the desert represented a retreat from language and civilization, Bowles sought the desert in order to sharpen his talent for writing. It was a journey both terrifying and exhilarating, and it was with an exhilaration approaching terror that Bowles, the composer, recovered the sounds that words made and began to put them on paper.

When asked about the similarities of Port, the protagonist of *The Sheltering Sky*, to the professor in "A Distant Episode," Bowles responded, "They're all the professor."[45] So too is the author himself. Like Mark Twain's Royal Nonesuch in *The Adventures of Huckleberry Finn*, the professor expressed the plight of the artist as showman, and Bowles, who wrote "A Distant Episode" in 1945, knew he had amused and entertained in the theaters of New York long enough. At times, the music he composed meant no more to him than the jangling sounds of the tin cans meant to the professor. He had cut out his own tongue to survive in New York, and now, nearly thirty-seven, he found a way to speak again.

The title *The Sheltering Sky* was inspired by memories of childhood and of the Sahara. One of his favorite records as a child had been "Under the Sheltering Palms." What had intrigued him most about the song was what he called the "strange" word *sheltering*. He had asked himself, "What did the palm trees shelter people from, and how sure could they be of such protection?" In this novel, Bowles transforms the vast, expansive sky of the North African desert into a claustrophobic, close-hanging canopy that is a thin shield from the terrors lurking behind and beyond it. The sky exists not as space extending ever outward but rather as a flat mask, a veil for unimaginable horror. The idea of shelter is not of a place in which one finds sanctuary and safety but rather of protection from beyond, from terrible forces, horrible secrets. The central question of the novel is the same one that had fascinated Paul as a child: From what are people being sheltered, and how certain can they be of that protection?

Having settled all the essential aspects of his book preparatory to the actual writing, Bowles resolved to let it rest. In May 1947, he and Gordon Sager, who had just published *Run Sheep Run*, boarded a ship for North Africa. After landing in Casablanca, Paul quickly left for Fez. From there he went north to Tangier, then crossed the sea to Algeciras, Spain, and continued to Córdoba and Ronda before returning to Tangier. During this two-to-three-month period, he repeatedly ran into a Mrs. Perrin and her son. The two seemed strange and thus interesting to Bowles.[46] He had decided to draw the "descriptive detail" for his novel from his own daily experiences, using whatever happened "during the day of writing, regardless of whether the resulting juxtaposition was apposite or not" (*WS*:278), and so he included in his novel the couple and the coincidence of meeting them throughout North Africa and Spain.

In Tangier, Paul settled in the Farhar hotel outside the city on the Mountain and wrote Jane to join him as soon as possible. It was not long before he had purchased a house with a view in the upper medina, the native quarter of the city. While he was having plumbing installed and repairs made, he left for Fez and then for the Sahara, reacquainting himself with the land he had left fourteen years earlier.

The characters Paul chose for his novel were fictional representations of himself and his wife, Jane. He resolved to work in a somewhat unconscious manner, clearing his mind of all conscious content and letting the unconscious take over as much as was possible. In this way, the characters Port and Kit, who began as painfully close representations of himself and Jane, acquired autonomous identities.[47]

The Sheltering Sky, a novel in three sections, tells about the troubled relationship between Kit and Port Moresby, two urban New Yorkers in their midtwenties who are emotionally estranged from each other. It is the story of the meeting of two disparate cultures: the modern, intellectual American with the timeless, sensual Saharan—a culture Bowles visited, remembered, and then re-created in opposition to a world he hoped to leave behind. The novel is also a travel book about an inner journey through states of consciousness. Finally, though least important to the novel, it is about Jane and Paul Bowles.

More than the relationship between Kit and Port, *The Sheltering Sky* discusses the inability to relate. The protagonist for the first two sections is Port, and he is the impetus for much of the action in the book. He is a tall, thin, almost haggard young man with a feverish aspect to his intense self-consciousness. Port Moresby is also the name of a city in Papua, New Guinea—the southernmost port in the Indian Ocean—a "small joke," according to Paul. In his high school literary magazine, Paul had published a poem called "Night Song at Papua." The poem describes an arid, salt-caked landscape through which the narrator wanders "hot and fevered," and the last lines of this juvenile poem presage the "sheltering sky" of the novel: "Lying dark under the burning moon / The air simmers like a brazen bowl; And I cannot move from thirst."[48]

Port and Kit Moresby are traveling through North Africa with a mutual friend, Tunner, a handsome, vacuous character who serves as a foil for Kit in her struggles with her loyalty to Port. Kit is small, thin, and nervous in an attractive way. She sees the world in terms of an elaborate system of omens. Only superstition saves Kit from complete inertia; she uses her omens to propel her through life. Without them she would be overcome by indecision. Like Jane Bowles, Kit feels herself at the mercy of other people: she guides her life by reacting to the signals she gets from those around her and is personally affected by everything that happens.

Port, on the other hand, is devoid of personal perspective. He is not a tourist but a traveler: "The difference is partly one of time, he would explain. Whereas the tourist generally hurries back home at the end of a few weeks or months, the traveller, belonging no more to one place than to the next, moves slowly, over periods of years, from one part of the earth to another. Indeed, he would have found it difficult to tell, among the many places he had lived, precisely where he had felt most at home."[49]

Travel emphasizes the Moresbys' emotional and philosophical rootlessness. Each feels adrift in a world of relative values. Port is not at home anywhere because he is not at home in himself; he is an other-directed person, "at home everywhere and nowhere."[50] Port's way of coping is to reject everything, "to deny all purpose to the phenomenon of existence." Kit distrusts her own judgment and fears the responsibility of decisions. Port is equally fearful of making the wrong move, and so they travel, staying always on the outside of life, with no destination to reach and no home to which they may return.

The novel concerns itself with things that are hidden, sheltered, or false. Although the desert is so important to the novel as to constitute a major character, the dominant metaphorical image is the sky, and a discussion between Kit and Port establishes Bowles's theme of shelter:

> "The sky here's very strange. I often have the sensation when I look at it that it's a solid thing up there, protecting us from what's behind." . . .
> "But what *is* behind?"
> "Nothing, I suppose. Just darkness. Absolute night." (*TSS*:101)

Kit and Port's relationship is full of pretenses and masks. In a minor disagreement, Port reproaches Kit—"with a certain ferocity which on the surface appeared feigned, but as Kit looked at him she felt that on the contrary he actually was dissimulating the violence he felt. She did not say the withering things that were on the tip of her tongue" (*TSS*:17). Both Kit and Port hold back certain truths from each other. The two characters are so interrelated, so dependent on each other, that to speak these truths might disturb the balancing of forces they have built, like wooden sticks in a child's game.

Port finds solace in Kit's presence. She is the only person to whom he is even remotely connected, and he needs her existence to remind him of his own. Kit validates his existence, and were she to leave, he would not be sure of his own presence in the world. He fantasizes about Kit, and in his fantasies, Kit is a "silent onlooker" whose watching soothes and calms him (*TSS*:40). Yet Port cannot open himself to Kit. He is "unable to break out of the cage into which he had shut himself, the cage he had built long ago to save himself from love" (*TSS*:100). To express love would mean to open himself to vulnerability, exposure, unmasking: to come out from behind his shelter. Most of all, it would mean accepting "emotional responsibilities." To be involved with Kit, especially, would entail enormous responsibility, because Kit accepts so little responsibility herself.

Kit uses Port as her lodestar. He serves her as do omens and all the people in her life—she uses him to make decisions for her. Knowing this, Port tries to avoid imposing his will on her and attempts to disguise his own wishes, so that Kit will be forced to reveal hers.

Port and Kit have more obvious reasons for being together. Port finds "her ability to decipher motivations [is] considerable. . . . Their long, rambling, supremely personal conversations always made him feel better" (*TSS*:92, 95). In turn, Kit feels there are times when she cannot do without Port. "In really bad moments she relied on him utterly, not because he was an infallible guide under such circumstances, but because a section of her consciousness annexed him as a buttress, so that in part she identified herself with him" (*TSS*:83).

Like Paul and Jane Bowles, Port and Kit are very much alike but not identical. Like a photograph with its negative, they manifest opposite aspects of essentially the same personal core, a fact that they both realize and deplore. Kit reflects, "In spite of their so often having the same reactions, the same feelings, they would never reach the same conclusions, because their respective aims in life were almost diametrically opposed" (*TSS*:99–100).

Port knows the source of the distance between them—their mutual unwillingness to make the first move, to risk the responsibility of independent action—yet he has not yet given up. "Always he held the fresh hope that she, too, would be touched in the same way as he by solitude and the proximity to infinite things. . . . Only if she were able to become as he was, could he find his way back to love" (*TSS*:100). Estranged from each other and from life itself, Kit tells Port, "We've never managed, either one of us, to get all the way into life" (*TSS*:101).

Kit and Port have fallen into a fatalism similar to that of the Muslim culture through which they are traveling. They use their fatalism as a reason for being carried along by events over which they feel they have little control and in which they exercise no control. They have resigned themselves to the eventuality of their own behavior without self-examination or philosophizing. They simply let their lives go unanalyzed save for noting their passage. Port fancies himself a writer but cannot write. He feels so long as he is living his life, he cannot write about it. To write as Port wishes demands absolute detachment, a point toward which he is traveling but has not yet reached. Port has no itinerary, no agenda, and no timetable. Indeed, he has already become so detached from any kind of normal existence that the concept of time itself has become meaningless. He has "made the fatal error of coming hazily to regard time as non-existent. One year was like another year. Eventually everything would happen" (*TSS*:133).

Through the characters of Kit and Port, Bowles embarks on the book's existential itinerary. Bowles's narrative moves from ordinary waking states to feverish halucinations to insanity. Port wakes from a dream at the beginning of the book and travels through several distinct stages of consciousness or awareness, passing from a state of nonbeing to a passive state of being, in which even waiting is too active for him. He lies in bed, "paralyzed in the airless room, not waiting for twilight but staying as he was until it should come" (*TSS*:12).

Port's dream recurs at several points in the novel. In his dream, he is traveling on a train that keeps going faster. He is offered the chance of living his life over again, and he refuses. Then he changes his mind, but by that point it is too late. He will never be able to go back to his youth nor to "smell the spring the way it used to smell when [he] was a kid" (*TSS*:18). Later in the book, Port realizes the dream has been "an epitome of life itself. The unsureness about the *no* and the *yes* was the inevitable attitude one had if one tried to consider the value of that life, and the hesitation was automatically resolved by one's involuntary decision to refuse participation in it" (*TSS*:74).

After several chapters, Port repeats the thought process, in nearly identical terms. "And it occurred to him that a walk through the countryside was a sort of epitome of the passage through life itself. One never took the time to savor the details; one said: another day, but always with the hidden knowledge that each day was unique and final, that there would never be a return, another time" (*TSS*:132).

These two metaphors for life are dependent on Paul's favorite childhood activities: train rides and long walks through the country near his house or on his grandparents' farm. The nostalgia that train rides and country walks evoke in Port clearly comes from Bowles's own experience of the emotion. Port's feeling of not being "inside of life," of having involuntarily "refuse[d] participation," is equally autobiographical.

Port's dream returns in a third form in the climactic scene of the novel. Kit and Port have traveled far south into a remote part of the Sahara where a French military outpost is the only available resting place. Port has already had some premonitions of his death: he has lost his passport, the "official proof of his existence." He falls ill; he has typhoid and becomes delirious with fever and racking chills. He is barely aware of his surroundings, but for Port, the past few weeks had been "one strict, undeviating course inland to the desert, and now he was very nearly at the center" (*TSS*:198).

As Port becomes decreasingly lucid, he moves into a state of mind where words cease to serve him. In contrast to the "strict, undeviating course" he followed to reach this point, his experience becomes nonlinear and irrational. Dimensions change, and he is in "exile from the world" (*TSS*:222). He experiences sensory distortion: he hears screams (they are his own, but he does not realize that); he sees spots of light; he feels as if his fingers are being thinly sliced along the edge of a sharp razor blade. He is in the state of nonbeing from which he had just returned when the novel opened. For a moment, Port rallies and tells Kit he has been trying to get back, to her, to life, but he feels himself falling farther and farther away: "Kit! All these years I've been living for you. I didn't know it, and now I do. I know it! But now you're going away" (*TSS*:217).

It is too late. As Port's head collapses onto Kit's chest, he closes his eyes, "and for a moment had the illusion of holding the world in his arms—a warm world all tropics, lashed by storm. 'No, no, no, no, no, no, no,' he said. It was all he had the strength to say. But even if he had been able to say more, still he would have said only, 'No, no, no, no'" (*TSS*:217–18). We do not know, when Port says "no, no, no" whether he is rejecting death or the way he lived his life, but at this point, it does not matter.

This is the center toward which Port has been traveling, the blankness of the Sahara, "the famous silence of the Sahara," where there is "no one in sight. There was nothing" (*TSS*:202). Life's illusion of an infinitude of possibilities for action is gone. He has reached the point that Sigmund Freud called the aim of all life: death, quiescence, utter peace, nothingness. In the chills of his fever, Port freezes to death in the middle of the desert. He has reached his destination, and as Gertrude Stein would have said, there is no there there.

Kit mourns as she sobs in Port's arms, until "within her, deeper than the weeping for the wasted years, she found a ghastly dread all formed and growing" (*TSS*:218). She is alone, without anyone to structure her existence. Port will never be conscious of her again, and so, "in reality, it would be she who would have ceased to exist" (*TSS*:237).

Kit packs a small bag with toiletries, emblems of civilization, and heads farther into the desert. She draws a curtain in her mind between her current state of being and the painful events of Port's death. "Like an insect spinning its cocoon thicker and more resistant, her mind would go on strengthening the thin partition, the danger spot of her being" (*TSS*:267). In the desert, a caravan approaches, and Kit asks to be taken along with it and the two riders at the head of the procession. Kit becomes the sexual slave of the younger of the two, Belqassim. She, too, cries "No, no, no!" as he first embraces her but then acquiesces to her helplessness. With the Bedouin, she travels only at night. Kit has pierced the fabric of the sky and passed beyond it into the absolute silence and night of the other side.

As Belqassim's victim, Kit reaches the logical conclusion of the way she has lived her life. In sexual bondage, she finds freedom from responsibility, guilt, and decisions of any sort. She is delighted "not to be responsible — not to have to decide anything of what was to happen!" (*TSS*:231). Belqassim takes her to his home where at first he disguises her as a young boy. Eventually he marries her. Kit no longer speaks, nor does she care to. She lives only for the times when Belqassim comes to her chamber, "her mind empty of everything save the memory or anticipation of Belqassim's presence" (*TSS*:292). She grows accustomed to acting without consciousness. "She did only the things she found herself already doing" (*TSS*:276).

But there comes a night when Belqassim does not visit her, and another night follows that, and Kit begins to fear that a servant is poisoning her. She begins her return to civilization, and like the professor in "A Distant Episode," the first step is recovering language. "In another minute life would be painful. The words were coming back, and inside the wrappings of the words there would be thoughts lying there" (*TSS*:302). She finds her way to a telegraph office and signals: "CANNOT GET BACK." As strangers help her prepare for her journey out of the desert, she struggles until she can no longer avoid the pain. She gives up, throws her head back, and stares at the sky. "Someone once had said to her that the sky hides the night behind it, shelters the person beneath from the horror that lies above. Unblinking, she fixed the solid emptiness, and the anguish began to move in her. At any moment the rip can occur, the edges fly back, and the giant maw will be revealed" (*TSS*:312).

Kit has gone completely mad.

Port and Kit have found what lies beyond the sheltering sky, and it is both nothingness and chaos. Port is headed toward death from the moment he is introduced in the novel. Although this knowledge makes him sad, it is not terrible because he knows death will release him from pain. At the moment of his death, he is aware only of a sense of merging: "A black star appears, a point of darkness in the night sky's clarity. Point of darkness and gateway to repose. Reach out, pierce the fine fabric of the sheltering sky, take repose" (*TSS*:235).

Port returns to the nothingness of death, to a state of peaceful repose. Kit's return is to life, awareness, and pain. Confined to Belqassim's chamber, she has been able to live a limited and therefore painless existence. Her return to the chaos of civilization forces her to face more pain than she can bear.

The Sheltering Sky quickly established Bowles as one of the new American existentialists."[51] Orville Prescott in the *New York Times* called the novel "unquestionably repellent in its subject-matter" yet "unquestionably compelling in its manner." He praised Bowles as an "accomplished technician in fiction, a master of narrative tension and of emotional atmosphere," and stated that Bowles was capable of holding the reader's complete attention while instilling a "sense of apprehension as a dentist with his drill boring closer and closer to an acutely vulnerable nerve"—unwittingly suggesting that Bowles was indeed his father's son. Prescott's conclusion that a "society populated by a large proportion of Ports and Kits would be in a dangerously advanced state of decomposition" was exactly the conclusion Bowles reached about modern civilization.[52] Tennessee Williams suggested that many readers might enjoy the novel as a "first-rate story of adventure by a really first-rate writer," without suspecting that it was a spiritual allegory, a "mirror of what is most terrifying and cryptic within the Sahara of moral nihilism, into which the race of man now seems to be wandering blindly."[53]

The book was a best-seller for eleven weeks in 1950, for Bowles had hit on a theme that resonated in the postwar world.[54] He wrote of lovers who could not love, who lived lives full of anxiety, trapped in cages of their own making. They ran to escape a world of absurd situations and people, and they met absurdity at every turn. Alienated from each other and from themselves, they rushed headlong toward death and nothingness, more afraid of making decisions than of the dreadful consequences that resulted from failing to decide. Bowles had written an existential travelogue that hit upon all the guideposts of the new philosophy in a chilling, compelling narrative. If for no other reason than this, he had produced a twentieth-century masterpiece.

Experimenting with Death

Death was a subject for the subconscious to handle, so for Port's death scene, Bowles decided to experiment with *majoun*, a jamlike paste made of *kif* (finely ground and sifted Moroccan marijuana). After eating some, he climbed to a mountain ledge and lay in the sun until the drug took effect. Returning to his cottage at sundown, he lit a fire and sat staring into it, with the sound of the waves below and the strong winds in the cypresses around him, and imagined Port's death. From this intense experience, Bowles took notes, and the next day he wrote much of the scene for his book, incorporating his fireside vigil into Port's last vision of a world "all tropics, lashed by storm."

In Morocco, cannabis derivatives such as *kif* and *majoun* were readily available, and Bowles availed himself of them. Although he had been in situations where marijuana was available for more than a decade, his steady use of cannabis did not begin until after his return to Morocco in the late 1940s. Of *majoun*, Paul wrote, "I felt that I had come upon a fantastic secret:

to change worlds, I had only to spread a bit of jam on a biscuit and eat it" (*WS*:280). He decided the best diet to accompany *majoun* was a clear soup, followed by a small steak, salad, and hot tea; the best time of day, twilight. "It is a delicate operation, the taking of *majoun*. Since its success or failure can be measured only in purely subjective terms, it is also a supremely egotistical pastime. Above all, there must be no interruptions, no surprises; everything must come about according to the timetable furnished by the substance itself" (*WS*:280).

Bowles continued his experiments with *majoun* and with other drugs (except alcohol, which he had abandoned in 1939). He showed equal interest in trance states brought on by music or hypnosis, and once in New York he and Jane had held a dinner party for John Huston, who was directing *No Exit*, to display Huston's abilities with hypnosis. Neither Paul nor Jane was able to fall into a hypnotic trance. Paul concluded that although he was eager to have the experience, in actuality he feared it: "Hypnosis involves a dubious action: the absolute relinquishing of power to another" (*WS*:268).

One of the strangest drugs Paul experimented with was *fasoukh*, which was reputed to have the power to intoxicate through its odor alone. In the Djema El Fna (the market) in Marrakech, Paul reported, "I remember smelling something and it gave me a very strange feeling when I smelled it and a promise, as it were, of something unknown. I didn't know what it was . . . but it was as though I'd smelled it before. . . . And I took someone named Abdul Kada ben Hammed ben Said there the next day . . . and recognized the odor and said, 'That's what I want to buy,' and he said, 'oh, that's bad, you don't want to buy that. Nobody nice buys such things.' . . . So of course, I insisted and got it."[55] According to Moroccans, *fasoukh*, a sticky tarlike resin made of dates, tree resin, and various other substances, among them rumored to be blood, had magical properties that could be used to ward off evil or to call evil to someone. Paul experimented with the *fasoukh* to see exactly what its effects might be: "In a closed room. I think there were eight people, without warning. I burned it. I gave them a bit of it to put on their cigarettes, and said smell and wave their hands. Everyone felt very strange in about ten minutes and everyone began looking at everyone else and said do you feel strange in your—and then one would say elbows and the other would say shoulders and then they all agreed that they felt dislocated in the joints everywhere."[56]

In Tangier, Paul could perform experiments that took their final shape in his fiction yet could remain ever the observer. At different times and under varying conditions, cannabis may erase psychological barriers or intensify them. As a traveler, Paul enjoyed the feeling of looking in from the outside at the culture in which he found himself. By using cannabis, he could observe others and himself. Cannabis seemingly magnified his sensations so that he could better analyze them, but it also left a part of himself detached from the experience. With *kif* he was aware of a "splitting of the self . . . the awareness and non-awareness at the same time," and he found the sensation interesting.[57] "I chain-smoked, all day, in a way I couldn't have done with tobacco."[58]

Paul had spent almost a year in Morocco by the time Jane joined him. Part of that time she spent in Paris studying Arabic. As soon as she arrived, she came up solid against Paul's new discovery. At a dinner party, she ignored his warnings about the strong effects of the sticky *majoun* that she ate like candy. Indeed, Paul was "the only European present who had had any experience with the substance." After going to bed, Jane endured a terrible, tortured sleep that seemed "ten nights long." Paul writes, "Illogically enough, from that day on she remained an implacable enemy of all forms of cannabis. The fact that her experience had been due solely to an overdose seemed to her beside the point" (*WS*:286).

Jane was not the only one of Paul's circle to suffer ill effects from the drug. Painter Robert Rauschenberg, living in Tangier in 1951, ate several helpings of Bowles's friend Ahmed Yacoubi's *majoun* one night and reportedly never forgave Paul for the episode, particularly since Paul seemed only to be making things worse with such comments as, "Yes, it sometimes has these terrible effects on people. . . . There have been a number of suicides."[59] Rauschenberg thought Ahmed had put a spell on him.[60] William Burroughs and others who met Paul in Tangier claimed that Paul and Ahmed often deliberately gave *majoun* to people and enjoyed their discomfort. Christopher Isherwood and Don Bachardy visited Bowles for a weekend in 1955 and had their first experience with *majoun*—"We didn't know what we were in for. Paul's friend Ahmed put hashish into these wonderful Moroccan pipes, so we were smoking it as well as eating it in *majoun*. When it hit us we were flying high as kites."[61] Ned Rorem remembers eating *majoun* "indiscriminately" when he was already drunk. Rorem had "hideous dreams" in which two or three seconds seemed like centuries. "I've never quite forgiven him for allowing me, though of course it was my fault, not his."[62] Perhaps Paul was simply a catalyst for these experiments. Perhaps his error was in failing to restrain his friends from indiscriminate consumption, or perhaps he had too much curiosity to do so. And in typical Bowles fashion, he refrained from intervening once the experiment was under way.

Jane in Morocco

Jane arrived in Morocco early in 1948, and Paul quickly took her to Fez, where he remained while she and a friend, Cory, went to Marrakech to see the festival *amara*, at a spot sacred to a local saint, Moulay Brahim. To see this *amara*, the two women had to climb a steep mountainside, through very rough country. After about half an hour, they heard sounds, which they assumed to be part of the festival, but were astonished to see thirty men running down the mountain toward them, eyes glazed and staring straight ahead at nothing, mouths screaming and dripping with blood. Unknowingly, Jane had come upon the brotherhood of Aissaoua, who had just finished a ceremony of sacrificing and devouring a live animal. They were probably in a trance state and completely unaware of the two women. The Aissaoua, followers of the cult of Sidi Aissa, wound themselves with knives while in drum-and-dance-induced trance states. Paul speaks of the men "ripping apart" a live bull and then eating it raw, but it is unclear as to what this ceremony might have been.[63]

Jane had prepared herself for life in Morocco, had even learned the language, but the sight of men with bloodied faces running headlong past her was terrifying. It was a far cry from Paul's first exposure to a ritual cult practice, safely sitting in a café in Fez, as hundreds of Aissaoua wound rhythmically through the streets.

Eventually, Jane found her own way to the center of Moroccan life through her involvement with several Moroccan women, their families, and their usually private domestic activities. She shared her experiences with Paul, but he had little interest in that aspect of Morocco. Although Paul and Jane traveled together through Morocco for a couple of years, their reactions to the country seldom coincided. Jane preferred Tangier and spoke the Tangier dialect; Paul gravitated to Fez and clung to Fez vocabulary and pronunciation. Paul's interest in Fez was "a touristic one," in that he enjoyed observing the city. Jane liked Tangier, because there she had Moroccan friends and could feel a part of the life of the people.

Throughout their first few "nomadic" years in Morocco, both Paul and Jane worked hard at their writing (*WS*:284). By May 1948, Paul had finished *The Sheltering Sky* and had ideas for other stories, while Jane was working on her long story "Camp Cataract." For years Paul assumed that Jane wrote so little because she was undisciplined. When they were in Fez in April and Paul was working on *The Sheltering Sky* and Jane on "Camp Cataract," Paul became more aware of her patterns and wrote to Peggy Glanville-Hicks: "Jane and I have communicating rooms, and as soon as I type she types. I imagine that she has got a good deal of work done too these past two weeks."[64] Later he recalled that Jane's constant questions for help with the construction details of a bridge perplexed him:

> After three or four mornings I became aware that something was wrong: she was still at the bridge. I got up and went into her room. We talked for a while

about the problem, and I confessed my mystification. "Why do you have to *construct* the damned thing?" I demanded. "Why can't you just say it was there and let it go at that?" She shook her head. "If I don't know how it was built, I can't see it."

This struck me as incredible. It had never occurred to me that such considerations could enter into the act of writing. Perhaps for the first time I had an inkling of what Jane meant when she remarked, as she often did, that writing was "so *hard*." (*WS*:287)

Writing was an excruciating activity for Jane because it involved conscious "constructions" and decisions. She tried to visualize every element of the scenario, to decide consciously exactly what each character would say in each specific situation. Thomson once asked Jane about her writing, and she produced a menu with notations of what all the characters had been eating.[65] Paul's approach to writing was the opposite. He let chance form the details and determine the action of the characters. Where Jane's writing was a constructive process, in which she labored over each detail, building her fiction brick by brick, Paul's process was deconstructive. He eliminated the conscious control on which Jane's work depended and used his characters to strip away layers of his own personality.

Much of Bowles's fiction describes the process of diving through the layers of the mind. Three of his four novels depend on a journey through the underworld or the unconscious for their plot. In *The Sheltering Sky*, each section is a further descent into the unconscious mind, such that by the final chapter, the reader sees Kit drop into complete insanity. Jane could never have written such a book, because she could not have descended so freely with each day's writing.

The edge of life on which Jane balanced was a cliff beyond which there was only madness. In her journal she once wrote, "Is it writing I'm putting off, or was it always something else—a religious sacrifice? The only time I wrote well, when I passed through the inner door, I felt guilt. I must find that again."[66] For Jane, a journey through the inner door might be one from which there was no return, but Paul passed easily through the inner door as he began writing each day and returned when he closed the cover of his notebook and quite easily distinguished the inner and outer parts of himself from each other. Such a complete separation was impossible for Jane. Eventually writing became more than hard; it became virtually impossible. What was a therapeutic activity for Paul, a way to reach that part of himself he had closed off to the outer world, was for Jane a glimpse into a world of terrible forces that she did not want to recognize, forces that controlled her all the more because she was afraid to confront them directly.

That summer of 1948 Paul received a wire from Tennessee Williams asking him to work on a score for *Summer and Smoke*. He left for New York in mid-July, leaving Jane at the Hotel Villa de France in Tangier. Her letters to Paul describe the delights she found daily in Tangier: "I love this spot geographically and I'm always pleased to have lots of blue around me. Here there's the water and the sky and the mountains in the distance and all the blue in the Casbah; even in the white, there's lots of blue."[67] She loved the marketplace and the women of the medina. A series of letters to Paul describes her attempts to win the affections of the women, to break into the "social structure, so different from the one you know — for certainly there are two different worlds here (the men's world and the women's)." At times she made progress, but at other times she wondered how "long it will take me to admit that I'm beaten." Later she wrote, "I am puzzled, vexed, and fascinated, but deep inside I have an awful feeling I shall never find out any more than I know now."

The complications of Jane and Paul's relationship are more clearly chronicled in these letters from Morocco than anywhere else or at any other time. Questions of where they were to live, how they were to support themselves and each other, with whom they were to spend their time, how much of each other they would reveal to other people, how intimate their work was, and how deep their involvement was with each other all arose at one point or another. Jane discussed her ambivalence over living in Tangier — her love for it and her frustration with it. She raised the unresolved dilemma of their different preferences: "I wish to hell I could have the same sort of adventures in Fez or that you liked Tangier. I cannot imagine a better time really than being in a place we both liked and each of us being free and having adventures . . . And I long to go now to Marrakech and Taroudant. It's a pity [I was reluctant in the past] and since reading your novel I take it very much to heart." She agonized over her "failure to like in it [Africa] what you do and to like what you do at all anywhere." She wrote of her jealousy of Paul's professional relationships and some of his friendships. She also alluded to Paul's jealousy of her affairs, writing, "I can see that I would hate to have someone waiting here at the hotel for me, with an eye on the watch and feeling very sad."

Interdependence is the undercurrent running through Jane's letters. There was nothing Jane would not discuss with Paul, including details of her flirtations with Moroccan women. She writes of agonizing over Cherifa, the woman who later became her live-in companion, a strong, hawk-faced woman, who Maurice Grosser said looked exactly like Georgia O'Keeffe. She also struggled to get to know Tetum, "the Mountain dyke," and wrote Paul, "If only you had been here it wouldn't have mattered — because frustrating as it all was, it was certainly ridiculous and you would have loved hearing about it."

Jane knew that their differences were part of their appeal to each other. She was a performer, and Paul a voyeur, an ideal audience for her antics. Whether she was acting out her dramas for him directly, at parties or in restaurants, or describing such a scene later on, she knew that of all the members of her audience, Paul was the most appreciative and the most astute critic because he knew her best.

Yet Jane also let Paul know that her very dependence on him disturbed her: "I wonder too if I would bother with all this if you didn't exist. . . . It is the way I feel about my writing too. Would I bother if you didn't exist? It is awful not to know what one would do if one were utterly alone in the world: You would do just what you've always done . . . but I don't exist independently."

She created in him dimensions of authority beyond any actually present in their relationship. His opinion and criticism of her, whether implicit or overt, gradually assumed huge proportions in her mind, and as their relationship continued, she became more fixated on this issue. Although Paul always encouraged Jane in her writing, his concern about her erratic and unpredictable behavior is clear in his letters to other people and in his autobiography. Jane could no more escape her desperate need for Paul's approval than she could the sense that she would never gain it, either personally or professionally. Jane's identification with her own writing was so complete that a failure in either writing or living was quickly reflected in the other.

Like the characters in their novels, neither Paul nor Jane chose to approach the difficulties in their relationship or themselves with any directness. Like Mr. Copperfield in *Two Serious Ladies*, Paul understood the sources of his and Jane's dissatisfactions. Like Mrs. Copperfield, Jane could not face her fears outright. Nor could Mr. Copperfield, who had to write his wife a letter to tell her what he could not say in person. Like that letter, *The Sheltering Sky* was Bowles's attempt to sort out the most difficult issues of his life and to make a statement of his deepest conviction: that he must face the abyss alone. Jane admired this aspect of his personality: "You have always been a truly isolated person so that whatever you write will be good because it will be true which is not so in my case because my kind of isolation is an accident, and not inevitable . . . not only is your isolation a positive and true one but when you do write from it you immediately receive recognition because what you write is in true relation to yourself which is always recognizable to the world outside." Paul understood solitude; he had accepted that each person is alone with his fate: death. In *The Sheltering Sky* he detailed the outcomes awaiting those who grapple with the horror beyond the sheltering facade of everyday life: one moves toward nothingness and embraces it, or fights the emptiness beyond and is driven mad by the chaos of existence.

Kit was selfish, self-centered to the point of petulance in the midst of Port's illness. But there was a difference between what was on the surface of her behavior and her deeper fears: "The formation of the words was really a screen to hide the fear beneath—the fear that he might be really ill" (*WS*:180). Here was love askew—out of place or misdirected and submerged, lost beneath the surface of verbal interplay. Like Kit, Jane sat balanced between chaos and nothingness on the edge of the giant maw in the sheltering sky. Paul had already recognized how the scales would tip in the end.

Jane saw Paul's unflattering portrait of Kit in the novel as an omen for her life, a prophesy, and insofar as that prophesy was negative, it was a judgment against her. As Paul recalled, "She thought that Kit was Jane Bowles. Well in a way she was, of course—but she wasn't. You know how those things are; you use a living model to build your mythical character. I remember that she said to me that the end made her very sad, because she didn't know what I meant. . . . I never found out why it made her sad. Did she think I felt she was going to have that kind of an end to her life?"[68]

Jane's response to his novel confirmed for Paul the fearful prophesy it held for his own life. For as much as *The Sheltering Sky* was a depiction of their relationship, it was also a statement of his fears of the empty center—the absolute nothing—of his own private universe. Jane could not face this aspect of the book or of their relationship. And Paul preferred not to learn why she reacted as she did. Like the characters in the novel, they remained separate from each other, each waiting for the other to make the move that would reunite them.

Nowhere and at no time did either of the Bowleses admit the reason each sought the other: because he was detached from his emotions; because she had no self-control. Each needed the exhausting extreme of the other for balance but to admit their psychological interdependence would have been to admit both individual and shared imbalance. Neither partner was willing to disturb the equilibrium.

Travelogue: 1947–1951

While working on *The Sheltering Sky* in the winter of 1947/48, Paul decided to take a trip into the Sahara. Traveling through Oujda, Colomb-Béchar (a town south of Fez and the last major stop on the Trans-Saharan railway line), Taghit, Béni-Abbès, Timimoun, and Adrar, he gathered impressions and experiences for the novel and for some short stories. In Taghit—"probably the most intensely poetic spot I had ever seen"—he admired the town built overlooking a river valley on one side and next to a tall orange-gold sand dune on the other (*WS*:282). There he met an elderly Swiss schoolteacher wintering in the Sahara, who became the model for the protagonist in his story "The Time of Friendship." At dinner with the French commanding officer in Timimoun, Paul heard a tale of three Muslim merchants, murdered for their desert caravan, which their murderer appropriated and sold in the next town. A year later Paul transformed this story into "The Delicate Prey."

In September 1948, Bowles went on tour with *Summer and Smoke* to Buffalo, Cleveland, and Detroit, returning to New York for the 6 October opening at the Music Box Theater. He stayed for the 14 November Town Hall premiere of his Concerto for Two Pianos and Orchestra and returned to Tangier in December, with Tennessee Williams and Frank Merlo in tow. As usual, traveling stimulated Bowles to write, and while crossing the Atlantic, he completed a short story he had begun in the Sahara, a story that horrified even such a staunch admirer as Williams.

Paul's publisher Doubleday rejected *The Sheltering Sky*, claiming the contract was for a novel and Paul had given them something else. His agent sent the manuscript to John Lehmann, a London publisher from a distinguished family with a long history of literary connections.[69] When he received Bowles's typescript, he "read it with mounting enthusiasm: I had not been so struck by an American novel since Saul Bellow's *Dangling Man. . . .* It proved one of our greatest successes."[70]

Bowles also sent the manuscript to James Laughlin at New Directions, who had earlier published "A Distant Episode" in *New Directions in Prose and Poetry*. Laughlin brought out the American edition of the novel in October 1949, a month after the English edition appeared. By December *The Sheltering Sky* had climbed to the *New York Times* best-seller list. Critic George Malcolm Thomson wrote of the book: "This is writing with an 'edge' on it, derived from the author's command over words, his uncomfortable insight into the elusive mainsprings of human action and human failure . . . a novel touched with genius."[71] The *Evening Standard* chose it as book of the month and applied their considerable marketing efforts to sell the book.

Lehmann's publication of *The Sheltering Sky* initiated a relationship that lasted throughout the 1950s. He published Bowles's second novel, *Let It Come Down*, in 1952 and included the short story "By the Water" in his anthology *Penguin New Writing*. He used Bowles's short stories "If I Should Open My Mouth" and "Tapiama," his review of Peter Mayne's *Alleys of Marrakesh*, and his travel piece "Letter from Tangier" in the *London Maga-*

zine. He also published Bowles's short story collection *A Little Stone* omitting "Pages from Cold Point" and "The Delicate Prey," fearing censorship problems.

Lehmann urged Paul to visit England in the autumn of 1949 to take advantage of the notices his book was receiving, and a friend in Morocco, David Herbert, invited the Bowleses to travel with him to his family estate at Wilton in England. Lehmann, eager to meet the author of his new acquisition, was not disappointed in Bowles. Nearly twenty years later, he described his impression of the author: "In his early middle-age, with his shock of gold hair, slightly curled and as stiff as if made of nylon bristles, he still looked like a slim Greek athlete who might have had a nervous breakdown and taken to an intellectual, bohemian life after just failing to win the *discus* championship. Neatly dressed, with imaginative eyes, over which he wore a shade in the early morning, he was much more reserved than most of the Americans of his generation I had met."[72]

Lehmann decided that Paul's years abroad had "left a deep impress not only on his behavior but also on his writing," making him more European than American, "in thought as well as in style. He struck me at once by his quiet charm and intelligence, his shrewdness about the ways of the world, and—when the reserve melted—a sharp wit that did not spare his contemporaries, of some of whom he could give very funny imitations."[73]

At first Paul was "a little at sea in the literary world of London," more of a listener than a talker. Paul's patient observation and recording of the details of conversation and scenery were just what made him so entertaining to those with whom he felt comfortable. During his stay with Herbert, Bowles admired a scrapbook of photographs of a small island called Taprobane, off the coast of Ceylon, which Herbert and his parents had visited in the mid-thirties. Bowles mentioned that he might be interested in passage to Siam or Ceylon. Suddenly, through the combined efforts of two of John Lehmann's friends, he found himself booked to travel to Colombo.

Sailing to India through the Strait of Gibraltar, Bowles was seized by "a rush of nostalgia for Tangier" (*WS*:296). He went inside, got into his berth, and began writing. He imagined a character, Dyar, standing at the edge of the cliffs, looking out at the freighters in the strait. By the time Bowles's ship had reached Suez, he had "made decisions about form and drawn diagrams clarifying motivations and was well into *Let It Come Down*" (*WS*:296). From Suez, Bowles continued his journey to Ceylon, and he kept on writing as he traveled through Ceylon and southern India for the first six months of 1950.

Paul had not lost his talent for meeting people, and during his first week in Colombo, he dined with the queen mother of Sarawak, then making a brief visit to Ceylon. His first friend on the island was an Anglican minister named

Padmanabhe, whom he met in a bookshop. Padmanabhe invited Paul to dinner and then to his mother's tea plantation, Maldeniya Estate, in the hills near Ginigathena.[74] Happy to find a piano there, Paul decided to work on the opera he was beginning at the request of his friend, singer Libby Holman. One afternoon, he was disturbed to find that the keys did not function. Only after he had attacked the keyboard with extra vigor did he notice a large snake rise straight out of the top of the piano and wrap itself securely around a ceiling beam, safe from further interruptions.

The light, climate, and lush vegetation of Ceylon and southern India exhilarated Bowles. When he decided to stay for a while at Cape Comorin to concentrate on his novel, he chose a large hotel overlooking the sea, but one without electricity. Bowles was the sole guest, and to escape the heat, he wrote naked at night by the light of oil lamps. He traveled in southern India about four to five months in all but never made it to the island he had heard about in England—Taprobane.

After meeting Jane briefly in Paris, Bowles returned to Tangier and invited Brion Gysin to come along. In Morocco, Bowles enjoyed "the last two or three months of the old, easygoing, openly colonial life" (*WS*:305). After he and Gysin settled in the house in the medina of Tangier, Paul traveled through Andalusia with Libby Holman, gathering material for their opera *Yerma*, to be based on García Lorca's poem of that name. Back in Tangier, he picked up Gysin and took a trip to Fez and Marrakech. When they returned to Tangier, Bowles moved to a hotel farther from town in order to immerse himself in a routine of writing. He tried to ignore the incessant and increasing chill of the Moroccan winter, but when the walls of the hotel no longer kept the rain from seeping onto and entirely covering the floor of his room, Paul decided to accept the request of a *Vogue* writer to travel to the Sahara. The trip was difficult, and they both became ill, but it gave Bowles the desire to travel more by car. Gysin suggested that Paul buy his own, which he did—a black Jaguar convertible. Shortly afterward, he acquired a chauffeur named Temsamany.

In the spring of 1951, Bowles and Gysin traveled to Fez and Marrakech and for hundreds of miles on a four-month trip through the desert in the south of Morocco and Algeria. Bowles worked on *Let It Come Down* throughout the trip. After a trip to Spain in the fall to meet Jane and bring her back to Tangier, he moved into the medina house where all three of them stayed. Trying hard to make progress on his book, Paul spent the mornings in bed next to a thermos of coffee, writing in his notebook until noon. While he was writing, Jane did the marketing with the chauffeur. Soon Paul moved to Xauen, a village about an hour away from Tangier, to work more steadily on his novel. Jane had to leave for a New York production of her play *In the*

Summer House, so Paul moved back into their house to stay with Jane before her trip. He finished his second novel in the medina of Tangier.

In writing *The Sheltering Sky*, Paul had begun to explore the psychological equivalent of his geographical retreat from Western civilization to North Africa—an adventure into the mind, into states of conscious and unconscious awareness, into the desert of the human psyche. Now he was beginning a new phase of this journey; he was about to push emotional extremes and existential choice beyond any horror he had yet discovered.

BOOK V

THE SAVAGE MIND,
1949–1957

The characteristic feature of the savage mind is its timelessness.[1]

Tangier

WHEN PAUL ARRIVED in Morocco in 1947, he still
thought of himself as a traveler, and Morocco was a pleasant
country in which to travel. He moved about and only
gradually settled in Tangier as a city where he might want to
stay a while. During a stay in Fez in the spring of 1948, he wrote to Charles
Henri Ford: "My room is full of orange blossoms from a garden outside the
walls where I was taken yesterday noon. Fez is at its best: birds, flowers,
fountains playing, and a warm wind most of the time. The lake in Bou Jeloud
is covered with little boats full of Arab ladies in pink and lavender
haiks. . . . We shall probably spend most of the Spring in Tangier on the
mountain, because Jane feels more at home there than here. (It's more like
Mexico to her.)"[2] Fez, the city he loved, was in many ways still a medieval city,
land-locked and remote, while Tangier had a large expatriate community,
was small enough that Jane felt she could get to know it, and was on the sea.
As in Mexico, Paul compromised in order to remain in the country of his
choice.

Because of its strategic location on the western tip of North Africa at the
entrance to the Mediterranean, Tangier had been the treasure of several
world powers over the centuries. Phoenicians, Carthaginians, and Romans
all established themselves in Tangier at one time or another. The Berbers of
Morocco might have descended from the Phoenicians, but it was the Arabs,
arriving in Tangier in 706 and remaining for several centuries, who gave that

city and others in Morocco a distinctive and alluring flavor. Starting in 1471, Tangier began changing hands. First, the Portuguese won the port city from the Arabs; then it went to the Spanish in 1580, to the Portuguese in 1643, to the British in 1661, and again to the Arabs in 1684.

The British never gave up on this city only a few miles across the ocean from Gibraltar, and in the late nineteenth century they began pressuring France and Spain to declare Tangier a neutral port. Following the First World War, the three European countries laid out boundaries for an international zone with an autonomous international administration. During the Second World War, Generalissimo Franco occupied the city and allowed Germany, Japan, and Italy to open consulates there. When the Axis powers lost the war, Tangier became international once again, and the Legislative Assembly of Tangier included representatives of France, Spain, Britain, the United States, Italy, Belgium, Holland, and Portugal.

Under the multinational administration, there were no foreign exchange restrictions, no trade restrictions, and no personal or corporate taxes. Import duties were low, and only the sale of firearms and narcotics was restricted. Additionally, there was a free market in gold, meaning it was possible to buy gold over the counter in a bank, by the pound. The International Zone minted its own coin, the Hercules, which in the midfifties was selling for $38.25, only a dollar over the price of gold in bullion form.

Conditions were fertile for growth in businesses of all kinds. Between 1945 and 1953, more than four thousand new companies and seventy-two banks were formed. Tourism and a boom in construction and real estate spawned many new businesses. The building boom eventually played itself out, leaving behind blocks of empty flats, which made housing inexpensive throughout the city. International holding companies swarmed to Tangier in order to avoid taxes. Smuggling and piracy, long associated with the city, were now rampant due to the free access of all nations to the port and to international banking in the city. Goods were transshipped through Tangier for Malta, Marseilles, or other Mediterranean cities, only to be hijacked en route—often by the ships' owners—and rerouted. Many times the ships simply reappeared in Tangier after several weeks absence, mysteriously empty, without having reached their reported destination.

Bowles found postwar Tangier very different from the Tangier of the early 1930s. In his words, it had become "the boom town of the Eastern Hemisphere. Night shifts keep the buildings going up fast. Everywhere the countryside is being cut into squares by the endless prolongations of the streets. And there is no room for all the people trying to get space to live. I think all Europe's black-market profiteers are here, still profiting away, since the whole International Zone is one huge black market."[3]

Despite the city's changing face, the old Arab quarter remained medieval. "Tangier is a basin that holds you, a timeless place; the days slide by less noticed than foam in a waterfall," Truman Capote wrote after a visit in 1949.[4] Tangier combined cheap living with a sense of history in a way that made it a magnet to those looking for a temporary or permanent retreat from the "civilized world."

The postwar years marked the heyday of the international set, whose denizens ranged from writer Robin Maugham (nephew of Somerset Maugham) to Conan Doyle (son of Sir Arthur), who won the 1950 Tangier Auto Association Race in a torrent of protests over the price of his Delahaye.[5] Paul wrote to Ford that they had made Tangier "so civilized that the latest number of Horizon hangs from each newsstand, Sartre, Beauvoir, Camus and Lorca decorate the bookshop windows, and the American Legation hangs a copy of the Random House Selected Writings of Gertrude Stein in a glass case outside the entrance so the mules can brush against it as they pass. Reading matter is snapped up in the first half hour after it arrives in the Zone."[6]

A few old-time Tangerines remained and ruled the social scene, such as the Greens—Feridah, Jessie, and Ada: daughter, niece, and daughter-in-law of Sir William Kirby Green, British minister in Tangier in the 1880s. For years Feridah Green ran the Infant Welfare Centre for Moroccan children, and once a week, sitting on a high wooden chair at the end of a barn, she distributed sacks of flour to destitute Moroccan women. She rented out her large house, lived in a small two-room house she built next to it, and to escape the flies, received visitors in a wire cage on her veranda. Ada Green had retired to Tangier from other parts of Africa, bringing her servant Putti, who dressed in white linen with a turban and gold earrings and carried a leather switch to swat flies from Miss Ada.

Wealthy and titled, artists, and bons vivants filled downtown cafés and bars and entertained each other in occasionally fabulous style. They exchanged gossip at bars such as that run by witty, sharp-tongued Joseph Dean. Dean, rumored to be living under an alias, could put anyone in touch with anyone else in Tangier and served as an unofficial information bureau. Gerald Hamilton, himself the model for Christopher Isherwood's notorious Arthur Norris in *Mr. Norris Changes Trains*, claimed Dean was the wickedest man in Tangier, an ex-gigolo and jewel thief. (Hamilton neglected to add that Dean had been his partner in several high-stake crimes.) Many of those who frequented Dean's cherished it, because it was the watering hole of "the highly coloured collection of fake and genuine, cruel and kind, which formed the international society of Tangier."[7] Owners of the competing Parade bar were two Americans—Jay Haselwood and Bill Chase—and a Russian—Ira

Belline—who had met while working for the Red Cross during the war.[8] The tall, lanky Kentuckian Haselwood became a fixture of the city, friend and confidant to all, and when he died of a heart attack in 1965, many declared that the heart of Tangier perished as well.

Despite the postwar boom in construction and profiteering, Tangier remained relatively unnoticed by the larger world, to Paul's satisfaction:

> Tourists don't exist of course. There is not a single good hotel since the Spanish took them all over. There are a great many Franco officials arriving every day on pleasure trips from Ceuta and Algeciras, but they merely flash their diamonds, give orders and go away again. They seem to run the town, however. . . . In spite of everything's being new it all looks much older and more dilapidated than ever, and in that everlasting wind the newspapers and refuse swirl through the streets against one's legs. And the construction goes on in all parts of town . . . [Bowles's ellipsis] always more and more big buildings going up, even in the Grand Socco. The Arabs are mostly dressed in rather awful European suits, and the poorer ones in ragged American uniforms and G.I. overcoats with the linings they have sewn in sagging to the ground.[9]

Paul assured his friends that Morocco was worth visiting and that Fez was even better: "It is so much more impregnable and so much larger that it's still an efficacious refuge from the twentieth century."[10] The country was also economical, important to Bowles who complained in March 1950 that he had "only $1091.79 to show for that damned [best-selling] book."[11]

Paul attracted a stream of visitors. Among the first was Edwin Denby, arriving only a few weeks after Jane in 1948. Both went with him to Fez but were "not very venturesome" and stayed in their rooms most of the time.[12] Oliver Smith arrived shortly afterward, in June. A month later Libby Holman came with her son Christopher, and Paul took them on a trip through the Anti-Atlas Mountains.

Tennessee Williams arrived in January 1949 and complained about nearly every aspect of the trip from Málaga to Tangier, ranging from the quality of the food to a mysterious ailment he called "vibrations." He protested that the lodgings in El Farhar, a collection of bungalows on a mountain overlooking the ocean, were "perfectly ghastly," combining a marvelous view with "every possible discomfort."[13] Williams expressed no interest in the history of the hotel, reputed to have been the residence of a famous Moroccan outlaw chieftain—Ahmed el Raisuli, "Sultan of the Mountains" and "Lord of the Jibala." Some said the bar, which Williams surely visited, had been El Raisuli's stable.

Paul and Jane spent early 1949 in the Sahara, Paul working on short stories and Jane on "A Stick of Green Candy." In April, Paul went to Paris to hear

Gold and Fizdale perform his Concerto for Two Pianos. The concert was a success.[14] In the postwar years the French welcomed Americans as at no other time except during their liberation. A favorable exchange rate made it possible for Americans to live more cheaply there than at home. A suite at the Ritz cost eleven dollars a day, and good hotels on the Left Bank could be found for much less. Paul took advantage of the conditions to visit other expatriates: Copland, Ned Rorem, James Baldwin, Williams, Gore Vidal, and Capote. Vidal remembers, "It was a glamorous, golden time for all of us. Prices were low, the food was marvelous, and there was little traffic and no pollution; the light was extraordinary."[15]

While in Paris Bowles tantalized Capote and Vidal, serious rivals, each trying to be more precocious than the other, with stories of Tangier. Capote decided to follow Bowles back to Tangier, and when Vidal heard this, he decided to get there first, chiefly to annoy Capote. According to Paul, in a now famous story, Capote leaned over the railing of his ship at the docks of Tangier, grinning and waving his long scarf in anticipation of seeing Paul. Then he spotted Vidal on the pier: "His face fell like a soufflé placed in the ice compartment, and he disappeared entirely below the level of the railing for several seconds. When he had assumed a standing position again, he was no longer grinning or waving" (*WS*:291).

The summer of 1949 remained in everyone's memory as one of parties and picnics for Tangier society, a final fling during the last years of colonial Morocco. The leader of the social season was David Herbert, son of the Earl of Pembroke and Montgomery and "unofficial social arbiter" of Tangier. As the second son, Herbert had received neither a title nor family property, but in Tangier he was able to live comfortably on his inheritance and to establish a small domain of his own. He gave dinner parties for everyone of note who passed through Tangier, from Italian countesses to Winston Churchill. The tall and thick-chested Herbert enjoyed greeting his guests in his carefully tended garden while costumed in a white-sequined burnouse and wearing a huge amethyst ring. Though he entertained with style and grace, no one was safe from Herbert's acerbic commentary, and he took it upon himself to determine the parameters of Tangier society. He shared his abode—the Marshan house owned by Joel Guinness—with society photographer Cecil Beaton, and in order to be near Beaton, Capote remained with Paul and Jane at the "hellishly hot" Farhar.[16]

Belgian Count de Faille and his American-Scots wife held several parties at their estate, where the countess kept more than four hundred pets, ranging from cats and parrots to foxes. For one such party the countess had straw strewn on the ballroom floor for the snake charmers, acrobats, and other Moroccan entertainers who proceeded to build a fire in the middle of the room and sit around it in perfect comfort. The party was a costume ball, and Capote had come dressed in tulle. When Ada Green spied him through her lorgnette, she asked him, "And what are you supposed to represent?" Capote lisped, "The spirit of spring," to which Green replied, "Well, you don't look it."[17]

At a party for the thirty-fifth birthday of Capote's lover, Jack Dunphy, Beaton decorated a seaside grotto at the famous Caves of Hercules overlooking the bay with flowers, lanterns, and hangings, while in an adjacent but hidden grotto, Moroccan musicians played. For refreshments, Beaton served only roasted marshmallows, champagne, and hashish. Capote, terrified of the scorpions that infested the cliffs above the grottos, insisted on being carried down the rocks.

Fashionable Europeans and prosperous Moroccans preferred the Marshan—the plain beyond the Casbah (fort)—or the Mountain, the wooded hill a short distance from town across the river. Colorful and less well-to-do writers, actors, journalists, and eccentrics lived in houses dotting the Casbah. In 1931 Bowles and Copland had stayed on the Mountain. Now in the late 1940s, Paul was drawn to the Casbah, and in the summer of 1949 he purchased a small house there. Because it lacked plumbing and had to undergo renovation before he and Jane could live in it, Paul and Jane accepted Herbert's invitation to move in with him while work on the house progressed.

Paul's house was tiny but lay around the corner from one of the most famous houses in Tangier, that of Woolworth heiress Barbara Hutton. Hutton had outbid Franco of Spain in paying one hundred thousand dollars for the house of an American diplomat who had made it into a showcase of Moroccan art with intricate plaster work, painted wooden ceilings, and mosaic tiles by artists from all over Morocco. (A master craftsman supervised the plaster carvings, which covered the walls throughout the house and took ten years to complete.) Paul hired as his cook a man who had formerly worked for both Hutton and David Herbert, and through this man, who still visited Hutton's house and gleaned stories about her, Paul became privy to a great deal of Tangier gossip.

Hutton gave legendary parties throughout the 1950s and into the 1960s. Paul finally wrote an article about one such extravaganza for which entertainment included Moroccan *djibli* dancers (boys disguised to look like girls), a Moroccan orchestra, a gypsy orchestra and dancers imported from Granada, and a pianist who played Mozart. One room displayed an American flag created completely from jasmine, hibiscus, and a blue flower that Bowles could not identify. Hutton received her guests in a nook on a throne of brocades, surrounded by feathers and spears. Standing outside were several disgruntled guests whom the doormen would not admit, because they had bought their invitations from Moroccans who, presumably, had stolen them. "They have been fetching up to 20,000 francs each," Bowles noted. From the terrace of Hutton's palace, Bowles looked out at the neighbors' houses, which Hutton had had freshly whitewashed, the woodwork painted, and brilliantly lit with floodlights for the party.

> There are Moroccans in all the windows and along the edges of the roofs, watching the show. But if the party is entertainment for them, the floodlighting of their dwellings makes it clear that these are meant to be a dramatic backdrop for the party, and indeed nothing in the house itself strikes me as being nearly so theatrical in effect as this unexpected view of the quarter of Amrah with its unmoving rows of shrouded women, merely sitting and looking. On the other side of the terrace, the native houses go down steeply toward the harbor, their flat white roofs making a kind of stairway in the moonlight.[18]

Of the expatriates, Bowles alone realized the shifting focus between those watching and those being watched. In his writings, the Moroccans were not dramatic backdrop. He wrote from the point of view of the other side, those unmoving rows of faces, sitting and looking.

Paul and Jane formed the center of a rotating creative enclave in Tangier. Gordon Sager, who had sailed with Paul from New York in 1947, returned to Tangier, and Bu Faulkner came to visit occasionally. Over the years, Maurice Grosser, Virgil Thomson, Francis Bacon, Vidal, Capote, Irving Thallberg, Jr., Robert Rauschenberg, Peggy Guggenheim, Timothy Leary, and Susan Sontag (eventually even the Rolling Stones) all made the trip to Morocco to see the Bowleses. One resident estimated that Paul and Jane brought "more world famous personalities to Morocco than all the other distinguished people in the city combined."[19] Lawrence Stewart said, "Jane always lived on 'people coming through'—it was her phrase for those, like . . . myself, Truman, Gore, Tenn, Oliver, who passed through Tangier, invariably headed somewhere else. But one liked to call upon Paul and Jane. They were genuine exotics and, despite everything, endearing."[20] "At their best they were an enchanting couple," said their friend Canadian Christopher Wanklyn. "Together they had a background of shared experience which could spark off a rich exchange of Bowlesian humour that none of their biographers has yet managed to even suggest, and indeed such an individual kind of humour is almost impossible to describe." Wanklyn remembers Jane announcing once, "Thank God Charles took the beans up on the mountain," referring to historian Charles Gallagher and a pot of leftovers. Paul heard the beginning of a spiritual in this proclamation and promptly wrote one on that theme.

One of Paul's most notable converts to Morocco was Brion Gysin, Canadian painter and writer, whom Paul ran into in Paris on his 1950 return from India. Gysin had been to the Sahara in 1937, "on a wild adventure with almost no money—$30."[21] Gysin stayed in Paul's newly renovated house in the Casbah, while Jane remained in Paris, Brion occupying the second floor of the small house and Paul the fourth, in a tower he had built on top of the tiny original structure. That summer the two men spent a couple of months in Fez, and when they returned to Tangier in the fall, Gysin occupied the Casbah house while Paul moved to what he hoped would be a more comfortable hotel in order to work on *Let It Come Down*. The friendship between Gysin and Bowles—and no one would suggest the relationship was anything other than friendship—was typical of many of Bowles's relationships: the two were opposites in many ways. Gysin was extroverted, outgoing, and unabashed; Bowles was reserved and passive. Gysin could "dance like a Moroccan and carry on like a Moroccan. He was a very 'down' person."[22] He must have been enormously entertaining for Paul.

When Paul took Gysin to a festival on the beach outside Tangier in 1950, Gysin heard Moroccan trance music for the first time and saw large groups of people falling into trances. One group of musicians in particular caught his ear. "Ah! That's my music . . . I just want to hear that music for the rest of my life."[23] Gysin spent a year searching for the musicians, and when he found them in the mountain village of Jajouka, he became so fascinated that he opened a restaurant in order to bring them to Tangier.

The Thousand and One Nights occupied a wing of the Menebhi Palace on the Marshan and became the premiere restaurant of Tangier for tourists and local celebrities throughout the 1950s. Gysin furnished it with red-tiled wooden tables, locally upholstered banquettes, and brass lanterns and candle-holders and served a variety of couscous, lamb, and other Moroccan specialties. In addition to the Jajouka musicians, he brought in young dancing boys from the Jibala hills south of Tangier. An evening's entertainment usually concluded with a fire-eater and a traditional Moroccan acrobatic dance, in which a boy dashed into the main salon carrying a large brass tray of glasses filled with tea on his head and performed without spilling a drop.[24]

Writer William Burroughs arrived in Tangier in 1954, at a time when Paul was in New York. Burroughs had published only one book, *Junkie, the Confession of an Unreformed Dope Addict* (under the name of William Lee), but was working on a mammoth free-form novel. Burroughs saw little of interest in the Moroccan culture—"And don't ever fall for this inscrutable oriental shit like Bowles puts down"—and reported to Allen Ginsberg that despite Bowles's presence, there was no writer's colony and no one of the slightest interest in Tangier.[25] But Tangier met Burroughs's minimal requirements: "Tangier has all the sex you want, it is cheap, and you are not a foreigner here."[26] Burroughs hoped to get to know Paul but seldom saw him and decided that either Paul was being "kept in seclusion by an Arab boy who is insanely jealous and given to the practice of black magic" or Paul was avoiding him because of an aversion to Burroughs's heroin addiction.[27] A year passed, and Burroughs still found Paul "very withdrawn and difficult to contact" but had begun to feel at home in Tangier.[28] Soon after, he reported that Paul and Jane had become "quite accessible" and that he had met a "good selection" of artists in Tangier: Christopher Wanklyn, Charles Gallagher, linguist and student of the occult Viscount de Iles, and writer Peter Mayne.[29] Burroughs eventually found Paul "a charming person"[30] and wrote, "[I] dig him like I never dig anyone that quick before. Our minds similar, telepathy flows like water."[31]

In 1954 and 1955, Burroughs lived at the front of a small rooming house overlooking the port. The house's Dutch owner, Anthony Reithorst, was famous for his ability to procure whatever could be bought in Tangier for his regular clientele. Burroughs wrote and relaxed by taking out his pistol and shooting at match boxes he lined up on a shelf in his room. Riots in the summer of 1955 made foreigners living in the Casbah uneasy, and Burroughs moved to the more secure and more respectable Villa Muniria off the Boulevard Pasteur. Beat writers Allen Ginsberg, Jack Kerouac, and Gregory Corso all arrived to visit and eventually to help him assemble the novel that became *Naked Lunch*. They also came to see Bowles, as an ascetic and mystical forerunner of the Beat movement.

Burroughs and Bowles were of the same generation and class. Both had come to writing relatively late in life, and both rejected their conventional upbringing by concentrating on the more disturbing aspects of human nature. Like Bowles, Burroughs found in Tangier a physical correspondent to the side of the imagination he wanted to explore. He set his novel in an imaginary city he called "Interzone," a composite of all the drug environments he had lived in and a reference to Tangier's International Zone.[32]

Mystery Writing and *The Delicate Prey*

In the two and one-half years between the publication of *The Sheltering Sky* (1949) and *Let It Come Down* (1952), Bowles struggled to find his place in literature and with his readers. The ennui that Paul had fled in coming to Morocco to write his first novel had caught up with him again. He wrote to David McDowell at Random House in the spring of 1950, "I'm working on the new book, but I'm a slow and unsure worker . . . unsure because from day to day, hour to hour, minute to minute, my concept changes, disappears, pleases me, disgusts me, seems not to exist, exists too much but means nothing. If only I knew what I believed I could at least keep my feet on solid ground. . . . But without that possibility one is completely alone on the raft of one's own existence, with nothing else in sight."[33] In February 1951, he told Peggy Glanville-Hicks that his writing was going well, but he was "waiting to escape to somewhere else." Writing at that point was mere therapy, a way of "working . . . in order to be able to forget one's life. . . . I suppose the trouble is that one thinks one's life instead of living it. Occasionally one enters into contact for a split second, when the wind blows across one's face, or when the moon comes out from behind a cloud, or a wave breaks against the rocks in some particular way which it would be impossible to recognize or define. Then one catches oneself being conscious of the contact, and it is lost. Thus, a great desire to lose consciousness. Yet in sleep nothing is different: there is always the same cage around."[34]

Phrases and ideas from this letter appear in both *Let It Come Down*, on which he was then working, and his next novel, *The Spider's House*. Dyar in *Let It Come Down* shares Bowles's desire to lose consciousness and has come to Morocco to escape the cage that had surrounded him in New York. The dilemma of the writer who uses his work as therapy became the basis of Stenham, the protagonist in *The Spider's House*. Like works of origami, Bowles's characters begin as two-dimensional representations of different aspects of himself and his acquaintances and then slowly achieve fullness through Bowles's folding and unfolding of previously hidden or unrecognized contours. If he had intended writing to distract himself from the cage within which he had shut himself, he was achieving the opposite. As happens with effective therapy, his work was making more of the unconscious conscious. Although conscious awareness of certain issues might have cleared the way for work in new areas, it did not provide him with peace of mind.

Bowles's volume of short stories *A Little Stone* appeared in England in August 1950 and in the United States as *The Delicate Prey* in November. English critics focused on technique. Michael Sadleir in the *Times* said: "The extreme beauty of Paul Bowles's writing, his vibrant response to colour and sound, render his book a 'must' to anyone on the watch for outstanding writing talent. These are tales of terror of a high order." The *New Statesman* proclaimed: "Mr. Bowles is probably the most promising writer to emerge since the war. That is to say he is not just 'promising' in the sense of being better than most of the other writers under review in one particular week. . . . He is promising because he is a mature writer, infinitely interested in and fascinated by the tension that exists in nature and between human beings." The *Times Literary Supplement* specifically cited Bowles's facility with language, writing: "Mr. Bowles is not concerned with the poetic possibilities of language but with prose as a means of coming to grips as quickly and as directly as possible with the culminating unease of the human situation . . . their [the stories'] brilliance comes from a subtle skill in suggesting a terrifying *denouement* without ever actually confirming it." The critic concluded that the stories were "terse, brilliantly suggested in their setting, dramatic and controlled in their development." A vindicated Bowles collected phrases from the reviews to send to his American editor for use as blurbs in future editions.[35]

"The Delicate Prey," the title story in the American collection, was even more gruesome than "A Distant Episode." A Moungari tribesman kills two merchants in the desert and then undertakes the torture of the third. He binds him, the youngest of the merchants, by his hands and feet, strips him below the waist, and in a swift motion, castrates him. As the boy screams, the Moungari further mutilates him and finally sodomizes him. Not until the next morning does he finally kill the boy, slitting his throat and leaving him among the rocks. Soon friends of the merchants discover the truth about the Moungari and carry out their revenge. They dig a large pit in the desert and bury him in it, leaving only his head exposed. The desert will finish their work.

As usual, Bowles describes the most shocking events of this story in bare outline form. He treats all actions equally, like a camera slowly panning across the desert, giving equal attention to everything that passes in front of the lens. Bowles is not casual in his treatment of the violent and the profane, but he does not emphasize the horror. In this way, the shocking is sometimes even more shocking, presented against a background of emotional blankness. Bowles does not need to dwell on the horrifying actions of the Moungari for the reader to feel their force.

Bowles's tale relies on atmospheric effects, and the atmosphere is one of silence, pierced only occasionally by the puny sounds that humans make. The young boy, Driss, plays a small flute that pierces the silence of the desert. The sounds of gunshots, "distant, but perfectly clear in the absolute silence," ring out to lure the boy's uncles over the rocks to their death (*CS*:167). The last sentence of the story leaves the sound of the Moungari's voice hanging in the desert dust, as he lies buried up to his neck: "The wind blew dust along the ground into his mouth as he sang" (*CS*:172).

As a composer Bowles was especially sensitive to such sounds. Against the silence of the desert, the music of a flute or a man's voice or even the camels' "grumblings" could be made as prominent as a figure suddenly appearing on a previously empty horizon. Existing as they do in relation to the emptiness of the desert, sounds accentuate such blankness, the void that only occasionally is pierced and never filled. Although any sound in the desert breaks the monotony of the silence, a man's song cannot last and does not travel far in the "infinite wasteland."

If Bowles had questioned his wisdom in leaving the United States, the American reviews of his short-story volume confirmed his decision. British critics had concentrated on Bowles's technique and control of language. American reviewers focused on the content and filled their columns with words such as "decay," "putrescent," "revolting," "loathsome," "sensational-ism," "horror," "disintegration," and that particularly American moral judgment, "evil." Even while Bowles labored over his second novel, he tried to make sense of this reception. He complained to McDowell that American readers had missed the point: his stories in fact belonged to a popular American genre—"a variety of detective story. Not the usual variety . . . but still, detective stories in which the reader is the detective; the mystery is the motivation for the characters' behavior, and the clues are given in the form of reactions on the part of the characters to details of situation and surroundings."[36]

Although Bowles objected to the reactions of moral indignation, his stories were as much morality tales as they were mysteries. Bowles wrote of violence, impermanence of the flesh, and sexual perversion in order to make a moral point. He wrote of a world in spiritual decline, not to glorify the savage and bestial nature of humans but to show what we are and what we are becoming. His romanticism was not only that of Poe, who first put into words the disintegration of the personality, but a later variety of spiritual disintegration, closer to Herman Melville, Joseph Conrad, and even Freud—a negative romanticism that looked beyond the personality deep into the soul and heart of humanity and saw only horror.[37]

McDowell quickly reassured Bowles that by the end of January sales had already passed the five thousand mark, that Random House intended to reprint the book when the original seven thousand five hundred copies had sold out, and that American reviewers were stupid and shallow. McDowell also told Bowles that the title for his new book, *Let It Come Down*, was "perfectly swell" and reminded Bowles that they had hoped to publish the novel that fall.[38] Shortly afterward, he asked for a synopsis of the new novel, which Bowles sent in March, along with notes and comments on the notes. As during the publication of *The Delicate Prey*, Bowles stressed the aspects of the book that linked it to the popular mystery genre. Although *Let It Come Down* had "intellectual and serious" elements, "the majority of people reading it will take it strictly at face value as a novel of action and adventure unless someone points out to them that it is something else."[39] The "some-thing else" that Bowles felt this book to be was a "novel of ideas."

In *Let It Come Down* Bowles followed his recipe for fiction: a novel or story whose plot had popular appeal through surface elements of intrigue and exoticism that veiled a deeper layer of meaning intended for discerning readers. He explained the existential philosophy behind this "novel of action and adventure" set in Tangier, "a complete epitome" of the "moral chaos of today's world": "No barriers can stop the decay of the spirit as it spreads throughout the earth. Salvation is for the individual who is willing to risk destruction at the hands of society in order to savor the consciousness of being alive."[40]

The book turned on the Bowlesian confrontation between Western rationalism and non-Western imagination. Yet the thrilling elements of international intrigue that were new to this novel took a back seat to the existential spiritual struggle that had also marked Bowles's first novel and his volume of short stories. The "mystery" was a "whydunnit." Bowles was disturbed that readers had not seen the mystery element in his writing, because the motivation, the "why," of the sometimes violent actions of his characters was indeed the point. It was not the writing that was "putrescent," "revolting," or "evil" but the modern world into which he and his readers had had the misfortune of being born. The twentieth century was one of moral decay and the human spirit a sad reflection of the terrible situation, and only this could explain the mysterious reactions of his characters.

In July of 1951, Bowles wrote McDowell saying that he was having trouble with the last few chapters, complaining how taxing it was to be "the sole arbiter of the behavior and destiny of a group of unsure, difficult people." He felt somewhat out of control and wrote despairingly about "the mess my characters have made of the final section of *Let It Come Down*."[41] Eventually, his "unconscious writing" paid off in a stunning and horrifying scene no serious writer could have planned consciously.

Let It Come Down

Bowles set *Let It Come Down*, his second novel, in postwar Tangier's International Zone. His protagonist, Nelson Dyar, is a bank clerk tired of his life and job in New York. Bowles had even more fun with this protagonist's name than with Port Moresby of *The Sheltering Sky*. Dyar is a man who is dying from within, and *Dyer* was an American cruiser lost in the Tangier bay in a storm in 1918.[42]

Dyar is not really living and has never really "been inside" of life. On a whim, he has written his friend Jack Wilcox, who runs a small travel agency in Tangier. Wilcox invites Dyar to join him in the International Zone, which he does.

The evening he arrives, Dyar accompanies Wilcox to Hesperides, the home of the beautiful Marquesa de Valverde (Daisy) and her darkly handsome husband, Luis, who are typically gracious International Zoners. Daisy grew up on a ranch somewhere in South America; Luis lost most of his family fortune in the civil war in Spain.

Wandering the streets after his evening with the de Valverdes, Dyar meets a less respectable group of Tangerines. Thami, a young reprobate son of the respected Behoudi family, takes him to a local bar, and there Dyar meets and falls in love with Hadija—young, beautiful, and a prostitute—who has come under the protection of a grotesque, rich, alcoholic American named Eunice Goode.

Dyar becomes a hapless victim in the middle of an intricate web spun around him. Wilcox intends to use Dyar to carry out a complicated international smuggling scheme. Daisy wants Dyar to cancel another traveler's reservations at an exclusive hotel in Marrakech so that she can stay there later in the season. Thami and Hadija see Dyar as they do all foreigners: as a potential bankroll.

Psychologically, Dyar is an unsophisticated version of Port from *The Sheltering Sky*. Like Port, Dyar feels confined and imprisoned, but unlike Port, he has not yet identified the prison as himself. As a bank clerk, he felt he had been "confined in a cage" by circumstances and blamed his predicament for his feeling of stasis and paralysis.[43] In Tangier he is still empty and numb, and his own life is as heavy on him as a "dead weight" (*LICD*:7). "It was a progressive paralysis, it gained on him constantly, and it carried with it the fear that when it arrived at a certain point something terrible would happen" (*LICD*:8). When Daisy asks Dyar what he wants out of life, his answer horrifies and intrigues her: "I want to feel I'm alive, I guess. That's about all" (*LICD*:24). Using language reminiscent of his poetry in the 1940s, Bowles has Dyar speaking of paralysis, motionlessness, and helplessness. The voice is passive. Things happen to Bowles's characters, settle upon them. Dyar falls prey to the schemes of others; he is a victim.

The relatively minor character Eunice Goode shares with Dyar a "progressive paralysis." Luxuriating in laziness, she claims movement of any kind disrupts contact with what she calls "the inner reality" (*LICD*:40). Yet she feels an "aching regret for a vanished innocence, a nostalgia for the early years of life" (*LICD*:49). Through her relationship with the Moroccan Hadija, Eunice seeks to return to "that infinitely distant and tender place—her lost childhood" (*LICD*:49)—the lost childhood from which we all are banished when we step into the cage of adulthood.

Hadija epitomizes the imagined innocence of simpler times that drew Bowles to North Africa. Naive and guileless, she is also manipulative like a crafty child. She perceives the world as existing only to fulfill her needs and sees nothing wrong in using others to get what she wants. Even though Hadija plans to use Dyar to her advantage, her scheming is so natural to her, so unconscious, that she appears blameless.

In Tangier, Dyar begins to think about the purpose of life, particularly his own, and the process disturbs him. "He was used to long stretches of intolerable boredom punctuated by small crises of disgust; these violent disturbances inside himself seemed no part of his life" (*LICD*:196–97). Dyar blames his internal struggles on Tangier, a dream city with a dreamworld's "tortuous corridors" (*LICD*:171). But Dyar always has been a sleepwalker—Tangier merely provided him with a physical setting appropriate to his somnambulism.

Dyar's passivity allows him to be drawn into two illegal Tangerine activities: money laundering and spying; and having fallen outside his own cultural mores, he begins to see his life as he imagines the Moroccans do. He discards his previous notion of "being on his way" and realizes "life is not a movement toward or away from anything; not even from the past to the future, or from youth to old age, or from birth to death" (*LICD*:186). He embraces the sense of timelessness and finds a greater apprehension of each individual moment as a point in time, in existence. He has passed from a sense of futility at the meaninglessness of his own existence into a transcendence of meaning: one is alive because one lives, and "in the meantime you eat" (*LICD*:187). Dyar rejoices in the feeling of being, and he basks in accepting a state of existence as sufficient in and of itself. By committing a crime, Dyar has stepped away from the "unquestioning herd" into the loneliness and fullness of his own being.

By the time Dyar meets Daisy de Valverde at her home for dinner, he has committed himself completely to his new life. In Daisy's bedroom, he confirms his new position outside Western society. Having left New York geographically and socially, he now leaves it psychologically through drugs and adultery. He takes a piece of *majoun*, and then he and Daisy make love. In a rhapsodic passage describing Dyar's impressions, Bowles's writing achieves a rare climactic intensity matched only by Port's death scene in *The Sheltering Sky* and a later scene in *Let It Come Down*. Each of these remarkable passages indicates a new plateau of psychological development, achieved through an altering of consciousness, by fever, drugs, or passion.

Sleeping with Daisy connects Dyar with a decidedly female (and timeless) life-force. As he lies on top of her, he feels the "soft endless earth spread out beneath him, glowing with sunlight, untouched by time, uninhabited, belonging wholly to him. How far below it lay, he could not have said, gliding soundlessly through the pure luminous air that admitted no possibility of distance or dimension" (*LICD*:226). Later, under the influence of *kif*, Dyar is "an animated extension of the sun-baked earth itself" (*LICD*:269). Having felt the connection with life, Dyar is sure of being able to continue his withdrawal from civilization. He has felt his own being stir; no longer will he be caged.

After Dyar leaves Daisy, he completes in every way the journey he began in leaving New York. With Thami, he crosses into the Spanish Zone where he believes he will be free from criminal prosecution. Thami helps Dyar settle into a little house on the mountain, and from that place Dyar launches into his final exploration of consciousness. Dyar's process of discovery takes him to the notion that one is fully alive when one is aware of being alive. But Dyar wants more than this. He wants to pass beyond an awareness of participation in life into a primitive, fully participatory and unselfconscious state of being. Thami's presence interrupts this final transcendence, and Dyar takes "dire" measures.

In a passage of hypnotic intensity, Dyar and Thami begin separate and yet shared hallucinatory journeys. Thami brings out a packet of *majoun*, and each is "conscious in his own fashion that as he swallowed the magical substance he was irrevocably delivering himself over to unseen forces which would take charge for the hours to come" (*LICD*:291). Earlier in the book, Dyar had longed for the sensation of timelessness, "the pinpoint of here and now, with no echoes reverberating from the past, no tinglings of expectation from time not yet arrived" (*LICD*:269). In his *majoun* hallucinatory state, Dyar sees the way to step outside time. He spies a "door ahead of him, but suddenly between him and it a tortuous corridor made of pure time interposed itself. . . . If it opened when he did not want it to open, by itself, all the horror of existence could crowd in upon him" (*LICD*:299).

This door is for Dyar what the sheltering sky was for Port—the door between him and the "horror of existence." Dyar slips into a corridor, the hallway between worlds, and hears the door banging in the wind. Slowly he reaches for a hammer and nail and walks over to where he thinks the noise is coming from. He puts the nail as far into Thami's ear as it will go and then carefully, deliberately, pounds it into his head. He has nailed shut the door to the world from which he came.

In killing Thami, Dyar not only has passed through the door but also has eliminated all reminders of what he has left behind. "'Thank God [Thami] hasn't come back with me,' he told himself. 'I never wanted him to know I was alive'" (*LICD*:302). Consistent with the female/life-force imagery established earlier in the book, the "humid, dangerous breeding place," the womb of ideas, is destroyed by hammering a spike into it, by impaling it with the manufactured phallus. In so doing he has achieved, at least symbolically what Norman Mailer later called the existential "apocalyptic orgasm."[44]

The overt sexual encounter between Dyar and Daisy encourages the reader to see the last meeting between Dyar and Thami in sexual terms. Dyar and Thami have shared an intensely sensual journey whose summit converts the "little death" of orgasm into a murderous climax, and Dyar is glad to be the "only survivor" of their orgiastic journey. Dyar now knows what it is to be alive. He sees Thami not as a partner but as a witness who must be eliminated. A witness would imperil Dyar's delicate state of unselfconsciousness and would also imply further involvement—a relationship, something that Dyar is too fragile to risk. The existential hero must complete his journey alone.

Daisy comes to the Spanish Zone to take Dyar back to the city, to help him "get back in," she tells him (*LICD*:313). Like Kit and other characters of Bowles's fiction who have succumbed to the world beyond the shelters of everyday life, Dyar cannot go back; he has gone too far to return. He must remain on the mountain to wait for whatever will happen to him. In solitude he must face the final state of nonexistence, nonbeing, and nothingness.

The Landscape of the Unconscious

Bowles's psychological makeup laid the foundation for his philosophy. As an artist, a romantic, and a rebel against his father's world, Bowles sided with mystery and the imagination, with the savage mind. But as a Westerner and his father's son, Bowles could not help but remain part of the civilization he so detested. In the conclusion to *Let It Come Down*, the schism that had always been Bowles's demon emerged suddenly and forcefully. The tension between the opposing impulses to abandon and to retain his origins exploded in a gruesome murder that makes sense only in terms of Bowles's own needs and the existentialism that dominated his thinking. Both sides of Bowles's personality were at work when Dyar committed his crime. Through his crime he liberated himself from all restrictions he had brought from the drudgery of his previous life. He broke forever with the European world, with all rules and restrictions, and with all morality, senseless or otherwise.

On a purely symbolic level, does the impaling of the brain represent an artistic death wish? A longing for sleep, death, stasis, and cessation of activity pervades Bowles's works, with his strongest statement occurring in his first novel: at the moment of death in *The Sheltering Sky*, Port find himself gazing at the "gateway to repose." Bowles intones, "Reach out, pierce the fine fabric of the sheltering sky, take repose" (*TSS*:235). Life is difficult in this "age of monsters," and compulsive personalities often feel desire for a rest from their inner drives. Freud based his notion of the death instinct on the assumption that one finds pleasure in freedom from tension: the aim of all life is death, because only in death is all tension truly resolved. In that sense, Dyar's symbolic murder of the brain, the seat of the intellect and imagination, is a logical extension of Bowles's psychological and philosophical beliefs.

Bowles's death wish was not for artistic death—a final stilling of the imagination. Rather, it was for intellectual death. The ending of *Let It Come Down* owes a lot to Bowles's latent interest in doubling and split personalities. At the point in the novel when Thami is murdered, Thami has ceased to exist as a sentient being on his own. Nor does he now signify the "savage mind," natural humanity. Instead, he has become for Dyer the objectification of the intellect: a witnessing consciousness. Thami has observed Dyer's transformation to aliveness. He represents conscious awareness of all the "horrors of existence" (*LICD*:307). Bowles often links intellectual activity with danger in his writing. Creation, according to Bowles, originates in the unconscious, which is not the same as the intellect or the brain or perhaps even the imagination. The unconscious lived on in Dyar, who had freed himself to live a new life in which all decisions would be made unconsciously, without premeditation.

Bowles reserved his greatest enthusiasm for that which stimulated the unconscious. Trance music, hypnotic states, mild hallucinogens and *kif*, the landscape and cities of Morocco, southern Spain, India, and Ceylon captivated him because they seemed to be ways of unlocking or gaining access to the unconscious mind. His writing has always depended on strict discipline to clear his mind of all distractions and to start each day's writing with little or nothing on his conscious mind. He has gone to great ends to reach the unconscious. So, too, did his character Dyar.

Let It Come Down did not match *The Sheltering Sky* in popular or critical success. John Lehmann wrote to Paul, "I fear that a couple of stupid reviews by nit-wits in the Sunday papers did it a lot of harm. Privately, people expressed enthusiastic admiration to me."[45] Lehmann's own opinion remained strong: "a descent into hell by a master of infernal landscape, with a dry macabre humor running through it that seemed to me an important gain over his first novel *The Sheltering Sky*; a book not to be put down till the very end."[46]

Lehmann's assessment captured the strength of the book—its descent into hell—but sidestepped its weakness. Reviewing the novel for the *New York Times*, Charles Poore summarized it as "a short and peculiarly violent season in hell," faulting the novel for a lack of plausibility that he decided was due to too rapid pacing. "It is as if [Bowles] had only a few days to stop over in Tangier, and had a tourist's ticket calling for his appearance at Taxco or Capri or Taormina within a very short time or in an already scheduled novel," he complained.[47]

Yet pacing was only a symptom of the problem Bowles faced in this novel. He later said that he worked on the book from the middle outward. This partially explains why the first section rushes by somewhat unconvincingly and why the last third is nothing short of magnificent. In the third section of *The Sheltering Sky*, Bowles had used an epigraph from Kafka: "From a certain point onward there is no longer any turning back. That is the point that must be reached." In writing *Let It Come Down*, he returned to this idea: "I strained to pass that crucial point; only then could I be sure of not having to turn back and abandon the book when I tried to continue work on it later."[48] It is from this point in the book that *Let It Come Down* gains its strength as a novel. The final pages are as compelling as anything Bowles has ever written.

In magazine articles and essays, Bowles's descriptions of the social scene and culture of Tangier capture the flavor and essence of the city. In *Let It Come Down*, the characters clutter the landscape. Bowles has many times stated that the most important element in his work is the landscape, and his strongest writing sets characters against the backdrop of a powerful natural field of action and explores the inner conflict that develops. Deprived of social distractions, his characters begin the unconscious struggle that always lies just under the surface.

The final scenes of *Let It Come Down* function as well as they do because in them Dyar's struggle turns inward and assumes its true form. Dyar's relation to other characters has been only circumstantial, and Bowles's description of these relationships is two-dimensional. When Dyar begins to treat other characters in the book as objects for use in his own psychic battle, we finally reach the deep psychological truth that is Bowles's strength. Bowles once wrote, "Relationships with other people are at best nebulous; their presence keeps us from being aware of the problem of giving form to our life" (*WS*:69). Nowhere has this statement proved truer than in *Let It Come Down*.

Sexuality and Eccentricity

Although sexuality clearly provides the subtext to the violent imagery of the murder scene in *Let It Come Down*, Bowles's interest in Moroccan male culture was multidimensional, going far beyond the single issue of sexual preference. Tangier had a reputation as a magnet for homosexual activity, and several of Tangier's expatriate residents readily admitted that the attractions of the city were its inexpensive life and the homosexuality. Moroccans regarded homosexuality with indifference, except in the case of boys who prostituted themselves or grown men who practiced passive pederasty.[49]

One longtime British resident of Tangier claimed that the attraction of Moroccan men was that although they preferred women, "there wasn't a one of them who wouldn't sleep with a man. So you lose the consciousness of being a homosexual."[50]

Paul Bowles was more discreet about this aspect of Tangier, replying to a 1947 question about Tangier's "sex-life": "I have a feeling it is completely changed. I never knew it very well, even when I was young"; adding, "Of course the people I knew when I was here before are middle-aged and fathers of families, and I'm inclined to avoid them."[51]

Most of Bowles's friends agree that Bowles was interested in something other than sex. Ned Rorem recalled talking with Paul after Tennessee Williams had visited Tangier. Rorem asked Paul how things had gone, and Paul answered, "Well, I've never gotten used to Tennessee's treating people as though they were just a hunk of meat." Rorem agreed with several of Bowles's friends on the subject of Bowles's sexuality. "I think that some people are sexual by nature, and I don't think of Paul as a sexual being. I think he likes to hear about it; he likes to look at it, write about it, and so on. But I don't know how much. Unlike Tennessee, he gets involved."[52]

Reserved and discrete, Bowles has never discussed intimacies in depth or in detail, stating that one's sexuality is a private matter. Like his character Dyar, Bowles has simply preferred that there be no witnesses. Then, too, as a foreigner in Morocco after Moroccan independence, Bowles lived in a precarious situation, and any admission on his part would have jeopardized his own safety and that of several of his friends.

In Tangier, where homosexuality was commonplace and the homosexual treated with indifference, a man might indulge or abstain with impunity. One would be suspected in either case, simply by virtue of association, yet the truth would be difficult to discover. In this city Bowles found a situation that perfectly met his youthful requirement of concealing his true feelings or motives and his adult conviction that homosexuality was not "a 'cause' to be defended. . . . That would necessitate that each individual conceive of himself as a member of a segregated community, that he see himself not as a free spirit, but as one of many. A definite diminution."[53]

Although Paul preferred to keep his private life private, in his own way he relished his public reputation. Paul often said that foreigners in Tangier were eccentric by definition. "Of course they're eccentric. They wouldn't be here if they weren't." In 1948 he reported to Charles Henri Ford, "When I arrived . . . I discovered a ridiculous, libelous article about me in the *Echo d'Alger*, describing me as distant, chilly, and eccentric, and, even worse, describing my parrot as skinny and featherless, which is certainly not the case. So that the staff of the Hotel Saint Georges seemed frightened to let me loose in the lobby, because as soon as I signed my *fiche* they all knew I was the crazy American from the desert. Of course I was really delighted. No one can ever heap enough insults upon me to suit my taste. I think we all really thrive on hostility, because it's the most intense kind of massage the ego can undergo."[54]

Perhaps living in Tangier did encourage an image of eccentricity. Yet Paul's habits as a middle-aged man were not markedly different from those of his childhood. As in his youth, he maintained a strict schedule for his work. Mealtimes were occasions for great fussiness, as they had been at his father's table, and he worried about his health. Maurice Grosser remembers that when Paul and Christopher Wanklyn took an extended trip through Morocco in the late 1950s to record folk music, Paul had the back seats of the Volkswagon removed so that he could fill them with his luggage, including "two bags Christopher couldn't understand the need for . . . [in] the desert. One was a suitcase full of cornflakes, and the other was a suitcase full of neckties. I never quite understood the cornflakes myself."

The cornflakes were essential to Paul, who claimed he could not regain full consciousness in the morning without them. Another staple for Paul was bottled water, even after years in Morocco. One way of rising above the inconveniences of travel was to follow a proved routine.

A need for precision, so characteristic of Bowles's writing, was evident in other areas of his life. An acquaintance from Tangier remembers that when Paul came to visit, he habitually spent part of his time rearranging the logs in his host's fireplace.[55] Yet his nomadic life meant that, among other inconveniences, he lived in rooms piled high with valises, and as a consequence, his personal belongings were often in disarray. He spent hours looking for misplaced manuscripts, some of which he never found. Still he preferred the discomforts of a life in transition, and though he complained, friends knew not to take his complaints seriously. As Thomson put it, "Paul complains about everything, always. That's the way he makes himself interesting. He does it quite charmingly."[56]

Grosser explained Paul's dietary fussiness as a logical and learned behavior: "He's had so many illnesses, and he's a bit of a hypochondriac, so he takes care of himself. He doesn't take any chances. There isn't any sense in being disturbed by anything. He sticks to his regime, and that's it." Such attention to health occasionally came at the expense of someone else's comfort. Famous among Paul's friends was a story Wanklyn related about one of the desert excursions, which Grosser remembered:

The car broke down right in the middle of a very deserted place. Of course it was a terribly hot, rocky expanse, and in the distance there was a sort of little hut. I suppose they were Moroccan farmers, but in this desperately hot landscape. Christopher had to go to the nearest town to get a mechanic to come back and help fix the car. He hitched a ride, leaving Paul there, and he came back four or five hours later. Paul wasn't there. So he went to this hut, the nearest spot, and there was Paul, sitting in the middle, in a bathtub, using up all the family's water.

Presumably, the bath had been "by invitation," since the family seemed quite happy about it. Grosser laughed, thinking of Paul in this situation, and then continued, "Paul could make himself at home anywhere. He was a marvelous traveler."

Moroccan Music

Some of the more fantastic scenes in *Let It Come Down* came directly from Bowles's experiences in Morocco. Working on the novel in a local café, he witnessed a brotherhood ritual. "A mountain Jilali came in, sat beside us, and soon went into a trance. As he danced, he slashed himself, covered his face with the blood, and licked it from his arms and fingers. It was tremendously impressive, the more so for having been done without a word being spoken" (*WS*:310). Bowles used this episode for a scene in which Dyar comes upon a café in a small village. Bowles's description mimics the compelling and hypnotic music: "The chanted strophes were now antiphonal, with 'Al-lah' being thrown back and forth like a red-hot stone from one side of the circle to the other. At the same time it was as if the sound had become two high walls between which the dancer whirled and leapt, striking against their invisible surfaces with his head in a vain effort to escape beyond them" (*LICD*:286). The narrative moves from the sound itself to the state of mind created by such a listening experience. The effect of the music is similar to the effect of *majoun*; it succeeds in "destroying the listeners' sense of time, forcing their minds to accept the arbitrary one it imposed in its place. With this hypnotic device it had gained complete domination" (*LICD*:286). The music creates a sense of "virtual time," in which the rhythmic structure of the music becomes so dominant that all sense of time outside that structure disappears.[57]

The dancer moves into a ritual of purification through self-mutilation. Watching, Dyar becomes a participant in a communal ritual through which the power of the spirit transcends the flesh: "It was his own blood that spattered onto the drums and made the floor slippery. In a world which had not yet been muddied by the discovery of thought, there was this certainty, as solid as a boulder, as real as the beating of his heart, that the man was dancing to purify all who watched" (*LICD*:287).

Although partly a carryover from indigenous tribal practices, the Moroccan brotherhood rituals are closely related to the Sufi branch of Islam, a mystic offshoot that developed in opposition to the more systematic theological and legalistic aspects of Islam. Sufi teachings approach spirituality from an intuitive and emotional stance and aim toward achieving a state of oneness with God. Music was out of place in Islamic worship, but it came to be of great importance to the Sufis. By the twentieth century, Sufi leaders, "dervishes," had acquired a full repertoire of techniques "to condition the person, open up his consciousness to the attractions of the supra-sensible world."[58] Their techniques assailed all the senses, using perfume and incense, music, chanting, drugs, dancing, and occasionally alcohol.

In Morocco, Sufi practices merged with the religious ceremonies of indigenous tribes in the Berber men's groups, or brotherhoods. Brotherhood members reinforced music's hypnotic or trance-inducing properties from early infancy on, training babies and children to the particular rhythmic patterns of their own brotherhood, often while burning certain herbs or grasses. Bowles reported occasions in which his Moroccan friends would leave the room when a certain incense was burning, because they were afraid of falling into a trance. His friend Mohammed Larbi would pass out whenever he smelled the herbal substance Djaoui,[59] and Mohammed Mrabet refused to dance when trance music was played, knowing that he would quickly become entranced.

In the brotherhoods, music could induce a trance in preparation for ritual burning, flagellation, or bloodletting, all in the service of reaching a state of ecstasy. The ceremonies of the brotherhoods all involved religious dancing, but from that point they varied according to the practices of the particular tribe. The Gnaoua, Negro descendants of central Mali, were exorcists and healers who used the trance state to cast out evil spirits. The Jilala practiced ritual self-mutilation with knives; the Hamatcha brotherhood, according to Bowles, "used rocks to drive the sharpened bones of animals into the flesh of the chest or thigh."[60]

Bowles brought a composer's awareness to his fascination with these rituals. For him the music of Morocco, to which the brotherhoods contributed much, was the country's single most important cultural possession. In 1958 he convinced the Rockefeller Foundation to fund a series of trips to record examples of Moroccan music for the Library of Congress. The $6,800 grant was to cover a six-month period, but Bowles ended up traveling two years through the mountains and lowlands ferreting out authentic music. Government officials were reluctant to cooperate and blocked Bowles's efforts, denied him permission, or subverted his detective work in locating the musicians. Young, educated, politicized Moroccans disapproved of the project altogether. They feared it would show Morocco to be a backward nation, a land of savages, and labeled the music *une musique des savages*.

Bowles traveled with Christopher Wanklyn, who admitted to "no particular interest in Moroccan music," outside the *rhaitas* (oboes) that play from the mosques during the nights of Ramadan. Yet Bowles's enthusiasm "rubbed off" on Wanklyn. On several trips, Bowles brought along Larbi Djilali, a Moroccan friend, to help, which perplexed Wanklyn:

> At times it seemed to me that Paul was coaching [Larbi] in how to sabotage the expedition, which was strange, since Paul had the purpose of his recording project very much at heart, and we faced constant problems placed in our path by various factions of Moroccan officialdom which regarded folk music as decadent and shameful. We had no need of Larbi's opposition as well. Yet Paul seemed helpless in the face of Larbi's machinations and the project was going down the drain, so I said that from now on if Larbi was coming I wasn't, and since my car was indispensable and Paul's meagre budget from the Library of Congress allowed no alternative, Larbi had to stay behind. I think Paul was relieved.

Despite the serious limitation of working with an electric Ampex recorder in remote areas, Bowles succeeded in recording many kinds of native music already nearing extinction. One five-and-one-half month trip alone, taken late in 1959, netted him two hundred fifty recordings.[61]

The hypnotic potential of Moroccan music fascinated Bowles. Both the highland Berbers isolated in the Atlas mountains and the lowland Muslims used music designed to induce trance states, and Bowles soon discovered that even the unconditioned or lay listener could be seduced by the music. Analyzing the musical hypnotic process, he wrote, "All the genres have in common a fundamental quality of deceptiveness and paradox: the music is sufficiently repetitive to discourage active listening, and yet it contains multiple variations which prove to be all-important once the mind has accepted the principle of unlimited recurrence."[62]

One of the basic purposes of Berber music was "to assist in effacing the boundaries between individual and group consciousness."[63]

> The sight of ten or twenty thousand people actively declaring their faith, demonstrating *en masse* the power of that faith, can scarcely be anything but inspiring. You lie in the fire, I gash my legs and arms with a knife, he pounds a sharpened bone into his thigh with a rock—then, together, covered with ashes and blood, we sing and dance in joyous praise of the saint and the god who make it possible for us to triumph over pain, and by extension, over death itself. For the participants exhaustion and ecstasy are inseparable.[64]

In addition to its role in religious rituals and trance induction, the Moroccan music had a place in the larger African tradition of tribal rituals that enforced the social interdependence of their members. For example, in the "Aqlal," a dance of the Draaoua tribe that Bowles recorded in the Moroccan pre-Sahara, "each participant carries a square hand-drum which, by a complex gymnastic pattern of overlaying and interlacing of arms, is being played by the men on either side of him, while he in turn is playing their drums, one with each hand."[65] Bowles recorded a piece by the Cheikhats, or courtesans, of the Haouz, the Moroccan plain of which Marrakech is the central city. The women sang while standing stiffly, each holding a small ceramic hand-drum and contributing a single tap to an ongoing percussive pattern. The Ouarzazat drummers of southern Morocco specialized in a group drumroll: while seated in a long line, the men struck their drums one after the other, "so that the sound move[d] down the line like a row of dominoes falling."[66]

In this socially oriented art form, in which the music exists to reinforce social bonds, the concept of individual expression is alien. Accordingly, Paul was pleased to discover one musician named Boujemaa ben Mimoun who agreed to perform alone, although he could not understand why anyone would want to hear his *qsbah* (transverse flute) without the accompanying songs. Reluctantly, the musician played several solos on his long reed flute. These solos were Bowles's favorites of the collection he made, even though they are not typical of the music of the North African tribes. In contrast to the rest of the socially functional music, the solos reminded Paul of the one aspect of North Africa to which he was ultimately drawn. "In a landscape of immensity and desolation it is a moving thing to come upon a lone camel driver sitting beside his fire at night while the camels sleep, and listen for a long time to the querulous, hesitant cadences of the *qsbah*. The music, more than any other I know, most completely expresses the essence of solitude" (*THAG*:119).

Ahmed Yacoubi

Paul first met Ahmed Yacoubi in Fez in 1947 at the home of Abdelsam Ktiri, where many students from the university in Fez gathered. For centuries the westernmost post of the religion of Islam had been Fez, a city forbidden to Christians until the early twentieth century. Many young men came to study Islam and other disciplines: astrology, alchemy, divination, and philosophy.[67] Yacoubi, however, was the son of a *cherif* (descendent of Allah) on both his mother's and his father's sides, and he was illiterate. He retained the flavor of his family's and his country's past. Yacoubi's father and grandfather were healers, and Ahmed had been educated in the laying on of hands, in herb collecting and brewing, and in legends, songs, and dances. Secretly, he aspired to paint and to sculpt, although he hid his work from his family, figurative art being forbidden by the Koran. When Jane first met him in Fez in spring 1948, he was drawing using a mixture of goat dung and water.[68]

In the summer of 1950, while Paul was in Fez with Brion Gysin, working on *Let It Come Down*, he renewed his acquaintance with Yacoubi. When he bought a car in the spring of the following year, he returned to Fez. That June, Jane cabled from Paris that she was ready to return to Morocco. Paul decided to meet her at the Spanish border, invited Yacoubi to travel with him, and Temsamany drove them north. The trip through Spain was full of the minor clashes among cultures that Bowles relished, with Yacoubi and Temsamany gargling and spitting the holy water in the cathedral at Cordoba, and Yacoubi marveling at Heironymus Bosch's paintings in the Prado. When Jane arrived at the border, Paul was there to meet her with his two traveling companions.

The trip back to Tangier was lighthearted, and once home the Bowleses established a comfortable household routine: Jane rose early to go with Temsamany to do the day's marketing, while Paul made his coffee and returned to bed where he wrote until noon. But after a few weeks Paul decided to go to Xauen, a mountain town slightly south of Tetuan, to try to finish his novel, now two years in the making. He worked there in relative solitude, interrupted only occasionally by visitors.

Initially, Jane spent some weekends with Paul in Xauen, but then she began to distract herself with the social life of Tangier. She spent much of her day with the native women at the market, her afternoons writing, and her evenings at dinner parties. Jane was having trouble working. She was also drinking more, and this disturbed Paul. He felt she was withdrawing from her work and from him. Paul continued to write, as he had always done during Jane's difficult periods, and his productivity only emphasized her "failure." "She became increasingly recalcitrant about showing me any of her work because of her block or whatever you want to call it. She wasn't able to carry anything through to completion and she hated everything she was doing. She wouldn't show her work to me and didn't even want me to mention it to her. Nor would I have dreamed of insisting. She wouldn't have done it. She'd have refused."[69]

While Jane struggled with her writing, Ahmed worked at his painting. Jane had bought him his first paints; now Paul coached him with his work and helped him in ways he could not help Jane. By December 1951, the two men had moved to a hotel in Tetuan, where Ahmed amassed enough work for an exhibition. In Tetuan, artist Robert Rauschenberg lived just down the street. Ahmed's most significant contact with him occurred on the night he fed Rauschenberg *majoun* without first explaining what it was. As Paul spent more time with Ahmed, he began to transfer the affection he had reserved for Jane. Paul found Ahmed open, unaffected, spontaneous, and unlike Jane, willing to travel. In January 1952, Jane returned to New York, hoping to take her play *In the Summer House* from its repertory production in Pennsylvania to Broadway. Paul booked passage for himself and Ahmed to Bombay. Curiosity and thrift were behind this move: it was cheaper to winter in India, and he wanted to "drop Ahmed Yacoubi, from the medina of Fez, into the middle of India and see what happened" (*WS*:311).

Ahmed's complete ingenuousness was charming: in him there was a certain naïveté, an immediacy of response to the world around him that a more sophisticated traveler such as Bowles had lost. Seeing the world with Ahmed was like seeing everything for the first time, and Bowles's descriptions of their journey through India are among the most vivid in his autobiography. A careful observer, Bowles took as much note of Ahmed's reactions to this completely foreign world as he did of his own. When Lehmann asked Paul for a travel essay on his experiences in India, Paul sent Lehmann a transcript of Ahmed's recollections of their trip, explaining his original essay revolved so much around Ahmed's experiences that he decided Ahmed should author it:

> You might want to know that the piece is by a completely illiterate and mediaeval-minded Arab boy who is so ingenuous about the world in general that when he heard organ music and hymns coming out of a church one Sunday evening he asked if it would be possible to go in and order only ginger beer, or if they would insist on his ordering whiskey! He's not retarded mentally by any means, however;—he's just had no experience outside the casbah of Fez. . . . Nothing could be more typical of an Arab than the calm assurance with which he speaks of the Moslems' superiority over everyone else, and the patronizing tone he uses when he mentions other people.[70]

Following their "thousands of miles of snaking back and forth across India," Yacoubi and Bowles went to Italy, where Albert Rothschild met them and took them to his house on the shore of Lago di Orta. There Brion Gysin was painting, and Rothschild's brother, Dadaist Hans Richter, was beginning a new film in which Yacoubi and Bowles (reluctantly) agreed to appear. From Orta, Yacoubi and Bowles went to Venice to stay with Peggy Guggenheim in the Palazzo Vénier dei Leoni. On their first morning there, Guggenheim invited them up to the terrace where she was sunbathing nude, a sight unprecedented in Ahmed's experience and one that made him forever wary of her.

With Paul's encouragement and his connections, Yacoubi's painting career blossomed. Jane took Yacoubi's larger works to New York for a 1951 exhibit at Betty Parsons's Fifty-seventh Street gallery. A critic and painter questioned their authenticity, stating that the work was certainly that of a European under an assumed name. From that point on, the works were shown alongside an angry letter Ahmed had dictated to Paul protesting his innocence. Paul arranged a show for Yacoubi at the Gallimard Agency bookshop in Tangier in December 1951, at which twenty-eight paintings sold, an unprecedented success for a local artist. On their way back from India and Ceylon in 1952, Paul arranged an exhibition at a gallery in Madrid, where Yacoubi's work attracted attention and sold well. In the autumn of 1954, he set up an exhibition in Paris at the Galeria Provensa. When English painter Francis Bacon came to Morocco in 1955, he and Paul struck an acquaintance, and Bacon introduced Yacoubi to oil paints. Throughout Bacon's stay in Tangier that winter, Yacoubi visited frequently in his studio in the Casbah in order to watch him paint. In the autumn of 1957, Bacon arranged a show of Yacoubi's work at the Hanover Gallery in London. Maurice Grosser also took an interest in Yacoubi's work.

Paul's friendship with Yacoubi suffered strains when he took Yacoubi to New York in March 1953. Jane's play was nearing production, and she had cabled Paul to come write a score for it. While Jane and Paul rehearsed and tried out the play in Washington, Ahmed stayed with Libby Holman at her Connecticut estate, Treetops. Paul wrote to him frequently and complained at not receiving news in return.[71]

During Yacoubi's stay at Treetops, the relationship between Yacoubi and Bowles suffered. In May, Libby reported to Paul that she had fallen in love with Ahmed (Gore Vidal says she "bedded him and Paul was not pleased"[72]). Paul decided to return to Tangier. Ahmed stayed behind. Shortly after that, Libby accused Ahmed of pushing her son, Christopher, into the swimming pool, and after a row during which Jane defended Ahmed, Ahmed returned to Morocco.[73] Paul encouraged him to go directly to Fez and spend some time with his family in order to regain a sense of himself.

Most acquaintances agree that Libby had long wanted desperately to have an affair with Paul, and in 1948 she asked Paul to marry her, with the provision that Jane would live with them at Treetops. Paul said nothing, and Libby dropped the subject. Perhaps her failure to win Paul six years earlier prompted her to turn to his traveling companion. It is also possible that Ahmed deliberately provoked an argument with Holman in order to force her to ask him to leave, because she had made him feel like a "slave."[74] Whatever the reason for the upheaval, the results were unhappy for all concerned.

By July 1953, Ahmed had rejoined Paul, and they were in Rome where Paul was writing the script for *Senso*, a film by Lucino Visconti, because Tennessee Williams had too little time to do so. Williams was convinced that Ahmed was "torturing Paul by not sleeping with him," because Libby had told him it was "evil" to do so, "and the opinions of a lady with thirty million dollars cannot be taken lightly by a young Arab whose family live in one room." More likely the entire episode with Holman had shaken Paul, who, according to Williams, was having liver problems again and complained constantly about his health. Paul looked haggard, Williams said, and was almost too disturbed to "do a good job on the film."[75]

When Paul finished the script and gave it to Visconti, Visconti complained that the love scenes were too "clinical" and cold-blooded, too devoid of emotion, and rejected Bowles's explanation that the love scenes matched the style of dialogue in the rest of the film. "It seems love is special, . . . either in films in general or to Italians in general, probably both. He said he wanted love scenes and not 'sex' scenes. I couldn't write tender love scenes. . . . I don't think I could at all, in any case, but certainly not in that film."[76] Williams agreed to do the two love scenes, and the two writers shared credit on the film.

Following so closely a long separation from Jane and the betrayal by both Holman and Yacoubi, Bowles's difficulty with the love scenes in this film is entirely understandable. Paul attributed the problem to his sense that a tender scene was incongruous with the relationship already established in the script, something that, ironically, made no difference to Williams.

Some friends found Paul's relationship with Ahmed puzzling. Edouard Roditi found Yacoubi "predatory in a very involved and egocentric way."[77] Gore Vidal "regarded him as decorative only."[78] Grosser called Ahmed "subtle and involuted" and suggested he was predatory in a very pragmatic way, as was evinced by some of Paul's unaccountable behavior. Christopher Wanklyn had never understood Paul's taking a suitcase full of neckties with him on their desert trips. "We were unlikely to need formal clothing on any of our trips, or if we had, one necktie would have been ample, and space in my Volkswagon 'bug' was at a premium." Grosser knew the reason. "Paul didn't dare leave them at home, because if he did, Ahmed Yacoubi would run away with all of them," probably to sell them. Ira Cohen, a photographer and poet who knew Ahmed well, said Ahmed was "not an easy person to get along with. He was very sensitive, always with a touch of suspicion. People he became close to had to be very sweet people, without cynicism or criticism. Paul doesn't show his emotion, but he's very caring."[79]

According to Wanklyn, who met Paul through Yacoubi, what Paul admired in Yacoubi was a quality of rootedness:

For all his travels around the world with Paul, Ahmed's roots were firmly imbedded in ancient Morocco, and this he recognized as a source of strength. Paul of course appreciated this, drawn as he was to the mysteries of primitive psychology, even when on the losing end of the perpetual struggle between the primitive and the modern. I somewhat regret that word "primitive" which suggests something that works less well than its modern counterpart. In Paul's *oeuvre* the opposite is frequently the case. There is no doubt that between Paul and Ahmed a battle always existed, not necessarily an unfriendly one, it was considered normal or at least inevitable, a power struggle sometimes mild sometimes savage but never quite out of mind. I don't think Paul regretted this. It was after all a situation he often explored in his fiction and translations.

Bowles had no illusions about Yacoubi. He saw Ahmed as he was, and he celebrated the differences between them. He once wrote about him to Allen Ginsberg: "Few people alive could have less sense of reality; is intelligence the ability to learn from experience? If so, he's stupid. . . . But of course, he's always told me his concept of intelligence was the ability to blend truth and falsehood so expertly that no one could possibly distinguish them, one from the other."[80]

During the years following the Holman episode, Paul and Ahmed remained close, but by 1957 the Moroccan government had begun to persecute some expatriate residents and all local residents who associated with foreigners or who were suspected to have sympathy for the French. Paul began to fear for his own and Ahmed's safety. When Ahmed was jailed in November for a supposed sexual liaison with a young German boy, Paul hired lawyers to secure Ahmed's release and for a few weeks visited him daily in jail. Soon, however, it appeared that the Moroccan government was intent on ridding itself of the expatriate community and silencing Moroccans like Yacoubi who had close associations with foreigners. Paul and Jane decided their best course was to leave the country until things had settled down. Paul continued to inquire about Ahmed, until Ahmed sent word through Temsamany that Paul must not write to him in jail. Over the next few years, the friendship between the two lessened. In the late 1960s Ahmed immigrated to New York, where he married. According to Cohen, Paul never understood Ahmed's wanting to leave. "Whenever Ahmed talked about going to America, Paul would say, 'But he doesn't even speak English.' As if that had anything to do with it."[81]

There was no definite break in Bowles's concern for Yacoubi. In September 1985, he wrote to a former student inquiring about Yacoubi: "I'm told that Ahmed Yacoubi is very ill. I've written him, but got no answer. If you ever have a chance, go and see him, and let me know."[82] Ten days later he wrote Buffie Johnson asking her to check on Yacoubi to see whether there was anything Bowles might do for him. Finally, he received an answer from friends. Ahmed was at Sloan Kettering Institute with a brain tumor. Shortly thereafter, Ahmed died. Paul's written reaction was even more chillingly restrained than usual, suggesting a great depth of emotion. He enclosed the news in the middle of an inconsequential paragraph as casually as, more than forty years earlier, his mother had dropped the telegram announcing his grandmother's death into the center of their Mah-Jongg game. "There's no news. Claude Thomas is here this week and returns to Paris on Saturday, taking her aunt with her. Ahmed Yacoubi died on Christmas Day. The weather has been much colder than usual, but at least it has rained a great amount between the cold clear spells, so the farmers are satisfied."[83]

In 1962 Bowles wrote the story he claimed was inspired by his 1947 visit with an elderly Swiss schoolteacher in the Sahara. Emotionally, "The Time of Friendship" is closer to his own friendship with Ahmed Yacoubi. The story focuses on the relationship between a proper Swiss schoolteacher and a young Arab boy, and their friendship is one of the few truly tender and loving relationships in Bowles's works, an intimacy made possible because the two are so different.

As Fräulein Windling, the schoolteacher, and Slimane, the boy in the story, become friends, the gentle unfolding of intimacies between the schoolteacher in woolen stockings and the Arab who owns no sandals reveals the difference between their two cultures. She tries to educate him but finds him maddeningly unwilling to pursue the "principle" of reading, so she shifts her focus to stories about important individuals in European history: Hitler, Martin Luther, Garibaldi, and Jesus. The one point on which Slimane will accept no instruction is Islam: on that subject he is convinced no Nazarene (European Christian) is the least knowledgeable.

One season when Fräulein Windling returns to Timimoun, she realizes that because of the hostilities between the inhabitants and the French colonial authorities, she is making her last visit. When the captain of the military announces the area closed to civilians and suggests Fräulein Windling return another year, she understands "it's the end, and the time of friendship is finished" (CS:355).

Early in the story, the Fräulein had gone with desert women to look for firewood in the sand but could not distinguish the "sign" the wind left of the "invisible roots" beneath the shifting grains. "What we have lost, they still possess," she realizes (CS:338). The other women are superior because they have not been exposed to the germ of European culture, and they alone can read the desert signs.

Time is central to the story. To go back to an earlier time is to become purer; to go forward is to become more corrupt. For the Fräulein, the beauty of the desert lies in its pristine character, undisturbed by time. As the Fräulein and Slimane near the end of their time together, the landscape itself becomes increasingly tawdry. The café in the town is "shabby, modern." They face an "empty lot strewn with refuse," the refuse of civilization: "Nearby, spread out like the bones of a camel fallen on the trail were the rusted remains of an ancient bus" (*CS*:359). The contrast between the past and the future is concentrated in the image of a "long, newly-felled date palm," which lies discarded across a vacant city lot. "Fräulein Windling turned to look at the wet orange fiber of the stump, and felt an idle pity for the tree. 'I'm going to have a Coca-cola,' she declared. Slimane said he, too, would like one" (*CS*:359). Slimane must abandon his timeless innocence in order to join the world Fräulein Windling has taught him so much about.

Their Heads Are Green

For a while after *Let It Come Down*, Paul pursued different types of projects. He returned to the more deliberate process of writing music: the opera for Libby Holman, the music for Jane's play *In the Summer House*, the cantata commissioned by pianists Gold and Fizdale, *A Picnic Cantata*. He also wrote several travel essays that appeared throughout the 1950s in the periodicals *Holiday* and *Vogue*, in which he recorded his reactions to India, Ceylon, North Africa, and other countries. Some of these essays were published as a collection in 1963 under the title *Their Heads Are Green*, a title he took from a poem by Edward Lear, and they focus on the differences between Westerners, North African Muslims, Hindi, Buddhists, and Indian Muslims — nonfictional accounts of the same material he pursued in short stories and novels. In the introduction to the book, Bowles emphasizes his interest in people as opposed to scenes of natural beauty and in diversity, stating, "It is the human element which gives [the traveler] the strongest impression of difference" (*THAG*:7). Throughout his essays, Bowles laments the trend toward homogenization of cultures and the "irrational longing" of non-Western people to Westernize societies. Bowles identifies with the people of the developing countries. He describes the incongruities of worlds whose inhabitants have been made to feel like "aliens," and he sides with the aliens.

Bowles was certain European civilization had forced people to assume all kinds of protection, to surround themselves with a variety of cages, the topic he explores in "All Parrots Speak." "The only macaws I have seen chained or caged belonged to Americans: they were vicious and ill-tempered, and the owners announced that fact with a certain pride" (*THAG*:28). In contrast, indigenous people, however rigid their social structure might be, remain free of psychological imprisonment. Their inner lives have more "satisfactory meaning" than those of Westerners. What gives the non-European such satisfaction? Beliefs and rituals. In Bowles's view, a twentieth-century continuation of the historical tradition of romanticism, the Westernizing process destroyed the basic wisdoms that all peoples once possessed. European civilization took away "the old harmony" (*THAG*:67). But in places where its tentacles have not yet reached, people have managed to preserve a "state of grace." "In Tunisia, Algeria and Morocco there are still people whose lives proceed according to the ancient pattern of concord between God and man, agreement between theory and practice, identity of word and flesh (or however one prefers to conceive and define that pristine state of existence we intuitively feel we once enjoyed and now have lost)" (*THAG*:67–68). These people have not fallen, have not yet experienced the split between man and nature, man and God. They have not yet become self-conscious, aware of their nakedness.

Bowles's indigenous inhabitant is in harmony with nature because of the ability to experience the world through the senses with no intellectual distancing. In the 1963 London edition of *Their Heads Are Green*, but not the 1984 edition,[84] Bowles included an essay titled "Mustapha and Friends." According to Grosser, this piece angered the Istiqlal, rumors of which instigated Paul's flight from Morocco to Portugal in 1958. On his part, Bowles stated that he had dropped the piece, "since everything it describes pertains to the colonial era and not to the present day."[85] Bowles describes a fictional Arab who, more clearly than anywhere else in Bowles's writing, embodies his idea of the indigenous person. Mustapha's

> powers of observation are extraordinarily acute, and his sense–impressions, while perhaps not highly differentiated, are intense; he is very conscious of smell, color, sound and texture, and he takes it for granted that the senses with which he perceives them were given him to be gratified on every possible occasion. He can spend hours merely sitting on the ground, looking out over a landscape, in a kind of contemplation that you and I will never know. He is not engaging in metaphysical reflections; you might say, rather that he is enjoying the act of existing. (*THAG*:94)

To enjoy the act of existing: this is the secret of the indigenous person, the treasure possessed without knowing. Self-awareness disrupts the unity, destroys the identity, obliterates the possibility of enjoying one's existence.

Bowles's interest in ethnography was a clear extension of his romanticism, which led him to pity and nearly despise the Western-educated Moroccans who were changing what he had first loved about the country. For Bowles, the Europeanized Moroccans failed to realize the importance of such immutables as fate and its relation to personal freedom. "The old helplessness in the face of *mektoub* (it is written) is gone, and in its place is a passionate belief in man's ability to alter his destiny. This is the greatest step of all; once it has been made, anything, unfortunately, can happen" (*THAG*:65).

With freedom of choice comes responsibility for one's own destiny. Those whom Bowles believed to be most satisfied were preliterates like Yacoubi or Bowles's amalgamate Mustapha. Mustapha "has not yet abrogated the pact between nature and man, according to whose terms she commands and he obeys" (*THAG*:94). In bondage to nature, Mustapha is the freest of all men. He is at one with nature and at peace with himself and Allah, knowing, "That which is all-powerful goes far beyond the realm of moral consideration. The supreme law of the universe is that what is inexorable is thereby right" (*THAG*:94).

Bowles considered the essays in *Their Heads Are Green* "reportage," not "travel writing." Most came directly from his travel journals with few alterations. He recorded his observations of the countries and people as events transpired. Reminiscent of his adolescent fantasies of the universe as a telekinetic sending station, Bowles suggests that the writer functions as a kind of lightning rod, an "instrument of reception." The writer must "ensure that the experiences which will constitute his material come into being, and this requires awareness, imagination, and flexibility."[86] Elsewhere he wrote, "He has got to draw the events themselves out of thin air, make them happen, before he can write about them. Obviously, he can never know what they are going to be; at the same time he is obliged to put himself in such a position, or create such situations, as will make some sort of continuation inevitable."[87]

For Bowles, "The best travel books, . . . are the ones where the writer has done little more than choose the locale in which the hypothetical events which will decide the course of his plot are going to take place. This done, he had gone there to live out the events in the most constructive way he can and with only the purpose of living in such a way that the events take place."[88] This description is remarkably close to how he approached writing fiction. As a profoundly passive travel writer, Bowles, like a character in one of his novels, placed himself in situations and then observed what transpired, often as a result of his being there. Remaining open to experience, he felt that he magnetized to himself the kinds of events he wished to write about and became someone to whom things happened. Things happened because he had actively assumed the passive role of one ready to receive them.

Bowles's eye for the fantastic and his deadpan style of describing the surreal in life occasionally compete handsomely with fiction. There is a passage in his autobiography that bears striking similarity to one in *The Asiatics* (1935), a best-selling novel of the 1930s by popular writer Frederich

Prokosch, an acquaintance of Bowles in New York.[89] Prokosch's protagonist comes out of a forest pool in India covered with leeches, "Soft and painless things that swelled up even while I watched them. It was hard to pluck them off my skin, for they stretched like a rubber band. They'd come rippling toward me from all sides, through the marsh and over the wet swamp, hundreds of them."[90] Bowles accounts in his autobiography: "At the hour when the rain ceased and the sun's first hot rays hit the steaming lawn, the leeches came out of the ground, glistening and black, thousands of them (they were only about an inch long) bending and stretching their bodies as they moved forward and waving their triangular snouts in the direction of whatever was there for them to attack. . . . It was like a scene out of science-fiction, as if the earth itself were sending out countless tiny black tubes, each with the sole aim of filling itself with my blood" (*WS*:303–4).

Prokosch had never visited Asia and thus drew on other sources to create his fictional world. Bowles, on the other hand, had traveled to the places Prokosch only fantasized about and then placed himself in the role of a fictional protagonist. As if in a dream, Bowles drifted from one situation to another, all the while relishing and recording every detail. He once wrote, "Since early childhood it had been a fantasy of mine to dream a thing in such detail that it would be possible to bring it across the frontier intact—the next best thing to being able to hang onto all those fistfuls of banknotes that must always remain behind when the eyes open" (*WS*:165). In only one composition (*Par le Détroit*) and in very few short stories did he achieve this ambition. Yet as he crossed geographical borders, Bowles's method of writing facilitated bringing his experiences across the frontier nearly intact.

Not everyone appreciated Bowles's approach to the genre. Travel writer Freya Stark complained Bowles combined "a superb gift for observation with an almost complete lack of the capacity to deal with it once it is made," a lamentable result of the fact-gathering nature of the documentary age.[91] Stark completely missed the philosophical point of Bowles's detached style of report-age. For Bowles, the act of observing and recording was all; he had cultivated a disinterest in analyzing his observations since his childhood Volga Merna stories. His job as a writer was not to convince or analyze but merely to select and describe. Philosophically, Bowles remains opposed to active intervention on the part of a writer. The readers must draw their own conclusions.

The Spider's House

In the spring of 1952, a crowd of Tangier Moroccans gathered to protest the international administration of the city and to demand Moroccan independence. As they spilled out of the Casbah into the large town square, the

Socco Grande, police suddenly opened fire and then inexplicably retreated into the station. The crowd went on a rampage through the town, smashing store windows, overturning and burning cars, and looting shops. In the end, eighteen Moroccans and one Dutch boy died, and more than one hundred Moroccans and forty police suffered injuries. Bowles was in India at the time but read of the riots and wondered whether the Tangier he knew had come to an end. By the winter of 1953/54, a full-scale terrorist campaign for independence against the French was under way. Leading the campaign was the Istiqlal (Independence) Party, founded in the 1920s by Allal al Fassi, who had studied at the university at Fez. In response to the demonstration, the French replaced the Sultan Mohammed bed Yussef with a figurehead of their own. Since they considered their sultan a direct descendant of the prophet appointed by God, this sacrilege caused the Moroccans to demonstrate daily in the streets, and shopkeepers spent most of their time rolling their storefront steel shutters up and down, preparing for riots.

Bowles "had the impression that everyone was waiting for a signal to be given, and that when it came, all hell would break loose" (*WS*:322). While Bowles was writing *A Picnic Cantata* for Gold and Fizdale (scheduled for a 23 March performance), he began to think about a short piece on Tangier for John Lehmann's *London Magazine*. The article, "Letter from Tangier," would discuss the cultural life of Tangier, although Bowles said it would no doubt have to encompass a great deal more than what *London* readers customarily considered "cultural," since "there is probably no city of this size in the civilized world that has so little [European] cultural life." By March 1954, Bowles knew that the piece would have to take on a different tone. "It will be difficult to keep political material out, inasmuch as political disagreements here have now reached the point where every two nights or so a policeman is murdered in the streets of Tangier."[92] Still, maintaining "the light touch" seemed to make such events, and perhaps their description in his article, palatable. In the finished version, which appeared four months later, Bowles concluded, "In spite of these shadows cast by coming events, the character of the city is one so intimate that it is somehow difficult to consider them seriously. 'We'll probably all be murdered in our beds,' people say smiling, and nobody believes it for a minute."[93]

Bowles spent three weeks in bed with typhoid in March–April 1954 and then drove to his favorite city—Fez. "A startling change had come over the city. Each day the newspapers published lists of the previous day's atrocities. No one knew where the next dead body would be found or whose body it would prove to be. The faces of passersby in the streets showed only fear, suspicion, and hostility" (*WS*:323–24). Writer Peter Mayne was wounded by a hand grenade at the Café de France in Marrakech. Jane just missed getting hit by the same explosion and then went to Fez where a bomb went off in the post office the day she arrived. Paul wrote to Lehmann, "The French papers have a special page each day consecrated to news of the previous day's terrorist attacks."[94]

Drawing on this experience and his years in Morocco, Bowles began a third novel, *The Spider's House*, the last to be set in Morocco. ("What would it be like," he wondered, "to see one's city, the only city one knows, falling to pieces from day to day before one's eyes?" [*WS*:324].) Bowles focused his book on a young Arab inhabitant of the native quarter of Fez, drawing political material from the current climate. Some aspects of Amar, the young Moroccan protagonist, resembled Ahmed Yacoubi, and the heart of the book consists of the friendship between Amar and an American writer, John Stenham. A third major character, who serves to balance Stenham's affection for Amar, is an American traveler, Lee Burroughs Veyron, who prefers to be called Lee (again Bowles played a name game: "Lee" was also the name of the protagonist in Burroughs's *Naked Lunch*).

The novel chronicles the effect of the uprising on the illiterate resident of the Fez Casbah and explores the interior world of this young man — the mind of a "savage" — the unlettered, untrained, pristine imagination. In the prologue Stenham says that "unaccountable behavior on the part of Moslems amused him, and he always forgave it, because, as he said, no non-Moslem knows enough about the Moslem mind to dare find fault with it."[95] Bowles retains this uncritical attitude even as he attempts to crawl inside the mind of the Muslim through Amar and through Stenham's relationship with Amar and other friends in Fez.

Amar's innocence and the purity of his belief in the principles of Islam prevent his personal involvement in the Muslim rebellion against the French, for he sees through the pious facade of the Istiqlal and finds the hypocrisy of its leaders appalling. He cannot accept the Istiqlal's manipulation of Islamic tradition in support of political independence, for he thinks only in terms of destiny and divine justice. The Istiqlal hope for an autonomous government like that of Westernized Egypt and envision "platoons of Moslem soldiers marching through streets where all the signs were written in Arabic script, they saw factories and power plants rising from the fields; he saw skies of flame, the wings of avenging angels, and total destruction" (*TSH*:104).

The difference between the politically radicalized young men of Morocco and traditionalists like Amar signified the widening gap between the Morocco Bowles had known in the 1930s and the Morocco of 1955. In the latter and in the novel, the world has changed to the point where the old doctrines of Islam no longer explain or govern existence. "Sins are finished," a potter tells Amar, and Amar finds he secretly agrees, knowing that if this is true,

Islam is finished as well (*TSH*:114). If Amar, the innocent, remains true to his heritage and to natural laws, he is in danger of extinction.

Stenham has more in common with Bowles than any previous protagonist. A writer living in Fez, he does not drink; he comes from a New England family that considered both religion and sexuality unmentionable subjects; and his fascination with Moroccan culture developed from a trip he made as a college freshman twenty years previously. Stenham's friendship with Lee contains elements of Paul and Jane Bowles's deep but frequently difficult relationship. In attempting to persuade Lee to accompany him on a ride through town, Stenham anticipates her possible arguments against the trip and states them before she has a chance to do so herself, feeling "that if it were he who made the objections for her, she might be more likely to accept" (*TSH*:179). Stenham also has a past as a Communist party member and admits to a friend that he lost his enthusiasm for the party when the United States became allied with Russia in 1940. As he lost faith in the party and Marxism, he came to question the concept of human equality, until "he had found no direction in which to go save that of further withdrawal into a subjectivity which refused existence to any reality or law but its own." Living in isolation and careful exclusion of news from the postwar world, he finds that "little by little he had had the impression that the light of meaning, the meaning of everything, was dying. Like a flame under a glass it had dwindled, flickered and gone out, and all existence, including his own hermetic structure from which he had observed existence, had become absurd and unreal" (*TSH*:195–96). As Bowles had complained while writing *Let It Come Down*, Stenham feels that his work serves little purpose other than that of therapy.

The Spider's House continues Bowles's search for the lost childhood as it furthers his theory that laws and rules are designed to restrain and even to deaden all that is young and free on earth. Amar's father has the mosque and the Koran to sustain him in times of crisis. This is "the immutable world of law, the written word, unchanging beneficence, but it was in some way wrinkled and dried up." Amar's world is that of "the live, mysterious earth," constantly changing and each day a surprise to those who walk it with their eyes open (*TSH*:29). Amar puts his trust in nature—the natural world and his own nature—rather than in humanly made or imposed discipline and rules. Like the young Paul Bowles who shunned a formal training for his musical gifts, Amar refuses to attend school. He makes himself strong by "allowing his body to express itself, to take complete command, and develop itself as it wished" (*TSH*:88). Stenham is attracted to a "natural wisdom" in Amar and decides that the key to it is "an unusually powerful and smoothly functioning set of moral convictions" (*TSH*:329). Amar's cultural heritage is a set of moral principles, not a learned set of rules. Illiteracy is a virtue that keeps him free from the shackles of the word.

Amar and the other Muslims that Stenham befriends in this novel have retained a sense of a timeless universe, and this more than any other feature fascinates Stenham and keeps him in Morocco. "They embodied the mystery of man at peace with himself, satisfied with his solution of the problem of life; their complacence came from asking no questions, accepting existence as it arrived to their senses fresh each morning, seeking to understand no more than that which was directly useful for the day's simple living, and trusting implicitly in the ultimate and absolute inevitability of all things, including the behavior of men" (*TSH*:217). Lee also enjoys the timeless Muslim world, as it represents something she lost as a child (the Bowlesian "lost childhood") and hopes to find again.

Stenham's opposition to independence is rooted in his belief that it will destroy the Moroccan world he cherishes. Lee hopes that it will at least improve the daily lives of the Moroccan people. Stenham rejects her assessment: "He would have liked to prolong the status quo because the décor that went with it suited his personal taste" (*TSH*:286). When he and Lee disagree over the possible outcome of the revolution, she calls him a "hopeless romantic without a *shred* of confidence in the human race," an assessment that he does not dispute (*WS*:239). Lee believes that Stenham praises Amar because even without knowing it, he stands in opposition to Western culture and civilization. Amar is a "perfect symbol of human backwardness," one who wears "the armor of his own rigid barbaric culture" and consciously defies progress (*TSH*:345).

When Lee and Stenham visit a religious festival outside the city, Lee's reaction to the incessant drumming reveals another aspect of the non-European world that recurs in Bowles's novels, one to which all his protagonists must reconcile themselves. Lee hears a message in the drumbeats: "It was saying, not precisely that she did not exist but rather that it did not matter whether she existed or not, that her presence was of no consequence to the rest of the cosmos" (*TSH*:319). Amar reminds Stenham that *Islam* means surrender and that submission to divine authority is the first duty of all people. In his opinion, Lee will never be happy because she has not yet accepted that she is powerless and can achieve nothing in this life save that which Allah wills.

It seems that the friendship between a Muslim boy and a Nazarene (Christian) is not part of Allah's will. Bowles echoed his own life when he allowed a Western woman to come between Stenham and Amar. Amar leaves the festival and Stenham when Lee gives him money to buy a gun, but he finds that he misses the Nazarene: "He had been a friend; perhaps with time they could even have understood one another's hearts" (*TSH*:394). The uprising in Fez puts an end to the relationship: Stenham decides to leave the city and cannot take Amar with him.

The Spider's House is Bowles's most finely crafted novel, his most measured assessment of the existential situation. It is, as well, his most complete exploration of the "savage mind" from the inside, a rare attempt in Western literature to see the world through the eyes of the other. In his earlier two novels, Bowles showed the results of the collapse of cultural authority: without a culturally imposed belief system, every choice is moral, and one must choose in order to define and become oneself. In *The Spider's House*, through the character of Amar, Bowles quietly explores what Western civilization has lost in the process of discarding earlier beliefs. Amar signifies the pre-Westernized citizen, at peace with himself, possessed of a sense of place and of self that comes from feeling secure in his culture and in his religion.

Bowles dedicated this novel to his father, which on the surface seems an appropriate, even conciliatory gesture. It is the least controversial of his novels, the only one with no gratuitous murder, no extended explorations of drug- or fever-induced trance states, and the existential problems lack the urgency of the earlier novels. It appears to be the one that Claude Bowles would have found the least objectionable.

Yet in the second chapter, Bowles describes a detached Amar undergoing a ferocious beating from his father. "[Amar] felt the lashes from a great distance. It was as if a voice were saying to him: 'This is pain,' and he were agreeing, but he was not convinced" (*TSH*:25). Amar takes solace in the thought that if he does not cry, "his hostile silence was in a sense a victory over his father" (*TSH*:16). The beating is more severe than any Paul ever suffered—indeed, Bowles stated in his autobiography that his father beat him only once—yet its inclusion in the opening pages of a book dedicated to his father suggests that a subtle form of revenge could be counted among the therapeutic qualities Bowles found in writing.

Amar's father is a holy man, a devout Muslim, and Amar has inherited and has learned his beliefs. Paul received no such inheritance from his own father; such a set of beliefs was part of the ideal childhood Bowles had lost. Bowles believed it was important to stay in the religion in which one was raised and wrote extensively about the impossibility of moving far beyond one's cultural belief system. In *The Spider's House* Bowles calmly and lovingly shows the beauty and tragedy of a boy born into a culture that is being destroyed.

Bowles finished his novel in March 1955 while on a visit to the Ceylonese island Taprobane. In Morocco, terrorists continued to plant bombs in cafés and markets, cut telephone lines, and destroy railways. In Tangier, demonstrations for independence continued until a massive, final street gathering on 18 November, when the Sultan Mohammed V returned from exile in Rabat to rule as chief of the new Moroccan government. Moroccans carried the blood-red Moroccan flag while tribesmen in djellabas marched through the streets banging drums and cymbals. Morocco became an independent nation on 2 March 1956, and on 29 October the International Zone of Tangier was formally ceded to Moroccan rule.

Taprobane

While Paul worked quickly on *The Spider's House*, convinced the end of the "old way of life" in Tangier was near, he and Jane found themselves more involved with their Moroccan friends. By May 1954, Jane had returned to Tangier after an absence of nearly two years, just in time to nurse Paul through a serious case of typhoid. As if giving in to the inevitability of remaining in Morocco, Jane asked Cherifa to join her in the house in the Casbah. Cherifa came, and though at first she insisted she was only visiting or working there as a housekeeper, she remained part of Jane's household for many years. As Cherifa became the dominant force in Jane's life, Jane's writing dropped into the background.

Cherifa was notorious in the Casbah as an aggressive and independent woman. Like Ahmed, she claimed descent from nobility. She was openly lesbian, and many suspected her of witchcraft and supernatural powers. In a male-dominated social structure, to profess magical abilities, to assume a shaman's role, was one way for a woman to assume a privileged position, and Cherifa craved power.[96] Her friendship with Jane, a "rich American," also gave her certain social esteem and notoriety. And by insisting on gifts of food, money, and articles of clothing in exchange for her companionship, she maintained her control of the relationship.

Paul distrusted Cherifa, and she in turn disliked him with an intensity bordering on hatred. He claimed she carried a switchblade and had murderous impulses toward him and all men. His biggest concern was Cherifa's influence on Jane. Cherifa was loud and tough, and with Cherifa around, Jane drank more and wrote less. Late in the summer of 1954, Jane told Paul she had found packets of *tseuheur* (magic) under her pillow. When Paul told Ahmed about the *tseuheur*, Ahmed called Cherifa a "witch" and refused to visit Jane in the house in the Casbah because Cherifa was there: then he insisted that Paul stay away as well, to which Paul agreed.

Like it or not, by mid-1954, the Bowleses were involved personally in the spiritual and mystical native underground that had fascinated Paul since 1931. Each was living with a present-day example of indigenous traditions. Their companions encouraged the Muslim separation of worlds, male and female, finding reasons why Jane and Paul should be spending even less time together than they did already. Cherifa made a point of pulling out a huge knife to study whenever Paul visited and threatened to castrate any man who touched her.[97] Jane told friends that Ahmed made her feel like a visitor in her husband's house.

Since his departure from New York in May 1953, Paul had been trying to convince Jane to join him in the upcoming trip to Ceylon. She had demurred, saying that she preferred the notion of the Sahara in the spring.[98] The trip to the Sahara, however, did not materialize, and in December 1954 Paul insisted Jane join him and Ahmed on their trip to the island of Taprobane. She agreed, he said, in order to have "something concrete to object to." Together, Paul, Jane, Ahmed, and Temsamany traveled to the "land of death."

Located in the Southern Hemisphere, Taprobane's December summers offered Paul a chance to escape winter entirely. Paul hated cold weather. Having spent November through February 1954 in New York, overseeing the music to *In the Summer House*, he was not about to spend another season battling the cold of Tangier where "one is conscious only of the cold. Now it's a little less cold, now it's much colder, in this room one must keep on one's overcoat, here it's too cold to sit down at all, we'll have to sit upstairs in this cafe because downstairs our feet will freeze, put the rug under your feet so they won't get so cold, have you enough fuel to last out the evening or ought we to buy more now while the bacals are still open?"[99]

Paul had visited the island on his 1952 trip to Ceylon and had written about it in the terms he reserved for the special places in his life: "It was far better even than I had expected, an embodiment of the innumerable fantasies and daydreams that had flitted through my mind since childhood. . . . The hot smell of the sun on the flowers, the sound of the sea breaking on the big rocks. . . . More than ever the island represented an unfulfilled desire, an impossible wish."[100] Soon after his first visit, he managed to purchase Taprobane for five thousand dollars. According to legend, the island was a rock pile where the Buddhists of Ceylon threw cobras, which their religion forbade them to kill.

In 1926, Comte de Mauny-Talvande built a huge octagonal house at the western end of the island with a circular central room thirty feet high. From the terrace surrounding the house, a garden of orchids and bougainvillea dropped steeply to the sea. The terrace views encompassed a bay on one side and the ocean on the other—an ocean that extended without interruption by land until it reached the South Pole.[101] At low tide, the Bowleses could wade to the island from the mainland, but at high tide they had to swim. It was, according to Peggy Guggenheim, the "southernmost inhabited spot in the Indian Ocean, . . . fantastically beautiful and luxuriant with every conceivable flower and exotic plant from the east."[102] Jane's reaction was different. Paul writes that when Jane first saw the island, "a mere tuft of rain forest rising out of the sea," she groaned. Later, looking up the "long series of stairways through the unfamiliar vegetation, toward the invisible house," she told him, "It's a Poe story. . . . I can see why you'd like it" (*WS*:325). Paul had tried to prepare Jane for some of the more unexpected aspects of life on Taprobane, such as the "nightly invasion of bats," but he had not told her about the three-foot wingspread of the bats called "flying foxes" nor had he mentioned their huge and visible teeth. Jane was terrified.

Knowing Jane's horror of the "forces of nature," only desperation to get her away from what he considered a destructive environment in Tangier can explain why Paul would have brought her to this wild, overgrown rain-forested island where she would be forced to undergo, without surcease, the very kinds of excesses of the primitive she loathed. Paul wrote, "The house is self-sufficient in eggs, orchids, lobsters and crabs, and that's all. Everything else has to be bought on the mainland."[103]

He hoped that isolated from the parties and people of Tangier, Jane would regain equilibrium and settle down to writing or resume their previously close relationship. But the estate house was completely without amenities. The central room opened onto several smaller rooms separated from the main room by curtains. The wind blew through the chamber at will, because the windows were simply open spaces in the walls, and the oil lamp that provided the only light cast monstrous and unpredictable shadows. Even Paul was affected by such extremes of nature as were found on Taprobane. He wrote his editor at Random House, "There is, I think, an interesting study to be made of the strange psychological effect this powerful world of vegetable life can have on the person who opens himself to consciousness of it . . . it's a rather unpleasant sensation on the whole, to feel very strongly that plants are not inert and not insentient. And here, of course, they grow so fast that one imagines one can almost see them moving, and when you watch their movements from day to day you see how diabolically ingenious they are in getting the better of one another."[104]

In addition to knowing Jane's feelings about untamed nature in general, Paul knew specifically how she felt about Taprobane before he brought her there, although perhaps he thought exposure to the island might change her mind. His private notebook describes her reactions in terms infinitely more forlorn than his autobiography reveals.

> I was pretty well prepared . . . by her reaction when I broke news of the purchase. "I think you're crazy" she cried. "An island off the coast of Ceylon? How do you *get* there?" My ingenuous delight in announcing the acquisition

of my prize prevented me from realizing that she was by no means asking for information. . . . "And once you're on the island there's nothing between you and the South Pole," I added. She looked at me for a long moment. "You'll never get me there," she said presently. But three years later she did allow herself to be persuaded, and she did stand on a black rock under a casuarin tree and look out across the Indian Ocean towards the South Pacific. "I'm going to die of the heat," she told me.[105]

Even so Paul did not allow Jane's distress to interrupt his routine. Each morning he strolled across the island, wearing only a sarong and sandals, to watch the sun rise. Then he wrote until noon, walking around the island with his notebook in hand. In the afternoons, he consulted with Ahmed on his painting.

Peggy Guggenheim visited and found Jane on the edge of a nervous breakdown. Jane found the island ghastly. She could not appreciate the elegance of the thirty-foot ceiling in the house Guggenheim likened to the Taj Mahal: Jane was afraid of shadows. Paul was working; Ahmed was working; but Jane was not and could not. Nor had she any escape. Except for occasionally wading through waist-high water to the mainland, she spent her time drinking with the chauffeur, Temsamany. The combination of her blood pressure medicine and as much as a fifth of gin daily only increased her wild mood swings. After two months on the island, early in February 1955, she and Temsamany left for Tangier.

Paul and Ahmed left to spend six weeks in Japan, and when they returned to the island in May, Paul found the house depressingly empty without Jane. He closed it up and returned to Tangier, sending a completed draft of *The Spider's House* to Random House before leaving Ceylon. By July he was back in Tangier working on corrections. It was published in November 1955, the last novel he would write for nearly ten years.

Paul was about to close several chapters of his own life. That summer he finished the opera on which he had been working for several years — *Yerma*. In February 1956, a group of Moroccan youths in the Casbah stabbed his friend Christopher Wanklyn. (Wanklyn claimed the stabbing was due to his own "foolishness" at strolling through the Casbah at four in the morning with his friend Jorge Jantus. Some "louts who had been carrying on a sort of vendetta against Jorge" attacked them, and when Wanklyn pursued them, one of the men stabbed Wanklyn in the back.[106]) The Wanklyn attack precipitated an exodus of Europeans from the medina.[107] Paul let go of his house in the Casbah, where Barbara Hutton was now the sole remaining non-Muslim, and moved to the modern apartment building across from the American consulate. Late in 1956, his parents came to visit Tangier, and when they left, he wrote the short story "The Frozen Fields," which openly discusses the conflict with his father, unresolved for years. Finally, he decided to sell Taprobane: Jane hated it, and he could no longer afford the expense of maintaining it. The buyer was Irish writer and editor of the *Illustrated Weekly* of India, Shaun Mandy. Bowles was never able to get his rupees out of the country.[108]

After a futile month in Ceylon trying to make legal arrangements to transfer moneys from the sale of the island, he and Yacoubi toured East Africa so he could write a piece on Kenya for the *Nation*. They had traveled as far as Las Palmas in the Canary Islands when, in April 1957, Paul received Gordon Sager's telegram informing him that Jane had suffered a stroke. For a decade, Paul had been living a timeless existence, writing, visiting with friends, traveling summer to summer from the desert of Morocco to the jungles of southern India. Now he suddenly became aware of time's passage—"I did not know it, but the good years were over" (*WS*:336).

BOOK VI

CLOSER TO THE SUN, 1957–

Oh I'm sad for never knowing courage,
And I'm sad for the stilling of fear.
Closer to the sun now, and farther from the heart.
I feel that my end must be near.

> —Jane Bowles, "The Old Woman"

Escape from Morocco

THERE WERE SEVERAL stories surrounding Jane's stroke. The night it occurred—4 April 1957—she and Cherifa had argued, and Jane had gone to Gordon Sager's apartment where, after fasting all day, she had drunk a lot. She probably ate some *majoun*. Several friends, and Paul, were sure that Cherifa had poisoned her, as Cherifa had threatened to do for years.

Jane's stroke left her with partial vision, partial paralysis of her right arm, a speech problem, and aphasia. Long before her stroke, Jane had written in a journal, "My father predicted everything when he said I would procrastinate until I die."[1] Jane had been putting off writing for years. Now she had a variety of medical reasons for not writing: she suffered seizures similar to those in epilepsy; her writing hand was dysfunctional; she could not see the material she typed with her left hand; she could not dictate clearly, she could not remember words, or she would say the opposite of what she meant.

In addition to her physical symptoms, Jane suffered from depression, paranoia, agoraphobia, and violent urges. Brion Gysin felt her mental state was "just a continuation of what she had been doing, of being out of the ordinary."[2] Joe McPhillips agreed: "She was always out of touch. Reality was different for her than most people.[3] In the summer and autumn of 1957 she made two separate trips to England to stay at clinics in London, Oxford, and

Northampton. Following these, Paul found her mental state "completely normal": "She has never been emotionally *normal*, and since her illness she has been even more inclined than usual to worry. But still, I should say she has been herself, but more so."[4] Shortly after her second return to Tangier in late November 1957, when she felt she was beginning to cope with her symptoms, Ahmed Yacoubi was arrested.

Morocco was changing rapidly in a wave of nationalism. Moroccans insisted that everything from striped awnings in front of cafés to the restaurant fare itself be changed to erase the memories of French and Spanish rule in the International Zone. The new regime declared it would reestablish morality and punish decadent Europeans. Police compiled a blacklist of the unemployed, tax avoiders, and homosexuals, including some of the most socially prominent Europeans on the Mountain.[5] The Bowleses escaped questioning, but Yacoubi was arrested and accused of having sexual relations with a fifteen-year-old German boy. Paul and Jane both visited him in jail and brought him food but finally decided for the safety of all to leave for Funchal, Madeira, in February 1958. In March, Christopher Wanklyn informed Jane:

> The Tangier situation is not too good, and I think it would be very unwise for you to go there for quite some time. Temsamani [*sic*] has been called in four times for questioning. He was asked about Paul's relations with Ahmed, and yours with Cherifa. He gave the right answers, that Cherifa was your maid, that Ahmed and Paul slept in separate rooms, and that he was only the chauffeur and didn't know anything about your private lives. . . . Temsamani has been very loyal in the whole affair, but has finally had enough, and asks me not to write to him anymore directly.[6]

Temsamany took the Jaguar that Paul had given him, sold it, and went to Germany. Cherifa left the city for her family's home in the hills.

In Funchal, Paul became a caretaker for his wife. It was not a job for which he was emotionally well suited, nor was she. Her illness restructured and restricted their lives in countless ways. Paul felt renewing Jane's interest in her work might be a key to her recovery. To provide therapy, each day he spent hours encouraging, almost forcing her to write. He would read to her whatever she had laboriously typed and would make suggestions, voicing his approval. "I would read it and say, 'It's marvelous,' and she would say, 'You're just saying it. It isn't true. I can't think the way I could. I can't visualize.'"[7] When she was able to write, other problems arose. She destroyed much of her work, and some of it just disappeared. Paul wrote to his parents, later, in 1961, "Jane works every day on her new play. Two pages of it blew out the window the other day. No copy. That always seems to happen to her. In Mexico a whole novel blew out of the hotel window once and she enlisted a dozen Mexicans to look for the loose pages."[8]

Paul was worn out. He had less help with Jane than before and felt isolated "in the intellectual emptiness of Portugal." He eagerly awaited the new James Purdy story in the June issue of *London Magazine*, he wrote, since Purdy's book sent by James Laughlin "provided the only bright spot in our Madeira sojourn. I read it aloud to Jane (who as you know can't read) and she liked the stories so much that she wouldn't let me read one every night, for fear the supply would run out too soon."9 News from Tangier continued to be depressing, and Jane's progress had slowed. A letter Jane wrote Paul later that year suggests that in Portugal he considered suicide preferable to the prospect of Jane's continued depression or their having to leave Morocco forever. "You threatened suiside [*sic*] if you had no money or if you were trapped with me and I didn't cheer up or if you were trapped in America," she reminded him.10

In mid-April, Jane was compelled to return to New York to renew her passport, while Paul remained in Portugal. Since the Bowleses had left most of their possessions in Tangier, Paul wanted to stay close until he was, as Jane put it, "once more joined together with your clothes."11 In June he and Maurice Grosser leased a house in the fishing village of Albufeira, only to receive a phone call from Libby Holman saying that his opera *Yerma* was about to go into production. He left for New York to attend rehearsals and to provide one last aria. During this time Jane began speech therapy at Lenox Hill Hospital in New York. Her therapist forced her to write for him, although her vision was so impaired that she could not read what she had written. The fragments that survive are pitiful, agonizing attempts to articulate her unnamable terrors. Following treatment of the physical side of Jane's problem, in early October her mother and Paul agreed on hospitalization at the Cornell Medical Center in White Plains, a psychiatric clinic.

Paul remained in the United States for as long as Jane was in New York, traveling to Denver for the 29 July 1958 opening of his opera *Yerma*, where he found the orchestra "lamentable" (*WS*:341). Reviews were lukewarm but noted Bowles's "outstanding musical score," calling his music "haunting, weird, mystical."12 Carlos Surinach conducted at the Ithaca College Theater performances, where Bowles thought the orchestra did a better job. Bowles confided to Tennessee Williams that *Yerma* was "pretty miserable" and blamed it on the direction and the choice of Rose Bampton for the Old Woman.13 A reviewer for the *Ithaca Journal* described the score as "an intricately woven score, textured to fit as a background to dialogue, accompaniment to the women's and men's choruses, rich and full when used as an interlude between scenes or to set a mood, 'torchy' and throbbing when in combination with solo voice, exotic and rhythmically exciting for the dance."14 The instrumentation for *Yerma* reflected Bowles's taste for strings, winds, and percussion, and consisted of harpsichord, harp, cello, winds, and percussion.[15] The opera never went on to a New York City debut; it closed after ten performances.

Actor and director José Ferrer asked Bowles to write a score for *Edwin Booth*. Bowles accepted, hoping the project would distract him while he waited for Jane to conclude her treatment in White Plains. The play had a tryout in Hollywood before opening in late November, and reviewer Brooks Atkinson noted simply, "Paul Bowles has composed background music to suit every mood."[16] Los Angeles, "The City of the Future," horrified him. It was "a truly exotic culture, and perhaps one of the strangest of all time" (*WS*:341). The boldness and casualness of the city's young people shocked him. The very existence of smog was astonishing. He heard twenties' jazz tunes resurrected to be played with *danzón* and *bolero* rhythms and wrote, "Decidedly civilization had turned and begun to devour its own body. One night I sat at a desk for forty-five minutes talking with Oscar Levant; the following night I watched our encounter on the television during a Chinese meal at the Gershwins' house. It was both horrible and fascinating" (*WS*:341).

As an expatriate Bowles saw for the first time the elements of modern civilization that other American writers in the late 1950s had seized upon: the fragmented, fast-moving, recycled world of technology, media, and environmental disaster. He considered moving to Santa Fe, New Mexico, but decided it was not his world. He belonged to a different time and place, hundreds of miles and years away from his native country. The United States had become the pinnacle of modern Western civilization, and to Paul, it was a foreign country. No matter how long he might remain in the United States, it was never again his home.

In October, Paul heard from William Burroughs, who was still in Tangier. The city was in chaos, with some friends being questioned by police, some fleeing the country, and others, such as himself, managing to remain relatively unmolested. He added: "I have it from Paul Lund who allegedly read it in *España* that you were officially expelled from the Sherifian Empire no reason given by Rabat. . . . For myself never passed a quieter and pleasanter month eating Majoun and working."[17]

Nevertheless, when Jane's condition improved, she and Paul returned to Tangier, and Paul found, to his surprise, "that more *kif* is smoked in the streets and cafes here than ever before. In fact, everything seems very much the same as always," he wrote to Tennessee Williams. By March 1959 Jane was "her old self again,—happy and joking about everything." Paul told Williams that returning to Tangier was the "best thing she could have done," because there she had a routine to follow and could do so easily. He and Jane were sharing their small apartment with Cherifa and two maids. "It's not quite my idea of a permanent set-up," he wrote. Perhaps just as important, Ahmed was now living with "an American girl" and preparing to leave Morocco. "I've seen very little of him, naturally, as he's completely taken up by his new life," Bowles wrote. With Ahmed involved and Jane apparently settled, Paul decided, "there seems little point in my hanging around here."[18]

Bowles had anticipated writing the music to Tennessee Williams's play *Sweet Bird of Youth* and was waiting for the word to return to New York and to work on the play. The decision was a long time in coming, and he wrote with some anxiety to Williams, "I came away from New York thinking that I should be back within a few weeks, and am now somewhat staggered by the sudden shift of plans. . . . I suppose I can only wait and see what comes in the mail."[19] Jane's illness had been expensive, and they needed the money a commission would bring. When all parties involved finally agreed, Bowles had six weeks in which to complete the score and present it in New York. He rented an apartment and a piano in Tangier to work on the score, finishing it on board ship while traveling to New York. The play opened on Broadway on 10 March 1959 to pleasing reviews of Williams, actors Paul Newman and Geraldine Page, and Bowles's music, "spidery and tinkling music of exquisite texture."[20]

The Beats

As a young composer in the 1930s and 1940s, Paul had been well known to artistic and intellectual sophisticates. Despite his solitary nature, he had sought the company of artists he respected, as if to increase his stature by association. The strategy, if it was such, had worked. Bowles established himself as a successful composer. By the time his first novel was published in 1949, his theater music and chamber works were widely respected. Friends and fans followed his new literary career and his move to Morocco with great interest.

The 1950s were expansive years for Paul. He went from the success of his first novel to publish two more novels, two collections of short stories, many travel essays, and a text for Peter Haeberlin's photographs of the Algerian Sahara, published as *Yallah*. He traveled throughout North Africa and southern Europe in his Jaguar. He bought an island and lived in eternal summer between Morocco and the jungle of Ceylon and took trips to India, Japan, and the east coast of Africa. Friends visiting him from abroad included the most celebrated artists of the era. As his New York friends had formed the hub of the theater and music circles, his Tangier friends were the elite of the expatriate community.

Almost forty when his first novel was published, in the space of a decade Paul had moved from the position of a promising young novelist to a writer's writer. James Purdy once wrote him, "I am deeply pleased and proud of what you say about *The Nephew*—because *you* say it and because this book nearly killed me to write. . . . Believe me Paul, nobody could have said anything finer than you about my book, and no finer writer could say it."[21]

The generation called the Beats took him as their unofficial literary elder statesman. In 1957 several of the Beats came to Tangier to help William Burroughs pull the "chaos of sheets of yellow paper" scattered around his room in the Villa Muniria into manuscript form. (Burroughs claimed he picked up after himself every day, but Paul remembered obvious shoe prints on the manuscript pages on the floor, along with rat droppings and pieces of cheese sandwich.) Jack Kerouac arrived in February and stayed till early April, retyping the manuscript and complaining to Burroughs that the material gave him nightmares.[22] Just before Kerouac left, Allen Ginsberg and Peter Orlovsky arrived, having made the trip on the strength of Ginsberg's two-hundred-dollar award from the National Academy of Arts and Sciences and Orlovsky's army disability pay. Soon afterward, Alan Ansen arrived and began indexing Burroughs's materials, while Ginsberg and Orlovsky edited and typed. They worked in six-hour shifts and in the evenings sat on the porch of the Villa Muniria drinking sherry and watching the sunset. By June, they had assembled two hundred finished pages of the manuscript that was published two years later as *Naked Lunch*.

Shortly after his arrival in 1957, Ginsberg called Jane Bowles and introduced himself as "Allen Ginsberg, the Bop poet." Paul was in Ceylon at the time, but when he returned he had Ginsberg and his friends over to his apartment, where he played Indian music and rolled *kif* cigarettes for them. He introduced them to Francis Bacon. Bacon and Burroughs became close, which seemed natural to those who knew them both and felt that Bacon painted the way Burroughs wrote. After Paul and Jane left for Portugal, Paul wrote a couple of letters to the entire group of Beats, "Allen, Peter, Gregory, and Jack (if present)."[23]

Back in New York for the opening of *Sweet Bird of Youth* in 1958, Paul attended a dinner party Libby Holman gave for Allen Ginsberg, Gregory Corso, and the Soviet consul, at which the Beats behaved outrageously, calling Krushchev and Eisenhower idiots, offering the Russians marijuana, and making overt sexual advances. Paul's description of the scene in his autobiography casts his sympathy alongside the Russians; like them, he was of the old school and considered high jinks indecorous. Showmanship went against every instinct in him and reactivated his lifelong conviction that the artist should remain invisible.

Yet because of the Beats, Bowles's work now had an American literary context. The work of Burroughs, Lawrence Ferlinghetti, Ginsberg, and Kerouac translated and made more accessible the topics and methods Bowles had first explored in the 1940s. Thanks to Kerouac's book *On the Road*, a genuine counterculture formed around the ideas of "hip" and "beat."

By 1961, the "Beatniks" had invaded Tangier. Paul found this development appalling. "Everyday one sees more beards and filthy blue jeans, and the girls look like escapees from lunatic asylums, with white lipstick and black smeared around their eyes, and matted hair hanging around their shoulders."[24] In May, Allen Ginsberg, Peter Orlovsky, and Gregory Corso returned to Tangier; in July, Alan Ansen arrived, and in August, Timothy Leary, who brought psilocybin capsules from the Swiss Sandoz laboratory. Although Paul often had the entire group over to his apartment, a guest that summer described Paul's attitude as barely disguised "what-fools-these-mortals-be."[25] To his parents, he wrote with amusement at the social success of the Beats in Tangier. "The residents have been outdoing themselves giving parties for them."[26]

Bowles's short stories and novels had charted the underside of modern civilization, a feat that put him at the tiller of a generation with which he otherwise had little in common. Norman Mailer wrote, "Paul Bowles opened the world of Hip. He let in the murder, the drugs, the incest, the death of the Square . . . the call of the orgy, the end of civilization."[27] For Mailer, Bowles was the new American existentialist, the "hipster" who knows that the only way to cope with the death sentence hanging over the twentieth century is "to divorce oneself from society, to exist without roots, to set out on that uncharted journey into the rebellious imperatives of the self."[28] In "The White Negro," Mailer identified two alternatives for the postwar American: the hipster and the square, which followed the same typology André Gide had laid out forty years earlier in a book that remained Bowles's favorite —*Les Caves du Vatican*. Gide's "crusted" and "slim" suggested alternatives for living: either in conformance with society or by rebelling against it. The "slim" were able to slip through social requirements untouched, yet their distinguishing characteristic was that they did not "present to all persons and in all places the same appearance."[29] For Bowles, who thought an artist should never look like an artist, this kind of rebel presented an elegance the hipster lacked.

In temperament and literary style Bowles was closer to Gide and his successors, the French existentialists, than to any of the American Beat generation who followed. Bowles grew up on Gide and translated Sartre for the American stage. His existentialism was psychological, and his characters fought intensely personal battles against a private and individual alienation.

Kerouac, Ginsberg, John Clellon Holmes, and other Americans writing in the early 1950s used existentialism to supply a philosophical foundation for their social commentaries. The Beat generation that Holmes described in his novel *Go*, that Kerouac immortalized in *On the Road*, and that Ginsberg lyricized in *Howl* was completely American. The Beats pitted themselves against a morally deficient cultural authority, while Bowles was at odds with existence itself. Bowles's work may have ushered in the world of hip, but Bowles himself was no hipster. He shared more with Victorians such as Oscar Wilde, late romantics such as Rimbaud, or early moderns such as Gide. Among literary existentialists, both French and American, he remained a romantic, convinced that pre-European societies lived according to ancient principles and beliefs that saved them from the existential anguish of modern civilization.

If the Beats were social democrats, Bowles was a social aristocrat. Privately, he preferred many of the old ways to the new. Illiterates interested him more than political revolutionaries, and he missed the comfortable, small, French-run restaurants and inns scattered through Morocco and the orderly English establishments in India. To Ginsberg and Orlovsky, he wrote in 1962, "I think the truth is that the India I liked is the India that no longer exists. My happiest memories are of the hotels and their impeccable service and the barefoot silent domestics who brought chhota hazri and pulled back the curtains on the gardens outside, and the crows that came down from the trees to rob strips of bacon and pieces of toast."[30] Although, in his own way, Paul enjoyed living on the fringes of Western society, he preferred those fringes to be comfortable and discreet. He had no need to perform or to shock deliberately in the way the Beats did. Further, Paul appreciated the long history of expatriate and disfranchised artists before him. Paul had not opened the world of hip. He merely stuck his foot in the door Rimbaud and Gide opened decades before and graciously held it there until the Beats claimed it for their own.

Bowles was a generation older than most of the Beats, except Burroughs, and though he formed strong friendships with some of the figures associated with this movement—Allen Ginsberg, Brion Gysin, and William Burroughs—he was unwilling to become part of any movement, whether literary, social, or cultural. For years Gysin said that he had tried to avoid the Beat Generation on Paul's advice, after Paul had written him, "I can't understand their interest in drugs and madness." Only later, Gysin said, did he understand that Bowles meant just the contrary, and Gysin forever regretted not having met Jack Kerouac.[31] Bowles's and Gysin's ambivalence toward the Beats was understandable; they saw the Beats embracing as if for the first time ever a set of interests and ideas with which Gysin and Bowles had matured. These two older writers had formed their ideas about artistic experimentation during the surrealist movement, had breathed in mystical notions during childhoods lived in clouds of Helena Petrovna Blavatsky incense. Brion Gysin, born six years later than Bowles, had aunts who had been to India, practiced theosophy, and followed the life of Krishnamurti, as had Bowles's relatives. Like Bowles, Gysin had been in Paris during the height of the surrealist movement. As a painter, he had shown in a 1935 surrealist exhibition until André Breton expelled him and his work, presumably for Gysin's acknowledged homosexuality.[32]

Bowles wrote about the Beats with scepticism, yet his letters to Ginsberg, particularly after the 1961 visit to Tangier, betray unmistakable fondness and contain plans for travel together in Ceylon or India, plans that fell through because of Jane's illnesses. These letters are chatty and rambling in a style that more resembles the younger Bowles writing to his friends Daniel Burns and Charles Henri Ford than the weary Bowles of the sixties. He signed them with "love."

Burroughs, born in 1914, was closer in age to Bowles and Gysin than to most of the Beats. He lacked Bowles's and Gysin's direct experience with the surrealists, but he had lived in Europe during the height of surrealism and had taken with him many of their ideas, particularly that of automatic writing. He once described his own work as "almost like automatic writing produced by a hostile, independent entity."[33] Like Gysin and Bowles, Burroughs had lived in New York in the 1940s, but his friends had been the younger, literary crowd that included Jack Kerouac and Allen Ginsberg. He collaborated with Kerouac on an unpublished novel, "And the Hippos Were Boiled in Their Tanks" (1945), which they considered the first American existential novel. Allen Ginsberg collaborated with him on two books: *Yage Letters* (1963) and *Queer* (1952). When Ginsberg, Corso, and Burroughs attended a party in Paris in honor of surrealists Man Ray and Marcel Duchamp, Ginsberg insisted that Duchamp kiss Burroughs, in a ritual succession of power from one generation to the next.[34]

Paul liked Burroughs's work enough to give *Junkie* to Brion Gysin to read. In so doing, Bowles set the wheels in motion for one of Burroughs's most infamous literary techniques—the "cut-up"—a way of combining pieces of narrative by cutting out sections of text and putting them together in different sequences. The cut-up was Gysin's discovery. Drawing on the surrealist tenet of demystifying art, Gysin had theorized about applying a painter's technique to writing. One day he accidentally cut through a pile of newspapers with a Stanley blade and suddenly realized that it was possible to treat written words as physical material, attacking them physically with scissors or a blade and rearranging the "raw words."[35] Burroughs saw this technique as a tool of enormous importance for his work and began applying it to all sorts of manuscripts he had written but never published. When he described it at a writers' conference at Edinburgh University in 1962, he caught the attention of writers from all over the world.

Bowles always doubted the value of the cut-up technique, but independent of Gysin and Burroughs's "discovery," he embarked upon some experiments of his own that predated the cut-up. In the early 1960s, during the day Bowles worked on various articles for such publications as *Holiday, London Magazine, Gentlemen's Quarterly*, and *Kulchur*, and at night he amused himself by writing "stories about Moroccans" (*WS*:347). Starting with fragments of narrative, "anecdotes, quotations, or simple clauses deprived of context—gleaned from separate sources and involving, if anything, entirely different sets of characters," Bowles then imposed on himself the task of connecting the fragments into a cohesive piece (*WS*:347). *Kif* smoking provided him with the glue to bind the fragments together.

Bowles had long been interested in *kif* and as a teetotaler preferred smoking it to drinking. In a notebook he wrote, "These . . . tales deal with aspects of twentieth century life in a region where the kif pipe, rather than the glass, is the key to the exit door from the phenomenological world."[36] He did not smoke *kif* in order to write the stories, rather, he used the idea of *kif* as a device to connect his arbitrarily selected incidents. First he listed several situations he had heard about or observed that year in Morocco and assigned each one a letter, from A to K. Then he created a pattern for three groups of letters (A, B, G, K; C, D, H; E, F, I, J) and used this formula to create three stories. For the fourth story in the collection, Bowles took three statements by a *kif* smoker and constructed a seven-paragraph story around them, the paragraphs being arranged in the story according to a pyramidal pattern based on the point of view of the characters involved. Thus the stories are not drug-induced hallucinations but literary puzzles through which Bowles gathered ethnographic notes. Since the episodes themselves are unique to Morocco, it is appropriate that the fictional device used to link them—*kif*—originated in that part of the world, as well. The overall effect is a collection that evokes the *kif* smoker's world, a parallel universe to which *kif* opens the door.

At Ginsberg's suggestion, Bowles contacted Lawrence Ferlinghetti about these stories, and Ferlinghetti quickly agreed to publish with his City Lights Press. Throughout production Ferlinghetti graciously deferred to Paul's wishes. The book appeared late in 1962, after an extended discussion between Bowles and Ferlinghetti concerning the cover design. Ferlinghetti had designed a cover with a drawing of a Moroccan scene, but Bowles wanted a photograph of *kif* pipes, and he wanted to keep all mention of North Africa off the cover and out of the title. Respectfully, Ferlinghetti relinquished his own cover design. The book came out with Paul's photograph on the front cover. Instead of "Three Kif Stories" or "Three Hashish Stories," the title was *A Hundred Camels in the Courtyard*, taken from the Moroccan saying, "A pipe of *kif* before breakfast gives a man the strength of a hundred camels in the courtyard."

For several years, Bowles had been using a tape recorder for the purpose of aleatory composition—composing by combining random combinations of sound. Bowles surely drew on his surrealist background for this technique, collecting "found" sounds from the world around him, slowing them down, mixing, and rerecording them. He called this music *musique concrète*. In 1960, he created a piece called "The Pool" from various recordings, including night noises of the city of Tangier.[37] He sent the piece to Burroughs, who wrote back exclaiming over its beauty. Five years later Burroughs was still writing to Bowles about new ways to use the tape recorder, which Burroughs preferred to the textual cut-up work. Burroughs suggested recording parrots, adding, "After all a parrot is a tape recorder but perhaps with limited storage space."[38] Bowles did not use the tape recorder for his fiction but did use it to record the tales of Moroccan storytellers and often left it running in his apartment to record random conversations. Burroughs continued his experiments, even creating chapter headings for his book *The Soft Machine* by folding together texts of *The Sheltering Sky*, "Pages from Cold Point," and "A Distant Episode." The results: "Last Hints" and "Where the Awning Flaps."[39]

A much later work by Bowles that bears the mark of the cut-up experiments of the 1960s is *Points in Time* (1982), a collection of narrative episodes divided into eleven sections, all on the subject of Morocco. The inspirations for the book came from historical writings, popular songs, legends, and stories from Morocco, with equal weight given to all sources. In it Bowles did not attempt to link the fragments but allowed their juxtaposition to create a literary collage of the jumbled country in which past and present still exist simultaneously. Stories of transformation, conspiracy, magic, piracy, saints, and holy men mingle with ancient sayings, a modern popular song, and enigmatic images. He tells a tale of a rabbi who devoted himself to Islamic texts for years in order to discuss them intelligently with his Moroccan friends, only to be accused by them of sorcery and subsequently executed for arguing against Islam. Bowles relates also the story of the Moorish sultan who studied Christianity in captivity and came to admire Paul's Epistles, telling his captors, "The only fault I find with Paul is that he deserted Judaism."[40]

Like Bowles's beloved city of Fez, the narrative is a maze of blind alleys, dead ends, and twisting passageways that surprises and delights the reader.

Bowles's use of language reached its highest austerity in this book that he called a "lyrical history." Its episodic form owes a debt to his musical background, but the condensed and powerful prose demonstrates the evolution of Bowles's language. In this slim volume Bowles's experiences as a poet, composer, ethnologist, and novelist coalesce into the mature expression of his artistry.

Nothing could be more typically Bowlesian than the fact that Paul's maid threw out the first section of *Points in Time* as he was working on the book. He wrote, "Nothing irreplaceable is lost, and I have to be optimistic enough to believe that the second version may be superior to the first."[41]

Up above the World

The Bowleses continued to receive visitors in Tangier. Ginsberg returned in 1962, and he and Bowles traveled to Marrakech only to find that the beautiful marketplace had burned down the day before. Tennessee Williams came to Tangier and took Jane each day to the beach, where, Paul said, they could be found "in an atmosphere of deck chairs, towels, highballs, and cold cuts" (*WS*:351). Jane supervised the household and the preparation of all meals, and with illness exaggerating her tendency to agonize over all decisions, this consumed nearly all her time. Interruptions occasioned a flurry of indecision. Paul wrote about the annual Barbara Hutton ball. "Jane has decided to go, but to stay away from the room with the jeweled tapestry and sofa-cushions. Also not to go into any part of the house directly under the terrace on the roof, for fear of being crushed when the house caves in . . . she is buying a series of evening gowns and matching accessories, and that of course augments her anguish, since she can't decide what to wear."[42]

Jane's friends occasionally invited her to make short trips with them, but she was reluctant to leave Paul, whom she felt would not eat well if she were gone. She was also terrified of being away from her doctor and her Moroccan companions, whom she paid to look after her. As she recovered from her stroke, other health problems emerged. A hernia required operations in 1960 and 1962. Early in 1962, she suffered a painful attack of shingles. She could not sleep, ate very little, and drank more. Paul later recalled, "Our combined worlds orbited around the subject of her poor health. Each week she seemed to have a new symptom to add to the old ones; the horizon of her illness was slowly widening" (*WS*:351).

Again, Paul tried to get Jane interested in her work. Late in 1961, she received a grant from the Ingram Merrill Foundation to write a play. She decided to set it in Camp Cataract, the site of an earlier short story that she still loved, but she found writing this play next to impossible. At Paul's urging, she allowed an off-Broadway company to produce *In the Summer House* in 1964, but when the play closed after a short run, Jane was devastated and felt her failure confirmed. Paul encouraged her to collect her stories for publication with Peter Owen, and she objected at every turn.

> It all seemed so simple, a reprint, twenty years after publication. But for her it assumed tremendous proportions. She was sure it would be reviewed, and *would* everyone understand it was an early work, and they would be sure to loathe it, and she couldn't bear reading adverse reviews, and having the whole thing raked over once again, and the first publication was already a traumatic experience, and did I want her to have a nervous breakdown or what?[43]

Paul gathered the stories together himself, fictionalized Jane's journalistic piece "East Side: North Africa," and mailed them to Owen for publication under the title *Plain Pleasures*, which appeared in 1966, as did another volume, *The Collected Works*. The reviews were quite good, and David Herbert gathered them together and took them to Jane to read to her. After he finished, Jane told David that he could not have done anything crueler. "It all makes me realise what I was and what I have become," she told him. Then she took his book and underneath *The Collected Works* she added, "of Dead Jane Bowles."[44]

Always a complainer, Paul complained surprisingly little throughout Jane's difficult illness. In his letters he mentioned the problems involved in caring for someone as nerve-rackingly indecisive and heedless as Jane, but the comments underscored his pain and growing sense of loss. Joe McPhillips "was absolutely dumbfounded by the intimacy and closeness between them, moreso than in any two people I've known. They had remarkable, unique rapport. They could sit together at a party and be totally unaware of others around them."[45] David Herbert found it "touching and extraordinary to hear them talking and laughing in the next room as though they had just met and were being at their most scintillating in order to charm each other." He added: "The Bowles' marriage is based on mutual admiration and deep affection; nothing could spoil this ideal relationship."[46] Jane's gradual decline left Paul "distraught and unable to write, compose or accomplish anything," Herbert wrote.[47]

Emotionally separated from his wife by her illness, Paul continued his psychological explorations. In their letters, Burroughs, Ginsberg, Rorem, and he discuss a variety of experiences with mescaline, *quaoujh*, *majoun*, and other indigenous substances. Paul even proposed using the proceeds from a project to release a set of records on Moroccan trance music to pay for the trial of Timothy Leary. But Bowles's drug experiments in the 1960s involved

African hallucinogens. As with his travels and travel essays, Paul was interested in reporting his experiences.

In 1963, Bowles began a new novel that was to include a diabolic drug experiment imposed by a deranged murderer on a couple he suspects to have witnessed his crime. Paul avoided synthetic hallucinogens and used his experiences with organic drugs to construct the hallucinations of that novel. He thought the experiment in the book would recreate the feeling of one with LSD, and William Burroughs assured him that it did.[48]

Although Paul has written in several different places that he pursued *Up above the World* as a lark, as a suspenseful "thriller" and a "purely pleasurable pastime," Jane's mental collapse figures into it. By exploring alteration of memory, dreams, sense of time, and state of mind through a drug experiment, the novel allowed Paul to test the limits of sanity. Ultimately, the question the novel asks is how much control one has over one's own mental well-being. Is the world, perhaps, a giant laboratory in which we have been placed so that forces outside our control might tinker with our psychological centers? The possibility still existed that Cherifa, still close to Jane, had poisoned her, just as the central characters in his novel would be poisoned by a diabolical young man. Certainly Jane was struggling with something over which she felt she had no power; likewise, Paul felt her dilemma had maneuvered them both into a bizarre and nearly unlivable situation. The novel could have provided a means of handling at a distance the chaos his life had become.

As always Paul insisted that the writing of the novel come from his unconscious and have as little connection with the ordinary world as possible. His habit had been to form a scenario and an idea of characters and then allow the direction of the story to develop from the writing itself. Yet writing never was to be a mechanical act but rather a journey each day into the unconscious with just enough reserve to be able to report on the expedition. While working on this novel, he explained, "With a novel the work is a good deal more than just consecrating so many hours of the day to sitting at a desk writing words; — it is living in the midst of the artificial world one is creating, and letting no detail of everyday life enter sufficiently into one's mind to become more real than or take precedence over what one is inventing. That is, living in the atmosphere of the novel has to become and stay more real than living in one's own life."[49]

In order to accomplish this task, in the spring of 1964 Paul rented a house in the country. It stood at the edge of a cliff overlooking the ocean and had twenty-five acres of forest. He wrote as he walked along the paths through the woods, with a notebook in hand. Jane and several maids came at noon to prepare a meal, and other guests occasionally came in the evening. After six months of following this routine, Paul had finished his novel.

Up above the World took Paul away from Morocco, back to the part of the world where he and Jane had spent their honeymoon. The central characters of the novel, Dr. Slade (a family name on Bowles's mother's side)[50] and his wife, Day, are on a tour of South America. He is older than she, protective of her, easily irritated, compulsive, and fussy. She is young, pretty, and trim. Her neuroses manifest themselves in the form of nervous energy, anxiety, and fatigue. The Slades are devoted to each other but somewhat estranged, "very separate indeed," as Dr. Slade realizes in the first few pages.

On board their ship, Day becomes entangled with a fellow passenger, Mrs. Rainmantle. Mrs. Rainmantle is one of those people to whom disasters continually happen. Her appearance reflects her personality, which is falling apart around the edges: matted, messy hair and makeup, and stained clothing. After spending an evening together and lending Mrs. Rainmantle some money, Dr. Slade and Day leave her and head for Puerto Farol. Later that day, Dr. Slade reads in a newspaper that Mrs. Rainmantle has burned to death in a fire in the hotel room where they had left her. He hides the newspaper from Day in order to keep her from discovering the tragedy.

In Puerto Farol, Day becomes involved with a second stranger, this time a young man named Grover Soto, or Vero—Vero to his lover, Luchita, but Grove to everyone else, a double identity that intensifies the ambiguity of his actions. Grove takes Day for a drive to his penthouse above the city. He invites Day and Dr. Slade to return later for cocktails. The evening at Grove's penthouse becomes surreal. To Slade, the apartment furnished in leather, glass, and fur resembles more an "over-poweringly elegant hotel than a home. A hotel or a department store."[51] Grove wants to take both Dr. Slade and Day on a drive to his hacienda, but Day decides to stay behind. Suddenly and separately, both she and her husband become very ill and enter feverish, delirious states that last an unspecified and unknowable amount of time. Slowly they come out of their hallucinatory states to the world with which Grove has surrounded them. They have memory gaps, feel weak, and are both completely dependent on him.

The novel reveals that Grove and his sidekick Thorny (who becomes a thorn in Grove's side) engineered Mrs. Rainmantle's death in order to inherit her money (she was Grove's mother) and tracked down the Slades to find out how much they knew. Having decided their secret was in danger, Grove concocted an elaborate plan to hold them hostage while altering their memories with drugs and sound effects. Day gradually comes to suspect Grove, whom she thinks is too watchful, and she has vague feelings of manipulation, as if her thoughts and memories were not her own but had been planted in her by some outside force. She also becomes convinced that Grove has killed her husband, though she does not know why. She escapes to a hotel in town, but Grove finds her, and she is not surprised. She wants only for the terrible night to be over. She sits with Grove in a café at the edge of town overlooking deep, remote canyons slightly visible in the moonlight. "As she sat letting her eyes follow their faint contours, she thought of the terrible expression she had caught on Grove's face in the kitchen, and it seemed to her that all the forces which had made this present scene inevitable had come into being at that time, and that nothing had changed since then" (*UAW*:216). Grove slowly pulls a revolver from his pocket and points it at Day. As we have come to expect with Bowles, the murder itself happens "offstage." In another typically Bowlesian twist, Thorny discovers the advantage of being a witness rather than an actual murderer and blackmails Grove.

Day's final sense of being trapped in a terrifying situation that refuses to change parallels statements Bowles made about his life after Jane's stroke. He had insisted before that his fiction should be seen as less-than-serious writing. His stories are detective fiction; *Let It Come Down* is a mystery novel; and *Up above the World* is a thriller that he wrote merely to pass the time. In truth, the novel was no further from his daily life and concerns than any of his previous three, and in some ways, even closer.

One of the most unusual aspects of the plot is Grove's experiments with Dr. Slade and Day using drugs and hallucinogens. In his autobiography Bowles relates several instances in which friends of his consumed too much *majoun* in his presence and suffered terribly as a result. Robert Rauschenberg, Christopher Isherwood, and Jane, among others, all fell prey to his casual nonintervening with regard to drug consumption. In some cases, the victim ate the *majoun* without knowing what it was or what its effects were to be.

Grove's use of tape recordings also came indirectly from Bowles's personal life. Paul often taped conversations and "generally had one of his tape recorders recording in a corner of the room, which sometimes picked up wonderful sequences of Paul/Jane conversations at their Bowlesian zaniest."[52] Gordon Sager wrote that Paul sometimes "recorded conversations without warning people that he was doing so, and I quarreled with him about that," but added that Jane "surreptitiously cooperated in Paul's surreptitious taping," as if it were another game they played.[53]

Bowles promised a thriller in *Up above the World*, but he could not bring himself to write within the tradition of any genre. The novel departs from the standard mystery thriller in several ways. Bowles was accustomed to writing about the extraordinary in an unemotional style, and this novel was no exception. Although the setting is exotic, the characters bizarre, and the plot filled with drugs and murder, the book lacks the excitement and intensity of a true thriller. Omens and portentous events abound—birds that screech like demons, bats, and storm clouds follow the Slades—yet such ominous signs do not point to immediate danger as in a thriller.[54] The charged atmosphere persists, with no climax and little relief, and the result is that the reader feels more confused than thrilled, a reaction in keeping with Bowles's underlying existential philosophy. The point of view shifts throughout the novel from the Slades to Grove to Thorny, adding to the reader's disorientation. Rather than finding vicarious pleasure in the thriller, the reader becomes a frustrated victim of the writer's refusal to follow literary conventions.

In *Up above the World* Bowles returns to the thread he dropped at the end of *Let It Come Down*. In that novel, as in this one, the protagonist commits a terrible crime, the difference being that Dyar's murder of Thami is an existential *acte gratuit* performed in a *majoun*-induced hallucinatory state. In *Up above the World*, the murders are deliberate. Grove wants to create a universe in which he has absolute control. "What he had in mind when he had fitted together the various possibilities that would form and maintain his present life was an eternally empty schedule in which he would enjoy the maximum liberty to make sudden decisions" (*UAW*:82). Grove writes scripts for the murders and even for discussions with his mistress and rehearses the parts ahead of time with the help of a tape recorder. He tries to control others in his life as easily as an artist takes charge of the characters in his fiction. Yet eventually his plot overtakes the boundaries of his script, and he too becomes a victim.

In his last novel, Bowles creates a criminal-artist who approaches his work (crime) with just the kind of control Bowles always claimed to lack over his writing. In the end, Grove discovers that his control is only an illusion. Bowles identified with his criminal. Like Grove, he experimented with tape recordings and drugs. Like Grove, he would have enjoyed an empty schedule with the liberty to make sudden decisions. In his youth, Bowles had seen the artist as a criminal, and Dyar in *Let It Come Down* and Grove in *Up above the World* fit both those roles. Yet for all the superficial resemblance to his protagonists, emotionally Paul Bowles had more in common with his victims. He used shifting narrative points of view, the changing roles of victims, and the criminal's illusion of control to describe a world in which control is illusory and all depends on fate and point of view.

Next to Nothing

The mental and physical collapse of Jane Bowles from 1957 on brought to recognition the final uncharted planets of Paul's psychological constellation.

For a few years in the early 1960s, the Bowleses both worked on separate works, novels entitled "Out in the World" (Jane's, never finished) and *Up above the World* (Paul's). While Jane struggled to keep from sinking further into mental disorder, Paul rose above the clutter of their lives with his experiments in writing, translation, and music, although he lacked solitude and large blocks of time. In 1966, Jane's condition deteriorated rapidly, and her lack of interest increased to the point of obvious self-destruction.

Jane had complained of being forced to live in Tangier but refused to stay in the clinics in New York, London, or Spain where Paul took her for treatment. She insisted she did not need his constant attention, but when he traveled or lived apart from her, she began to drink and to refuse her medication or to use it indiscriminately. At one point, she took to wandering the streets of Tangier in various states of undress and writing bad checks in the name of Barbara Hutton, checks that Paul was forced to cover. One evening she planted herself outside the gate of the American consulate and began calling the name of the consul's wife and stripped when the woman failed to appear.[55] She went to see Brion Gysin before a trip to the hospital in Málaga. "Well, I'm off to the nuthouse tomorrow," she called through his closed door. "Let me in or I'll take my clothes off."[56]

It was a twisted fulfillment of the prophesy Bowles had made inadvertently in *The Sheltering Sky*. The issues of emotional bondage and personal responsibility became the central forces of the Bowleses' lives. Like Kit, Jane slowly lost her mind. Yet, though increasingly enslaved to her illness, she was freeing herself from the self-imposed requirement that she write.

Becoming a victim of her stroke, she began to divest herself of all personal responsibility. In July 1966, Paul took Jane to New York where she was to stay while he was in Thailand writing a book on the city of Bangkok for Little, Brown. Both of them had agreed it would be better for her to be with friends than alone in Tangier. After he had departed for San Francisco, Jane changed her mind and returned to Tangier, where she indeed proved unable to care for herself. Neither would she write to Paul, who wrote often, begging her for even one line at the typewriter. He urged her to take care of herself, to use caution in taking her medication.

Paul arrived in Thailand in late September, and by October he was bored and frustrated with his attempts to secure permission for an extended stay. Adding to his problems was a cut in his knee, from his having run into a hotel glass door in San Francisco, which refused to heal. He wrote a friend, "You could sum up Thailand in four words: smile, war, green, golden-yellow."[57] He was lonely without Jane and without Mohammed Mrabet, a Moroccan with whom he was now working on several translations. Paul repeatedly urged Mrabet to obtain a passport so that he could leave Tangier and stay with Paul in Bangkok. He asked Mrabet to give him news of his storytelling, his attempts to get his passport, and whether he had been able to get the tape recorder repaired and to send photographs. In November he began planning for his return to Tangier, since it did not appear that Mrabet would be joining him there. Long after he had left Thailand, Bowles continued to pester Mrabet about his passport, writing from Malaysia, Singapore, and Penang that had he taken care of his passport sooner, Mrabet would have been able to see these places for himself.[58] Bowles seemed to excel at placing himself outside the realm of influence in other people's lives and then making futile attempts to control their actions.

Late in December, Dr. Roux wrote that Jane needed him at home. Following a violent epileptic seizure brought on by "too many whiskeys," Jane had entered a "state of depression with obsessive ideas." The doctor found Jane resisted her attempts at regular medical treatment. "Mrs. Bowles stays quietly at home with Cherifa and Aicha. She goes out very seldom, does not read, writes to no one, and spends all day ruminating. . . . Perhaps your return will give her the necessary impetus to come out of her depressive state, but I am not certain."[59]

Paul left Bangkok in January 1967, without having finished his research for the book that consequently, he never published. As was his custom, he insisted on traveling by boat, which delayed his arrival in Tangier until the first of March. By the time of his return, Jane was severely depressed and refused to take even the most basic interest in her own bodily functions. She suffered intestinal adhesions from a lack of bowel activity due to her immobility. In early April, he took her to a psychiatric clinic for women in Málaga.

In July, Paul brought Jane back to Tangier. Nervousness and constant agitation had replaced her depression. In her absence, Paul had found a packet of *tseuheur* in her apartment, and Mrabet warned Paul that Cherifa was using this plant in some evil way. Given the past accusations against Cherifa, the fact that Paul's parrot had died of poisoning in 1966, Cherifa's constantly dunning Jane for money, and her aggressive attitude toward Paul, the only wonder is that he waited so long to act. Although he fired Cherifa, soon after Jane returned, so did Cherifa. As the months passed, Jane's agitation increased, and she suffered painfully after two operations for hemorrhoids, the second of which, Paul wrote to Oliver Evans, left her "screaming all night, and there doesn't seem to be anything the doctors can do for her. No injection calms the pain. This preoccupation has kept me from doing much of anything, as I'm always on the alert for poundings on the ceiling by one of the maids, summoning me; it happens any hour of the day or night. The trouble is that she sometimes tries to get out of bed by herself, and falls, and that always makes things worse."[60]

Toward the end of that year, Jane wrote: "It was only after the end of World War II that I came to Morocco. Paul had come ahead of me and bought a house in Tangier. From the first day, Morocco seemed more dreamlike than real. I felt cut off from what I knew. In the twenty years that I lived here I have written only two short stories, and nothing else. It's good for Paul, but not for me."[61]

In January 1968, Jane retured to Málaga, but her treatment gave her no relief from her symptoms, to say the very least. Electroshock therapy left her more disoriented and unable to remember chunks of her life. She begged to return to Tangier, and Paul tried a number of different arrangements to appease her.

In June 1968, Paul took Jane to a pension run by Americans in Granada, where he hoped she might be happy, but within ten days he was called to come retrieve her. The owners recalled:

> She was very gentle and quiet on arrival, and went almost straight to bed. She was *very* particular about personal cleanliness, and had a "thing" about it. She was nervous about a major accident in the bed, although we begged her not to worry on that score, as we had catered for such a possibility. She would have barely left the bathroom when she would go back in again, sitting for ages on the john—and furiously and meticulously washing herself. All the while she was rather tearful because she could not feel properly clean.[62]

Jane required full-time attention day and night. Attached to the pension was a bar, at which Jane often appeared wearing full makeup but only a sheer nightgown. The bar was dangerous for her, and she frightened the customers. When Paul came for Jane, he brought Mrabet, who went out on the town after smoking a fair amount of *kif* and began insulting local gypsies. The police brought him back to the pension, and he started an argument with Paul, waving a knife about and screaming at Jane, who was sobbing and screaming as well at the thought of being taken back to Málaga. While Paul sought to assure Jane that Málaga was over and done with, Mrabet was insisting on leaving immediately, even before Jane could be calmed. They all took off "at top speed, with Mrabet cursing behind the wheel. Mrabet . . . seemed to have complete control over both Paul and Jane."[63]

Paul then took Jane to a different hospital in Málaga. Finally in February 1969, against the advice of Jane's doctor in Tangier, he brought her home. By now she had deteriorated physically as well as mentally. She had a great deal of difficulty moving by herself and shuffled loose-jointed as she went for walks with Paul, mouth hanging open and eyes glazed. She had trouble following conversations and sat in silence. Two months later, Paul wrote, "Jane herself is pretty low, not wishing to come out of her depression long enough to look at it for what it is. However, I still believe she is getting slowly better, and I'm determined to pull her out of the dark place where she would like to stay. (The doctors don't think it can be done.)"[64] Two weeks later: "Jane continues the same. She has one firm decision in her mind, and that is not to get better."[65] At David Herbert's for dinner one evening, she threw her egg aspic on the floor and started weeping, pleading with Paul to take her home.[66] Herbert said that she was so much better, he was going to plan a party for her. "If you do, you'd better give it in the cemetery because I'm dead," she retorted.[67] The next day she returned to Málaga.

Jane's illness reinforced Paul's feelings of being a bystander in his own life. Although he took steps to intervene in Jane's slow deterioration, for the most part he was resigned to watching his wife's sanity, her health, their life together, and his own freedom slowly slip away from any reason and all order. Some friends felt he did too little in the way of overseeing Jane's recovery. They questioned his agreeing to electroshock therapy, contraindicated in the case of organic damage. At the time he too questioned it and answered his critics, "You pay doctors to tell you what to do and you have to do it then, don't you?"[68] Burroughs, for one, felt that Paul's passivity disguised a secret but conscious method for destroying Jane (one might well question his theory, coming as it did from a man who had accidentally shot and killed his own wife).[69] Yet Paul was powerless over Jane's own self-destructive impulses. "You could see he was distraught after he came back from seeing her," McPhillips said, "It was very difficult for him."[70] Poet Allen Sillitoe wrote that Jane "was right early on when she intimated that Paul would be the death of her, yet at the same time Paul was never to blame for what happened. On another level, his saintliness was amazing."[71]

Reflecting on those years, Paul wrote, "It took me a long time to realize that my life had undergone a tremendous change. The act of living had been enjoyable; at some point when I was not paying attention, it had turned into a different sort of experience, to whose grimness I had grown so accustomed that I . . . took it for granted" (*WS*:351).

While Jane waited to die in Málaga, Paul worked on his autobiography and wrote about both waiting and dying.

> In my tale . . . there are no dramatic victories because there was no struggle. I hung on and waited. . . . "Good-bye," says the dying man to the mirror they hold in front of him. "We won't be seeing each other any more." When I quoted Valéry's epigram in *The Sheltering Sky*, it seemed a poignant bit of fantasy. Now, because I no longer imagine myself as an onlooker at the scene, but instead as the principal protagonist, it strikes me as repugnant. To make it right, the dying man would have to add two words to his little farewell, and they are: "Thank God!" (*WS*:367)

Jane Bowles was catatonic and completely blind when she died in Málaga on 3 May 1973. With her death, Paul was forced to acknowledge the extent of his dependence on her. Jane's fears and excesses of indecision, self-indulgence, and childlike playacting allowed Paul to persevere in his own act, that of the polite onlooker. He played the adventurer, but perhaps, psychologically, she had taken the risks. As is the case with his writing, Paul's awareness of what he had done to keep himself going and his reluctance to change in the face of this knowledge is astounding. After reading Millicent Dillon's biography of Jane, Paul wrote Dillon, "I saw myself as a consistently blithering idiot who stood by and watched the process of destruction, instead of taking hold and stopping it. And yet I know there would have been no way."[72] Commenting on the impact of Jane's death, Paul told her, "You never get over it. It's always with you. At least I don't, because it's disconnected me. I think I lived vicariously largely and didn't know it. And when I had no one to live through or for, I was disconnected from life."[73]

Though Bowles used the technique he called unconscious writing, it was in reality a way not of opening up the unconscious but of separating himself from his unconscious. Though he wrote from within, he treated his inner self as a separate entity and refused identification with his own creative genius. To the fastidious, compulsive Bowles, the unconscious was messy, gushy, and uncontrollable. Its dark fertility, that "damp breeding place of ideas" he had discussed in *Let It Come Down*, was rich with the stuff of life— soil, mud, and blood—and of death, and it repelled Bowles more than any force of nature ever terrified his wife. During one of Jane's worst periods following her stroke, when Paul was in New York and she in Tangier, he wrote to her, "Of course everything's a mess, but please forget the mess now and then each day, because otherwise you won't ever work. The mess is just the decor in which we live, but we can't let the decor take over, really."[74] Paul preferred to believe the "mess" was external, separate from the self. His wife, on the edge of insanity, knew better. In a poem Paul wrote after Jane's death, he acknowledged what she had succumbed to in her madness and what he had tried to deny.

> At first there was mud, and the sound of breathing,
> and no one was sure of where we were.
> When we found out, it was much too late.
> Now nothing can happen save as it has to happen.
> And then I was alone, and it did not matter.
> Only because by that time nothing could matter.
> . . . .
> We thought there were other ways.

> The darkness would stay outside.
> We are not it, we said. It is not in us.[75]

The title of this poem, "Next to Nothing," comes from a one-act play he wrote in 1958 and then used as the scenario for the novel *Up above the World*.[76] Bowles began his most successful and perhaps most personal poem at the request of a friend, Ira Cohen, who asked him for a ten- to twelve-page poem that was a dream. Bowles's response reaffirmed his unconscious approach to poetry: "As far as I'm concerned, all poems are dreams, in the sense that the relationships between words and the relationships between thoughts operate as in dreams. One goes into reading a poem as one goes into living a dream, with no preconceived ideas, totally absorptive, and making no judgment until it is over."[77]

To think of Bowles's poems as dreams explains why some of the images in them seem so familiar. "The tiger at the window smiles," he wrote in a 1940 poem from Taxco.[78] This image returns in the form of a wolf in his short story "The Frozen Fields." In the same poem, he wrote, "The mind turned scorpion lives among its stones." This image had previously occurred in his short story "The Scorpion." Dream images, or images from the unconscious, returned again and again until Bowles had found their best expression. The poem "Next to Nothing" turns out to be the most eloquent and final expression of ideas that had obsessed Bowles for years. "When there was life, I said that life was wrong. / What do I say now?" he wrote,[79] as elsewhere he had said that he did not know the good years were over until they were gone. One section, beginning with the words "The woman pointed," paraphrases Libby Holman's reaction to a ride through the Anti-Atlas.[80] References to an increasingly violent world abound—machine guns and macabre "knifing matches in the stadium":

> I think the people are ready for it, the mayor said.
> Total involvement. A new concept in sports.
> The loser does not leave the ring alive.[81]

Qualitatively, "Next to Nothing" stands apart from the rest of Bowles's poetry. For a reader familiar with his life story, it holds great emotional power. In a section that could refer with equal strength to the Bowleses' marriage or to their life in Tangier, the poem reads:

> On our way out we used the path that goes around the swamp.
> When we started back the tide had risen.
> There was another way, but it was far above and hard to get to.
> And so we waited here, and everything is still the same.

> There were many things I wanted to say to you
> before you left. Now I shall not say them.
> Though the light spills onto the balcony
> making the same shadows in the same places,
> only I can see it, only I can hear the wind
> and it is much too loud.
> The world seethes with words. Forgive me.[82]

Shortly after the biography of Jane Bowles was complete, Paul wrote to Millicent Dillon: "I've read and reread the book so often that it's made me dream of Jane. The scene I remember most vividly is one where she and I were sitting with others around a table talking. Suddenly she became fractious and began to upbraid me. I was angry, so I rose and walked toward the door. I heard her call out: Good bye. And then I heard myself saying: There is no good bye from me to you."[83]

Translating and Teaching

One of the consistent thematic concerns of Bowles's literary work is transformation. Throughout his career, Bowles explored turning something expressed in one set of signifiers into another. In his writing he occasionally tried to turn dreams or hallucinations into a fictional existence in this world. He enjoyed crossing the boundaries between different forms of creative expression, bringing ideas from one world intact into another. He wrote *Par le Détroit*, which he called Dream Cantata, in 1933, precisely as he had heard it in a dream. When caught in a London epidemic of the Asian flu, he wrote his short story "Tapiama" (1957) while under the influence of a raging fever. Only the short story "You Are Not I" came from a dream in which the words on a page appeared in front of him. "Afterwards, I realized this must be about a crazy woman," he said, and invented her story.[84] He once compared writing itself to dreaming, saying, "The periods of writing are rather like long and short dreams in the midst of living the life, but dreams long since forgotten, and of which the only record is the writing itself."[85]

Another way of crossing boundaries for Bowles was to translate, to bring ideas from one culture to another. In the late 1950s, Bowles began working with language that had never before been committed to paper. With Ahmed Yacoubi, Bowles had transcribed a few stories. In 1963, Bowles began translating Larbi Layachi, a Moroccan he had met on an isolated beach outside Tangier. Larbi could neither read nor write, but as they talked, Bowles marveled at his rhetorical skills and sense of detail. Out of their first meeting came a series of interviews that Bowles taped, transcribed, and then translated for publication. *A Life Full of Holes* was the first of many works Bowles would translate for Moroccan storytellers. In the years immediately following Jane's death, he devoted the bulk of his creative energy to these translations, which he called "a vicarious sort of creativity."[86]

Bowles's interest in the illiterate storyteller grew from his faith in the unschooled imagination, which he came to believe provided the richest source of uncensored, ungoverned narrative. In his own writing he tried to suspend judgment, to let the narrative flow of its own accord. He felt that a similar process must be going on with the illiterate, who had never had to harness his thoughts to a written language. Like anthropologist Claude Lévi-Strauss, Bowles believes the illiterate lives in a state of grace because he has escaped the fundamental method by which civilization imposes its will.[87] Thus, storytelling itself began to hold a great fascination for an intellectual of Bowles's inclination. Like Burroughs, who wrote that language is a virus, Bowles distrusted the written word. In 1936, Walter Benjamin suggested that the story is meaningfully related to communal experience, to the organic flow of life into death, where time is ordered by the sequence of events, and the experience of the story is shared. Benjamin argued against the novel, differentiated from all other forms of literature in that it had no connection to an oral tradition.[88] Benjamin praised the artisan class among whom storytelling arose, the peasants and seamen who were its masters. Of storyteller Mohammed Mrabet, Bowles said, "I don't know if he knows the difference between fantasy and fact. I don't think he cares much." Bowles left the impression that he thought Mrabet was thus better off.[89] It was as if in the minds of these storytellers, Bowles had finally found his lost childhood, and he set out to capture it on paper.

Ted Morgan, a frequent visitor to Bowles's apartment, described Mrabet as "a husky young fisherman with . . . a sullen expression, who was always bragging and showing off. . . . One day when Brion came to see Paul, he found Mohammed carrying him around the apartment over his shoulder, like a fireman. 'There's only one thing to do when he's like this,' Paul said, 'and that is to make yourself a limp rag.' Mohammed growled, 'Yo soy bruto.'"[90] Yet Mrabet showed his devotion to Bowles in countless ways. When Bowles was recuperating from an operation in 1984, Mrabet prepared all his meals without missing a day.[91] Mrabet visited Bowles daily, often to prepare breakfast or later for tea, when he amused Bowles's frequent guests with tall tales, jokes, and colorful opinions on world affairs. Cohen said, "You have to understand a lot more than just Mrabet. You have to understand the whole Moroccan culture. It's a very subtle relationship that Paul and Mrabet have. But as they say, it takes two to tango."[92] Bowles translated Mrabet's work and assisted him with paperwork connected with his books. Despite his success in publishing, Mrabet maintained his Muslim outlook, remarking to Paul's visitors, "We're all going to die. I'm going to die. I am nothing. My friends say, 'But you are an author of books.' I say to them, 'Yes, and I will die the same as you.' My friend told me, 'You're crazy.' I told him, 'Thank you.'"93

Mrabet became Bowles's most prolific source of indigenous stories and following the dissolution of his relationship with Yacoubi, a close friend, despite or because of the many obvious differences between them. Their first book together was *Love with a Few Hairs* (1967), a novel about a young Moroccan, Mohammed, who lives with Mr. David but with the help of a spell cast by a Moroccan witch falls in love with and marries Mina. Mr. David owns a hotel near the beach, and Mohammed helps with the bar and, when he is not with Mina, sleeps with Mr. David. Mohammed has learned many things about Westerners from Mr. David, such as that Mr. David prefers that Mohammed ask for money outright rather than hinting, as Mohammed considers more normal. The straightforward narrative simply presents a glimpse of a culture whose relations with the outside world have modernized, while the interrelations of its people have seen little change. Mohammed and Mina's marriage and divorce become a complex game of the sort that had intrigued Bowles for years. "If I play a good game I'll win," Mohammed says at one point, and much later on tells himself, "If I hold out I can win. If a man can keep going long enough he can win."94

Through this and other translations, Bowles brought another point of view into the cultural discourse between Morocco and the West. In introducing such voices as those of the indigenous Moroccans, Bowles has been instrumental in creating what Edward Said has longingly described as a cultural counterpoint, in which several voices weave through and around each other, no one voice more privileged than any other, each of comparable interest and worth, all interdependent.95 Typical of many of Bowles's creative acts, his translations have also been essentially destructive in a social sense in that they are helping to tear down the fortress of Western literary hegemony.

In 1968, Bowles accepted an appointment at San Fernando State University to teach one course in creative writing and another on the existential novel, though he protested, "I'm really a composer with a composer's mind, and I don't even have the normal cerebral functioning of a writer."96 He wrote several letters to his liaison at San Fernando State, Oliver Evans, asking how he should approach the course. Later, from California he wrote to Virgil Thomson, "The classes seem a farce, in that I don't feel I'm 'teaching' at all, and very probably I'm not. However, the students seem satisfied, and I suppose that's what matters."97

During this stay in California, Bowles wrote music for a one-act play by

James Bridges, which premiered at Schoenberg Hall at the University of California at Los Angeles in January 1969. He often dined with Christopher Isherwood and Don Bachardy, and Bachardy recalls Bowles working on a tape for the play. "I remember he got one of the effects by flushing the toilet. It was very mysterious and very effective."[98] Mrabet came to stay with Bowles for a few weeks and soon left, saying California was uncivilized. Once back in Tangier, he then wrote Paul asking to return. Paul answered, "It seems impossible that you want to return here when you hated it so much. If you couldn't stand it two months ago, you won't like it now either." He continued, "You must be joking when you ask whether I want you to send me some *kif* by mail!"[99] As he had written from Thailand, Bowles told Mrabet that he was lonely and bored in California. For diversion, he took long walks along the beach "in a crisp white suit, pink shirt and bow tie. . . . He was a stunning apparition in the bright sunlight there on the beach, fully dressed."[100] Bowles returned to Morocco at the end of the term, by way of Florida.

Beginning in 1980, Bowles again taught writing in Tangier in a program sponsored by the School of Visual Arts out of New York. Bowles did not particularly enjoy the classes, although he found that when they attracted older students, teaching was less a chore. "Perhaps also it's easier to make contact personally with those nearer my own age, and making that contact is all-important if the teacher is to establish credibility. . . . In general, the younger, the less receptive on the surface."[101] To one student he wrote, "Satisfying? Not terribly. No, it doesn't pay very well. It makes me feel a little less isolated."[102] These classes further increased the demands students and visitors made on Bowles's time.

To all visitors, correspondents, and friends, Bowles extended the same graciousness: he refused no interviews or manuscripts and answered all questions patiently. Even after his classes ended, he continued to receive manuscripts with requests for comments. He met such queries meticulously. Of one such writer he asked for patience, explaining, "I've received six items since you left Tangier—including an entire novel and another novel in parts, not complete. . . . To read a story the length of yours carefully and make notes takes many hours; it can't be done in an hour or two."[103] Many of Paul's friends have marveled at his patience with these intrusions, but such behavior is perfectly understandable given his passive, fatalistic acceptance of what life brings his way.

At least two of his students from those summer programs went on to publish novels. The Guatemalan writer Rodrigo Rey Rosa so impressed Bowles that he referred the young writer to City Lights Books, which published Rosa's stories in a collection titled *The Beggar's Knife* (1985).

Bowles translated the stories into English and continued to translate for Rosa.

A second student, Joel Redon, eventually published a novel called *Bloodstream*, but for several years before finishing this work, he sent Bowles short stories, asking for advice and corrections. Bowles responded patiently and in detail, and his suggestions concerned the most basic elements of prose, which to Bowles were of primary importance. Regarding narrative style, he wrote, "I wish you could imagine the story as a filmscript. No flashbacks, no commentary—merely what happens, from beginning to end. . . . A short story shouldn't have explanations; they weigh it down. It shouldn't have descriptions of personality. All these things should be implicit in the action and dialogue, which tell everything."[104] In another letter he reiterated, again using film as a means of explanation: "Information, if it's essential, should be given in terms of action. (Action and dialogue before the camera, as it were, not offstage, and not narrated.) Tell only a small part of what you *could* tell, and imply the rest."[105] As he had after reading Jane's first manuscript, Bowles cautioned his student to be more careful with grammar, spelling, and punctuation: "Above all you must pay stricter attention to your language and the business of getting it on paper with a minimum of orthographical errors and punctuational oversights, which for me constitute your principal weakness. No matter what you may have in your head, the finished manuscript is all anyone else can use in determining your strength as a writer."[106]

To Bowles's way of thinking, such attention to detail constituted the true work of the writer, which is to use language precisely, if not beautifully. "The 'story' exists only inside the mind until it has been made communicable by the act of writing. It's the writing itself that clothes the 'story' in language and makes it alive."[107] To make language come alive, he suggested not just reading carefully but also hearing the prose, just as a composer would play the notes he had written to hear exactly how they sound. "I often wonder if you read over your paragraphs *aloud* after you've written them; it would seem that you don't, or you'd unearth a lot of the weaknesses in the writing. . . . You must ask yourself with regard to every sentence: *Is this sentence exact?*"[108]

As to his own writing, Bowles said he wrote slowly and laboriously but with such attention to detail that he seldom needed to rewrite anything. "The first draft is the final draft; I almost never change anything. I write the story in longhand, copy it on the typewriter, go through it carefully, making any necessary cuts or additions, then retype it, and date it. It's really all one operation."[109] Although he might have written only two pages a day, he so completely dedicated himself to that task that the two pages usually emerged in nearly finished form. He explained elsewhere that he was able to write this way because he completely submerged himself in the imaginary world of his novel and then simply reported on the events that took place there. He has called himself a "peripatetic writer," referring to his practice of writing while strolling, notebook in hand, as at Taprobane, and after seeing his first tape recorder in 1956, he began dictating his prose into the tape recorder.

Since he prefers not to plan before he writes, it is not surprising that over the course of his career Bowles has excelled at the short story rather than at longer forms such as the novel. To write without stopping to judge, review, or determine what comes next is risky, and a strain. Bowles said he quit writing novels because he lacked the energy necessary to conjure up an alternative existence for long periods of time and because Jane Bowles was no longer around to read what he had written.

Midnight Mass

In 1981, Black Sparrow Press published *Midnight Mass*, a collection of twelve stories written by Bowles since 1976. These stories focus more on revenge, deceit, and treachery than any previous collection. They recall the Western-Muslim confrontations of earlier stories located on the frontier where civilization and savagery meet, but here the intersection is psychological and moral.

In "Madame and Ahmed," Ahmed secures his position as gardener for Madame by discovering treachery on the part of a potential rival, short-circuiting that gardener with some treachery of his own, and then using his superior knowledge of the situation to win his position and to disgrace the rival. The husband in the story of that name manages to leave his wife and girlfriend, but both later exact their revenge and ruin him in his new life. Counter to Western morality, both stories imply that one prospers through treachery; the more cunning one is, the better.

In "Midnight Mass," the title story, a Moroccan painter and a European woman seemingly conspire to take possession of a Tangier home that has been left to an exile by his mother. In "The Little House," there is a poisoning, perhaps intentional, perhaps simply bad luck. The Islamic combination of belief in fate—*suerte* in Tangier—and a passion for vengeance fascinates Bowles.

In a key story in the collection, "Rumor and a Ladder," an elderly man named Ducros accidently breaks his leg falling from a ladder in his study. It has been rumored that he is about to sell his house, along with several valuable artworks, although he claims to have no interest in this direction. After being stopped at the airport and accused of trying to smuggle money out of Morocco, he suddenly decides to do just that. "I've already been punished," he declares. "Now I want to *deserve* that punishment."[110] What was a question of ethics now becomes a question of honor.

Ducros expresses Bowles's distillation of the curious game he had observed the Moroccans playing for years concerning the question of honor, a thing quite apart from ethics, connected more with destiny, fate, and luck. At the center of these quarrels with destiny lies the paradox of "dishonorable" deeds performed to preserve or restore one's honor. In a world in which all is preordained by Allah, fortune and honor become the essential variables — fortune completely independent of anyone's actions; honor completely dependent on one's actions. One cannot choose one's destiny, beyond the use of certain potions or charms that have only limited power. Events happen for reasons only Allah understands, perhaps for no reason at all. But what one does with these events after the fact, how one plays the cards, is another matter — a matter of honor. And any hand, no matter how poor or unlucky, can be played with honor. As Bouayad says in "Bouayad and the Money," "It is in the hands of Allah." Luck may shine or not, but one may at least pursue this little game with fortune — this game of retribution and revenge.

Psychologists say that the character type obsessed with revenge, having been disappointed in expectations of love from his or her parents, is engaged in a lifelong battle with them or, by extension, with their world view. Vindictiveness functions to effect a reunion through mutual suffering or mutual annihilation. "Time does not heal the hatred of the pathologically vindictive person. He savors his fantasies and carefully plots revenge. For him, vengeance readily becomes a vital, coordinating principle on the basis of which he organizes his life."[111] One might choose an artistic credo, romantic existentialism, in vindictive opposition to a modern, middle-class world view. In place of civilization, one might construct savagery.

Paul Bowles had many quarrels of his own with destiny, yet he never questioned it as a concept. His was a philosophy that he came to very early in life: one does not choose one's destiny any more than one chooses one's parents or even to be born. From a very early age, Bowles believed himself helpless to change his fate, felt powerless to escape it. He could only wait for it to pass. Bowles saw in the Moroccans he wrote about a people who, like himself, felt powerless to change their situations but were able to invent numerous plots and schemings to manipulate to their advantage what had been dealt them.

In the last story in *Midnight Mass*, "The Eye," the European narrator wants to "find someone on whom the guilt might be fixed" (*MM*:162). Yet he cannot do so without determining criminal intent. The European alone — and perhaps the reader who identifies with him — is concerned with guilt. The Moroccans in the story care about what has happened only in terms of how it affects them, whether or not they can profit by it. For them, there is no absolute wrong or right. There is personal gain or loss, a balancing of the accounts. The narrator muses, "What constitutes a crime? There was no criminal intent—only a mother moving in the darkness of ancient ignorance. I thought about it on my way home in the taxi" (*MM*:162).

Bowles writes from the point of view of his Moroccan characters. By not assuming a Western moral position, by reporting the events neutrally, he implicity supports the position that whatever is, is. He does not stand in judgment, thus aligning himself with the Moroccans, who do not judge but react. Reaction, as opposed to action, is consonant with Bowles's lifelong mode. On whom then can the guilt be affixed? We are, all of us, only moving in the darkness of ancient ignorance.

In Absentia

Bowles first went to Tangier on a lark in 1931 and returned after World War II in order to write a novel. He had not intended to immigrate to Morocco but one day found that he had done exactly that. Even in 1947, he had written Charles Henri Ford: "Certainly I never meant to stay in Tangier again, but for no reason at all I have remained on and on, perhaps because one can get everything one wants here and the life is cheap as dirt, and travel is so damned difficult . . . and mainly the great fact that I haven't the energy to pack up and go anywhere else."[112] By 1963, he was writing to William Burroughs that "the only way to live in Morocco now is to remember constantly that the world outside is still more repulsive."[113] Twenty years later he assessed the city where he had spent nearly the past forty years: "Tangier is now the last word in shabbiness; it has become European only in the sense that the Moroccans have become European. The population consists of partially Westernized Moroccans and the tourists who arrive in tens of thousands."[114]

Throughout his life, Paul bewildered his friends by turning his back on opportunity and success, each time moving farther away from what might have been for him. He wrote in his autobiography that as a youngster he preferred the unmarked paths in the woods, yet increasingly he seemed to scorn paths of any sort. Copland regretted that Bowles had not further developed his considerable talent as a composer. Thomson felt he could have had a long, successful career in the theater. There is no question that although Jane's writing may have initially inspired Paul, her illness robbed him of years of productivity. After that, Paul continued to work on the translations that he admitted interrupted his own writing. His longtime friend Edouard Roditi said, "We have many friends and memories in common, but I've been leading in the past 30 or 40 years a much less withdrawn life than Paul. In a way, I suspect that he has missed much that life might have offered him."[115]

Roditi wrote about Paul's "flight" to Tangier in his poem "Lot's Wife," which he dedicated to Paul Bowles, who had "fled" from those he once loved, "driven to this / Small city where my soul may live." For Roditi, Bowles was "escaping for [his] life from all [his] life," longing to turn and look at the past he left behind but compelled instead to "strive / Ahead into the unknown that awaits me / In the bleak mountains where I'll be safe." In the final lines of the poem, Lot's wife turns back to "join in the stillness of death the life that I feared and failed to live."[116]

Today, Paul lives in the modern section of Tangier across from the American consulate in the same apartment in which he has lived since 1958. The living room is small and dark, with red and yellow Moroccan rugs on the floor and black and gray cushions below the bookcases lining the wall as one enters. A sofa faces the doorway, and the only other furniture consists of two round tables, one in front of the sofa and one in the corner piled with books, and a trunk. The fireplace mantel contains small exquisite art objects, and the fire is usually lit. "One must have a fire," Bowles insists. He greets his visitors cordially, shakes hands with a squeeze. At home he dresses casually, a turtleneck sweater or shirt and tie under a pullover, Wrangler corduroy jeans, brown Hush Puppies. He wears two rings on his right hand. His eyes are clear blue, and he does not wear glasses. His chauffeur has just returned from the market. "For once he got everything he wanted," Paul says, as he prepares tea. "I've noticed Americans don't take sugar these days. I suppose it's bad for you. Of course, eating is bad for you. It will kill you. You can eat for seventy-five, eighty years, and then suddenly one day you're dead."

After years of problems with his digestion and his liver, Paul eats plain food: first a clear soup of chicken broth, tapioca, and soy sauce, over which he shrugs, "It's good if you like it." A small steak, asparagus, and a green salad make up his dinner, "if you call this dinner," he says. "Paul complains about everything, always," said Thomson, "it's part of his charm." Yet as he chats with visitors, one feels this is not complaining, just amused exasperation that the world can be so much the way it is. "It isn't much, this life, but it's all we've got," he says, smiling. "It's not such a wonderful thing." Characteristically, his next thought involves money. "Considering the inevitables, I don't know which is worse: the taxes or the dying that gets you out of paying them."[117]

He has no telephone, and visitors must write or arrive unannounced. Paul prefers it this way: "Talking on the telephone is very much like flying; one always wishes it were over. The nervous tension is terrible. One is definitely out of contact in both cases, and nothing brings one back to reality except hanging up or landing."[118]

He says he often has no idea what he is going to write when he sits down at his paper. "Writing isn't about an idea. It comes more from a kind of feeling." He continues with an inscrutable smile, "But if it comes from the unconscious, how can it be wrong?" He has not forsaken his belief in the integrity of the unconscious. "It's all I've got," he says.

Paul Bowles still dreams at night, but he does not record his dreams or use them for his fiction. "I'm purely hedonistic about dreaming. It doesn't give me anything, but it's the pleasantest part of the day," he says. "What I dream about is places. I very seldom dream about anybody I know. There are people, but they are only passersby, people I met traveling. I dream about landscapes. Or New York. Most of the time I'm in New York."[119]

Several new generations of readers have come to appreciate his prose. This too he shrugs off. "I'll probably be dead before it does me much good." He insists he has not profited by the sale of the rights to *The Sheltering Sky* for Bernardo Bertolucci's movie. Although his agent states the sales figure was in the six figures, Bowles claims he received nothing.

He continues to write, prose that is increasingly journalistic, as if he were only recording the words of a consciousness from which he is completely detached. His writing is sparse, economical, operational, and fascinating. His latest works take the form of letters and journal entries, a narrative form he had first used in "Pages from Cold Point," the story he wrote on board the ship that brought him to Morocco in 1947. They closely resemble his own correspondence, filled with domestic details, observations on the state of the world and Tangier, and in the case of letters, suggestions to his correspondents that he knows even at the time of writing to be futile. The voice of these stories is one of a man removed and detached from the world, powerless over his own life and other people in it, compelled nevertheless to comment and report. It is as if, as he wrote about his adolescence, he were viewing rather than participating in his own existence; as if, as he wrote during his twenties, he were pretending to be living. Only a portion of this work takes the form of unanswered letters, yet in a sense, all his work is a one-sided correspondence with the world. "One day my words may comfort you," he wrote in "Next to Nothing," "as yours can never comfort me."[120]

Paul Bowles waits in Tangier, and everything and nothing are still the same.

NOTES

WORKS BY PAUL BOWLES

SELECTED BIBLIOGRAPHY

INDEX

NOTES

Introduction

1. Paul Bowles to author, 5 December 1988.
2. Paul Bowles to author, 5 December 1988.
3. Walter Kaufmann, *Existentialism from Dostoevsky to Sartre* (New York: New American Library, 1975), pp. 11–12.
4. Kaufmann, *Existentialism*, p. 17.
5. Jean-Paul Sartre, *Existentialism and Human Emotions* (New York: Philosophical Library, 1957), p. 32.
6. Paul Bowles to author, 9 February 1989.
7. Paul Bowles to David McDowell, 15 December 1950, Random House Collection, Butler Library, Columbia University (hereafter cited as Butler).
8. In Kaufmann, *Existentialism*, p. 46.

Book I. The Landscape of the Child, 1910–1929

1. Paul Bowles, "The Worlds of Tangier," *Holiday* 23 (March 1958): 66.
2. Paul Bowles, *Without Stopping* (New York: G. P. Putnam's Sons, 1972), p. 106. Further references to this work will be noted parenthetically in the text as *WS*.
3. For a rich description of Stein in her studio, see James R. Mellow, *Charmed Circle: Gertrude Stein and Company* (New York: Avon, 1974).
4. Paul Bowles, in Oliver Evans, "An Interview with Paul Bowles," *Mediterranean Review* 1, no. 2 (Winter 1971): 4.
5. See correspondence between Rena Winnewisser Bowles and family members, Paul Bowles Collection, Harry Ransom Humanities Research Center, University of Texas, Austin (hereafter cited as HRHRC).
6. Guy Flint to Rena Bowles, 29 January 1924, HRHRC.
7. Paul Bowles, draft of "The Frozen Fields," HRHRC.
8. Henry Ashby, *Health in the Nursery* (London: Longman, 1898).
9. For a detailed historical discussion of child-rearing practices, see Christina Hardyment, *Dream Babies: Three Centuries of Good Advice on Child Care* (New York: Harper and Row, 1983).
10. I am grateful to Betty Fish, librarian for the Rockingham Free Public Library in Bellows Falls, Vermont, who located undated clippings confirming Marjorie Winnewisser's trip to Berlin to study opera, where she reportedly learned that the family name was Vennevitz and that the family was Jewish.
11. Paul Bowles, conversation with author, February 1986.
12. Paul Bowles to Millicent Dillon, 22 January 1983, HRHRC.
13. Millicent Dillon, *A Little Original Sin: The Life and Work of Jane Bowles* (New York: Holt, Rinehart, and Winston, 1981), pp. 44–45.

14. *Springfield City Directory, 1929* (Massachusetts), pp. 891, 1188.

15. Thomas Mulford Farquhar, *The History of the Bowles Family* (Philadelphia, 1907), p. 205.

16. Death notice, *Elmira Star Gazette*, Elmira, New York, 30 December 1933.

17. For information on the Water-Cure, see the 1860 Elmira, New York, *Gazetter*, under "Elmira."

18. I am grateful to Belva Dickinson, George Kloppel, and the Schuyler County Historical Society in Montour Falls, New York, for assistance in locating death notices for Christiana A. and Fox Holden and Darwin W. Mead, husband of Mary Robbins Mead.

19. See listings in *Williams' Elmira City Directory*, Elmira, New York, 1896–1907.

20. Paul Bowles, "Autobiography," *Antaeus* 55 (Autumn 1985): 7.

21. *Catalog*, Simmons College, Boston, Massachusetts, 1907–8, p. 110. Rena was one of six students to complete the program that year, whereas the four-year class of 1907 had fifty graduates. I am grateful to Brenda M. Favreau, assistant archivist of Simmons College, for providing me with this information.

22. *Catalog*, Simmons College, 1906–7, pp. 34–35.

23. Bowles recalls the author as "Dr. Riker." Searches have not uncovered the book or the physician.

24. Rena's last letter to her mother gave details of recent losses in a poker game: nine cents for Rena and thirty cents for Claude (Rena Bowles to Mother & All, Tuesday afternoon, HRHRC).

25. United States Census, 1900.

26. Her poem "The night is long, the night is dark," survives among Paul's papers at the HRHRC.

27. Oliver Smith, conversation with author, April 1985.

28. The New York Department of Health lists simply, "Bowels [*sic*], Paul F.," born 30 December 1910 in the borough of Queens. Although Paul had a grandfather, uncle, great-uncle, and great-grandfather named "Frederick," he has always spelled his name "Frederic." His high school literary magazine, the *Oracle*, notes him as "Paul Frederic Bowles."

29. Buffie Johnson, conversation with author, 1 October 1984.

30. Christopher Sawyer-Lauçanno, in his book *An Invisible Spectator: A Biography of Paul Bowles* (New York: Weidenfeld and Nicolson, 1989), states that Bowles lived at 108 Hardenbrook Avenue until he was five and a half (p. 6). But I have found only 317 Fulton in the *Queens Borough 1913 Directory*.

31. Harvey Green, *Fit for America: Health, Fitness, Sport, and American Society* (Baltimore, Md.: Johns Hopkins University Press, 1986), pp. 294–95.

32. H. T. Finck, "Horace Fletcher, Gluttony's Opponent," *New York Evening Post*, 14 January 1919, p. 79.

33. Green, *Fit for America*, p. 295.

34. Paul Bowles, in Regina Weinreich and Catherine Warnow, *Paul Bowles: The Complete Outsider* (New York: Waterfall Productions, 1993), film.

35. David Handlin, *The American Home: Architecture and Society, 1815–1915* (Boston: Little, Brown), p. 90.

36. Handlin, *American Home*, p. 157.

37. Kenneth T. Jackson, *Crabgrass Frontier: The Suburbanization of the United States* (New York: Oxford University Press, 1985), p. 175.

38. United States Geological Survey, Map, 1910, New York 28, Brooklyn.

39. Robert A. Caro, *The Power Broker: Robert Moses and the Fall of New York* (New York: Vintage Books, 1975), pp. 143–71.

40. Although in *Without Stopping* Paul gives the year as 1916, the *Queens City Directory* shows Dr. C. D. Bowles residing at 76 Herriman Avenue as late as 11 October 1917. I am grateful to William Asadorian for his help in finding a flat map of Jamaica Estates, 1910, 69a, Long Island Collection, Queens Borough Public Library.

41. Paul Bowles, Notebook, Paul Bowles Collection, HRHRC (unless noted otherwise, manuscript materials are part of the Paul Bowles Collection, HRHRC).

42. Again, Bowles says he was in the seventh grade, which would place this move about 1922, since Paul entered high school in January 1924. However, in 1924, Rena Bowles received correspondence addressed to both 207 De Grauw Avenue and 34 Terrace Avenue, suggesting that the move took place that year.

43. Rena Bowles to Mother & All, Tuesday afternoon, HRHRC.

44. There are several World War I era recordings of "Down among the Sheltering Palms," but the earliest listed in the Victor Catalogue is the 1915 Victor Military Band. Since Bowles states he listened to this record from the age of four on (he turned four on 30 December 1915), he probably heard the Victor Military Band recording.

45. See Hardyment, *Dream Babies*, for a fuller description of the upper-middle-class child in the early twentieth century.

46. George Orwell, "Such, Such Were the Joys," in *A Collection of Essays* (Garden City, N.Y.: Doubleday, 1954), p. 52.

47. Orwell, "Such, Such Were the Joys," p. 53.

48. Paul Bowles, in Weinreich and Warnow's film.

49. I am grateful to William Kelly, local historian, for helping me locate clippings related to the Holden and Robbins family, for sharing with me his memories of Mary Robbins Mead, and for showing me Holden Hall. Particularly useful were death notices in the *Watkins Review and Express* on 5 March 1941 (for Mary Robbins Mead) and 23 January 1890 (for Fox Holden).

50. Robert Laurence Moore, *In Search of White Crows: Spiritualism, Parapsychology, and American Culture* (New York: Oxford University Press, 1977), p. xii.

51. Ruth Brandon, *The Spiritualists: The Passion for the Occult in the Nineteenth and Twentieth Centuries* (New York: Alfred A. Knopf, 1983), pp. 1–3.

52. Brandon, *Spiritualists*, p. 37.

53. Brandon, *Spiritualists*, p. 44.

54. Brochure, HRHRC.

55. Mary [Crouch] Oliver to Gertrude Stein, no date, Gertrude Stein Collection, Beinecke Library, Yale University (hereafter cited as Beinecke).

56. One of Bowles's earliest surviving poems, "A Chatting as of Unfetters" (9 December 1927), bears an inscription of dedication to Daniel Burns (HRHRC).

57. Dell's comments in *Intellectual Vagabondage* and *Love in Greenwich Village* are cited in Van Wyck Brooks, *The Confident Years: 1885–1915* (New York: E. P. Dutton, 1952), pp. 488–89.

58. Albert Parry, *Garrets and Pretenders: A History of Bohemianism in America* (New York: Dover Publications, 1960), p. 327.

59. André Gide, *Lafcadio's Adventures (Les Caves du Vatican)*, trans. Dorothy Bussy (New York: Alfred A. Knopf, 1927), p. 95.

60. R. D. Laing, *The Divided Self: A Study of Sanity and Madness* (New York:

Penguin Books, 1969), p. 71. For a discussion of R. D. Laing in relation to Bowles's fiction, see Wayne Pounds, *Paul Bowles: The Inner Geography* (New York: Peter Lang, 1985).

61. André Gide, *If It Die: An Autobiography (Si le grain ne meurt)*, trans. Dorothy Bussy (London: Secker and Warburg, 1950), p. 159.

62. R. D. Laing tells of a patient of his who occasionally felt as if she had "blended" into the landscape around her. Like the young Paul Bowles, she repeated her name over and over to bring herself back to life (*Divided Self*, p. 111).

63. See James S. Grotstein, *Splitting and Projective Identification* (New York: Jason Aronson, 1981), pp. 9–11, 66.

64. Paul Bowles, "You Are Not I," in *The Collected Stories of Paul Bowles, 1939–1976* (Santa Barbara: Black Sparrow, 1979), p. 163. Further references to short stories in this volume will be noted parenthetically in the text as *CS.*

65. Sigmund Freud, "The Uncanny," *An Infantile Neurosis and Other Works*, in *The Standard Edition of the Complete Psychological Works of Sigmund Freud*, ed. James Strachey (London: Hogarth, 1955), p. 234.

66. Gore Vidal, Introduction to *Collected Stories of Paul Bowles*, p. 8. Vidal listed three categories of stories: stories based on locale, stories of "how the inhabitants of alien cultures regard the creatures of our civilized world," and "stories of transference."

67. Paul Bowles, in Evans, "Interview with Paul Bowles," p. 5.

68. Sigmund Freud, *Beyond the Pleasure Principle, Group Psychology, and Other Works*, in *Standard Edition.*

69. Walter Benjamin, "On Some Motifs in Baudelaire," in *Illuminations*, ed. Hannah Arendt, trans. H. Zohn (New York: Schocken Books, 1969), pp. 203–18.

70. Like Edgar Allan Poe, Bowles leaves the reader many clues to the autobiographical nature of the story, even giving a birthdate near his own birthday to the protagonist of the story, as did Poe in "William Wilson." In the original draft, Bowles gave his own birthdate, 30 December, but later he changed it to 2 January (draft of "The Frozen Fields," HRHRC).

71. Paul Bowles to Gertrude Stein, 18 September [1931], Beinecke.

72. Paul Bowles, *Oracle*, November 1927, p. 22, Alderman Library, University of Virginia.

73. Paul Bowles to Millicent Dillon, 7 November 1978, HRHRC.

74. Edna Bockstein Madway to author, 25 November 1983.

75. In the program notes for the 10 and 12 April performances of *Kiss-A-Miss Alley*, Paul Bowles is listed in the part of "The Second Harlequin" (HRHRC).

76. This statement seems another nod to Walter Benjamin, who believed conscious awareness incompatible with remembrance. Benjamin cites Freud's *Beyond the Pleasure Principle*: "Becoming conscious and leaving behind a memory trace are processes incompatible with one another in one and the same system" ("On Some Motifs in Baudelaire," p. 114).

77. See Brandon, *Spiritualists*, p. 50, for a description of the process.

78. Editors' introduction, *transition* 3 (June 1927): 178–79.

79. Lawrence D. Stewart, *Paul Bowles: The Illumination of North Africa* (Carbondale: Southern Illinois University Press, 1974), pp. 152–53.

80. "Spire Song," *transition* 12 (March 1928): 120–22; "Entity," *transition* 13 American Number (Summer 1928): 219–20.

81. Paul Bowles to Daniel Burns, no date [1928], HRHRC.

82. Paul Bowles to Daniel Burns, no date [1930], HRHRC.
83. Paul Bowles to Daniel Burns, no date [1928], HRHRC.
84. Paul Bowles to Daniel Burns, no date [1928], HRHRC.
85. Paul Bowles to Daniel Burns, no date [1928], HRHRC.
86. Paul Bowles to Daniel Burns, no date [1928], HRHRC.
87. Paul Bowles to Daniel Burns, no date [1928], HRHRC.
88. Paul Bowles to Daniel Burns, no date [1928], HRHRC.
89. Paul Bowles to Daniel Burns, no date [1928], HRHRC.
90. Paul Bowles, undated fragment, HRHRC.
91. Paul Bowles, autobiographical fragment, [late 1960s], HRHRC.
92. In a surprising analogy to this story, in 1912, while debating what to do with his life — whether to leave teaching and pursue his writing abroad — Robert Frost tossed a coin, he later told a friend, to make the decision. In England, Frost published his first two volumes of poetry, the second of which, *North of Boston*, marked his breakthrough into use of the New England language patterns that formed the substance of his genius from that point on. Clearly both artists felt that in order to begin a creative life, one had to leave the United States. For Bowles, as perhaps for Frost, no other life was worth living.
93. John Glassco, *Memoirs of Montparnasse* (New York: Oxford University Press, 1970), p. 14.
94. Bowles states that Hubert was an orphan from Alabama whom Ida and Frederick Bowles had adopted on a tour of the South in the 1880s. Curiously, Charles Frederick Robbins, brother of Ida Bowles and Mary Robbins Mead, lived for many years in Aldrich, Alabama. When Christiana Robbins Holden died in 1890, she left no will but instead a letter of administration, which left her home to her daughter Mary, one thousand dollars to her daughter Ida, and one dollar to Charles, although her reasons for doing so are impossible to determine. It might have been simply that Charles was in need of no money. When Mary Robbins Mead died in 1941, she left her house to this brother, Charles, and her nephew Claude Bowles "to be divided between them equally," according to her will filed in the Schuyler County Clerk's office. Most interesting of all, in light of this possible connection between Charles Frederick Robbins of Alabama and Uncle Hubert is that the hated brother and uncle in Bowles's story "Pages from Cold Point" is named Charles. However, in Bowles's notes for his autobiography in the HRHRC, he cryptically jotted: "Billy H. as envoy from father." Surely this is the real life "Uncle Hubert."
95. Paul Bowles, "In Absentia," *Antaeus* 58 (Spring 1987): 26.

Book II. Pretending to Be Living, 1929–1933

1. Paul Bowles to Gertrude Stein, no date [1933], Beinecke.
2. For a complete discussion of the roles of the naïf and the dandy with relation to English writers from 1918 to 1957, see Martin Burgess Green, *Children of the Sun: A Narrative of "Decadence" in England after 1918* (New York: Basic Books, 1976).
3. Green, *Children of the Sun*, p. 13.
4. Composers are listed in order of presentation on the programs. Aaron Copland and Vivian Perlis, *Copland: 1900 through 1942* (New York: St. Martin's, 1984), pp. 143–49.
5. Aaron Copland, conversation with author, 3 October 1984.

6. Aaron Copland to author, 21 November 1984.

7. Paul Bowles to Charles Henri Ford, no date, HRHRC.

8. Paul Bowles, "A White Goat's Shadow," *Argo, an Individual Review* 1, no. 2 (December 1930): 50–51.

9. Gertrude Stein to Charles Henri Ford, no date, HRHRC.

10. Djuna Barnes to William Aspenwall Bradley, no date, Charles Henri Ford Collection, HRHRC.

11. Paul Bowles to Edouard Roditi, no date [1931], the University Library, University of California at Los Angeles (hereafter cited as UCLA).

12. Paul Bowles to Millicent Dillon, 23 October 1981, HRHRC.

13. Buffie Johnson, conversation with author, 5 October 1984.

14. Marilyn Moss discusses the metaphor of adolescent rebellion as the dominant principle structuring Bowles's autobiography in her essay "The Child in the Text: Autobiography, Fiction, and the Aesthetics of Deception in *Without Stopping*," *Twentieth Century Literature* 32, nos. 3–4 (Fall–Winter 1986): 314–34.

15. Paul Bowles to Gertrude Stein, no date [1930], Beinecke.

16. Paul Bowles to Daniel Burns, no date [1930], HRHRC.

17. Paul Bowles to Daniel Burns, no date [1930], HRHRC.

18. Paul Bowles to Daniel Burns, no date [1930], HRHRC.

19. Paul Bowles to Edouard Roditi, 2 March 1931, UCLA.

20. Edouard Roditi, "Works and Days of the Young and Evil," *Paris exiles* 1, no. 1 (Winter 1984): 5.

21. Paul Bowles to Edouard Roditi, 20 April 1931, UCLA.

22. Stephen Spender, *World within World* (New York: Harcourt, Brace, 1951), pp. 98–99.

23. Spender, *World within World*, pp. 118–19. For Stefan Zweig's indictment of Berlin as "Babel of the world" in 1931 and the despair of German intellectuals, see Peter Gay, *Weimar Culture: The Outsider as Insider* (New York: Harper and Row, 1968), pp. 129, 140.

24. Paul Bowles to Daniel Burns, no date [1931], HRHRC.

25. Paul Bowles to Edouard Roditi, 19 May 1931, UCLA.

26. Paul Bowles to Daniel Burns, no date [1931], HRHRC.

27. Paul Bowles to Daniel Burns, no date [1931], HRHRC.

28. Maurice Grosser, conversation with author, 5 October 1984. Further statements by Grosser are from this conversation.

29. Paul Bowles, unpublished interview with Ira Cohen, 1965, Butler Library, Columbia University (hereafter cited as Butler).

30. Paul Bowles, conversation with author, 13 February 1986.

31. Paul Bowles to Daniel Burns, [1931], HRHRC.

32. Gertrude Stein to Paul Bowles, no date [1931], HRHRC.

33. Gertrude Stein to Paul Bowles, 20 January 1932, HRHRC.

34. Paul Bowles, Cohen interview, Butler.

35. Paul Bowles to Daniel Burns, no date [1931], HRHRC.

36. Paul Bowles, "In the Creuse," HRHRC.

37. Paul Bowles, Cohen interview, Butler.

38. See Paul Bowles, "The Worlds of Tangier," p. 66; see also Lawdom Vaidon [David Woolman], *Tangier: A Different Way* (Metuchen, N.J.: Scarecrow, 1977), pp. 195–234.

39. Copland and Perlis, *Copland*, p. 188.

40. Gertrude Stein to Paul Bowles, 9 August 1931, HRHRC.

41. Paul Bowles to Daniel Burns, no date [September 1931], HRHRC.

42. Paul Bowles to Gertrude Stein, no date [September 1931], Beinecke.

43. Paul Bowles to Edouard Roditi, no date [August 1931], UCLA.

44. Paul Bowles to Edouard Roditi, no date [August 1931], UCLA.

45. Paul Bowles to Gertrude Stein, 18 September [1931], Beinecke.

46. Paul Bowles, conversation with author, February 1985.

47. Paul Bowles to Gertrude Stein, 18 September [1931], Beinecke.

48. See Kathryn Cavarly Hulme, *Arab Interlude* (Philadelphia: Macrae Smith, 1931), p. 145, for an evocative description.

49. "Mr. Copland and I came to Fez over a week ago and he left two or three days afterward" (Paul Bowles to Gertrude Stein, 9 October [1931], Beinecke). In Copland and Perlis, *Copland*, Bowles states that Copland returned to Berlin "about 1 October" (p. 190).

50. Paul Bowles, "Worlds of Tangier," p. 66.

51. Paul Bowles, "Worlds of Tangier," p. 67.

52. Paul Bowles to Gertrude Stein, 1931, Beinecke.

53. Virgil Thomson, conversation with author, 1 October 1984.

54. Virgil Thomson to Aaron Copland, 26 November 1931, Virgil Thomson Collection, Jackson Music Library, Yale University (hereafter cited as Jackson).

55. Aaron Copland to Virgil Thomson, Saturday, Jackson.

56. Paul Bowles to Virgil Thomson, 21 January 1932, HRHRC.

57. Virgil Thomson to Aaron Copland, 17 October [1931], Jackson.

58. Aaron Copland to Virgil Thomson, 5 December [1931], Jackson.

59. Virgil Thomson, *Virgil Thomson* (New York: Da Capo, 1966), p. 206.

60. Copland, conversation with author, 3 October 1984.

61. Paul Bowles to Daniel Burns, 1 December 1931, HRHRC.

62. Copland and Perlis, *Copland*, p. 191.

63. Paul Bowles to Edouard Roditi, no date [1931], UCLA.

64. Virgil Thomson, conversation with author, 1 October 1984.

65. Paul Bowles to Edouard Roditi, 12 January 1932, UCLA.

66. Paul Bowles to Edouard Roditi, 12 January 1932, UCLA.

67. Paul Bowles to Gertrude Stein, 10 January [1932], Beinecke.

68. Gertrude Stein to Paul Bowles, 20 January 1931, HRHRC.

69. Paul Bowles to Gertrude Stein, 1 February [1931], Beinecke.

70. Virgil Thomson, conversation with author, 1 October 1984.

71. Paul Bowles, conversation with author, 14 February 1986.

72. Paul Bowles to Edouard Roditi, no date [September 1931], UCLA.

73. Roditi, "Works and Days," p. 6.

74. Sawyer-Lauçanno, *Invisible Spectator*, p. 124.

75. Paul Bowles to Edouard Roditi, no date [1931], UCLA.

76. Virgil Thomson, conversation with author, 1 October 1984.

77. Paul Bowles to Jennie Skerl, 6 February and 21 March 1988.

78. Joan Peyser, *Bernstein: A Biography* (New York: William Morrow, 1987), p. 56.

79. Paul Bowles to Gertrude Stein, no date [1933], Beinecke.

80. Trounstine had assured a future by selling the book *Little Caesar* to be made

into the movie *Scarface* and later changed his name to Turner (Roditi to author, 7 November 1990).

81. Edouard Roditi to author, 7 November 1990.

82. Paul Bowles to Virgil Thomson, no date, Jackson.

83. Gertrude Stein, *The Autobiography of Alice B. Toklas* (New York: Harcourt, Brace, 1933), p. 309.

84. Manuscripts to the Sonatina for Piano, dated "Monte Carlo 1932," and *Scènes d'Anabase* (1932) are available in the HRHRC.

85. Bowles used the same formula when he based his opera *The Wind Remains* on García Lorca's *Así que Pasen Cinco Años*.

86. George Antheil, *Bad Boy of Music* (Garden City, N.Y.: Doubleday, 1945), p. 265.

87. Paul Bowles to Charles Henri Ford, no date, Charles Henri Ford Collection, HRHRC.

88. Richard S. Barbe Baker, *Sahara Challenge* (London: Lutterworth, 1954), p. 44.

89. Paul Bowles to Gertrude Stein, 6 January 1933, Beinecke.

90. Paul Bowles to Charles Henri Ford, no date [January 1933], HRHRC.

91. Paul Bowles to Gertrude Stein, 14 February [1933], Beinecke.

92. Paul Bowles, note dated November 1950, HRHRC.

93. Paul Bowles to Gertrude Stein, 14 February [1933], Beinecke.

94. Paul Bowles to Charles Henri Ford, 23 March [1933], HRHRC.

95. Paul Bowles to Gertrude Stein, 7 March 1933, Beinecke.

96. Paul Bowles to Charles Henri Ford, 23 March [1933], HRHRC.

97. The holiday in the United States lasted from 6 to 10 March, but it might have lasted longer in Tunis, where Bowles posted a card to Stein on 7 March.

98. Paul Bowles to Charles Henri Ford, 23 March [1933], HRHRC.

99. Paul Bowles to Charles Henri Ford, 23 March [1933], HRHRC.

100. Paul Bowles to Charles Henri Ford, 23 March [1933], HRHRC.

101. Paul Bowles, Cohen interview, Butler.

102. Paul Bowles to Gertrude Stein, 14 February [1933], Beinecke.

103. For a full discussion of dandyism in the nineteenth century, see Ellen Moers, *The Dandy* (London: Secker and Warburg, 1962).

104. Roditi, "Works and Days," p. 7.

105. Gertrude Himmelfarb, *Marriage and Morals among the Victorians* (New York: Alfred A. Knopf, 1986), p. xiii.

Book III. A Nomad in New York, 1933–1948

1. Frederick Douglass, *Narrative of the Life of Frederick Douglass, an American Slave* (New York: Signet, 1968), p. 45.

2. Paul Bowles to Gertrude Stein, no date [1933], Beinecke.

3. Paul Bowles to Virgil Thomson, June 1933, Jackson.

4. Paul Bowles to Gertrude Stein, no date [1933], Beinecke.

5. Paul Bowles to Edouard Roditi, no date [1931], UCLA.

6. Paul Bowles to Virgil Thomson, no date [1933], Jackson.

7. Paul Bowles to Gertrude Stein, no date [1933], Beinecke.

8. Paul Bowles to Virgil Thomson, no date [1933], Jackson.

9. For comments about the performance, see Arthur Berger, "The Young Composers' Group," *Trend* 2, no. 1 (April–May–June 1933): 26–28.

10. Copland and Perlis, *Copland*, p. 192.

11. Oscar Levant, *A Smattering of Ignorance* (New York: Doubleday, 1940), p. 225.

12. Paul Bowles, conversation with author, February 1986.

13. Paul Bowles, "Portrait of Five," HRHRC.

14. Paul Bowles to author, 25 February 1988.

15. Paul Bowles to Bennett Lerner, 23 March 1985.

16. Paul Bowles to Bennett Lerner, 23 March 1985.

17. Paul Bowles to Gertrude Stein, no date [1934], Beinecke.

18. All quotations from David Diamond are from an interview with the author, 5 October 1984. David Diamond lent me correspondence to him from Paul Bowles, from which I quote.

19. Paul Bowles to David Diamond, no date [1935–36].

20. Paul Bowles to David Diamond, no date [1935–36].

21. Paul Bowles to Jennie Skerl, 6 February 1988.

22. Green, *Children of the Sun*, p. 8.

23. Ned Rorem, conversation with author, 27 September 1984.

24. Paul Bowles to Daniel Burns, no date [October 1934], HRHRC.

25. Paul Bowles, in Gary Conklin, *Paul Bowles in Morocco* (New York, 1970), film.

26. Charles Seeger, quoted in Rita Mead, "The Amazing Mr. Cowell," *American Music* 1, no. 4 (Winter 1983): 65.

27. Mead, "Amazing Mr. Cowell," p. 69.

28. Paul Bowles to author, 25 February 1988.

29. Paul Bowles to Gertrude Stein, 1 February [1935], Beinecke.

30. Paul Bowles to Gertrude Stein, no date [March 1935], Beinecke.

31. As late as February 1936, he wrote Charles Henri Ford complaining that he never saw him in New York, giving Fuhrman's Saint Martin's Road address in return (5 February 1936, HRHRC).

32. Paul Bowles, conversation with author, February 1986.

33. Jean-Paul Sartre joined the Communist party in France because of his opposition to the status quo and his belief that only the Communist party could bring it down, even though he did not believe in the party doctrines himself.

34. Paul Bowles to John Lehmann, 16 November 1955, John Lehmann Collection, HRHRC.

35. Recorded Chemung County Surrogate Court, no. 15661.

36. Paul Bowles to Virgil Thomson, 8 January 1936, Jackson.

37. Jan Morris, *Manhattan '45* (New York: Oxford University Press, 1987), pp. 21–22.

38. Program for *Yankee Clipper*, Ballet Caravan, Lincoln Kirstein, Director, HRHRC.

39. Paul Bowles, *Yankee Clipper*, HRHRC.

40. It also prepared him for his work as jazz critic for *View*, *Modern Music*, *Vogue*, and the *New York Herald Tribune*, where he inaugurated jazz columns.

41. Paul Bowles, "Negro and Non-Negro Music," *Modern Music* 17, no. 1 (October–November 1939): 45.

42. Colin McPhee, "New York's Spring Season, 1936," *Modern Music* 13, no. 4 (May–June 1936): 40.

43. Aaron Copland, "America's Young Men—Ten Years Later," *Modern Music* 13,

no. 4 (May–June 1936): 10.

44. Thomson, *Virgil Thomson*, p. 265.

45. Virgil Thomson, conversation with author, 1 October 1984; Virgil Thomson to Alexander Kroff, 11 April 1951, Jackson.

46. Quoted in John Houseman, *Entertainers and the Entertained: Essays on Theater, Film, and Television* (New York: Simon and Schuster, 1986), p. 19.

47. Brooks Atkinson, *New York Times*, undated clipping, HRHRC.

48. Charles Higham, *Orson Welles: The Rise and Fall of an American Genius* (New York: St. Martin's, 1985), p. 90.

49. Paul Bowles, "On the Film Front," *Modern Music* 17, no. 3 (March–April 1940): 186.

50. Elliot Carter, "With the Dancers," *Modern Music* 15, no. 2 (January–February 1938): 122.

51. Paul Rosenfeld, "The Newest American Composers," *Modern Music* 15, no. 3 (March–April 1938): 158.

52. Paul Bowles to Charles Henri Ford, no date [Summer 1937], HRHRC.

53. Paul Bowles to Charles Henri Ford, 2 October 1937, HRHRC.

54. Juanita Hall was later to become famous as Bloody Mary in *South Pacific*. For now, she led her nine singers in a chorus.

55. Virgil Thomson, *Selected Letters of Virgil Thomson*, ed. Tim Page and Vanessa Weeks Page (New York: Summit Books, 1988), p. 154.

56. Paul Bowles to Charles Henri Ford, 10 January 1939; no date [Spring 1939], HRHRC.

57. Brooks Atkinson, "Set My People Free," *New York Times*, 14 November 1948, sec. 2, p. 1.

58. Paul Bowles to Charles Henri Ford, no date [Spring 1939]; 13 December 1947; 22 March [1948], HRHRC.

59. Paul Bowles to Charles Henri Ford, 25 January [1948], HRHRC.

60. Paul Bowles to Charles Henri Ford, 22 March [1948], HRHRC.

61. Paul Bowles to Charles Henri Ford, no date [Summer 1938], HRHRC.

62. Paul Bowles to Bennett Lerner, 13 October 1988.

63. Paul Bowles to Virgil Thomson, 6 December 1976, Jackson.

64. Paul Bowles to Virgil Thomson, 6 December 1976, Jackson.

65. See Bowles's articles on film music in the *Herald Tribune* for 17 January, sec. 6, p. 7; 31 January, sec. 7, p. 7; 29 June, sec. 6, p. 6; and 21 November, sec. 4, p. 6, all from 1943; and in *Modern Music*, from 1939 through 1941, when he wrote "On the Film Front" for each quarterly issue.

66. Rudy Burckhardt to author, 15 June 1988.

67. Paul Bowles to Gertrude Stein, [1936], Beinecke.

68. This film is listed in Jeffrey Miller, *Paul Bowles: A Descriptive Bibliography* (Santa Barbara: Black Sparrow, 1986), as *Roots in the Earth*, but Bowles recalls it as *Roots in the Soil* in his autobiography and in conversation with the author.

69. Rudy Burckhardt to author, 15 June 1988.

70. Paul Bowles to Bennett Lerner, 13 February 1988.

71. Ninety-four percent of the inhabitants had radios, but seventy-one thousand of the total six hundred thousand dwelling places had no private lavatories, and three thousand five hundred had no running water (Morris, *Manhattan '45*, p. 155).

72. Truman Capote, "Brooklyn Heights: A Personal Memoir," *Holiday* (February

1959), as quoted in Susan Edmiston and Linda D. Cirino, *Literary New York: A History and Guide* (Boston: Houghton Mifflin, 1976), p. 114.

73. Capote, as quoted in Edmiston and Cirino, *Literary New York*, p. 113.

74. Capote, as quoted in Edmiston and Cirino, *Literary New York*, p. 114.

75. Paul Bowles to Virgil Thomson, no date [February 1938], Jackson.

76. Virgil Thomson to Paul Bowles, no date [1938], Jackson.

77. Paul Bowles to Gertrude Stein, no date [Spring 1938], Beinecke.

78. Paul Bowles to Charles Henri Ford, no date [1938], HRHRC.

79. Paul Bowles to Charles Henri Ford, no date [1938], HRHRC.

80. Higham, *Orson Welles*, pp. 117–19.

81. Paul Bowles, conversation with author, February 1986.

82. Burns Mantle, *New York Daily News*, 13 April 1939; and Richard Watts, Jr., *New York Herald Tribune*, undated clipping, HRHRC.

83. Brooks Atkinson, "The Play," *New York Times*, 20 November 1940.

84. Virgil Thomson, *New York Herald Tribune*, 9 November 1940.

85. Samuel L. M. Barlow, "In the Theater," *Modern Music* 18, no. 3 (March–April 1941): 190.

86. Paul Bowles, "Autobiography," p. 16.

87. Anaïs Nin, as quoted in Edmiston and Cirino, *Literary New York*, pp. 348–53.

88. Anaïs Nin, as quoted in Edmiston and Cirino, *Literary New York*, pp. 348–53.

89. Edmiston and Cirino, *Literary New York*, p. 353. The first suite for this work is in the HRHRC dated "1941 New York–Taxco."

90. Paul Bowles, as quoted in Edmiston and Cirino, *Literary New York*, p. 353.

91. Other recipients were Marc Blitzstein, David Diamond, Alvin Etler, Hunter Johnson, and Earl Robinson.

92. Paul Bowles to Virgil Thomson, 27 June [1941], Jackson.

93. Paul Bowles, *Pastorela* (*Danza Mexicana*), CBS Symphony Orchestra, Bernard Herrmann conducting, no date.

94. Jane Bowles to Virgil Thomson, October 1941, Jackson.

95. On the same program, Bernstein conducted *Homenaje a García Lorca* by Silvestre Revueltas, which Bowles had first heard in Mexico five years earlier.

96. Paul Bowles, Works 7, HRHRC. The work has been published by American Music Edition. Bowles prepared a condensed version of *The Wind Remains* for Peggy Glanville-Hicks's annual New Works for Chamber Orchestra concert at the New York Metropolitan Museum of Art. The concert took place on 19 February 1957, and about a week later the piece was recorded by MGM, with Carlos Surinac conducting the MGM Chamber Orchestra (E3549).

97. Thomson, *Virgil Thomson*, p. 339.

98. Howard Taubman, "New Bowles Score Gets First Hearing," *New York Times*, undated clipping, HRHRC.

99. Ned Rorem, conversation with author, 27 September 1984.

100. Paul Bowles, *The Wind Remains: Orchestral Suite* (overture only), Nicolai Berezowsky conducting, orchestra unknown, 1943.

101. Thomson, *Virgil Thomson*, p. 280.

102. Paul Bowles, conversation with author, February 1986.

103. Peyser, *Bernstein*, p. 118.

104. Ned Rorem, conversation with author, 27 September 1984.

105. Paul Bowles, conversation with author, 13 February 1986.

106. Paul Bowles, "Autobiography," p. 17.

107. Ned Rorem, conversation with author, 27 September 1984.

108. Virgil Thomson, conversation with author, 1 October 1984.

109. Arthur Hartmann, Drama Mailbag, *New York Times*, 24 October 1948, sec. 2, p. 2. Of the scores mentioned in this section, *The Dancer* and *Summer and Smoke* are held by the HRHRC; others are presumed lost.

110. Edna Bockstein Madway to author, 25 November 1983.

111. Gina Lalli, conversation with author, December 1983.

112. The HRHRC holds the score for *A Picnic Cantata*; the Sonata for Two Pianos was published by G. Schirmer in 1949. The Concerto for Two Pianos, Winds and Percussion is alternately called Concerto for Two Pianos; an orchestral version is called Concerto for Two Pianos and Orchestra. Both versions have parts on rental from American Music Edition.

113. Peggy Glanville-Hicks, liner notes to Paul Bowles, Concerto for Two Pianos, Gold and Fizdale, Columbia LP 2128.

114. Paul Bowles to author, 5 November 1988.

115. "Gold and Fizdale Play Five New Works," *New York Times*, 15 November 1948, p. 22.

116. Arthur F. Berger, "Duo-Pianists," *New York Herald Tribune*, 15 November 1948.

117. *American Composers Today* (New York: H. Wilson, 1949), s.v. "Bowles, Paul."

118. *American Composers Today*, s.v. "Bowles, Paul."

119. *American Composers Today*, s.v. "Bowles, Paul"

120. Rudy Burckhardt to author, 25 June 1988.

121. Paul Bowles, "Autobiography," p. 19.

122. Paul Bowles, Internal Revenue Service return for 1946, HRHRC. The six works were *Ballet Theatre*, *Twilight Bar*, *The Dancer*, *Cyrano*, *Land's End*, and *On Whitman Avenue*.

123. Thomson, *Virgil Thomson*, p. 207.

124. Paul Bowles to Charles Henri Ford, 19 November 1947, HRHRC.

125. Paul Bowles, "The Jazz Ear," *View* 3, no. 1 (April 1943): 28.

126. Virgil Thomson, conversation with author, 1 October 1984.

127. Paul Bowles to Millicent Dillon, 21 November 1980, HRHRC.

128. Rudy Burckhardt to author, 25 June 1988.

129. Jane Bowles to Paul Bowles, no date, HRHRC.

130. Among the "primitives" in which Bowles might have been interested was prisoner Joe Massey, who carried on a correspondence with Bowles begging him to set his poetry to music.

131. William Carlos Williams, *View* 2, no. 2 (1942): 3.

132. Randall Jarrell, *View* 2, no. 2 (1942): 3.

133. Paul Bowles, "Bluey," *View* 3, no. 3 (1943): 81.

134. In 1939, living in Brooklyn Heights, he had written "Tea on the Mountain"; it was first published in *The Delicate Prey* (1950).

135. Paul Bowles to Marian Chase, no date [1945], Jackson. In Havana they met the painter Wilfredo Lam and then the writer Lydia Cabrera, who guided them to an African religious ritual at Guanabacoa but then whisked them away in her limousine before they could see the ritual fully under way. For *Modern Music* he kept a journal of the trip, a combination of ethnography and wry observation on the "dubious meaning

our culture holds for the members of less evolved groups," the autochthonous peoples of the area ("In the Tropics," *Modern Music* 22, no. 1 [Winter 1946]: 19).

136. Harvey Breit, "Talk with Paul Bowles," *New York Times Book Review*, 9 March 1952, sec. 57, p. 10.

137. Jane Bowles to Paul Bowles, no date [1947], HRHRC.

138. Michael Griffin, "Maroc of Ages," *Guardian*, 9 April 1988.

139. Jane Bowles to Paul Bowles, no date [1947], HRHRC.

140. Gordon Sager to author, 24 March 1988.

Book IV. The Sheltering Relationship, 1938–1951

1. Paul Bowles, journal, HRHRC.

2. Paul Bowles to Millicent Dillon, 13 March 1978, HRHRC.

3. Paul Bowles, "Delicate Song," in *The Thicket of Spring* (Los Angeles: Black Sparrow, 1972), p. 20.

4. Dillon, *Little Original Sin*, p. 15. I am indebted to Dillon's biography for the information on Jane Bowles's early years.

5. Although tuberculosis commonly locates in the lungs, the tubercle bacillus may form in various tissues of the body.

6. No copies remain.

7. On a train trip to see *Yankee Clipper* in Philadelphia in 1937, which involved a number of drinks and much wild laughter, Rena decided that despite her dainty appearance, Jane was quite wild.

8. Brion Gysin, unpublished interview with Jennie Skerl, July 1985.

9. Paul Bowles to Millicent Dillon, 16 January 1981, HRHRC.

10. Paul Bowles to Millicent Dillon, 14 March 1983, HRHRC.

11. Christopher Wanklyn to author, 28 March 1991. Further statements by Wanklyn are from this letter.

12. Joe McPhillips, conversation with author, 13 February 1986. Further statements by McPhillips are from this conversation.

13. Dillon, *Little Original Sin*, p. 51.

14. Dillon, *Little Original Sin*, p. 119.

15. Bowles, *Without Stopping*, p. 223.

16. Jane Bowles, notebook no. 22, HRHRC. The manuscript version differs significantly from the posthumous "Iron Table."

17. Dillon, *Little Original Sin*, p. 133.

18. The name Bupple Hergesheimer referred to one of the parrot's words "budupple" and the writer Joseph Hergesheimer, whom Jane and Paul had known in New York. Edouard Roditi to author, 7 November 1990.

19. Don Bachardy, conversation with author, 15 November 1990.

20. Cohen interview, Butler.

21. Tennessee Williams, *Memoirs* (Garden City, N.Y.: Doubleday, 1975), p. 59.

22. Gordon Sager to author, 24 March 1988.

23. Gordon Sager to author, 24 March 1988.

24. Gordon Sager, *Run Sheep Run* (New York: Vanguard, 1958), p. 74.

25. Gordon Sager to author, 24 March 1988.

26. Gordon Sager to author, 24 March 1988.

27. Paul Bowles, conversation with author, February 1986.

28. Paul Bowles to Joel Redon, 8 November 1985, HRHRC.

29. Sager, *Run Sheep Run*, p. 69.

30. Paul Bowles to Virgil Thomson, no date [1940], Jackson.

31. Paul Bowles to Virgil Thomson, 27 June [1941], Jackson.

32. Paul Bowles to Virgil Thomson, 27 July [1941], Jackson.

33. Paul Bowles to Virgil Thomson, 27 July [1941], Jackson.

34. Paul Bowles, "Scene V," HRHRC.

35. Oliver Smith to Virgil Thomson, no date [August 1941], Jackson; Paul Bowles to Virgil Thomson, 27 July [1941], Jackson. Although Dillon states Jane stayed in Taxco, Oliver Smith writes in his letter to Thomson that Jane and Mrs. Perkins were also at the house in Acapulco with him, Paul, and Bob Faulkner.

36. Dillon, *Little Original Sin*, p. 98.

37. Jane Bowles to Paul Bowles, no date [August 1948], HRHRC.

38. Jane Bowles, *Two Serious Ladies*, in *My Sister's Hand: The Collected Works of Jane Bowles* (New York: Ecco, 1978), p. 62.

39. Jane Bowles, *Two Serious Ladies*, p. III. Perhaps only conincidence, but in Paul's novel *The Sheltering Sky* the protagonist's name would be Port and his wife would be leaving him, as in Jane's novel.

40. Paul Bowles to Virgil Thomson, no date [1942], Jackson.

41. Paul Peters to Nancy Wilson Ross, 1 October 1941, Nancy Wilson Ross Collection, HRHRC.

42. "I Heard the Sea," HRHRC.

43. Edna Bockstein Madway to author, 25 November 1986.

44. Paul Bowles, in Conklin's film.

45. Paul Bowles, in Evans, "Interview with Paul Bowles," p. 12.

46. Paul Bowles to Millicent Dillon, 6 February 1984, HRHRC.

47. Dillon, *Little Original Sin*, p. 176.

48. Paul Bowles, "Night Song," *Oracle*, Christmas Issue, December 1927, p. 27.

49. Paul Bowles, *The Sheltering Sky* (New York: Ecco, 1978), p. 14. Further references to this novel will be noted parenthetically in the text as *TSS*.

50. David Riesman, *The Lonely Crowd* (New Haven: Yale University Press, 1961), p. 25.

51. Norman Mailer, "The White Negro," in *Advertisements for Myself* (New York: G. P. Putnam's Sons, 1959), p. 339.

52. Orville Prescott, *New York Times*, 5 December 1949, p. 21.

53. Tennessee Williams, "An Allegory of Man and His Sahara," *New York Times Book Review*, 4 December 1949, p. 7.

54. "'The Best Books I Read This Year,' Twelve Distinguished Opinions," *New York Times Book Review*, 4 December 1949, p. 4. *The Sheltering Sky* appeared on the *New York Times Book Review* "Best Sellers" list first on 1 January 1950 and remained there until 12 March 1959.

55. Paul Bowles, Cohen interview, Butler.

56. Paul Bowles, Cohen interview, Butler.

57. Paul Bowles, Cohen interview, Butler.

58. Paul Bowles, in Michael Rogers, "Conversations in Morocco: The *Rolling Stone* Interview," *Rolling Stone*, 23 May 1974, p. 50.

59. Ted Morgan, *Literary Outlaw: The Life and Times of William S. Burroughs* (New York: Henry Holt, 1988), p. 378.

60. Paul Bowles, in Conklin's film.

61. Don Bachardy, conversation with author, 15 November 1990.

62. Ned Rorem, conversation with author, 27 September 1984.

63. Katharine Hulme observed this ceremony in 1930 in her experiences with the Asawa tribe and describes it in similar language in *Arab Interlude*. Elizabeth Warnock Fernea also reports the ceremony but without the gory sacrifice in *A Street in Marrakech* (Garden City, N.Y.: Doubleday, 1975). Anthropologist Edward Wester-marck discusses the celebration of the prophet's birth during the month of the Mulud, the third month of the Islamic year. On the ninth day of the month, the Esáwa of Fez begin a pilgrimage to Meknes, during which people along the way toss them sheep and goats, which they "tear to pieces and eat raw." On some sacrificial occasions, a bullock or small camel is slaughtered along with a sheep, but sacrificial animals are cooked or cured before being eaten. At Fez, some blood fresh from the sacrifice is smeared on the hands and feet to prevent swelling and chapping in cold weather or as a means of keeping away dijinn, or evil spirits (*Ritual and Belief in Morocco*, vol. 2 [London: Macmillan, 1926], pp. 88, 114, 122).

64. Dillon, *Little Original Sin*, p. 157.

65. Andrew Drummond to Millicent Dillon, 7 March 1978, HRHRC.

66. Jane Bowles, unpublished journal, HRHRC.

67. Jane Bowles to Paul Bowles, undated. This and other undated letters from Jane to Paul are in the HRHRC.

68. Dillon, *Little Original Sin*, p. 176.

69. Lehmann's mother's family had founded the Edinburgh publishing firm W & R Chambers, and his father frequently wrote light verse and autobiographical sketches for *Punch*. Lehmann published books under his own imprint and founded the literary magazine *London*.

70. John Lehmann, *The Ample Proposition* (London: Eyre and Spottiswoode, 1966), p. 81.

71. Lehmann, *Ample Proposition*, p. 81.

72. Lehmann, *Ample Proposition*, p. 110.

73. Lehmann, *Ample Proposition*, p. 111.

74. Paul Bowles to Allen Ginsberg, 12 December 1961, Butler.

Book V. The Savage Mind, 1949–1958

1. Claude Lévi-Strauss, *The Savage Mind* (Chicago: University of Chicago Press, 1962), p. 263.

2. Paul Bowles to Charles Henri Ford, 22 March [1948], HRHRC.

3. Paul Bowles to Charles Henri Ford, 24 October 1947, HRHRC.

4. Truman Capote, *Local Color* (New York: Random House, 1950), p. 74.

5. Vaidon, *Tangier*, p. 257.

6. Paul Bowles to Charles Henri Ford, 24 October 1947, HRHRC.

7. Robin Maugham, *Escape from the Shadows* (London: Hodder and Stoughton, 1972), p. 204.

8. Vaidon, *Tangier*, p. 248.

9. Paul Bowles to Charles Henri Ford, 13 December 1947, HRHRC.

10. Paul Bowles to Charles Henri Ford, 13 December 1947, HRHRC.

11. Paul Bowles to David McDowell, 30 March 1950, Random House Collection, Butler.

12. Tennessee Williams to Donald Windham, 20 February 1948, Tennessee Williams, *Tennessee Williams' Letters to Donald Windham, 1940–1965*, ed. Donald Windham (New York: Holt, Rinehart, and Winston, 1947), p. 209.

13. Tennessee Williams to Donald Windham, 26 January 1949, Williams, *Tennessee Williams' Letters*, p. 228.

14. Alice Toklas praised the music of her "Freddy," who, she wrote, had "considerable endowment and more understanding," and whose works she preferred over those by John Cage and Aaron Copland (Alice B. Toklas, *Staying on Alone: Letters of Alice B. Toklas*, ed. Edward Burns [New York: Liveright, 1973], p. 172).

15. Gerald Clarke, *Capote: A Biography* (New York: Simon and Schuster, 1988), p. 168.

16. Cecil Beaton, *The Strenuous Years: Diaries, 1948–1955* (London: Weidenfeld and Nicolson, 1973), p. 49.

17. David Herbert, *Second Son* (London: Peter Owen, 1972), p. 121; Paul Bowles, conversation with author, February 1986.

18. Paul Bowles, "The Ball at Sidi Hosni," *Kulchur* 2 (Winter 1960/61): 8–14.

19. Vaidon, *Tangier*, p. 269.

20. Lawrence Stewart to Millicent Dillon, 28 July 1977, HRHRC.

21. Brion Gysin, unpublished interview with Jennie Skerl, July 1985.

22. Ira Cohen, conversation with author, 17 August 1993.

23. Brion Gysin, *Here to Go: Planet R-101* (San Francisco: Re/Search Publications, 1982), p. 27.

24. Vaidon, *Tangier*, p. 289.

25. William Burroughs, *Letters to Allen Ginsberg, 1953–1957* (New York: Full Court, 1982), p. 50.

26. Burroughs, *Letters*, p. 50.

27. Burroughs, *Letters*, p. 24.

28. Burroughs, *Letters*, p. 104.

29. Burroughs, *Letters*, p. 114.

30. Burroughs, *Letters*, p. 155.

31. Burroughs, *Letters*, p. 163.

32. Jennie Skerl, *William S. Burroughs*, Twayne's United States Authors Series 438 (Boston: G. K. Hall, 1985), p. 37.

33. Paul Bowles to David McDowell, 25 March 1950, Butler.

34. Paul Bowles to Peggy Glanville-Hicks, 25 February 1951; quoted in Dillon, *Little Original Sin*, p. 212.

35. Reviews quoted in a letter from Paul Bowles to David McDowell, 15 December 1950, Butler.

36. Paul Bowles to David McDowell, 15 December 1950, Butler.

37. For a full discussion of the influence of Poe and the disintegration of the personality on Paul Bowles, see Wayne Pounds, "Paul Bowles and Edgar Allan Poe: The Disintegration of the Personality," *Twentieth Century Literature* 32, nos. 3–4 (Fall–Winter 1986): 424–39; or Catherine Rainwater, "'Sinister Overtones,' 'Terrible Phrases': Poe's Influence on the Writing of Paul Bowles," *Essays in Literature* 11, no. 2 (Fall 1984): 253–56.

38. David McDowell, 30 January 1951, Butler. The Miller bibliography, *Paul Bowles: A Descriptive Bibliography*, states that six thousand copies were published, with six thousand eight hundred sets of sheets being ordered from the printers (p. 23).

39. Paul Bowles to David McDowell, 6 March 1951, Butler.

40. Paul Bowles to David McDowell, 6 March 1951, Butler.

41. Paul Bowles to David McDowell, 14 July 1951, Butler.

42. Sawyer-Lauçanno notes that Bowles and Bruce Morrissette knew a Professor Dyar in Baltimore (*Invisible Spectator*, p. 162).

43. Paul Bowles, *Let It Come Down* (New York: Random House, 1952), p. 7. Further references to this work will be noted parenthetically in the text as *LICD*.

44. Mailer, "White Negro," p. 347.

45. John Lehmann to Paul Bowles, 30 May 1952, HRHRC.

46. Lehmann, *Ample Proposition*, p. 110.

47. Charles Poore, *New York Times*, 28 February 1952, p. 25.

48. Paul Bowles, "Introduction: Thirty Years Later," in *Let It Come Down* (Santa Barbara: Black Sparrow, 1980), pp. 7–8.

49. For a full discussion of the subject, see Westermarck, *Ritual and Belief in Morocco*.

50. Quoted in Ted Morgan, *Rowing toward Eden* (Boston: Houghton Mifflin, 1981), p. 81.

51. Paul Bowles to Charles Henri Ford, 12 November 1947, HRHRC.

52. Ned Rorem, conversation with author, 27 September 1984.

53. Paul Bowles to Joel Redon, 18 August 1987, HRHRC.

54. Paul Bowles to Charles Henri Ford, 25 January [1948], HRHRC.

55. Morgan, *Rowing toward Eden*, p. 97.

56. Virgil Thomson, conversation with author, 1 October 1984.

57. Virtual time is discussed in John Blacking, *How Musical Is Man?* (Seattle: University of Washington Press, 1973), p. 27.

58. John Spencer Trimingham, *The Sufi Orders in Islam* (London: Oxford University Press, 1971), p. 2.

59. Paul Bowles, Cohen interview, Butler.

60. Paul Bowles, "Notes on Moroccan Hypnotic Music," p. 5, Butler.

61. Paul Bowles to John Lehmann, 18 February 1960, HRHRC.

62. Paul Bowles, "Moroccan Hypnotic Music," p. 2, Butler.

63. Paul Bowles, "Moroccan Hypnotic Music," p. 3, Butler.

64. Paul Bowles, *Their Heads Are Green* (London: Peter Owen, 1963), p. 72. Further references to this volume will be noted parenthetically in the text as *THAG*.

65. Paul Bowles, "Moroccan Hypnotic Music," p. 3, Butler.

66. Paul Bowles, "Moroccan Hypnotic Music," p. 6, Butler

67. Elizabeth Warnock Fernea and Robert Fernea, *The Arab World* (Garden City, N.Y.: Doubleday, 1985), p. 51, point out that by 1956, forty Moroccans had taken degrees in European and United States colleges.

68. Dillon, *Little Original Sin*, p. 214.

69. Dillon, *Little Original Sin*, p. 214

70. Paul Bowles to John Lehmann, 15 May 1952, HRHRC.

71. Paul Bowles to John Lehmann, 9 January 1954, HRHRC. Since Yacoubi was illiterate, he dictated his letters to Paul.

72. Gore Vidal to author, 30 July 1991.

73. In correspondence with Millicent Dillon on the subject, Paul continued to protect Ahmed, asking her to omit use of the word *push* in her description (HRHRC).

74. Ben Henry to Millicent Dillon, 25 May 1979, HRHRC.

75. Tennessee Williams to Donald Windham, 28 July 1953, Williams, *Tennessee Williams' Letters*, p. 281.

76. Paul Bowles, Cohen interview, Butler.

77. Edouard Roditi to author, 7 November 1990.

78. Gore Vidal to author, 30 July 1991.

79. Ira Cohen, conversation with author, 17 August 1993.

80. Paul Bowles to Allen Ginsberg, 1 November 1961, Butler.

81. Ira Cohen, conversation with author, 17 August 1993.

82. Paul Bowles to Joel Redon, 29 August 1985, HRHRC.

83. Paul Bowles to Buffie Johnson, 14 January 1986, HRHRC.

84. The 1984 edition bears a fuller title: *Their Heads Are Green and Their Hands Are Blue*.

85. Paul Bowles to Joel Redon, 18 August 1984, HRHRC.

86. Paul Bowles, journal, HRHRC.

87. Paul Bowles, journal, HRHRC.

88. Paul Bowles, journal, HRHRC.

89. Paul Bowles to Joel Redon, 8 November 1983, HRHRC.

90. Frederich Prokosch, *The Asiatics* (New York: Press of the Readers' Club, 1941), p. 306.

91. Freya Stark, "Beyond the Bazaars, the Hushed Air of the Sahara," *New York Times Book Review*, 25 August 1963, sec. 7, p. 3.

92. Paul Bowles to John Lehmann, 20 March 1954, HRHRC.

93. Paul Bowles, "Letter from Tangier," *London* 1, no. 6 (July 1954): 53.

94. Paul Bowles to John Lehmann, 27 March 1954, HRHRC.

95. Paul Bowles, *The Spider's House* (Santa Barbara: Black Sparrow, 1982), p. 6. Further references to this novel will be noted parenthetically in the text as *TSH*.

96. See I. M. Lewis, *Ecstatic Religion: An Anthropological Study of Spirit Possession and Shamanism* (Middlesex, England: Penguin Books, 1971), pp. 94–96.

97. Paul Bowles, Cohen interview, Butler.

98. Paul Bowles to John Lehmann, 9 January 1954, HRHRC.

99. Paul Bowles to John Lehmann, 4 February [1954], HRHRC.

100. Paul Bowles, "How to Live on a Part-Time Island," *Holiday* 21, no. 3 (March 1957): 41–47.

101. Robin Maugham, *Search for Nirvana* (London: W. H. Allen, 1975), pp. 121–23.

102. Peggy Guggenheim, *Confessions of an Art Addict* (New York: Macmillan, 1960), p. 151.

103. Paul Bowles to David McDowell, 1 March 1955, Butler.

104. Paul Bowles to David McDowell, 1 March 1955, Butler.

105. Paul Bowles, notebook, HRHRC.

106. Christopher Wanklyn to author, 28 March 1991.

107. Vaidon, *Tangier*, p. 277.

108. Paul Bowles to Allen Ginsberg, 12 December 1961, Butler.

Book VI. Closer to the Sun, 1957–

1. Jane Bowles, unnumbered notebook, HRHRC.
2. Morgan, *Rowing toward Eden*, p. 100.
3. Joe McPhillips, conversation with author, 13 February 1986.
4. Paul Bowles to Katharine Hamill, 26 April 1958; Dillon, *Little Original Sin*, p. 302.
5. Vaidon, *Tangier*, p. 325.
6. Christopher Wanklyn to Jane Bowles, 21 March 1958, HRHRC.
7. Dillon, *Little Original Sin*, p. 299.
8. Paul Bowles to Claude and Rena Bowles, 12 September 1961, HRHRC.
9. Paul Bowles to John Lehmann, 23 March 1958, HRHRC.
10. Jane Bowles to Paul Bowles, no date [Autumn 1958], HRHRC.
11. Jane Bowles to Paul Bowles, no date [Autumn 1958], HRHRC.
12. Reviews quoted in Jon Bradshaw, *Dreams That Money Can Buy: The Tragic Life of Libby Holman* (New York: William Morrow, 1985), p. 329.
13. Paul Bowles to Tennessee Williams, 7 September, HRHRC.
14. Forrest Sanders, "Music," *Ithaca Journal*, 16 August 1958, p. 3.
15. Paul Bowles, *Yerma*, HRHRC.
16. Brooks Atkinson, *New York Times*, 25 November 1958.
17. William Burroughs to Paul Bowles, 19 October 1958, HRHRC.
18. Paul Bowles to Tennessee Williams, 1 March 1959, HRHRC.
19. Paul Bowles to Tennessee Williams, 1 March 1959, HRHRC.
20. Brooks Atkinson, "Sweet Bird of Youth," *New York Times*, 11 March 1959, p. 39.
21. James Purdy to Paul Bowles, 12 September 1960, HRHRC.
22. Morgan, *Literary Outlaw*, p. 263.
23. Paul Bowles to Allen Ginsberg, Peter Orlovsky, Gregory Corso, and Jack Kerouac, 27 April [1957], Butler.
24. Paul Bowles to Rena and Claude Bowles, 6 December 1961, HRHRC.
25. Morgan, *Literary Outlaw*, p. 375.
26. Paul Bowles to Rena and Claude Bowles, 6 December 1961, HRHRC.
27. Mailer, *Advertisements for Myself*, p. 468.
28. Mailer, *Advertisements for Myself*, p. 339.
29. Gide, *Lafcadio's Adventures*, p. 252.
30. Paul Bowles to Allen Ginsberg and Peter Orlovsky, 2 August 1962, Butler.
31. Gysin, *Here to Go*, p. 194.
32. Gysin, *Here to Go*, p. 17.
33. Burroughs, *Letters*, p. 20.
34. Morgan, *Literary Outlaw*, p. 291.
35. Gysin, *Here to Go*, p. 51.
36. Paul Bowles, Works I, pp. 16–18, HRHRC.
37. William Burroughs to Paul Bowles, 9 October 1960, HRHRC.
38. William Burroughs to Paul Bowles, 28 October 1965, HRHRC.
39. William Burroughs to Paul Bowles, 21 November 1962, HRHRC.
40. Paul Bowles, *Points in Time* (New York: Ecco, 1982), p. 12.
41. Paul Bowles to Millicent Dillon, 4 February 1981, HRHRC.
42. Paul Bowles to Allen Ginsberg and Peter Orlovsky, 2 August 1962.

43. Paul Bowles to Peter Owen, 26 January 1964, Peter Owen Collection, HRHRC.

44. Herbert, *Second Son*, p. 127.

45. Joe McPhillips, conversation with author, 13 February 1986.

46. Herbert, *Second Son*, p. 122.

47. Herbert, *Second Son*, p. 126.

48. William Burroughs to Paul Bowles, 15 April 1968, HRHRC.

49. Paul Bowles to Rena and Claude Bowles, 26 July 1961, HRHRC.

50. Ida Barker Slade, second wife of Henry Slade from Walpole, New Hampshire, was Henrietta Winnewisser's sister, Rena's aunt, and Paul's great-aunt.

51. Paul Bowles, *Up above the World* (New York: Simon and Schuster, 1966), pp. 99–100. Further references to this novel will be noted parenthetically in the text as *UAW*.

52. Christopher Wanklyn to author, 28 March 1991.

53. Gordon Sager to Richard Scaramelli, 9 May 1988.

54. For ideas regarding Bowles's relation to the thriller genre, I am indebted to Ellen G. Friedman, "Variations on Mystery-Thriller: Paul Bowles' *Up above the World*," *Armchair Detective* 19, no. 3 (Summer 1986): 279–84.

55. Morgan, *Rowing toward Eden*, p. 100.

56. Morgan, *Rowing toward Eden*, p. 101.

57. Paul Bowles to Ira Cohen, 9 January 1967, Butler.

58. Paul Bowles to Mohammed Mrabet, [1966–67], Alderman Library, University of Virginia.

59. Translation of a letter from Dr. Roux to Paul Bowles, 9 January 1967, HRHRC.

60. Paul Bowles to Oliver Evans, 13 November 1967, HRHRC.

61. John Wakeman, ed., *World Authors, 1950–1970* (New York: H. W. Wilson, 1975), pp. 202–3.

62. Ursula D. K. Hart to Millicent Dillon, 6 October 1978, HRHRC.

63. Ursula D. K. Hart to Millicent Dillon, 6 October 1978, HRHRC.

64. Paul Bowles to Jane Howard, 9 April 1969, Butler.

65. Paul Bowles to Jane Howard, 22 April 1969, Butler.

66. Morgan, *Rowing toward Eden*, p. 103.

67. Herbert, *Second Son*, p. 128.

68. Morgan, *Literary Outlaw*, p. 421.

69. Morgan, *Literary Outlaw*, p. 421.

70. Joe McPhillips, conversation with author, 13 February 1986.

71. Allen Sillitoe to Millicent Dillon, 18 August 1981, HRHRC.

72. Paul Bowles to Millicent Dillon, 7 February 1980, HRHRC.

73. Dillon, *Little Original Sin*, p. 421.

74. Paul Bowles to Jane Bowles, 11 December 1962, HRHRC.

75. Paul Bowles, "Next to Nothing," in *Next to Nothing: Collected Poems, 1926–1977* (Santa Barbara: Black Sparrow, 1981), pp. 65, 70.

76. Paul Bowles, "Next to Nothing," HRHRC.

77. Paul Bowles to Ira Cohen, 20 February 1975, Butler.

78. Paul Bowles, "Scene VIII," *Next to Nothing*, p. 59.

79. Paul Bowles, "Next to Nothing," in *Next to Nothing*, p. 66.

80. Paul Bowles to Millicent Dillon, 7 February 1980, HRHRC.

81. Paul Bowles, "Next to Nothing," in *Next to Nothing*, p. 65.

82. Paul Bowles, "Next to Nothing," in *Next to Nothing*, pp. 70–71.

83. Paul Bowles to Millicent Dillon, 1 July 1991, HRHRC.

84. Paul Bowles, conversation with author, 13 February 1986.

85. Paul Bowles to Millicent Dillon, 13 December 1983, HRHRC.

86. Paul Bowles to Allen Ginsberg and Peter Orlovsky, 2 August 1962, Butler.

87. In "A Writing Lesson," Lévi-Strauss states that writing favors the "exploitation of human beings rather than their enlightenment" (*Tristes Tropiques*, trans. John and Doreen Weightman ([New York: Atheneum, 1975], p. 239).

88. Walter Benjamin, "The Storyteller: Reflections on the Work of Nikolai Leskov," in *Illuminations*, pp. 83–110.

89. Paul Bowles, conversation with author, 1986.

90. Ted Morgan, *Rowing toward Eden*, p. 98.

91. Paul Bowles to Buffie Johnson, 24 December 1984, HRHRC.

92. Ira Cohen, conversation with author, 17 August 1993.

93. Mohammed Mrabet, conversation with author, 14 February 1986.

94. Mohammed Mrabet, *Love with a Few Hairs* (San Francisco: City Lights Books, 1986), pp. 89, 150.

95. Edward Said, *Culture and Imperialism* (New York: Alfred A. Knopf, 1993), p. 51.

96. Paul Bowles to Oliver Evans, 8 January 1968, HRHRC.

97. Paul Bowles to Virgil Thomson, 26 November 1968, Jackson.

98. Don Bachardy, conversation with author, 15 November 1990.

99. Paul Bowles to Mohammed Mrabet, 26 December 1968 (translated from Spanish by author), Alderman Library, University of Virginia.

100. Don Bachardy, conversation with author, 15 November 1990.

101. Paul Bowles to Millicent Dillon, 28 August 1981, HRHRC.

102. Paul Bowles to Joel Redon, 23 April 1983, HRHRC.

103. Paul Bowles to Joel Redon, 3 November 1982, HRHRC.

104. Paul Bowles to Joel Redon, 19 November 1982, HRHRC.

105. Paul Bowles to Joel Redon, 1 October 1982, HRHRC.

106. Paul Bowles to Joel Redon, 25 November 1982, HRHRC.

107. Paul Bowles to Joel Redon, 20 January 1983, HRHRC.

108. Paul Bowles to Joel Redon, 3 March 1983, HRHRC.

109. Paul Bowles to Joel Redon, 23 April 1983, HRHRC.

110. Paul Bowles, *Midnight Mass* (Santa Barbara: Black Sparrow, 1981), p. 147. Further references to this work will be noted parenthetically in the text as *MM*.

111. Marvin Daniels, "Pathological Vindictiveness and the Vindictive Character," *Psychoanalytic Review* 56, no. 2 (1969): 173.

112. Paul Bowles to Charles Henri Ford, 19 November 1947, HRHRC.

113. Quoted in Morgan, *Literary Outlaw*, p. 393.

114. Paul Bowles to Buffie Johnson, 8 April 1982, HRHRC.

115. Edouard Roditi to author, 20 May 1991.

116. Edouard Roditi, "Lot's Wife," in *Thrice Chosen* (Santa Barbara: Black Sparrow, 1981).

117. Paul Bowles, conversation with author, February 1986.

118. Paul Bowles to Millicent Dillon, 5 March 1980, HRHRC.

119. Paul Bowles, conversation with author, 14 February 1986.

120. Paul Bowles, "Next to Nothing," in *Next to Nothing*, p. 71.

WORKS BY PAUL BOWLES

Works are listed chronologically

Books

Two Poems. New York: Modern Editions, 1933.

The Sheltering Sky. London: John Lehmann, 1949; New York: New Directions, 1949; New York: Ecco, 1978; London: Peter Owen, 1981; New York: Vintage Books, 1990; New York: Paladin, 1990.

The Delicate Prey. New York: Random House, 1950; New York: Ecco, 1972, 1980, 1984.

A Little Stone. London: John Lehmann, 1950.

The Lost Trail. By R. Frison-Roche. Translated by Paul Bowles. New York: Prentice-Hall, 1951.

Let It Come Down. London: John Lehmann, 1952; New York: Random House, 1952; Santa Barbara: Black Sparrow, 1980; London: Peter Owen, 1984; London: Arena, 1985; London: Abacus, 1990.

The Spider's House. New York: Random House, 1955; Santa Barbara: Black Sparrow, 1982; London: Peter Owen, 1985; London: Abacus, 1991.

Yallah. Photographs by Peter W. Haeberlin, with text by Paul Bowles. Zurich: Manesse, 1956; New York: McDowell, Obolensky, 1957.

No Exit. By Jean-Paul Sartre. Adapted by Paul Bowles. New York: Samuel French, 1958.

The Hours after Noon. London: W. Heinemann, 1959.

A Hundred Camels in the Courtyard. San Francisco: City Lights Books, 1962, 1986.

Their Heads Are Green. London: Peter Owen, 1963; New York: Random House, 1963; New York: Ecco, 1984; London: Abacus, 1990.

A Life Full of Holes. By Driss ben Hamed Charhadi. Translated by Paul Bowles. New York: Grove, 1964.

Up above the World. New York: Simon and Schuster, 1966; London: Peter Owen, 1967; New York: Pocket Books, 1968; New York: Ecco, 1982; London: Peter Owen, 1982; London: Arena, 1984; London: Abacus, 1991.

Love with a Few Hairs. By Mohammed Mrabet. Taped and translated by Paul Bowles. London: Peter Owen, 1967; New York: George Braziller, 1968; San Francisco: City Lights Books, 1986; London: Arena, 1986.

The Time of Friendship. New York: Holt, Rinehart, and Winston, 1967.

Pages from Cold Point. London: Peter Owen, 1968; New York: Zenith, 1983; London: Arena, 1986; London: Abacus, 1990, 1991.

Scenes. Los Angeles: Black Sparrow, 1968.

The Lemon. By Mohammed Mrabet. Translated and edited by Paul Bowles. London: Peter Owen, 1969; New York: McGraw-Hill, 1972; San Francisco: City Lights Books, 1986.

M'Hashish. By Mohammed Mrabet. Taped and translated by Paul Bowles. San Francisco: City Lights Books, 1969.

The Thicket of Spring. Los Angeles: Black Sparrow, 1972.

Without Stopping. New York: G. P. Putnam's Sons, 1972; London: Peter Owen, 1972; Ecco, 1985, 1991; London: Hamish Hamilton, 1989.

The Boy Who Set the Fire. By Mohammed Mrabet. Taped and translated by Paul Bowles. Los Angeles: Black Sparrow, 1974; San Francisco: City Lights Books, 1988, 1989.

For Bread Alone. By Mohamed Choukri. Translated and with an introduction by Paul Bowles. London: Peter Owen, 1974; London: Grafton, 1987.

Jean Genet in Tangier. By Mohamed Choukri. Translated by Paul Bowles. New York: Ecco, 1974, 1990.

Hadidan Aharam. By Mohammed Mrabet. Translated by Paul Bowles. Los Angeles: Black Sparrow, 1975.

The Oblivion Seekers. By Isabelle Eberhardt. Translated by Paul Bowles. San Francisco: City Lights Books, 1975.

Three Tales. New York: Frank Hallman, 1975; New York: School of Visual Arts, 1983.

Harmless Poisons, Blameless Sins. By Mohammed Mrabet. Taped and translated by Paul Bowles. Santa Barbara: Black Sparrow, 1976.

Look & Move On. By Mohammed Mrabet. Taped and translated by Paul Bowles. Santa Barbara: Black Sparrow, 1976; London: Peter Owen, 1989.

Next to Nothing. Kathmandu, Nepal: Starstreams 5, 1976.

The Big Mirror. Santa Barbara: Black Sparrow, 1977.

Things Gone and Things Still Here. Santa Barbara: Black Sparrow, 1977.

The Collected Stories of Paul Bowles, 1939–1976. Santa Barbara: Black Sparrow, 1979, 1989.

Five Eyes. By Abdeslam Boulaich, Mohamed Choukri, Larbi Layachi, Mohammed Mrabet, and Ahmed Yacoubi. Edited and translated by Paul Bowles. Santa Barbara: Black Sparrow, 1979.

Tennessee Williams in Tangier. By Mohamed Choukri. Translated by Paul Bowles. Santa Barbara: Cadmus, 1979.

The Beach Café & the Voice. By Mohammed Mrabet. Taped and translated by Paul Bowles. Santa Barbara: Black Sparrow, 1980.

The Husband. 1980.

In the Red Room. Los Angeles: Sylvester and Orphanos, 1981.

Midnight Mass. Santa Barbara: Black Sparrow, 1981, 1983, 1989; London: Peter Owen, 1985; New York: Harper and Row, 1991.

Next to Nothing: Collected Poems 1926–1977. Santa Barbara: Black Sparrow, 1981.

The Path Doubles Back. By Rodrigo Rey Rosa. Translated by Paul Bowles. New York: Red Ozier, 1982.

Points in Time. London: Peter Owen, 1982; New York: Ecco, 1982, 1984, 1986.

The Chest. By Mohammed Mrabet. Translated by Paul Bowles. Bolinas, Calif.: Tombouctou Books, 1983.

Selected Songs. Santa Fe, N.M.: Soundings, 1984.

The Beggar's Knife. By Rodrigo Rey Rosa. Translated by Paul Bowles. San Francisco: City Lights Books, 1985; London: Peter Owen, 1988.

International Poem. 1985.

She Woke Me Up So I Killed Her. Translations by Paul Bowles. San Francisco: Cadmus, 1985.

Marriage with Papers. By Mohamed Mrabet. Translated by Paul Bowles. Bolinas, Calif.: Tombouctou Books, 1986.

For Bread Alone. London: Grafton, 1987.

Call at Corazón and Other Stories. London: Peter Owen, 1988; London: Abacus, 1989.

A Distant Episode: The Selected Stories. New York: Ecco, 1988, 1989.

Unwelcome Words: Seven Stories. Bolinas, Calif.: Tombouctou Books, 1988.

Al Maghrib: Photographs. Edinburgh: Polygon, 1989; Third Eye, 1989.

A Thousand Days for Mokhtar. London: Peter Owen, 1989; London: Abacus, 1990.

Two Years Beside the Strait. London: Peter Owen, 1990.

Days, Tangier Journal: 1987–1989. New York: Ecco, 1991, 1992.

Too Far from Home: The Selected Writings of Paul Bowles. New York: Ecco, 1992.

The Letters of Paul Bowles. New York: Farrar, Straus, Giroux, 1993.

Musical Compositions

Instrumental

Sonata for Oboe and Clarinet, 1931.
Sonata No. 1 for Flute and Piano, 1932.
El Bejuco, 1934.
Sonata for Violin and Piano, 1934.
Mediodía, 1937.
Music for a Farce, 1938.
Huapango No. 1 and No. 2, 1939.
La Cuelga, 1946.
Orosí, 1946.
Sayula, 1946.
Six Preludes for Piano, 1947.
Sonatina for Piano, 1947.
Concerto for Two Pianos and Orchestra, 1949.
Sonata for Two Pianos, 1949.
Night Waltz for Two Pianos, 1958.
Cross Country, 1976.

Vocal

Scènes d'Anabase (text based on a poem by St. John Perse), 1932.
"Memnon," 1935.
Blue Mountain Ballads (text by Tennessee Williams), 1946.
A Picnic Cantata (text by James Schuyler), 1954.
Selected Songs. Santa Fe, N.M.: Soundings Press, 1984.

Opera

Denmark Vesey (libretto by Charles Henri Ford), 1939.

The Wind Remains (original libretto based on a play by Federico García Lorca), 1943.
Yerma (original libretto based on a play by Federico García Lorca), 1958.

Ballet

Yankee Clipper, 1937.
Pastorela, 1941.
Colloque Sentimental, 1944.

Incidental Theater Music

Horse Eats Hat, 1936.
Who Fights This Battle? 1936.
The Tragical History of Dr. Faustus, 1937.
Too Much Johnson, 1938.
My Heart's in the Highlands, 1939.
Love's Old Sweet Song, 1940.
Twelfth Night, 1940.
Liberty Jones, 1941.
Watch on the Rhine, 1941.
South Pacific, 1943.
'Tis Pity She's a Whore, 1943.
The Glass Menagerie, 1944.
Jacobowsky and the Colonel, 1944.
Ondine, 1945.
Cyrano de Bergerac, 1946.
The Dancer, 1946.
Land's End, 1946.
On Whitman Avenue, 1946.
Twilight Bar, 1946.
Summer and Smoke, 1948.
In the Summer House, 1953.
Edwin Booth, 1958.
Sweet Bird of Youth, 1959.
The Milk Train Doesn't Stop Here Anymore, 1962.
Electra, 1965.
Oedipus the King, 1966.
The Garden, 1967.
Wet and Dry/Alive, 1968.
The Bacchae, 1969.
Bachelor Furnished, 1969.
Caligula, 1978.
Birdbath, 1981.
Hippolytus, 1992.

Film Music

Bride of Samoa, 1933.

Venus and Adonis, 1935.
145 W. 21, 1936.
Seeing the World, 1936.
America's Disinherited, 1937.
Chelsea through the Magnifying Glass, 1938.
How to Become a Citizen of the U.S., 1938.
Roots in the Soil, 1940.
Congo, 1944.
Dreams That Money Can Buy, 1947.

For a complete annotated bibliography of works by Paul Bowles, see Jeffrey
  Miller's *Paul Bowles: A Descriptive Bibliography*. Santa Barbara: Black Sparrow, 1986.

SELECTED BIBLIOGRAPHY

Books

Ackerly, Joe Randolph. *Hindoo Holiday: An Indian Journal*. New York: Viking, 1932.

Allen, Walter. *The Modern Novel in Britain and the United States*. New York: E. P. Dutton, 1964.

Antheil, George. *Bad Boy of Music*. Garden City, N.Y.: Doubleday, 1945.

Antoun, Richard T. *Rural Politics and Social Change in the Middle East*. Bloomington: Indiana University Press, 1972.

Aries, Phillipe. *Centuries of Childhood: A Social History of Family Life*. New York: Vintage Books, 1965.

Ashby, Henry. *Health in the Nursery*. London: Longman, 1898.

Baker, Richard S. Barbe. *Sahara Challenge*. London: Lutterworth, 1954.

Barker, E. Frye. *Barker Genealogy*. New York: Frye, 1927.

Baumbach, Jonathan. *The Landscape of Nightmare: Studies in the Contemporary American Novel*. New York: New York University Press, 1965.

Beaton, Cecil. *The Strenuous Years: Diaries, 1948–1955*. London: Weidenfeld and Nicolson, 1973.

Benjamin, Walter. *Illuminations*. Edited by Hannah Arendt. Translated by H. Zohn. New York: Schocken Books, 1969.

Bertens, Johannes. *The Fiction of Paul Bowles: The Soul Is the Weariest Part of the Body*. Amsterdam: Costerus, 1979.

Blacking, John. *How Musical Is Man?* Seattle: University of Washington Press, 1973.

Bloom, Harold. *The Anxiety of Influence*. New York: Oxford University Press, 1973.

Bradshaw, Jon. *Dreams That Money Can Buy: The Tragic Life of Libby Holman*. New York: William Morrow, 1985.

Brandon, Ruth. *The Spiritualists: The Passion for the Occult in the Nineteenth and Twentieth Centuries*. New York: Alfred A. Knopf, 1983.

Brooks, Van Wyck. *The Confident Years: 1885–1915*. New York: E. P. Dutton, 1952.

Burroughs, William. *Letters to Allen Ginsberg, 1953–1957*. New York: Full Court, 1982.

Canetti, Elias. *The Voices of Marrakesh: A Record of a Visit*. New York: Seabury, 1978.

Caplovich, Judd. *Blizzard! The Great Storm of '88*. Vernon, Conn.: VeRo, 1987.

Caponi, Gena Dagel, ed. *Conversations with Paul Bowles*. Jackson: University Press of Mississippi, 1993.

Capote, Truman. *The Dogs Bark: Public People and Private Places*. New York: Random House, 1973.

————. *Local Color*. New York: Random House, 1950.

Caro, Robert A. *The Power Broker: Robert Moses and the Fall of New York*. New York: Vintage Books, 1975.

Chase, Stuart. *Mexico: A Study of Two Americas*. In collaboration with Marian Tyler. New York: Macmillan, 1931.

Clarke, Arthur C. *The Reefs of Taprobane*. New York: Harper and Brothers, 1956–57.

Clarke, Gerald. *Capote: A Biography*. New York: Simon and Schuster, 1988.

Clurman, Harold. *The Fervent Years: The Group Theatre and the Thirties*. New York: Harcourt Brace Jovanovich, 1975.

Cohen, Ronald, and John Middleton, eds. *From Tribe to Nation in Africa: Studies in Incorporation Process*. Scranton: Chandler, 1970.

Coon, Carleton. *Caravan: The Story of the Middle East*. New York: Holt, Rinehart, and Winston, 1958.

Copland, Aaron, and Vivian Perlis. *Copland: 1900 through 1942*. New York: St. Martin's, 1984.

Croft-Cooke, Rupert. *The Caves of Hercules*. New York: W. H. Allen, 1974.

————. *The Tangerine House*. New York: St. Martin's, 1956.

Cunninghame Graham, R. B. *Mogreb-el-Acksa: A Journey in Morocco*. 1898. Reprint. New York: Viking, 1930.

De Mauny, Count. *The Garden of Taprobane*. London: Williams and Norgate, 1937.

Dillon, Millicent. *A Little Original Sin: The Life and Work of Jane Bowles*. New York: Holt, Rinehart, and Winston, 1981.

Douglass, Frederick. *Narrative of the Life of Frederick Douglass, An American Slave*. New York: Signet, 1968.

Duke, Vernon. *Passport to Paris*. Boston: Little, Brown, 1955.

Edmiston, Susan, and Linda D. Cirino. *Literary New York: A History and Guide*. Boston: Houghton Mifflin, 1976.

Eickelman, Dale F. *Moroccan Islam: Tradition and Society in a Pilgrimage Center*. Austin: University of Texas Press, 1976.

Eisinger, Charles. *Fiction of the Forties*. Chicago: University of Chicago Press, 1963.

Ellwood, Robert S., Jr. *Alternative Altars: Unconventional and Eastern Spirituality in America*. Chicago: University of Chicago Press, 1979.

Erenberg, Lewis A. *Steppin' Out: New York Nightlife and the Transformation of American Culture, 1890–1930*. Westport, Conn.: Greenwood, 1981.

Farquhar, Thomas Mulford. *The History of the Bowles Family*. Philadelphia, 1907.

Fernea, Elizabeth Warnock. *A Street in Marrakech*. Garden City, N.Y.: Doubleday, 1975.

Fernea, Elizabeth Warnock, and Robert Fernea. *The Arab World*. Garden City, N.Y.: Doubleday, 1985.

Fiedler, Leslie A. *Waiting for the End*. New York: Stein and Day, 1964.

Finney, Brian. *Christopher Isherwood: A Critical Biography*. New York: Oxford University Press, 1979.

Flandrau, Charles Macomb. *Viva Mexico!* 1908, 1937. Reprint. Urbana: University of Illinois Press, 1964.

Ford, Charles Henri, and Parker Tyler. *The Young and Evil*. Paris: Obelisk, 1933.

Freud, Sigmund. *The Standard Edition of the Complete Psychological Works of Sigmund Freud.* Edited by James Strachey. London: Hogarth, 1955.

Fussell, Paul. *Abroad: British Literary Traveling between the Wars.* New York: Oxford University Press, 1980.

Gass, William H. *Fiction and the Figures of Life.* Boston: Nonpareil Books, 1971.

Gay, Peter. *Weimar Culture: The Outsider as Insider.* New York: Harper and Row, 1968.

Geertz, Clifford. *The Interpretation of Cultures.* New York: Basic Books, 1973.

———. *Islam Observed: Religious Developments in Morocco and Indonesia.* New Haven: Yale University Press, 1968.

Gide, André. *Lafcadio's Adventures (Les Caves du Vatican).* Translated by Dorothy Bussy. New York: Alfred A. Knopf, 1927.

———. *If It Die: An Autobiography (Si le grain ne meurt).* Translated by Dorothy Bussy. London: Secker and Warburg, 1950.

Girard, René. *Deceit, Desire, and the Novel: Self and Other in Literary Structure.* 1961. Reprint. Baltimore, Md.: Johns Hopkins University Press, 1965.

Glassco, John. *Memoirs of Montparnasse.* New York: Oxford University Press, 1970.

Green, Harvey. *Fit for America: Health, Fitness, Sport, and American Society.* Baltimore, Md.: Johns Hopkins University Press, 1986.

———. *The Light of the Home: An Intimate View of the Lives of Women in Victorian America.* New York: Pantheon Books, 1983.

Green, Martin Burgess. *Children of the Sun: A Narrative of "Decadence" in England after 1918.* New York: Basic Books, 1976.

Green, Michelle. *Dream at the End of the World: Paul Bowles and the Literary Renegades in Tangier.* New York: Harper Collins, 1991.

Greene, Graham. *Collected Essays.* New York: Viking, 1969.

———. *Journey without Maps.* London: W. Heinemann, 1953.

———. *Ways of Escape.* New York: Simon and Schuster, 1980.

Grobel, Lawrence. *Conversations with Capote.* New York: New American Library, 1985.

Grosser, Maurice. *The Painter's Eye.* New York: Rinehart, 1951.

———. *Painting in Public.* New York: Alfred A. Knopf, 1948.

Grotstein, James S. *Splitting and Projective Identification.* New York: Jason Aronson, 1981.

Guggenheim, Peggy. *Confessions of an Art Addict.* New York: Macmillan, 1960.

———. *Out of This Century: The Informal Memoirs of Peggy Guggenheim.* New York: Universe Books, 1979.

Gysin, Brion. *Here to Go: Planet R-101.* San Francisco: Re/Search Publications, 1982.

Handlin, David. *The American Home: Architecture and Society, 1815–1915.* Boston: Little, Brown, 1979.

Hardyment, Christina. *Dream Babies: Three Centuries of Good Advice on Child Care.* New York: Harper and Row, 1983.

Harris, Walter. *France, Spain, and the Rif.* London: Edward Arnold, 1927.

Hassan, Ihab. *Radical Innocence: Studies in the Contemporary American Novel.* Princeton, N.J.: Princeton University Press, 1961.

Herbert, David. *Second Son.* London: Peter Owen, 1972.

Hibbard, Allen E. *Paul Bowles: A Study of the Short Fiction*. Boston: Twayne Publishers, 1993.

Higham, Charles. *Orson Welles: The Rise and Fall of an American Genius*. New York: St. Martin's, 1985.

Hill, Derek. *Islamic Architecture in North Africa*. Hamden, Conn.: Archon Books, 1976.

Himmelfarb, Gertrude. *Marriage and Morals among the Victorians*. New York: Alfred A. Knopf, 1986.

Holin, Nils G., ed. *Religious Ecstasy*. Stockholm: Almquist and Willsell, Uppsala, 1982.

Hopkins, John. *Tangier Buzzless Flies*. New York: Atheneum, 1972.

Houseman, John. *Entertainers and the Entertained: Essays on Theater, Film, and Television*. New York: Simon and Schuster, 1986.

Hulme, Katharyn Cavarly. *Arab Interlude*. Philadelphia: Macrae Smith, 1930.

Inge, Thomas, ed. *Conversations with Truman Capote*. Jackson: University Press of Mississippi, 1987.

Isherwood, Christopher. *The Berlin Stories: "The Last of Mr. Norris" and "Goodbye to Berlin."* New York: J. Laughlin, 1945.

———. *Down There on a Visit*. 1959. Reprint. New York: Popular Libray, 1963.

Jackson, Kenneth T. *Crabgrass Frontier: The Suburbanization of the United States*. New York: Oxford University Press, 1985.

Josephson, Matthew. *Life among the Surrealists: A Memoir*. New York: Holt, Rinehart, and Winston, 1962.

Kaufmann, Walter. *Existentialism from Dostoevsky to Sartre*. New York: New American Library, 1975.

Kazin, Alfred. *Starting out in the Thirties*. Boston: Little, Brown, 1965.

———. *A Walker in the City*. New York: Harcourt, Brace, 1951.

Lahr, John, ed. *The Orton Diaries*. New York: Harper and Row, 1987.

Laing, R. D. *The Divided Self: A Study of Sanity and Madness*. Chicago: Quadrangle Books, 1960; New York: Penguin Books, 1969.

Lane, Margaret. *The Day of the Feast*. New York: Alfred A. Knopf, 1968.

———. *A Smell of Burning*. New York: Alfred A. Knopf, 1966.

Lears, T. J. Jackson. *No Place of Grace: Antimodernism and the Transformation of American Culture, 1880–1920*. New York: Pantheon Books, 1981.

Lee, Lawrence, and Barry Gifford. *Saroyan: A Biography*. New York: Harper and Row, 1984.

Lehmann, John. *The Ample Proposition*. London: Eyre and Spottiswoode, 1966.

Levant, Oscar. *A Smattering of Ignorance*. New York: Doubleday, 1940.

Lévi-Strauss, Claude. *The Savage Mind*. Chicago: University of Chicago Press, 1962.

———. *Tristes Tropiques*. Translated by John and Doreen Weightman. New York: Atheneum, 1975.

Lewis, I. M. *Ecstatic Religion: An Anthropological Study of Spirit Possession and Shamanism*. Middlesex, England: Penguin Books, 1971.

Lewis, Robert. *Slings and Arrows: Theatre in My Life*. New York: Stein and Day, 1984.

Lilius, Aleko E. *Turbulent Tangier*. London: Elek Books, 1956.

Loti, Pierre [Julien Vivaud]. *Morocco*. New York: Frederick A. Stokes, 1919.

Ludlow, Fitz Hugh. *The Hasheesh Eater.* 1857. Reprint. Upper Saddle River, N.J.: Literature House, 1970.

McCarthy, Mary. *How I Grew.* New York: Harcourt Brace Jovanovich, 1987.

Mailer, Norman. *Advertisements for Myself.* New York: G.P. Putnam's Sons, 1959.

Mangione, Jerre. *An Ethnic at Large: A Memoir of America in the Thirties and Forties.* New York: G. P. Putnam's Sons, 1978.

Martin, Jay. *Always Merry and Bright: The Life of Henry Miller: An Unauthorized Biography.* Santa Barbara: Capra, 1978.

Maugham, Robin. *Escape from the Shadows.* London: Hodder and Stoughton, 1972.

———. *Search for Nirvana.* London: W. H. Allen, 1975.

———. *The Wrong People.* London: W. Heinemann, 1970.

Mayne, Peter. *The Alleys of Marrakesh.* Middlesex, England: Penguin Books, 1957.

Mellow, James R. *Charmed Circle: Gertrude Stein and Company.* New York: Avon, 1974.

Memmi, Albert. *The Colonizer and the Colonized.* Boston: Beacon, 1967.

Merriam, Alan P. *The Anthropology of Music.* Chicago: Northwestern University Press, 1964.

Miles, Barry. *Ginsberg: A Biography.* New York: Simon and Schuster, 1989.

———. *William Burroughs: El Hombre Invisible, a Portrait.* New York: Hyperion, 1993.

Miller, Alice. *For Your Own Good: Hidden Cruelty in Child Rearing and the Roots of Violence.* New York: Farrar, Straus, Giroux, 1983.

Miller, Jeffrey. *Paul Bowles: A Descriptive Bibliography.* Santa Barbara: Black Sparrow, 1986.

Miller, Karl. *Doubles: Studies in Literary History.* New York: Oxford University Press, 1985.

Moers, Ellen. *The Dandy.* London: Secker and Warburg, 1962.

Moore, Robert Laurence. *In Search of White Crows: Spiritualism, Parapsychology, and American Culture.* New York: Oxford University Press, 1977.

Morgan, Ted. *Literary Outlaw: The Life and Times of William S. Burroughs.* New York: Henry Holt, 1988.

———. *Rowing toward Eden.* Boston: Houghton Mifflin, 1981.

Morris, Jan. *Manhattan '45.* New York: Oxford University Press, 1987.

Mrabet, Mohammed. *Love with a Few Hairs.* San Francisco: City Lights Books, 1986.

Nadal, Norman. *A Pictorial History of the Theatre Guild.* New York: Crown Publishers, 1969.

Naphegyi, Gabor. *Ghardaia: Ninety Days among the B'ni Mozab: Adventures in the Oasis of the Desert of Sahara.* New York: G. P. Putnam's Sons, 1871.

Orwell, George. *A Collection of Essays.* Garden City, N.Y.: Doubleday, 1954.

Parry, Albert. *Garrets and Pretenders: A History of Bohemianism in America.* 1933. Reprint. New York: Dover Publications, 1960.

Patteson, Richard F. *A World Outside: The Fiction of Paul Bowles.* Austin: University of Texas Press, 1987.

Peckam, Morse. *The Triumph of Romanticism.* Columbia: University of South Carolina Press, 1970.

Peyser, Joan. *Bernstein: A Biography*. New York: William Morrow, 1987.

Pounds, Wayne. *Paul Bowles: The Inner Geography*. New York: Peter Lang, 1985.

Preuss, Arthur. *A Dictionary of Secret and Other Societies*. Detroit: Gale Research Company, 1966.

Prokosch, Frederich. *The Asiatics*. New York: Harper and Brothers, 1935; New York: Press of the Readers' Club, 1941.

Putnam, Samuel. *Paris Was Our Mistress: Memoirs of a Lost and Found Generation*. New York: Viking, 1947.

Read, Herbert, ed. *Surrealism*. 1936. Reprint. London: Faber and Faber, 1971.

Rhys, Jean. *Smile Please: An Unfinished Autobiography*. New York: Harper and Row, 1979.

Riesman, David. *The Lonely Crowd*. New Haven: Yale University Press, 1961.

Robbe-Grillet, Alain. *Djinn*. Translated by Yvonne Lenard. New York: Grove, 1982.

Roditi, Edouard. *Thrice Chosen*. Santa Barbara: Black Sparrow, 1981.

Rorem, Ned. *Music and People*. New York: George Braziller, 1968.

———. *The New York Diary*. New York: George Braziller, 1967.

———. *Setting the Tone: Essays and a Diary*. New York: Coward-McCann, 1983.

Roussel, Raymond. *Impressions of Africa*. 1910. Reprint. Berkeley: University of California Press, 1967.

Sager, Gordon. *Run Sheep Run*. New York: Vanguard, 1950, 1958.

Said, Edward. *Culture and Imperialism*. New York: Alfred A. Knopf, 1993.

———. *Orientalism*. New York: Vintage Books, 1979.

Salzman, Jack. *The Survival Years*. New York: Pegasus, 1969.

Sartre, Jean-Paul. *Being and Nothingness: An Essay on Phenomenological Ontology*. New York: Philosophical Library, 1956.

———. *Existentialism and Human Emotions*. New York: Philosophical Library, 1957.

———. *Nausea*. London: New Direction, 1949.

———. *No Exit*. 1946. Reprint. New York: Alfred A. Knopf, 1972.

Sawyer-Lauçanno, Christopher. *An Invisible Spectator: A Biography of Paul Bowles*. New York: Weidenfeld and Nicolson, 1989.

Sayers, Frances Clarks. *Anne Carroll Moore*. New York: Atheneum, 1972.

Skerl, Jennie. *William S. Burroughs*. Twayne's United States Authors Series 438. Boston: G. K. Hall, 1985.

Spencer, Sidney. *Mysticism in World Religion*. Baltimore: Penguin, 1963.

Spender, Stephen. *World within World*. New York: Harcourt, Brace, 1951.

Spratling, William. *Little Mexico*. 1932. Reprint. New York: Peter Smith, 1947.

Stanton, Robert J. *Views from a Window: Conversations with Gore Vidal*. Secaucus, N.J.: Lyle Stuart, 1980.

Steen, Mike. *A Look at Tennessee Williams*. New York: Hawthorne Books, 1969.

Stein, Gertrude. *The Autobiography of Alice B. Toklas*. New York: Harcourt, Brace, 1933.

Stewart, Angus. *Tangier: A Writer's Notebook*. London: Hutchinson, 1977.

Stewart, Lawrence O. *Paul Bowles: The Illumination of North Africa*. Carbondale: Southern Illinois University Press, 1974.

Tanner, Tony. *City of Words: American Fiction, 1950–1970*. London: Jonathan Cape, 1971.

Thomson, Virgil. *Selected Letters of Virgil Thomson*. Edited by Tim Page and Vanessa Weeks Page. New York: Summit Books, 1988.

———. *Virgil Thomson*. New York: Da Capo, 1966.

Toklas, Alice B. *Staying On Alone: Letters of Alice B. Toklas*. Edited by Edward Burns. New York: Liveright, 1973.

———. *What Is Remembered*. New York: Holt, Rinehart, and Winston, 1963.

Tomkins, Calvin. *Living Well Is the Best Revenge*. New York: Viking, 1971.

Trilling, Diana. *Reviewing the Forties*. New York: Harcourt Brace Jovanovich, 1978.

Trimingham, John Spencer. *The Sufi Orders in Islam*. London: Oxford University Press, 1971.

Tytell, John. *Naked Angels: Lives and Literature of the Beat Generation*. New York: McGraw Hill, 1976.

Vaidon, Lawdom [David Woolman]. *Tangier: A Different Way*. Metuchen, N.J.: Scarecrow, 1977.

Van Loon, Hendrik Willem. *A Short History of Discovery from the Earliest Times to the Founding of Colonies in the American Continent*. Philadelphia: D. McKay, 1917.

Wakeman, John, ed., *World Authors, 1950–1970*. New York: H. W. Wilson, 1975.

Westermarck, Edward. *Ritual and Belief in Morocco*. 2 vols. London: Macmillan, 1926.

Wharton, Edith. *In Morocco*. London: Macmillan, 1920.

Williams, Tennessee. *Hard Candy: A Book of Stories*. New York: New Directions, 1954.

———. *Memoirs*. Garden City, N.Y.: Doubleday, 1975.

———. *Tennessee Williams' Letters to Donald Windham, 1940–1965*. Edited by Donald Windham. New York: Holt, Rinehart, and Winston, 1977.

Wilson, Colin. *The Outsider*. 1956. Reprint. London: Picador, 1963.

Wilson, Edmund. *Axel's Castle*. New York: Charles Scribner's Sons, 1931.

———. *The Thirties: A Study in the Imaginative Literature of 1870–1930*. New York: Farrar, Straus, and Giroux, 1980.

Zweig, Paul. *The Adventurer*. New York: Basic Books, 1974.

———. *Against Emptiness*. New York: Harper and Row, 1971.

———. *Three Journeys: An Automythology*. New York: Basic Books. 1976.

Articles

Excluding reviews of works by Paul Bowles

Alameda, Soledad. "Paul Bowles: *Tocado por la Magia*." *El País Setional* (15 February 1990): 26–29, 32.

Alenier, Karen LaLonde, Francine Geraci, and Ken Pottiger. "An Interview with Paul Bowles." *Gargoyle* 24 (Spring 1984): 5–32.

"Aspects of Self: A Bowles Collage." *Twentieth Century Literature* 32, nos. 3–4 (Fall–Winter 1986): 259–300.

Bailey, Jeffrey. "The Art of Fiction 67: Paul Bowles." *Paris Review* 23 (Fall 1981): 62–89.

Barlow, Samuel L. M. "In the Theater." *Modern Music* 18, no. 3 (March–April 1941): 190.

Berger, Arthur. "The Young Composers' Group." *Trend* 2, no. 1 (April–May–June 1933): 26–28.

Breit, Harvey. "Talk with Paul Bowles." *New York Times Book Review*, 9 March 1952, sec. 57, p. 10.

Butscher, Edward. "Paul Bowles as Poet: Excursions of a Minimal Anti-Self." *Twentieth Century Literature* 32, nos. 3–4 (Fall–Winter 1986): 350–72.

Butscher, Edward, and Irving Malin, eds. Paul Bowles Issue. *Twentieth Century Literature* 32, nos. 3–4 (Fall–Winter 1986).

Caponi, Gena Dagel. "Conversation with Paul Bowles." In *Conversations with Paul Bowles*, edited by Gena Dagel Caponi, pp. 193–200. Jackson: University Press of Mississippi, 1993.

Carter, Elliot. "With the Dancers." *Modern Music* 15, no. 2 (January–February 1938): 122.

Collins, Jack. "Approaching Paul Bowles." Paul Bowles/Coleman Dowell Number. *Review of Contemporary Fiction* 2, no. 3 (Fall 1982): 55–63.

Copland, Aaron. "America's Young Men—Ten Years Later." *Modern Music* 13, no. 4 (May–June 1936): 10.

Dagel, Gena. "A Nomad in New York: Paul Bowles, 1933–1947." *American Music* 7, no. 3 (Fall 1989): 278–314.

Daniels, Marvin. "Pathological Vindictiveness and the Vindictive Character." *Psychoanalytic Review* 56, no. 2 (1969): 173.

Davis, Stephen. "Interview: Paul Bowles." *Stone Age* 2 (Spring 1979): 38–40, 59.

———. "Mercury at 80." *Boston Globe Magazine*, 4 March 1990, pp. 14–20, 24–25.

Ditsky, John. "*The Time of Friendship*: The Short Fiction of Paul Bowles." *San Jose Studies* 12, no. 2 (Spring 1986): 61–74.

———. "*The Time of Friendship*: The Short Fiction of Paul Bowles." *Twentieth Century Literature* 32, nos. 3–4 (Fall–Winter 1986): 373–87.

Emerson, Stephen. "Endings and *The Sheltering Sky*." Paul Bowles/Coleman Dowell Number. *Review of Contemporary Fiction* 2, no. 3 (Fall 1982): 73–75.

Evans, Oliver. "An Interview with Paul Bowles." *Mediterranean Review* 1, no. 2 (Winter 1971): 3–14.

———. "Paul Bowles and the 'Natural' Man." *Critique* 3 (1959): 43–59.

Finck, H. T. "Horace Fletcher, Gluttony's Opponent." *New York Evening Post*, 14 January 1919, p. 79.

Friedman, Ellen G. "Variations on Mystery-Thriller: Paul Bowles' *Up above the World*." *Armchair Detective* 19, no. 3 (Summer 1986): 279–84.

Glanville-Hicks, Peggy. "Paul Bowles: American Composer." *Music and Letters* (April 1945).

Greene, Graham. "The Lost Childhood." In *Collected Essays*, pp. 13–19. New York: Viking, 1969.

Halpern, Daniel. "Interview with Paul Bowles." *TriQuarterly* 33 (Spring 1975): 159–77.

Hamovitch, Mitzi Berger. "Release from Torment: The Fragmented Double in *Let It Come Down*." *Twentieth Century Literature* 32, nos. 3–4 (Fall–Winter 1986): 440–50.

Harrison, Jay S. "Composer at Home Abroad." *New York Herald Tribune*, 17 May 1953, sec 4, p. 5.

Hassan, Ihab H. "Love in the Modern American Novel: Expense of Spirit and Waste of Shame." *Western Humanities Review*: 149–61.

———. "The Pilgrim as Prey: A Note on Paul Bowles." *Western Review* 19 (1954): 23–26.

Hauptman, Robert. "Paul Bowles and the Perception of Evil." Paul Bowles/Coleman Dowell Number. *Review of Contemporary Fiction* 2, no. 3 (Fall 1982): 71–73.

Hibbard, Allen E. "Expatriation and Narration in Two Works by Paul Bowles." *West Virginia University Philological Papers, 1986–1987* 32 (1986–87): 61–71.

Hunt, Tim. "Paul Bowles: Past and Present." Paul Bowles/Coleman Dowell Number. *Review of Contemporary Fiction* 2, no. 3 (Fall 1982): 52–55.

Lesser, Wendy. "Murder as Social Impropriety: Paul Bowles's 'Evil Heroes.'" *Twentieth Century Literature* 32, nos. 3–4 (Fall–Winter 1986): 402–7.

———. "Paul Bowles' *Collected Stories*." Paul Bowles/Coleman Dowell Number. *Review of Contemporary Fiction* 2, no. 3 (Fall 1982): 50–52.

McInerny, Jay. "Paul Bowles in Exile." *Vanity Fair* 48, September 1983, pp. 69–76, 131.

McPhee, Colin. "New York's Spring Season, 1936." *Modern Music* 13, no. 4 (May–June 1936): 40.

Malin, Irving. "Drastic Points." Paul Bowles/Coleman Dowell Number. *Review of Contemporary Fiction* 2, no. 3 (Fall 1982): 30–32.

Massot, Josep. "Paul Bowles: *Un Nomado Varado en Tanger*." *La Vanguardia Magazine*, 15 April 1990, pp. 10–16.

Mead, Rita. "The Amazing Mr. Cowell." *American Music* 1, no. 4 (Winter 1983): 63–89.

Metcalf, Paul. "A Journey in Search of Paul Bowles." Paul Bowles/Coleman Dowell Number. *Review of Contemporary Fiction* 2, no. 3 (Fall 1982): 32–41.

Moss, Marilyn. "The Child in the Text: Autobiography, Fiction, and the Aesthetics of Deception in *Without Stopping*." *Twentieth Century Literature* 32, nos. 3–4 (Fall–Winter 1986): 314–34.

Mottram, Eric. "Paul Bowles: Staticity and Terror." Paul Bowles/Coleman Dowell Number. *Review of Contemporary Fiction* 2, no. 3 (Fall 1982): 6–30.

Olson, Steven E. "Alien Terrain: Paul Bowles's Filial Landscapes." *Twentieth Century Literature* 32, nos. 3–4 (Fall–Winter 1986): 334–49.

Patteson, Richard F. "The External World of Paul Bowles." *Perspectives on Contemporary Literature* 10 (1984): 16–22.

———. "Paul Bowles: Two Unfinished Projects." *Library Chronicle of the University of Texas* 30 (1985): 57–65.

Pounds, Wayne. "*Let It Come Down* and Inner Geography." Paul Bowles/Coleman Dowell Number. *Review of Contemporary Fiction* 2, no. 3 (Fall 1982): 42–50.

———. "Paul Bowles and Edgar Allan Poe: The Disintegration of the Personality." *Twentieth Century Literature* 32, nos. 3–4 (Fall–Winter 1986): 424–39.

———. "The Subject of Paul Bowles." *Twentieth Century Literature* 32, nos. 3–4 (Fall–Winter 1986): 301–13.

Rainwater, Catherine. "'Sinister Overtones,' 'Terrible Phrases': Poe's Influence on the Writing of Paul Bowles." *Essays in Literature* II, no. 2 (Fall 1984): 253–56.

Roditi, Edouard. "Works and Days of the Young and Evil." *Paris exiles* I, no. I (Winter 1984): 4–7.

Rogers, Michael. "Conversations in Morocco: The *Rolling Stone* Interview." *Rolling Stone*, 23 May 1974, pp. 48–50, 52, 54, 56, 58.

Rondeau, Daniel. "Paul Bowles: *Un Americano en Tanger.*" *Quimera* 48: 27–33.

Rosenfeld, Paul. "The Newest American Composers." *Modern Music* 15, no. 3 (March–April 1938): 158.

Rountree, Mary Martin. "Paul Bowles: Translations from the Moghrebi." *Twentieth Century Literature* 32, nos. 3–4 (Fall–Winter 1986): 388–401.

St. Louis, Ralph. "The Affirming Silence: Paul Bowles's 'Pastor Dowe at Tacate.'" *Studies in Short Fiction* 24, no. 5 (Fall 1987): 381–86.

Seidner, David. "Paul Bowles Interview." *Bomb* 4 (November 1982): 10–13.

Spilker, John. "Paul Bowles Interviewed." *oboe* 5 (1982): 74–86.

Stewart, Lawrence D. "Paul Bowles and 'The Frozen Fields' of Vision." Paul Bowles/Coleman Dowell Number. *Review of Contemporary Fiction* 2, no. 3 (Fall 1982): 64–71

Talmore, Avital. "Beyond 'Wedlock' and 'Hierogamy'": Non-Marriage in Modern Fiction." *Durham University Journal* 77 (December 1984): 79–85.

Wells, Linda S. "Paul Bowles: Do Not Appropriate *My* Object." Paul Bowles/Coleman Dowell Number. *Review of Contemporary Fiction* 2, no. 3 (Fall 1982): 75–84.

Williams, Marcellette G. "'Tea in the Sahara': The Function of Time in the Work of Paul Bowles." *Twentieth Century Literature* 32, nos. 3–4 (Fall–Winter 1986): 408–23.

Personal Communications

Bachardy, Don. Series of correspondence and telephone conversation with author, 1990.

Bowles, Paul. Series of correspondence with author, 1980–93. Series of conversations with author, February 1986.

Burckhardt, Rudy. Series of correspondence with author, 1988.

Cohen, Ira. Telephone conversations with author, 1993.

Copland, Aaron. Series of correspondence with author, 1984. Telephone conversation with author, 3 October 1984.

Diamond, David. Series of correspondence with author, 1983–85. Conversation with author, 5 October 1984.

Grosser, Maurice. Interview with author, 5 October 1984.

Isherwood, Christopher. Letter to author, II December 1984.

Johnson, Buffie. Conversation with author, 4 October 1984.

Lerner, Bennett. Series of correspondence and telephone conversations with author, 1986–89.

McPhillips, Joe. Conversation with author, February 1986.

Madway, Edna Bockstein. Series of correspondence with author, 1982.

Roditi, Edouard. Series of correspondence with author, 1990.

Rorem, Ned. Conversation with author, 27 September 1984.
Sager, Gordon. Series of correspondence with author, 1988.
Smith, Oliver. Telephone conversation with author, April 1985.
Thomson, Virgil. Conversation with author, 3 October 1984.
Vidal, Gore. Letter to author, 30 July 1991.
Wanklyn, Christopher. Series of correspondence with author, 1991.

Manuscript Collections

Bowles, Jane Auer. Papers. Harry Ransom Humanities Research Center, University of Texas, Austin.
Bowles, Paul Frederic. Papers. Alderman Library, University of Virginia, Charlottesville.
———. Papers. Harry Ransom Humanities Research Center, University of Texas, Austin.
———. Papers. Library for the Performing Arts, New York.
———. Papers. Rare Book and Manuscript Library, Butler Library, Columbia University, New York.
———. Papers. Special Collections, University of Delaware Library, University of Delaware, Newark.
Dillon, Millicent. Papers. Harry Ransom Humanities Research Center, University of Texas, Austin.
Ford, Charles Henri. Papers. Harry Ransom Humanities Research Center, University of Texas, Austin.
Ginsberg, Allen. Papers. Rare Book and Manuscript Library, Butler Library, Columbia University, New York.
Lehmann, John. Papers. Harry Ransom Humanities Research Center, University of Texas, Austin.
Owen, Peter. Papers. Harry Ransom Humanities Research Center, University of Texas, Austin.
Random House. Papers. Rare Book and Manuscript Library, Butler Library, Columbia University, New York.
Redon, Joel. Papers. Harry Ransom Humanities Research Center, University of Texas, Austin.
Roditi, Edouard. Papers. Special Collections, Universitiy Research Library, University of California, Los Angeles.
Stein, Gertrude. Papers. Beinecke Library, Yale University, New Haven.
Thomson, Virgil. Papers. Jackson Music Library, Yale University, New Haven.

City Directories and Local Sources

Albany, New York. Division for Historic Preservation. Building-Structure Inventory for 629 West Church Street, Elmira, New York, May 1980.
Bellows Falls, Vermont. *Business Directory 1869.*
———. Rockingham Free Public Library. Scrapbooks and death files for Frederick C. Winnewisser and Marie Winnewisser.
Boston, Massachusetts. Simmons College catalogs, 1906–8.
Chemung Country, New York. *Chemung County Business Directory, 1868–1869.*

Elmira, New York. City directories (various titles), 1896–1907.
———. *Elmira Star Gazette*, 30 December 1933.
———. *Gazetter*, 1860.
———. *Williams' Elmira City Directory*, 1896–1907.
Montour Falls, New York. Schuyler County Clerk's Office. Deeds and estate records for Ida Bowles, Christiana Holden, and Mary Robbins Mead, 1890–1941.
———. Schuyler County Historical Society. Death files for Christiana A. Holden, Fox Holden, and Darwin W. Mead.
New York, New York. Department of Health, Borough of Manhattan, Births, 1917.
———. Department of Health, Borough of Queens. Births, 1911.
———. *Herald Tribune*, 18 May 1943, p. 17, col. 4. Death notice for Adelaide Bowles Maltby.
———. Marriage License Bureau. 1938.
Queens, New York. City directories (various titles), 1910–12 through 1924.
Springfield, Massachusetts. City directories (various titles), 1915–30.
United States Census. (Various counties), 1840–1920.
United States Geological Service. Map 1910, New York 28, Brooklyn.
Walpole, New Hampshire. Walpole Historical Society genealogical records.
Watkins, New York. *Watkins Review and Express*, 1941.
Windham County, Vermont. *Gazetteer and Business Directory*, 1884.

Films

Conklin, Gary. *Paul Bowles in Morocco*. New York, 1970.
Weinreich, Regina, and Catherine Warnow. *Paul Bowles: The Complete Outsider*. New York: Waterfall Productions, 1993.

INDEX